The Eighteenth-Century
WYANDOT

Indigenous Studies Series

The Indigenous Studies Series builds on the successes of the past and is inspired by recent critical conversations about Indigenous epistemological frameworks. Recognizing the need to encourage burgeoning scholarship, the series welcomes manuscripts drawing upon Indigenous intellectual traditions and philosophies, particularly in discussions situated within the Humanities.

Series Editor

Dr. Deanna Reder (Métis), Assistant Professor, First Nations Studies and English, Simon Fraser University

Advisory Board

Dr. Jo-ann Archibald (Sto:lo), Associate Dean, Indigenous Education, University of British Columbia

Dr. Kristina Bidwell (Labrador–Métis), Associate Professor, English, University of Saskatchewan

Dr. Daniel Heath Justice (Cherokee), Associate Professor, English, Canada Research Chair in Indigenous Literature and Expressive Culture, University of British Columbia

Dr. Eldon Yellowhorn (Piikani), Associate Professor, Archaeology, Director of First Nations Studies, Simon Fraser University

For more information, please contact:

Lisa Quinn
Acquisitions Editor
Wilfrid Laurier University Press
75 University Avenue West
Waterloo, ON N2L 3C5
Canada
Phone: 519-884-0710 ext. 2843
Fax: 519-725-1399
Email: quinn@press.wlu.ca

THE Eighteenth-Century WYANDOT

A Clan-Based Study

JOHN L. STECKLEY

This book has been published with the help of a grant from the Canadian Federation for the Humanities and Social Sciences, through the Awards to Scholarly Publications Program, using funds provided by the Social Sciences and Humanities Research Council of Canada. Wilfrid Laurier University Press acknowledges the financial support of the Government of Canada through the Canada Book Fund for our publishing activities.

Library and Archives Canada Cataloguing in Publication

Steckley, John, 1949–, author
    The eighteenth-century Wyandot : a clan-based study / John L. Steckley.

(Indigenous studies)
Includes bibliographical references and index.
Issued also in electronic formats.
ISBN 978-1-77112-200-9 (pbk.).—ISBN 978-1-55458-957-9 (pdf).
ISBN 978-1-55458-958-6 (epub).

    1. Huron Indians—Kinship. 2. Huron Indians—Social life and customs—18th century. 3. Huron Indians—History—18th century. I. Title. II. Series: Indigenous studies series

E99.H9S74 2014   305.897'555   C2013-905915-6
                                                 C2013-905916-4

Cover design by Heng Wee Tan. Text design by Daiva Villa, Chris Rowat Design.

Front-cover image: *Wendat/Wandat People of the Circle* (2012), a digital recreation of an original work in pencil, by Richard Zane Smith, Sǫhahiyǫh, hatinyǫnyéʔrunǫʔ (Bear Clan), Wyandot Nation of Kansas, and Catherine Tammaro, *Taǫmęʔšreʔ*, date:žátǫ ⁿgyaʔwiš hatiyerunǫʔ (Spotted or Small Turtle Clan), Wyandot of Anderdon Nation. Red represents male (fire, sun), black is female (fertile soil, rain clouds), yellow shades represent the three phratries. The centre represents the sacred fire of a Wandat community core, its source of life, its heartbeat the black oblongs representing twelve clan longhouses and its matriarch, whose voice/power influences both warrior societies (arrowheads) and those selected as clan chiefs and diplomats defending and representing the village and its nation.

© 2014 Wilfrid Laurier University Press
Waterloo, Ontario, Canada
www.wlupress.wlu.ca

This book is printed on FSC recycled paper and is certified Ecologo. It is made from 100% post-consumer fibre, processed chlorine free, and manufactured using biogas energy.

Printed in Canada

Every reasonable effort has been made to acquire permission for copyright material used in this text, and to acknowledge all such indebtedness accurately. Any errors and omissions called to the publisher's attention will be corrected in future printings.

No part of this publication may be reproduced, stored in a retrieval system, or transmitted, in any form or by any means, without the prior written consent of the publisher or a licence from the Canadian Copyright Licensing Agency (Access Copyright). For an Access Copyright licence, visit http://www.accesscopyright.ca or call toll free to 1-800-893-5777.

Contents

Preface vii

CHAPTER 1 Introduction 1
2 Two Questions 21
3 Five Wyandot Strategists of the Late Seventeenth Century: Sastaretsi, Kandiaronk, Sk8tache, the Baron, and Quarante Sols 51
4 Other Nations and the Clans of the Wyandot: Missionaries and Other Strangers Enter Their Midst 75
5 Wyandot Participation in "Christian" Rituals 107
6 Wyandot Leadership: Male Political Roles 135
7 The Political Roles of Wyandot Women 171
8 A Summary 203

Appendix A: The Census 217
Appendix B: Wyandot Correspondence 235
    Appendix B1: Father Richardie's Introduction to Father Potier 235
    Appendix B2: Governor Longueuil 237
    Appendix B3: The Wendat Response 247

Appendix B4: Father Richardie to the Huron of Wendake   251

Appendix B5: Father Richer to Father Potier   261

Appendix C: N'endi   265

Appendix D: Festin des Noces   271

Notes   273

References   291

Index   299

Preface

Early in 1974, I discovered the Huron/Wendat language. It held a fascinating paradox. It was no longer spoken, but it may have had more written in and about it than any currently spoken Aboriginal language in Canada. Further, the ideas that I could help a people recover their lost linguistic treasure and that I could use my knowledge of the language as a research tool for uncovering what no one else could see captured my heart and intrigued my mind. In 1978, I published my first academic paper, "Brébeuf's Presentation of Catholicism in the Huron Language" (Steckley 1978), based on my first academic paper presented at a conference. The same year I received my master's degree after my thesis, "The Soul Concepts of the Huron," was approved. Its 350-some pages included appendices of my translations from Huron that stood as much of my source material. Before my work could be assessed, my supervisor had to know to what it was I was referring. This put me on a path from which I have never strayed (except for very brief side trips) and from which I will never leave. I can truly say that the Huron or Wendat language is my life's work.

I have long said that the Wendat language is my best teacher. It continually instructs me. The words of Jesuit Father Jean de Brébeuf are appropriate here, in his instructions in 1636 to his fellow Jesuits who were going to join the Huron mission: "The Huron language will be your saint Thomas and our Aristotle" (JR10:91). It has been such for me.

I have so far published six books about the Wendat and their language, with another to be published probably about the same time as this work. The first such book was *Untold Tales: Four 17th Century Huron* (1992d). It contains the biographies of four Huron whose stories I used to tell when I was a historical interpreter at the historic site of Sainte-Marie Among the Hurons in 1977 and 1979 and I was taking school tours through the site. These stories were particularly useful when there was a group in the building in which I wanted to go, and we were left standing outside, just me and the class: time to tell a story. Sainte-Marie Among the Hurons was the site of a Jesuit mission community between 1639 and 1649, and had the first two people called Hechon working there (an explanation of the significance of this can be found in the next chapter). Father Jean de Brébeuf (the first Hechon) was buried there for a few centuries. His skull rests in the Martyrs' Shrine across Highway 12 in Midland, Ontario. I self-published this book twice (1981, with three biographies, and 1992d with four). Kandiaronk or Rat was the fourth story (included only in the second version). You will encounter him in the second chapter.

In 2004, I published *De Religione: Seventeenth Century Jesuits Telling Their Story in Huron to the Iroquois*. For this I translated and edited what appears to be the longest surviving text written in the Wendat language (fifty-three pages). I began that translation in 1979 as an exercise in keeping my experience with the language a living one. Then one day the text was fully translated. I strongly felt that others interested in the Wendat needed to know what was covered in this text. What I learned was communicated not only in the book, but in my most often referenced academic article, "The Warrior and the Lineage: Jesuit Use of Iroquoian Images to Communicate Christianity," published in *Ethnohistory* (Steckley 1992a).

In 2007, I published *Words of the Huron* with Wilfrid Laurier University Press (2007a). This publication included material from a long series of articles I had written for publications of the Ontario Archaeological Society (*Arch Notes* and *Ontario Archaeology*), updated with new insights. In essence, I was saying to the readers of the book, "This is what I have learned from the language so far." The same year, *A Huron English/English Huron Dictionary (Listing Both Words and Noun and Verb Roots)* came out (2007b). I developed a new appreciation for the Jesuits who wrote their Wendat dictionaries. It is not an easy task. You always feel that you are missing something. I am hoping for a second edition.

The year 2010 saw two more Wendat dictionaries come out. Both of them involved editing and translating the oldest surviving such works, one collected and written by Recollect Brother Gabriel Sagard, *Gabriel Sagard's Dictionary of Huron* (2010a), and the other, what I believe to be the oldest Jesuit dictionary, *The First French–Huron Dictionary by Father Jean de Brébeuf and His Jesuit Brethren* (2010b). I meant them to be tools of discovery that could be used by historians, anthropologists, and Wendat people not trained in linguistics to enable them to discover what they want to know and otherwise cannot find.

My favourite quotation from the American author John Steinbeck goes like this: "All my life has been aimed at one book, and I haven't started it yet. The rest has all been practice" (letter written to John Murphy, 12 June 1961). For me, this just might be that one book.

Chapter One

Introduction

This book is about linking together two photographs in time for the Wendat people, one of a remarkably well-recorded year in the mid-eighteenth century, the other of a very significant event that brought peoples with a shared history together in the late twentieth century.

A PHOTOGRAPH IN TIME: 1747

It was early in the year of 1747. The people were the Wyandot.[1] They lived in the Detroit/Windsor area on Bois Blanc Island in the Detroit River. The island is about 4 kilometres long (2.5 miles), and 0.8 kilometres wide (0.5 miles). A Jesuit missionary living with them, Father Pierre Potier, had compiled a census of their two communities, actually two, only slightly different. I cannot stress too much the uniqueness of this source. In it we see how many houses the people were living in. We see who is living in each house. Most of the names are given, if not at least the relationship between the unnamed person and those previously named. Sometimes ages of the individuals are presented as well.

Strangely, Potier identified the two villages as Petit Village and Grand Village. I say "strangely" as Petit Village was the larger of the two with a population of roughly 309, while the smaller Grand Village had around 232 (see Appendix A for how these numbers were calculated). The Wyandot were in significant ways living a traditional life despite having over one hundred years of contact with Europeans and living a few hundred kilometres away from a homeland of at least a few hundred years. Most people still lived in traditional bark, rectangular, round-roofed longhouses[2] with more than one nuclear family living inside, not in squared-off one-family European-styled dwellings. In the Petit Village, houses ranged in resident number from five to forty-nine. In the Grand Village, houses ranged in resident number from five to seventy-four. The average number of dwellers in a house was nineteen. The smaller houses tended to be lived in by people who were not born into the culture, adopted outsiders (e.g., Catawba and Iroquois).

In the following chart you can see a brief listing of the houses in each village, along with their estimated population. One of the most useful and fascinating features of Potier's census is that he listed members of the elders' council, male and female. I have indicated for each house how many elders lived there. Authority in the communities seems to have been fairly broadly distributed. Those houses without an elder typically had living in them peoples of different ethnicities, including "Iroquois" (PV3), Catawba (PV9), and Wendake Huron (GV1 and GV7). One was the house of a traditional healer (GV3).

Petit Village	House Population	Number of Elders in House
PV1	45	2
PV2	31	5
PV3	7	0
PV4	9	2
PV5	0	0
PV6	11	2
PV7	10	2
PV8	7	1
PV9	6	0
PV10	42	7
PV11	49	4
PV12	9	1
PV13	39	4
PV14	17	2
PV15	10	2
PV16	14	2
PV17	0	0
PV18	24	6

Grand Village	House Population	Number of Elders in House
GV1	5	0
GV2	8	4
GV3	8	0
GV4	30+	3
GV5	6	0
GV6	28	6
GV7	6–7	0
GV8	16	1
GV9	10	2
GV10	0	0
GV11	13	0
GV12	29	3
GV13	74	11
GV14	0	0
GV15	13	1

Clan was strong at this time. Despite the presence of patrilineal and patrilocal Europeans and Algonquians, they stayed matrilineal (determining kinship and clan membership along the female line) and matrilocal (families living primarily in the longhouse of the wife/mother). People did not marry people of their own clan; they practised clan exogamy, even though that cut the number of potential mates down, not an easy thing to deal with when you are a small people among larger nations. The clan-owned names that people bore were still passed on as they had been traditionally, that is with individuals going through more than one such name in a full lifespan. And a significant number of people appear to have been adopted by the Wyandot, including the missionaries and Aboriginal people from other tribes. Clan was a way of placing those people into the social networks of the Wyandot.

Identifying the clan membership of individuals is work that was very difficult, but proved to be quite fruitful and productive of insight. I was able at the end to identify the clan membership of 376 out of 576 individuals. This also means that in a significant number of instances, the clan identity of a house, that is the clan that numerically dominates, can also be determined, and will be shown shortly in an illustration of where houses are situated.

VILLAGE PLAN

Having the basic layout of the village in terms of how the houses are positioned relative to each other is useful in understanding the socio-political structure of the people in 1747, as well as, hopefully, helping archaeologists whose work centres on pre-contact and early contact Iroquoian villages. A village plan for the Wyandot in 1732 has been published (Tooker 1978, 400), based on a report by Henri-Louis Deschamps de Boishébert, in which there are twenty-eight longhouses of equal size lined up in two rows of five, with an additional building about half the size of the others at a ninety-degree angle. The pattern in the two villages described here is not so symmetrical.

We can also see how different clans and ethnicity dominance worked its way in the housing pattern as well. The houses listed on the left are those that would be on your right as you walked into the village. The estimated number of residents of each house is listed to the right. The houses are identified as much as possible with respect to clan and ethnic identity.

Village Plan Chart

PV3 (I) PV2 (Po/S) PV1 (Po) central pathway   PV4 (Sn)
(7)   (31)   (6)   (9)

                                                         PV5 (abandoned)
                                                         (0)
                                                         PV6 (D) PV7 (Sn) PV8 (?)
                                                         (11)   (10)   (7)
                                                         PV9 (C)
                                                         (5)
                                                         PV10 (S) PV11 (Pr)
                                                         (42) . (49)
                                                         PV12 (C)   PV13 (D)
                                                         (9)   (39)
                                                         PV14 (Po) PV15 (S)
                                                         (17)   (10)
                                                         PV16 (B)
                                                         (14)
                                                         PV17 (Pr – abandoned)
                                                         (0)
                                                         PV18 (B) PV19 (Po – abandoned)
                                                         (24)   (0)

Grand Village Housing Pattern: Location and Size

GV1 (?) GV2 (Pr)
(5)   (8)
GV3 (?) GV4 (L)
(8)   (30)
GV5 (?)
(6)
GV6 (L)
(28)
GV7 (H)
(6)
GV8 (D)
(16)
GV9 (D) GV10 (D – abandoned)
(10)   (0)
GV11 (Sn)
(12)
GV12 (W)
(29)
GV13 (B) GV14 (L – burned down)
(74)   (0)
GV15 (?)
(14)

Identity Key

Clans

B	Bear
D	Deer
L	Large Turtle
Po	Porcupine
Pr	Prairie Turtle
S	Striped Turtle
Sn	Snake
W	Wolf

Nations Other Than Wyandot

C	Catawba
H	Huron of Lorette
I	Iroquois

What we can see with the housing is a tendency towards phratry linking. Phratries, to be discussed in the next chapter, are groupings of clans. In the case of the 1747 Wyandot, we have Deer, Turtle, and Wolf phratries.

In both villages we can see Deer and Snake houses in close proximity. The two clans are linked by phratry (both belong to the Deer phratry) and by history, the Snake being derived from the Deer, the third member of the Deer phratry, the Bear, is the odd clan out, never having a house beside a Snake or Deer clan house. This may reflect their being "more Huron" than the other two clans of the phratry, having a significant number of names also found in *The Jesuit Relations'* accounts of the Huron. The Turtle phratry houses tend to cluster as well, with Striped Turtle and Prairie Turtle in two side by side, and with Striped Turtle and Porcupine in another in the Petit Village. Not enough clan identities of houses are known for the Grand Village for me to comment about the linking there of Turtle phratry houses. Only one clan of the Wolf phratry, the Wolf clan, has a house identified with it.

CENTRAL THESIS

The central thesis of this book is that clan kept the Wyandot strong, which enabled them to survive a forced migration and a splitting up of the villages and tribes that made up the ancestors of the Wyandot. Clans gave them options for adaptive responses to the powerful presence of French, English, Iroquois, and various Algonquian-speaking peoples all around them. Clans gave the Wyandot links with the ancestors and provided the foundations necessary for building their political structure to survive the uncertain winds of the future. Their clans provided the kernels for planting from which the newly formed Wyandot people would grow like the corn that sustained their lives. And leading female figures would be central to that new growth, although such is not obvious in the ethnohistorical literature.

The discussion in this work of the dynamic—as opposed to static—nature of clans is something under-reported in the classic anthropological literature, despite often detailed looks at clans appearing in the early literature.[3] This is because of the phenomenon of the ethnographic present, which I critique in *White Lies about the Inuit* as follows:

> This kind of study often involved two flawed forms of "as if" thought. The culture was described as if the people were not then and had not earlier been in contact with the broader world, typically Western society, and as if the society was static prior to contact. The anthropologists had a salvage mentality, thinking that they had to quickly salvage the pristine, untouched culture before it disappeared completely under Western influence. (Steckley 2008, 33)

ANOTHER PHOTOGRAPH IN TIME: 1999

The Kikuyu writer Ngũgĩ wa Thiong'o, in writing about colonialism in Kenya in his excellent *Something Torn and New: An African Renaissance* (2009), talks about the process through which colonized people have their metaphorical heads dismembered from their bodies. The colonizers do this by separating the people from their memory, that being their stories, cultural traditions, and the names, characters, and achievements of their key individuals. In the case of the peoples discussed in this book, this dismembering involved to a significant extent the fragmenting of memory into separate identities limited by space and time.

In 1999, there was a homecoming of descendants of an Aboriginal people spread across much of North America—Quebec, Michigan, Kansas, and Oklahoma—each carrying in their metaphorical hands a fragment of history they called their own, a fragment they wanted to fit with the pieces the others carried, to try to piece together their collective memory. The occasion was the reburial of some five hundred of their ancestors, laying down in honour bones that had been buried first in the turbulent, disease-filled times of 1636, then dug up by archaeologists in the early 1950s, studied by generations of graduate students, and were now going back to the earth in the homeland (see Seeman 2011, 140–44 for a longer description of the Homecoming).

The people were Wendat, a self-designation used from before European contact to the present. Several writers have guessed at the meaning of Wendat, "islanders" being particularly popular (see Steckley 1992b),[4] but there is no agreed-upon translation of the word. Some of the Wendat have since European contact been called "Huron" (an insulting reference, as you will see in the next chapter). This group now is based on a reserve in Wendake, Quebec, a place name meaning "at Wendat." The fragment of time they carried was of early contact and how it flowed into their present. The others are now typically called Wyandot (based on the word Wendat).

Some Wendat carried fragments of time that focused on the Windsor/Detroit area in the eighteenth century and of the loss of their reserve and official status late in the late nineteenth century. Some Wyandot have had until recently a sense of their history that seemed to begin with the War of 1812, carrying into a forced migration west and the early opening of a cemetery in Kansas City, Kansas, and their loss of official status. Some had ancestors that had moved on from there, ending up finally in what was then called "Indian Territory," but is now known as the state of Oklahoma. The last speakers of the Wendat language belonged to this most-distant-from-the-homeland community. As with the other communities, they want to change the designation of their language from "extinct" to "dormant and being awakened."

In the rest of this chapter I will be expanding on my discussion of these fragments a bit, to familiarize readers with the Wendat peoples, and have these readers come to share the belief that Wendat stories are important ones. All of this material will be incorporated in different degrees into my telling of the story of the Wyandot of the eighteenth century.

I use the plural "peoples" when talking about the Wendat because, in the time of first contact with Europeans, there were two Wendat peoples perceived as different by the French, the Huron and the Petun, the latter given their name as they (through their southern neighbours) provided tobacco (in French "petun") in trade with their neighbours, which they had received in trade with their Neutral partners to the south.[5] The Petun and the Huron spoke essentially the same language. They certainly would have had no problems communicating with each other (see Steckley 1992c, 1993b, 1997, and 2007a for discussions of Wendat dialects).

THE HURON FRAGMENT OF WENDAT HISTORY

The first Huron fragment of Wendat written history extends from first contact with Samuel de Champlain until the Wendat people were driven out of southern Ontario in the late 1640s and early 1650s by the Iroquois. The period is known well by the Wendat of Wendake, the community just a little outside of the city of Quebec. It is a period also fairly well known to school children in Canada, particularly in the area of southern Ontario, where they learn this part of the story in grade six (Aboriginal people unit) and grade seven (the fur trade unit). These young students may have gone on a school trip to visit the historic site of Sainte-Marie Among the Hurons on the outskirts of Midland and beside the southern shores of Georgian Bay. This is where the ten-year (1639–49) Jesuit mission community stood. By the early 1650s, the remaining Jesuits and some of the Wendat mission charges had moved east to the relative security of the area surrounding what is now the city of Quebec. The historic site Sainte-Marie Among the Hurons was reconstructed in the 1960s as a way of telling an important part of the history of New France and of Canada. Each year thousands of tourists get to hear the story and see something of what the community would have been like. Catholics would have extra reasons for knowing the story of this mission as this period produced the eight martyred saints of North America: Fathers Isaac Jogues (1646), Antoine Daniel (1648), Jean de Brébeuf (1649), Noël Chabanel (1649), Charles Garnier (1649), and Gabriel

Lalement (1649), and their donné assistants René Goupil (1642), and Jean de Lalande (1646). They may have visited the Martyrs' Shrine across Highway 12 from Sainte-Marie. And then there is the song the "Huron Carol," probably first written by one of the saints, Jesuit Father Jean de Brébeuf, in the early 1640s, and possibly the most frequently recorded of all Canadian songs, even if it is usually recorded in an English form that is not a translation of the original Wendat.

Interestingly, this fragment is so well known in comparison to the times that followed that many people think that the Wendat as Huron became extinct, that they died out when they were driven out of their southern Ontario homeland. Certainly that is an opinion often held by grade six students that I have talked to. And adults have often asked me, when I say that I study the Huron and their language, "But aren't they extinct?" I have a Wendat friend in Ontario who has a t-shirt that proudly declares, "I am not extinct."

One reason why this historical fragment is known as well as it is comes from the fact that the primary documentary sources are rich from this time. Samuel de Champlain (1574–1635), long regarded as "the Father of New France," wrote about the Wendat. He fought alongside them in 1609 in his attack on the Mohawk, and later wintered with the Huron in 1615–16. This was included in his *Voyages de la Nouvelle France*, first published in 1632. The words "Champlain" and "Huron" share many pages in the history books discussing this time.[6]

An even better early source involves the writings of Recollect Brother Gabriel Sagard. He wrote based on his 1623–24 life with the Wendat people called Huron. He borrowed some of the work from the earlier experiences of Champlain, plagiarism not being the issue then that it is now. Sagard's *The Long Journey to the Country of the Hurons* is a great source of the culture of the Huron, their music, customs, political structure, and religion. Not only has it provided information about the Wendat of a particular time, but scholars of the French and Scottish enlightenment of the eighteenth century used Sagard's writings to inform themselves about Aboriginal people generally, helping them foster the image of the "noble savage."

Underused, but of equal value, is his *Dictionnaire de la langue huronne*. It is the first Wendat dictionary ever published. Although this book was ignored or simply not seen by the Jesuits who composed an impressive set of dictionaries afterwards, Sagard's work saw a flicker of fame when the prolific French writer, historian, and philosopher Voltaire (1694–1778) made reference to it in his work *Ingénu*, a book in which a Huron "noble savage" or "innocent" is used as a voice to criticize the corruption of French society. The dictionary is used to identify the individual who washed up on the shores of France as a true Huron. That scholars could have learned much more about the Huron from this vital primary document can be seen in two recent works of mine (Steckley 2010a, 2012), one an edited version of this dictionary (2010a). They could have learned about Sagard's personality[7] and the somewhat surprising ethnicity of some of his informants, as well as the trade items that were popular among the Huron and the French (Steckley 2010a, 168–76). At least one of these informants was St. Lawrence Iroquoian, the people who gave us the word "Canada," some of the dictionary entries coming from an apparent trade or pidgin language based on their language.

The largest source or better put series of sources of information concerning the Huron is *The Jesuit Relations*, seventy-three volumes of annual reports sent back to Europe to say how the Jesuit missions were faring. These covered the period from 1610 to 1791. Initially, and in great detail, there were stories of the Algonquian speaking peoples to the east of the Huron, then the Huron themselves. Here we learn much about the lives of such people as Chihoatenh8a (shee-hoh-ah-ten-hwa) and his brothers Te haondechoren (the-hah-on-deh-shoh-ren) and Hatironta (ha-tee-ron-tah), the latter two names to be discussed in later chapters, and many more, as well as learning about the basic social structure, beliefs, and ritual practices of the people. Unfortunately, we do not get the same rich documentary background for the other Wendat people of the time, the Petun. And only a few of their names are mentioned in passing. This puts a Huron bias on the material.

These sources were gleaned brilliantly for information about the Huron/Wendat by Bruce Trigger (1937–2006; see Trigger 1969, 1976), Elisabeth Tooker (1927–2005; see Tooker 1967, 1978), Conrad Heidenreich (1971), and Wendat scholar Georges Sioui (1992, 1999). These authors represent the sources where most scholars have obtained the bulk of their information about the Wendat. They used to be only available in reference sections of university libraries or from pricy book dealers (I bought my own copy of the set for $2,000 in 1989), but now they are easy to find online through Early Canadiana Online and through Canadian Libraries sites (e.g., http://archive.org/). There are weaknesses in *The Jesuit Relations* as documents. They had something of a public relations spin to them, "We're doing well, but there are huge obstacles. Please send money." Patriarchal and other European-based biases are articulated. Translations into English sometimes are somewhat inaccurate, and sometimes fail to capture crucial subtleties in the French and Latin of the original texts. The following is a small such mistake based on a failure to change the word order from French to English:

"*Achitetsi* [It is a long foot], *vn pied long* [a long foot]" (JR10:116)
"*Achitetsi*, a foot long." (JR10:117)

A stranger example involves a missionary talking about a procession and translating a passage as "and having at their rear," when the word translated as "rear" was "tete" or "head" (JR61:114–15; see discussion of this passage in the next chapter).

Works that are likewise very useful, but have long been neglected are the manuscript French–Huron and Huron–French dictionaries written by the Jesuits. I regularly use nine of them: five that are French–Huron FHO (French–Huron Onondaga), FH62 (edited and published in Steckley 2010b), FH67, FH1693, FH1697—and four that are Huron–French—HF59, HF62, HF65, and Potier. The numbers here represent the manuscript number in the Archives Seminaire de Quebec, except for the two with dates, and these are my additions, my hypothesis of when they were written. Only the Potier dictionary was published, and that in 1920, the grammar attached to his work, with badly transposed Wendat, in 1831 (Wilkie 1831). The others were put on microfilm over forty years ago by Victor Hanzeli (1969) as part of the work he did for his important linguistic study, *Missionary Linguistics in New France*. I had the microfilm blown up into paper copy some thirty years ago. The pages are a bit faded now, but most of the text can still be read. One of them (FH62) I have been fortunate enough to have edited and published recently so that scholars can have access to it as a new kind of source (Steckley 2010b) that can provide a lot of information, if they know how to look. I believe it to be the oldest surviving Jesuit dictionary of Wendat. These dictionaries are remarkable sources, among the best dictionaries of any language of their time (all from the seventeenth century except for Potier's dictionary of the mid-eighteenth century), certainly much better than anything that then existed for the English language. The Jesuits themselves were master linguists, having been trained in and being teachers of a number of languages, including Latin, Greek, and Afro-Asiatic languages such as Hebrew and Aramaic (the language that Jesus is presumed to have spoken). In Jesuit missions of the time that were located in Asia, they learned a variety of languages including Mandarin (see Brockey 2007, 243–86 "Learning the Language of Birds"), Japanese, and Sanskrit.

In the late 1640s, terminating in 1649–50, the Wendat were driven out of their southern Ontario homeland by the five nations of the Iroquois Confederacy. After this dispersal, other Aboriginal peoples were included in *The Jesuit Relations*, as the Jesuits expanded their mission to the Iroquois and to peoples living farther west. The Wendat close at hand, near the city of Quebec, were reported on frequently after the dispersal, but in less detail than before. Even fewer are the references to the Wendat (primarily Petun) who moved west and eventually settled in and around Michilimackinac, near the joining of Lake Michigan and Lake Superior. We learn almost nothing about their lives. The often intimate personal sketches the reader had become familiar with in the first part of the seventeenth century are missing during this period of Wendat history.

As you will see from the next chapter, other sources become useful at this point, including primarily the New York Colonial Documents, which will be referenced frequently (as NYCD) in the third chapter. They include the writings of the French translated into English. Like *The Jesuit Relations*, these used to be found only in dusty reference obscurity in university libraries. Now, however, they are also found online (e.g., http://archive.org/).

There is a brief focus that links this fragment with the next one. The life of Kandiaronk or Rat (discussed in the third chapter), a leader based in the Upper Great Lakes, has a relatively concentrated focus in the series of events leading to the great peace of 1701 in Montreal, which temporarily stopped the fighting between the Iroquois and the Wendat as well as their more numerous Algonquian speaking neighbours. His name is linked with this peace, and he is accepted as a heroic figure by the people of Wendake (the Wendat reserve in Quebec). His name, written as Kondiaronk, is given to the building where the band council meets and where many cultural events take place. My wife and I have eaten and danced there.

THE WYANDOT OF THE DETROIT/WINDSOR AREA

In the early years of the eighteenth century, the people who would become known as the Wyandot left the Michilimackinac region to settle in a new home in the Windsor/Detroit area, shortly after the French founding of the community of the latter name. Antoine Laumet de La Mothe, Sieur de Cadillac, the commander of the local fort there (the first Cadillac parked in the Detroit area, Pontiac would come later), and the French traders wanted the Wyandot there to improve the trade and to provide warriors against their enemies.

They were initially primarily just a people included in lists as "and the Wyandot" by the French writers of the time, small in number but not in political influence. Historians might notice them in reports concerning the Fox wars, the battles pitting the Algonquian-speaking Fox, against the French and their Aboriginal allies. Scholars of this time and general area may also have heard of Porcupine clan leader Nicholas Orontondi and his brief resistance to the French in 1747. A little more mention is made of the

Pontiac resistance of 1763, where some Wyandot (called the "good Wyandot" in the primary documents) resisted while others (called the "bad Wyandot") were more amenable to joining up with the Ottawa leader, at least temporarily.

The one exception to the general lack of sources referencing the time of the 1740s into 1781 is the work of Father Pierre Potier. He seems to have been a compulsive recorder, and for that we should all be thankful. He left an amazing documentary legacy. Part of Jesuit language training in Wendat was copying down language-related texts that had been written before, with at least some of the missionaries adding to the copied material what they heard in the community themselves. Potier's dictionary and grammar represent the culmination, the final product of that process of over a century. He added to what had been written before some forms, depicted in superscript, that he heard among the Wyandot.[8] In so doing, he was the first one to systematically record the Wyandot dialect of Wendat. Added to that material were the religious texts explaining Christianity that had been written before Potier's time. The longest of those works, *De Religione*, was written in the 1670s and was composed by Father Philippe Pierson. I translated and edited *De Religione*, publishing the result in 2004. In addition, he recorded the baptisms, Christian marriages and funerary ceremonies, and, even more significantly, a pair of Wyandot censuses of 1747, the most important primary document providing information for my work here. Most of this material was published in 1920 as an archive report of the province of Ontario (Potier 1920). However, it took another Jesuit scholar, Father Robert Toupin, to add to this collection another census, and the Christian ritual record (e.g., baptisms, marriages, and funerary rituals), as well as important material for the study of French-Canadian society during the eighteenth century, completing the Potier collection. I could not have accomplished what I have in this work without Father Toupin's collection and his diligent work (Toupin 1996).

While in the late eighteenth and early nineteenth centuries Ohio became the main focus of the Wyandot, some of the people remained in Michigan and southwestern Ontario, on the other side of the border, where they would have a reserve in Ontario, named Anderdon. There was a process known as "enfranchisement" originally legislated in 1857 in the linked colonies of Upper (Ontario) and Lower (Quebec) Canada. Through this process, individual people of official Indian status could sign away their treaty and Aboriginal rights and, in return, they could own land as individuals, vote federally and provincially (if they were male and owned land), go to university and become lawyers, and drink alcohol legally, things they could not do as card-carrying "Indians," as created by the Indian Act of

1876. Not many Aboriginal people took advantage of this "opportunity." But members of the Anderdon Wyandot band did during the 1880s. Eventually, by 1892, everyone was forced to enfranchise and the reserve was no longer Indian land. Wyandot stayed in the area and have maintained their identity to this day. This identity is recognized by their fellow Wendat of Quebec, Kansas, and Oklahoma.

THE WYANDOT OF OHIO, KANSAS, AND OKLAHOMA

The next historical fragment carefully carried to the Homecoming in the minds of the American Wyandot, primarily those of Kansas and Oklahoma, begins with Tarhe (1742–1818), who was also referred to in English as "the Crane" and in French as "La Grue" (see "Tarhe" by Mrs. Thelma Marsh, and "Tarhe Grand Sachem" by C.A. Buser, both on the Wyandot of Kansas website, www.wyandot.org). He belonged to the Porcupine clan (see next chapter for clan designation). Wyandot history that came before his time has long been relatively vague, indeterminate in their minds, something embedded in other people's history. When I first heard the people speak about Tarhe, I was a bit confused. In my ignorance, I had never heard of Tarhe, after what was then about twenty-five years working on Wendat material. Checking the dictionaries, I found that his name is similar, perhaps cognate with the Wendat word *orhe*, referring to a swan (Steckley 2010b, 44). The usual word for crane was Atochin,ot or Aθochingot (Steckley 2010b, 44; Steckley 2007b, 78). He is not a significant figure in the story I am telling here; he arrived on the scene too late. I mention him because to the Wyandot he often signals the beginning of their known part of the story.

It turns out this story starts in Ohio, with Tarhe being first on the list of leaders signing treaties (in 1795, 1805, and 1815) and focuses primarily on the War of 1812. He was a leader of the Wyandot who chose to fight on the side of the Americans against the British and Canadians, on what we Canadians would call the "losing side." They attacked us and we successfully defended ourselves.

In contrast to the American Wyandot and their connection with Tarhe, on the Canadian side of the border, there is no recognition of Wyandot leaders. This includes my favourite War of 1812 Wyandot Hostayehtak or Bark Carrier (for some strange reason usually referred to as Roundhead), who also signed the treaty of 1795, and who was a close associate of the much more famous Shawnee leader, Tecumseh. In January 1813, Bark Carrier embarrassed the American forces by capturing their General, thus leading to a quick surrender. In all the Canadian bicentennial hoopla about the War of 1812, I have yet to hear or read Bark Carrier's name. He is not a big part of the social imaginary of Canadian history. Bark Carrier lives in the perpetual long shadow cast by Tecumseh.

In the story that starts with Tarhe, the Wyandot of Ohio are Methodists (with a sprinkle of Catholics faithful to their people's mixed religious traditions) settled into a life of farming familiar Aboriginal crops (corn, beans, and squash) probably mixed with alien European crops (e.g., wheat and oats) and animals (cows, horses, sheep, goats, and pigs).[9] To show how the recording of names changed to reduce possibilities of one fragment connecting with others, the Orontondi prominent among the Wyandot of Detroit/Windsor in the mid-eighteenth century had his name inscribed in a treaty of 1817 as Runtunda or Warpole. His name lives on in Wyandot County, Ohio, as the name of a creek (Warpole). In their former Upper Sandusky home, there is Warpole Street. Another important name, recorded reasonably accurately as Otiokwandoron, was recorded in 1828 as Hoocuyquondooroo (www.wyandot.org/1828us.htm).

The Wyandot did not stay in Ohio long, but would have their own story of forced migration to add to the narratives of such events in the history of the Wendat (see Steckley 1999, 206–9 for my telling of this story). When the American government passed the infamous Indian Removal Act of 1830, which was instituted by President Andrew Jackson, it was with the intent and declared purpose of moving all Aboriginal peoples west of the Mississippi River. In exchange for homelands they received promises (there are always promises) of good land in the west. The Sauk and Fox to the west of the Wyandot resisted, causing the short-lived series of battles known as the Blackhawk War, named after their leader, whose name is now borne by the Chicago NHL hockey team. The most hideous story related to the Indian Removal Act took place among the Cherokee:

> Of the 14,000 or more Cherokee who were forced marched west by 7000 troops for 116 days during the hard winter of 1838–39, at least 4000 died of malnutrition, exposure and disease. They thereafter referred to that trek as Nunna daul Tsunyi, "the trail where we cried," better known to history as the Trail of Tears. (Steckley 2011, 204)

The Wyandot of Ohio passively resisted the forced migration until 1843, when they ran out of quiet forms of resistance. The Wyandot elder known best as Squire Grey Eyes captured the mood of the departing people most eloquently when he said:

> My people, the time of our departure is at hand.... It remains only for me to say farewell.... Here our dead are buried. We have placed fresh leaves and

flowers upon their graves for the last time. No longer shall we visit them. Soon they shall be forgotten, for the onward march of the strong White Man will not turn aside for the Indian graves.... Farewell our hunting grounds and homes. Farewell to the stately trees and forests. Farewell to the Temple of the Great Spirit [the Methodist church]. Farewell to our White Brothers, and friends and neighbours. (www.wyandot.org/farewell.htm)

The group headed west numbered 609 (www.wyandot.org.muster.htm), with 150, or roughly a quarter, being under ten years old. While the trip did not bring death to the people, the conditions along the Missouri River where they came to stay did. Measles and cholera took their toll, particularly of the children. A cemetery was soon established that would hold their cold bodies. This cemetery would become the focal point of the identity of the Wyandot of Kansas. The three Wyandot Conley sisters would become locally famous for their fight for the survival of the cemetery around which grew Kansas City, Kansas. Lyda did her part as the first Native American woman to present a case to the Supreme Court of America. Lena (Helena) who wired the cemetery shut and put up a sign that read, "You Trespass at Your Own Peril" (the shed outside the cemetery was known for good reason as Fort Conley) fought with threats of potential violence. Stories say she patrolled the cemetery with a gun. Ida more quietly fought the good fight, financially supporting the sisters' long successful fight to preserve the sanctity of the burial place their dead. The cemetery still exists today. Plans were made by an independent producer to make a movie, called "Whispers Like Thunder," about the Conley sisters but, lacking funding, it has never come to a theatre near you. I was the translator for the Wendat lines. I learned in that work a lot about what you cannot say in Wendat (e.g., "favourite," "wild flowers," and "government").

The Wyandot of Kansas lost their official status (but maintained their identity and strong sense of heritage) in a treaty of 1855. Those who opposed the treaty left for what was then called Indian Territory, eventually to become the state of Oklahoma. There, with a touch of historical irony, they were offered land by the Seneca that lived there, one of the descendant groups of one of the Iroquois nations that drove them out of their homeland almost two hundred years earlier. The Wyandot of Oklahoma have maintained their official tribal status to this day.

The Wyandot became the subject of study of a number of writers during the late nineteenth century. One was William Elsey Connelley (1855–1930), a self-taught historian focused on the Kansas area, who was adopted by the Deer clan and given their greatest name, that of Sastaretsi (see the third chapter for the story of this name), written as Sahr-stahr-ra-tseh. He compiled a Wyandot vocabulary, as well as a collection of their stories and a discussion of their social structure in *Wyandot Folklore* (1899). It was primarily among the Wyandot of Oklahoma that the anthropologist Marius Barbeau (1915, 1917, 1960) collected stories, songs, and material items of Wyandot heritage in 1911–12, a wonderful source of information concerning the language and culture of the people at that time.

PIECING FRAGMENTS TOGETHER

This book is about putting some of these fragments together, hoping and expecting that works developed on a grander scale will follow. Petun archaeologist Charles Garrad's (2011) magnum opus is a noble effort in that regard. He brings a large part of another fragment to the story, the archaeological story of the Petun both before and during early contact. The archaeological fragment is complex, both for the Huron and the Petun, as it covers hundreds of years and locations south of the contact period Wendat. One wish for this book is that the illustrations of how clan is involved with migration might inform this fragment as well as the others. Archaeological researchers should look for clans leading the way. Look for images of key totem animals.

It is important that the big picture of the Wyandot with fragments of narratives of pre-contact migrations and resettlements, from the archaeology of southern Ontario until the settlements in Quebec, Michigan, Kansas, and Oklahoma, get linked together in one well-connected story. This work is directed towards taking a few steps towards the eventual accomplishment of this monumental task.

The reasons I am engaged in this project are several. My long-term work with the language and the people is foremost. Two special events of many come particularly to mind. One summer in Wendake, Quebec, during a wonderful week in which I had the privilege of teaching the Wendat language to descendants of speakers, I was given the name Hechon, a name that had been first given to Father Jean de Brébeuf, and after him Fathers Pierre Chaumonot and Daniel Richer. I felt truly honoured. A few summers later, I attended the homecoming in 1999, first mentioned at the beginning of this chapter. A few hours after I had been adopted into the Wyandot of Kansas, and given the name Te haondechoren, "He splits the country in two," the bones were reburied. I had a gut feeling that my ancestors were being buried in the ground in front of me. In writing this book, I am making sure that those and other ancestors are remembered.

Basic Wendat Chronology (for purposes of this book)

1609	Huron fight alongside Champlain, the Montagnais, and the Algonquin against the Mohawk
1615–16	Champlain winters with the Huron
1623–24	Recollect Brother Gabriel Sagard lives with the Huron
1639–49	Jesuit mission community of Sainte-Marie Among the Hurons
1649–50	Wendat driven out of southern Ontario
1671	Some Wyandot settle at Michilimackinac
1673	Huron settle in Lorette (now called Ancienne-Lorette)
1697	Huron resettle at their current site (Jeune-Lorette), later called Village des Hurons, now called Wendake
1701	Great Peace of Montreal
Early 1700s	Wyandot move to Detroit/Windsor area
1728	Father Armand de la Richardie establishes a mission among the Wyandot of the Detroit/Windsor area
1746	Father Pierre Potier moves into the Wyandot mission
1747	Potier takes two censuses of the Wyandot people Orontondi movement
1763	Pontiac movement
1843	Wyandot move west to Kansas from Ohio
1855	Wyandot of Kansas lose official status
1867	Wyandot settle in Oklahoma
1892	Anderdon band loses official "Indian" status
1911–12	Marius Barbeau records linguistic and cultural material on the Wyandot
1999	The Homecoming of all four Wendat groups

LINGUISTICS

Orthography

A short note should be added here concerning my choice of orthography. As with all of my publications concerning the Wendat language, I have chosen to represent the sounds of the language with a strict adherence to how the Jesuits did it. Such was the first writing system used consistently for the language. It is reasonably linguistically accurate, with a few minor flaws and eccentricities. Glottal stops (the sound ending the first 'uh' in uh uh) are largely missing. We know from a later recording of Wendat by Marius Barbeau and of related languages by modern scholars that it is not the sound that is missing but Jesuit representation of the sound. Pre-aspiration (breathing or an -h- like sound before a consonant) is typically symbolized or represented by the symbol -'-. Post aspiration (after a consonant) is represented by a theta θ if it is after a -t- and by an -x- if it comes after a -k-. An -8-, actually more of a -u- written over an -o-, represents a -w- sound before a vowel, and a -u- sound before a consonant. The Jesuits used this with other languages as well as Wendat. They used the iota subscriptum, like a backwards comma to represent a -y- like sound that existed in most of the dialects of Wendat that they encountered in the early years of their mission, but not the dialect that I have termed Northern Bear. I prefer to use this system as it was used in the literature to which I am referring. I have chosen not to impose a phonological analysis on it, but to leave that to work done currently in teaching the language by such phonetically talented linguists as Michel Gros-Louis, Craig Kopris, and Megan Lukaniec. They have converted the Wendat writings of the Jesuits and of Marius Barbeau into systems that can be learned and used by the Wendat people living today.

Translations

There is quite a number of translations included in this text. The reader might wonder how I did this, given that I was not raised with the language, or learned from native speakers. My translations come essentially from entries in eight different manuscript dictionaries written by the Jesuits in the seventeenth and eighteenth centuries. When I composed a dictionary in the language (Steckley 2007b), I included in the entries for most of the verb and noun roots, cognate terms and their translations from dictionaries of related languages such as Mohawk, Oneida, Onondaga, Cayuga, and Tuscarora. These assisted me in determining what the best possible translation could be of each root.

Chapter Two

Two Questions

In this chapter, two main questions will be addressed. The first is, simply, "Who are the Wyandot?" The second, the more difficult one, is "What does a clan-based study of the Wyandot entail?"

WHO ARE THE WYANDOT?

To address the first question, you have to look first to the early seventeenth century to see their origin from two, possibly three, different peoples.[1] When the French first travelled to what is now southern Ontario, they encountered three groupings of Iroquoian people. The name Iroquoian refers to both their language and culture. It links these three peoples linguistically and culturally with, among others, the St. Lawrence Iroquoians that the French encountered along the St. Lawrence in the 1530s and 1540s, as well as with the then five nations (from west to east Seneca, Cayuga, Onondaga, Oneida, and Mohawk) now six nations[2] of the people that came to be known to the French and English as the Iroquois (sometimes with the words "Confederacy" or "League" attached). The Iroquois are known today primarily by the Iroquoian name Haudenosaunee. This means "they (masculine)[3] build or extend a house" a metaphor for the Confederacy bringing together formerly separate and sometimes warring peoples. José António Brandão (2000, 1) estimates that the five nations together numbered about twenty-five thousand in the first half of the seventeenth century. (For his calculations, see his Appendix C, 131–67.)

21

South of Lake Erie were the Erie, or Nation du Chat (i.e., with the meaning "it is a long tail" referring to the cougar). Further east were the Andaste or Susquehanna. Both groups were Iroquoian.

Iroquoian cultures at the time were involved with what anthropologists call "horticulture," in their case the growing of corn, beans, squash, and sunflowers, along with fishing, hunting, and gathering of plant products (fruit, bark, and hemp for rope and such).

The three groupings of Iroquoian peoples in the area were known to the French as the Huron, the Petun, and the Neutre or Neutral. As we have seen, the first two groups bore the name Wendat, from which the word "Wyandot" was derived. Estimates of the population of the Huron vary. Early contemporary recorders had what we would now call high estimates. Champlain (1929, 122) reckoned there were thirty thousand, and Sagard (1939, 92) thirty to forty thousand. They may have been including the Petun and even some of the Neutral in their calculations. The estimates of contemporary scholars are lower, with Bruce Trigger (1976, 32) favouring eighteen thousand and Conrad Heidenreich going with twenty-one thousand. The range of medians for the three methods of calculation extends from 16,000 to 22,500 (Heidenreich 1971, 15, 103; for his methods of calculation, see 96–103). Judging from a series of different calculations, Garrad (2011, 537) reckons that the Petun numbered about eight thousand at the beginning of the seventeenth century, and about fifteen hundred at the time of the dispersal in 1650. In Gary Warrick's (2003, 266, table 1, using data from Warrick 1990) classic series of estimations of population of the Huron and Petun based on the number of hearth sites per village, he reckoned that their combined population was 29,400 in 1615, and after the epidemics and initial Iroquois attacks hit the people, this dropped to 11,520 in 1647.

We do not know what specific event might have caused the two Wendat peoples to be socially divided while linguistically and culturally linked, to be in separated clusters side by side geographically, with Petun to the west and Huron to the east. According to Father Jerome Lalemant, in 1640:

> These nations formerly waged cruel wars against one another; but they are now on very good terms, and have recently renewed their alliance, and made a new confederation against some other peoples, their common enemies. (JR20:43)

The Huron called the Petun, *Etionnontateronnon*, "people where there is a mountain,"[4] referring to the northern extension of the Niagara escarpment to Georgian Bay, the Blue Mountain area. Unfortunately, we do not know what the Petun called the Huron.[5] That might have told us a useful story.

The Neutral lived to the south and west of the Wendat peoples, including the areas of the Niagara Peninsula, western Lake Ontario, and north of the shores of Lake Erie. The Huron referred to the Neutral as *Hati8endaronk*,[6] probably meaning something like "their (m) words (or language) are some distance away." This may refer to the differences between the Neutral dialects or languages and those of the Wendat-speaking Huron and Petun. Again, we have no idea what the Neutral may have called the Huron (or the Petun). It is unfortunate that we have the perspective of only one people in the major sources, *The Jesuit Relations* and the Jesuit dictionaries, or we might know a lot more about the early relationships between these three groups. Although Brébeuf is said to have composed a Neutral dictionary, there is no evidence that it survived. That is too bad, as it would be an invaluable historical resource that would lead to a rewriting of the history of this time and place.

The Jesuits, from Father Jean de Brébeuf on, made their primary Iroquoian contact with the Huron. They seemed ideal mission subjects. They were a trading people, facilitating the French fur trade. They were relatively sedentary, so the Jesuits would not have to chase them around the countryside like they might the more nomadic Algonquian peoples. Additionally, the Huron had contacts with Algonquian-speaking peoples near the French, the Innu (Montagnais), and the Algonquin.

The Huron were made up of four tribes or nations.[7] The Bear (*Hatinnia8enten* "they (m) are of bear country," see Steckley 2007b, 192) and the Cord (*Hatingeennonniahak* "they (m) used to make cord, i.e., for fish nets")[8] had been in the area the longest. The former were linguistically (and probably to a certain extent culturally and politically) divided into two dialect groups, Northern and Southern Bear (see Steckley 1990b, 1991a, 1991b, 1997, 2007a). The dialect of the Southern Bear and that of the Cord were more similar to that of the Petun (as represented in the Wyandot dialect of the eighteenth century) than were the dialects of the Northern Bear and the Rock (and probably also the Deer). The other two tribes, the Rock (*Arendaenronnon* "people at the rock")[9] and the Deer (*Atahonta,enrat*[10] "she, one has two white ears") were smaller, and were relative newcomers to the Georgian Bay area at the time of contact, entering within the last generation. The Rock lived east of Georgian Bay, their greater closeness to the French a factor in their early contact with those people. The Deer lived the furthest south, in only one village that we know of.

The Petun were divided into two groups, the Deer and the Wolf (JR33:143). The nature of these two groups, whether they were separate tribes or merely phratries, i.e., linked clan groups (see discussion below), is not clearly known. Again, scholars lose because of the narrow Huron-focused experience of the Jesuits.

The late 1640s were hard times for the three Ontario Iroquoian groups. The nations of the Iroquois Confederacy won more and more of their battles with their Iroquoian foes, and became more aggressive in their push into the area. There have been debates as to why they pushed this hard and why they won relatively easily.[11] It is enough for this work to say that the member nations of the Iroquois Confederacy needed to replenish their numbers, and they wanted a larger share of the growing fur trade. They ultimately won, I believe, because they were united by the Great Law of Peace, in a relatively tight union of five peoples (from west to east, the Seneca, Cayuga, Onondaga, Oneida, and Mohawk) with a unity that the Ontario Iroquoians could not match, especially with the Huron having a new divide between Christians and non-Christians in their midst.

By 1650, the Huron and Petun were driven out of their centuries-old (for the Petun and the Bear and the Cord) homeland near the southern shores of Georgian Bay. The Huron went in three directions. Some went east to be close to the French, which resulted in the community formerly called Lorette, now known as Wendake. Others went south, by choice or by force to join the Iroquois, a path traditionally under-reported in the old historical canon of New France. It looks bad when your allies choose to join with your enemies. Finally, some went toward the Western Great Lakes with the Petun to eventually become the Wyandot. A significant portion of the Petun became the core of the Wyandot. A Neutral component is still there amongst the Wyandot, but it is not well documented, or easy to determine. I suggest below that the Neutral may have contributed to both the Wolf and the Hawk clans.

By 1671, the Wyandot finally settled for a while at Michilimackinac, where Lake Huron meets Lake Michigan, not far away from Lake Superior. They stayed there until the early 1700s, when they settled (again for a while) in the Detroit/Windsor area, stretching out east into north Ohio. It is their stay in the Detroit/Windsor area that is the main subject of this book.

At all these locations the people had to choose carefully when, and under what circumstances, they supported the combating forces of the more numerous and usually more powerful peoples with whom they came into contact. They had to closely watch the fluctuating fortunes of the opposing European forces, the French and the English, while keeping one eye on the moves of the ever-threatening Iroquois. Even their usual allies, the numerically superior Algonkian speakers of the upper Great Lakes (e.g., the Ottawa, Ojibwa, Sauk, Miami, Illinois, and Potawatomi) required vigilance. The Wyandot were newcomers in their country. This definitely affected the politics and policies of the Wyandot of the eighteenth century. All around them, neighbouring eyes were watching their every move.

As long as the people were with the French they were called Huron. It is in their dealing with English speakers, less linguistically schooled than the Jesuits, and people that generally seemed to have had a harder time wrapping their ears and mouths around the sounds of the Wendat language,[12] that the name Wyandot began to appear. The Wyandot had to deal with the English after the defeat of the French in the Seven Years War, 1756 to 1763, also called the War of the Conquest, in Canada and the French and Indian war in the United States. In the treaties with the United States, in my reading beginning with the Treaty of Greenville in 1795 (www.wyandot/grenvil.htm), the people were referred to as Wyandot.

A CLAN-BASED STUDY

The second question addressed is the following: What does a clan-based study of the Wyandot entail? Here we will be looking basically at the nature of the Iroquoian clan. This involves investigating how it relates to the clan leadership names or titles that operate as threads of continuity throughout the seventeenth and eighteenth centuries. Further, it entails a discussion of how the flexible nature of the clan structure functioned as a constant identity when larger-scale identity (e.g., tribe or nation) had been more seriously compromised. When an Iroquoian nation breaks into pieces, its most important constituent parts are clans.

It is unfortunate that the anthropological literature, while good at providing the odd decent study on clans, has yet to produce a major comparative work on the subject. It is not studied now as often as it was in the past. Obviously, other Aboriginal nations went through similar socio-political pressures. Matrilineal peoples were surrounded by powerful patrilineal neighbours that could influence their social practices. The Cherokee, for example, a fellow Iroquoian group and likewise matrilineal, did not "officially" give up matrilineal inheritance until their National Council made a decision in 1810 (Mooney 1900, 86–87). At the same time, they officially began referring to husbands/fathers as "heads of the household."

It is good to keep in mind that what the French may have called "nations," that is the Huron, the Petun, and the Neutral, were not fixed entities such as France or Britain at the time (themselves formerly unstable in boundary and in constituent elements). The Huron were at the time of first contact in the early seventeenth century experiencing the socio-political adjustments necessary for the entry of two tribes, the Rock and the Deer, into the territory of the Bear and the Cord, extending from the southern shores of Georgian Bay. Their prior "war" with the Petun had split apart peoples who spoke the same language (Wendat) and who doubtless shared most of their cultural features.

Also important to keep in mind is that part of the colonization process is the power to name, and to sever the capacity of the colonized to perpetuate their own names in the historical record. The Huron had no distinctive national name they called themselves, as opposed to the Petun. The name Huron is colonially imposed. Father Jérôme Lalemant presented the word's origin in the following way:

> Arriving at the French settlement, some Sailor or Soldier seeing for the first time this species of barbarians, some of whom wore their hair in ridges...this fashion of wearing the hair making their heads look to him like those of boars [hures], led him to call these barbarians "Hurons" and this is the name that has clung to them ever since. (JR16:229–31)

The haircut now known as a "Mohawk" was in fact at the time popular among a number of nations in the area, most particularly the Ottawa. It was not unique to the Wendat, even though it may have given them the name they are usually known by in history books and classrooms.[13]

Neither do we know what the Petun called themselves apart from the Huron, if anything. The Neutral were named such because the French thought them neutral in the conflict they saw between the Wendat speakers and the Haudenosaunee. We do not know the links and divides between "Neutral" tribes. Nor do we know whether they had their own collective name for themselves. As we will see later in this chapter, the Wenro, one of the groups the French termed Neutral, in their time of need were aided by the Huron, not by any other "Neutral" tribe.

As these ebbs and flows of unification and division were going on, people would always belong to a clan. The number of clans a tribe or "nation" of linked tribes may have could grow or shrink, but there would be little doubt among the people what constituted that unit. It was more constant than the more fluctuating larger socio-political entities.

This work is a clan-based study of the Wyandot. Readers would be well within their rights to wonder what is meant by that. First of all, I must offer a definition or explanation of what the nature of a clan was, as historically experienced by the Wendat peoples. Like all social scientific terms that also have use in common speech, there are sources of confusion when discussing the term "clan." I hope to handle this discussion piece by piece, examining the basic characteristics of the Iroquoian clan.

A clan is a unilineal descent group. That means that it is, to a significant extent, family determined because it follows one line or side of the family. This can be on the mother's side, called matrilineal, as with Iroquoian peoples, or, more commonly across the world and through time, on the father's side, called patrilineal. This does not necessarily mean that everyone that belongs to the clan is related by "blood" to the others. Although all may be said to descend from one real or mythic ancestor or family, that would not actually be the case. Families would have formed alliances, individuals, families, and even other peoples (see below regarding the Wenro) would be recruited or brought into the clan. The family social principle of the clan trumps its genetics. By that I mean that people considered family because they were clan members often did not directly depend on whether there was a blood kin connection.

NAMES FOR THE CLAN

The word "clan" was not used in the primary documents of the ethnohistorical literature. What then did the French and the Wendat call this social unit? Although in current French usage the word "clan" translates as the same word in English, the French writers of the seventeenth and eighteenth centuries represented Wendat clans with the words "bande" or more typically "famille," as in the following French–Wendat dictionary example:

Famille…de quelle famille est tu?	[Family…of which family are you?]
ndia8eron esendio'k8ten?	[Which clan are you (singular)?]
andia8ich de la tortue	[of the turtle][14]
annion,en de l'ours	[of the bear]
(FH1697:74; c.f. FH1697:15; FHO:58; and FH1693:141)	

The Wendat noun stem[15] used to refer to clans here is -,entiok8-, with the verb root -8ten- "to be of such a nature" added (Potier 1920, 441; Steckley 2007b, 310). This noun stem is derived by adding the instrumental suffix -k8-[16] to the verb root -,entio- (Potier 1920, 391; HF62, HF59, HF65; Steckley 2007b, 286), which referred to relatives on the mother's side.[17] The meaning of the noun stem so created was also generalized to refer to a "group," a meaning found in other Iroquoian languages (see Steckley 2007b, 310 for terms in Mohawk, Oneida, Onondaga, Cayuga, and Tuscarora) that do not still have the verb that originally generated the noun stem.[18]

Examples from Appendix B2 are:
Sa,onditiok8enh8a	he brings them (ind) as a group
Ehonditok8ichien	they (m) will investigate it as a group (i.e., the Standing Trees or councillors)

With the external locative noun suffix -,e- (meaning "at" or "on") added to the verb root, you get dictionary entries such as the following:

Gentio,e[19]   1. etre parens de c[oté] maternal
[to be relatives on the mother's side]
On,8entio,e
[we are matrilineal relatives]
....

2. av[oir] les par[ens]. matern[al]. en tel lieu
[to have maternal relatives in such a place]
θo a,itio,e
[there, they (ind) are clan members on my mother's side]
J'ay la des parens du c[oté] de ma mere
[I have there relatives on my mother's side]
(HF59; c.f. HF62; Potier 1920, 391)

The Characteristics of Wyandot Clans

There appear to have been five basic qualities of traditional Wyandot clans. They were matrilineal; they possessed names that they revived or resuscitated; they were exogamous; they were recruited; and they were organized into phratries.

(1) Wyandot Clans Were Matrilineal

The matrilineality of clans, which was discussed above, was remarked on by late-seventeenth-century French traveller and occasionally imaginative recorder of places and people Louis Armand, Baron de Lahontan. He spent time with the Wyandot and created the (partially imaginary) Wyandot character Adario. In his *New Voyages to North America*, he wrote the following, concerning the matrilineal nature of Wyandot clans:[20]

> The Savages always go by the Mother's Name [i.e., her clan]. To make this plain by an example: the Leader of the Nation of *Hurons* [i.e., Wyandot], who is called *Sastaretsi*, being Married to a Daughter of another *Huron* family [i.e., clan], by whom he has several Children, that General's Name is extinct at his Death, for that his Children assume the Name of the Mother. Now it may be ask'd how the name of *Sastaretsi*, has been kept up for the space of Seven or Eight Hundred Years among that People, and is likely to continue to future Ages? But the Question is easily Answered, if we consider that the Sister of this *Sastaretsi* being married to another Savage whom we shall call *Adario* [i.e., the name Lahontan sometimes used to refer to Kandiaronk or

Rat, see next chapter], the Children Springing from that Marriage, will be called *Sastaretsi*, after the Mother, and not *Adario* after this Father. (Lahontan 1970, 2:461)

Linked with this is the Wyandot practice of not having a first and last name distinction. One Jesuit remarked that among the Huron:

> In this Country, there are no Names [i.e., surnames or family names] appropriated to Families, as in Europe. The Children do not bear their Father's name, and there is no name that is common to the whole Family,—each one has his own different name. (JR23:165)

Interestingly, although French naming with patrilineality and multiple names at one time clashed with Wyandot matrilineality and single names at one time, the Wyandot did not adopt a European naming pattern of first name plus last name until the nineteenth century.

(2) Wyandot Clans Possessed Names

Choosing the Right Person

A second characteristic of Wendat clans is that they owned names. Every Wendat name was possessed by a clan. As such, names could be sociologically labelled, particularly with the leading names, as specific statuses, with a set of role expectations attached to each one. Therefore, for these leading names, the suitability of the prospective bearers for the status was considered to be important before they would be permitted to obtain the name. Names were not automatically inherited by specific individuals. Assigning the name involved deliberation within the clan as to who might be the best candidate. To use the language of sociology, they were not totally ascribed statuses like primogeniture, where the eldest son inherits titles in the system that was the general practice in Europe at the time. The names were at least partially achieved statuses. Potential candidates had to be declared by those in authority (female and male) as suitable for the name. Jesuit Father Jean de Brébeuf remarked:

> They reach this degree of honor, partly through succession, partly through election; their children do not usually succeed them, but properly their nephews [i.e., sister's sons] and grandsons. And the latter do not even come to the succession of these petty royalties, like the Dauphins of France, or children to the inheritance of their fathers; but only so far as they have suitable qualifications and accept the position, and are accepted by the whole Country. (JR10:233)

Another Jesuit commented on the same matter a few years later:

> [W]hen one of the Family dies all the relatives assemble, and consult together as to which among them shall bear the name of the deceased, giving his own to some other relative. He who takes a new name also assumes the Duties connected with it, and thus he becomes a Captain [i.e., clan leader] if the deceased had been one. (JR23:165–67)

It should be pointed out that despite the Jesuits' constant use of the masculine in talking about names, there were important female names as well. This will be discussed further when we talk about the elders' council and about female positions of authority.

There appears to have been a kind of hierarchy of names. When someone bearing a great name died, it was important that someone else gave up what can be called a lesser name to replace him or her. The great names of the people were passed down with solemn ceremony. It was important that these names lived on. To continue the quotation above, "Thus it happens that a Captain never has any other name than that of his predecessor, as formerly in Egypt all the Kings bore the name of Ptolemy" (JR23:167).

Resuscitating Names through Ceremony

New owners of the important names had to prove themselves worthy upon receiving the name. In *The Jesuit Relations* (10:275–77) of 1636, Father Jean de Brébeuf, whose own Wendat name, Hechon, would be treated as a great name to be passed down to others (Father Pierre Chaumonot, Father Daniel Richer, and more recently, myself) recorded that if the name was an especially esteemed one, the appropriateness of its new bearer had to be publicly demonstrated:

> [T]he one who resuscitates him,—after a magnificent feast to the whole country, that he may make himself known under this name—makes a levy of the resolute young men and goes away on a war expedition, to perform some daring exploit that shall make it evident to the whole country that he has inherited not only the name, but also the virtues and courage of the deceased.

Among Iroquoian peoples, as with other peoples whose clan names are important, reviving the name, bringing it back to life, involves formal ceremony. The ceremony for renaming had itself several names when it involved the rebirth of the name/title of a leader. In the literature directly pertaining to the Six Nations Iroquois it is usually referred to as the Condolence Ceremony.[21] The Wendat had two main terms for it. They used the noun root *-chiend-* "name" (Steckley 2007b, 76–77) and the verb root *-ohare-* "to wash" (Steckley 2007b, 292–93), to get the expression "to wash a name." The other term, resuscitation (literally causing one's life to return) is a translation of the Huron verb form *onsa8-atonnhonti* (Potier 1920, 415, based on the verb root *-onnhe-* "to live"; Steckley 2007b, 300–301) used to describe the process.

The ceremony was laced with metaphor. Each gift is a word or voice,[22] expressing a specific message, most relating to the physical actions of bringing back to life from inside the earth the spirit of the name that has "died" with the death of its previous owner:

> When this was done, each Nation gave its presents, which, according to custom, were differently characterized. Some, as they presented their gifts, said "May this grasp the arm of the deceased, to draw him from the grave." Others said: "May these support his head, lest he fall back again." Another, giving still a new present, would add volubly, that he gave him weapons to repel the Enemies. And a fourth would say, "I make the Earth solid under his feet, so that it may remain immovable during his reign." (JR23:167–69)

Atironta: Reviving a Great Wendat Name in the Seventeenth Century
A classic seventeenth-century example of Wendat name resuscitation is that of the Deer clan name Hatironta, usually spelled Atironta,[23] meaning "He draws or attracts." (Steckley 2007b, 52, verb root *-atironta-*). It was first recorded as a Wendat name of significance among the Arendaenronnon or Rock tribe of the Huron of the seventeenth century, and later with the Huron of Wendake in New France, and with the Wyandot of the eighteenth century. The written story of this name begins when Governor Samuel de Champlain first met a Hatironta in 1615 while visiting Huronia. Champlain stayed in Hatironta's home in Cahiagué, then the primary village of the Rock, located centrally in their territory. In the spring of 1616, Hatironta followed Champlain back to Quebec to become the first Wendat headman to establish a firm relationship with the French. He returned home with a pile of gifts and, most probably, trading rights that other Huron traders would envy. One of the ways of distinguishing the status of Huron leaders was in terms of the trade routes that they established and owned. And they guarded those rights jealously, as Brébeuf outlines in *The Jesuit Relations* (10:223–25) of 1636:

> Besides having some kind of Laws maintained among themselves, there is also a certain order established as regards foreign Nations. And first, concerning commerce; several families have their own private trades, and he is considered Master [i.e., great in voice] of one line of trade who was the first to discover it. The children share the rights of their parents in this respect, as do those who bear the same name; no one goes into it without permission, which is given only in consideration of presents; he associates with him as many or as few as he wishes. (emphasis mine)

I emphasize the words "as do those who bear the same name" as suggesting the inheritance of rights with the resuscitation of a name.

The connection between the name Hatironta and the Rock tribe was so well established for both the French and the Huron that to speak of the former was often to refer to the latter. In Recollect Brother Gabriel Sagard's dictionary, based on the monk's experiences with the Huron in 1623–24 and published in 1632, we find the following:

Nation Datironta [The nation of Atironta]
Renarhonon...[24] [People at the rock] (Steckley 2010a, 307; my translation)

In 1639, when the Jesuits were extending their Wendat mission in earnest to the Rock tribe, and they stayed in Contarea, then the principal Rock village, they lived in the house of a headman named Hatironta. The community was at the furthermost point of the territory of the Rock and the Huron, not far from the joining of Lake Couchiching and Lake Simcoe in present day Orillia. This Atironta was possibly a nephew (sister's son) of the individual first recorded as bearing the name. He set up a meeting in which the Jesuits, who were being accused of killing people through spreading European diseases, could defend themselves by explaining why they were there. Hatironta's home was a safe haven for the visitors.

In *The Jesuit Relations* of 1642, we read of how he and his brother Aeotahon had been instructed in Christianity, but were not yet considered ready to be baptized. This would change after the two men were captured by the enemy Iroquois. Hatironta was killed; his brother escaped.

Upon returning home, Aeotahon completed his Christian preparation and was baptized as Jean Baptiste, named after the Jesuit mission (St. Jean) to the Rock tribe. He also received his brother's Wendat name. Those that directed the ceremony effecting this change said to the Jesuits (and the other members of the audience):

"We..." said they, "cast our eyes on that man," pointing out Jean Baptiste to us; "and we do not wish his name to be any longer Aeoptahon [sic], but Atironta, since he brings him back to life." (JR23:167)

The Jesuits involved themselves in the ceremony with gifts and statements of their own, part of the mixing of traditional and Christian elements in rituals that would be a part of Wyandot life in the eighteenth century:

On our part, we gave three presents; and, as we produced the most valuable, we said: "This gift is intended to restore the Voice of the deceased, but a Voice that will no longer be the instrument of the Demons to proclaim and command forbidden Ceremonies,—I say, a Voice worthy of a Christian, who loves and encourages every one to defend his Country, to overthrow Impiety, and to promulgate the holy Gospel." To these words the entire Audience replied: "Ao!" which with them indicates a sentiment of approval. May GOD bless this new Christian Captain, and grant him the grace to do all in his power. (JR23:169)

In the fall of 1646, Jesuit Father Gabriel Lalemant (1610–49) came to live with the Huron. At some point, not specified in the literature, he received the name Hatironta, evidence of the close connection of the name and the Deer clan with the French, especially the Jesuits. The future saint suffered a martyr's death at the hands of the Iroquois in the spring of 1649. Within a year, the Huron Jean Baptiste Atironta would also be killed by the Iroquois.

Sometime within the next ten years, a new holder of the name, Pierre Atironta, was captured by the Iroquois. He was either released by them, or he escaped. Either way, he was back with his people in 1666. Over a six-year period, he became a Christian leader of his people and was credited with initiating the practice of Christian visitation of the sick. On 16 December 1672, as a sick old man, he died. There is a street in the Huron reserve community of Wendake that bears his complete name. We will return to the story of this name when we discuss, in chapter 7, the female leaders of the Deer clan.

Wyandot Name Resuscitation
Some changing of names is documented among the Wyandot of the eighteenth century, with both male and female names being resuscitated. It can often be confusing to the researcher, especially with entries in which first names are not given. Here are some examples. The main sources used are the census of 1747 (with the short form PV standing for Petit Village and GV standing for Grand Village), and the abundant baptismal records.[25] These records show the baptized, father, mother, and godparent. Using the name of the spouse as a guide can be tricky for three reasons. One is that her or his name might have changed over the years. Another is that they lived in dangerous times, so sudden violent death of a spouse, particularly a husband, might happen. Finally, someone might just have switched partners, which seems not to have been unusual for the Wyandot during the eighteenth century.

The following chart shows some of the names that were demonstrated as being resuscitated during the eighteenth century.

Resuscitated Name Chart

Men's Names	Clan	First Name	Years on Record
Te Hatontaratase (he is a twisted lake)	Striped Turtle	Jacob	1734–47
		Martin	1747
		?	1754–64
Ha8endaraties	Bear	?	1729–32
		Jean Baptiste	1743–47
		?	1760
Taniendonien (Hanniendo,en or Nniendonien)	Prairie Turtle	Jean Baptiste	1736–47
		?	(1747)–75
Ennons	Bear	Pierre	1747–52
		?	1765
		?	1777
Women's Names			
Onnonrachien	Porcupine	Catiche	(?)–1747
		Catharine	1748
Taronngiahak (Torondgiahak)	Bear	?	(?)–1747
		Dorothy	1747–49

New Names

It seems, as well, that new Wendat names could be created. Names based on the meaning or sound of the appellations of outsiders could be added to the list of names. We have seen this with Hechon, the name held by Fathers Brébeuf, Chaumonot, and Richer. It began with an attempt to say 'Jean,' the ž of the -j- being replaced by the phonetically close š of the -ch-. It was also true of the name Onnontio, "it is a great mountain," based on a translation of the French appellation of Governor Charles de Montmagny, Governor of New France from 1636 to 1648. Every French governor after him received that name from the Wendat and other Iroquoian-speaking people.

Could new names be added to the set that the Wyandot drew upon to name themselves? There is one example that would give the answer "possibly" to that question. The leader of the Bear clan in 1747 was Michel A,a8as (Toupin 1996, 226). In his entry in the elders' council, there is added the French word "general," followed by the Wendat phrase "ha8endio d'hotiskenra,et" (Toupin 1996, 228) meaning "he is great in voice, in authority of those who are warriors," which fits well with the French addition.

In the PV11 house entry for Michel A,a8as, we have ",a,a8as (asari-8oin—)" (Toupin 1996, 209). The latter name is found on a list of names of European officials: "asarei8oin..gouv: de la caroline [governor of Carolina]" (Toupin 1996, 233). The name can be translated as "large knife," which seems in line with the term "long knives" that would later generally be used by Aboriginal groups to refer to Americans. The name comes from another Iroquoian language, as the meaning of 'knife' for the noun root appearing here exists in related languages, not in Wendat, and as the noun root would be -achra- in Wyandot (Steckley 2007b, 13). In the recording of Michel's death in September 1752, we have "asarei8oin, Michel vieux a,a8as" (Toupin 1996, 924, E69). The baptismal record is not very useful here, as we only have two references to a,a8as as a godfather in 1736 (Toupin 1996, 841, B384, B391), and nothing after that for either of his names.

Name Sharing
Connolly declared dogmatically that names were the unique property of each clan:

> Each clan had its list of proper names, and this list was its exclusive property which no other clan could appropriate or use. These were necessarily clan names. They were formed by rigid rules prescribed by immemorial custom.... Custom was inflexible—exacting—and could be modified only by long and persistent effort... or by national disaster. (Connolly 1900, 107)

Yet in the record of the elders' council we see names that appear to be shared by more than one clan. Perhaps the "national disaster" of being driven from one homeland and establishing themselves in others made that necessary:

Barnabe Anien8indet	Snake clan elder
Etienne Enie8indet	Deer clan elder
Christine A8innonke[26]	Bear elder
Anne A8innonke	Large Turtle elder
Te ondise8a (tiaondise8a)	Snake clan elder
Marie-Marguerite Te ondise8a	Striped Turtle

This is difficult to explain. Perhaps these names related to specific roles that were not limited to a particular clan, or to some connection between the clans. I will be suggesting below that clans recruited members and that the Snake clan was perhaps "recruiting members" at this time. Name-sharing may have been one such form. It could perhaps be seen as honouring the clan from which the name came.

(3) Wyandot Clans Were Exogamous

A third Wyandot clan characteristic is that they were exogamous, meaning that marrying outside the clan was mandatory. Marrying another clan member would be considered a kind of incest. The very articulate, if often racist and Francophobic, nineteenth-century American historian Francis Parkman clearly identified the value placed on clans by a number of Aboriginal groups in North America (Parkman 1894, 405). One important point he made referred to clan exogamy, that is, the practice of having to marry outside one's clan at the tremendous social risk of violating an incest taboo:

> The members of the same clan, being connected, or supposed to be so, by ties of kindred, more or less remote, are prohibited from intermarriage. Thus Wolf cannot marry Wolf; but he may, if he chooses, take a wife from the clan of Hawks, or any other clan but his own. It follows that when this prohibition is rigidly observed, no single clan can live apart from the rest; but the whole must be mingled together, and in every family the husband and wife must be of different clans. (Parkman 1894, 5)

The Wyandot appear to have adhered to this rule throughout the eighteenth century, despite their relatively small numbers, and their exposure to societies that had no such practice. Going through the baptismal and marriage records, I noted that when clan could be determined for husband and wife, father and mother, they were almost never of the same clan. Clan exogamy ruled in the country of the Wyandot.

The single exception that proves the rule appears in an entry for a baptism taking place in 1746. The later fate of the individual involved would seem to provide evidence for the condemnation that would fall on someone who broke the incest rule. The entry runs as follows:

> Josephus...P[ere] jos[ephus] so,a8enda...M[ere]...Matrikina...Pa[rraine; godfather] jos[ephus] s. Martin (Toupin 1996, 855, B676)

The entry is for a Striped Turtle member of the elders' council named Tso,a8enda. He must have had some significance, as least in war councils at the time as the word "general" was placed after his name. It is noteworthy that his name was not included elsewhere in the census. His name is not recorded as being that of a resident in any of the homes of Wyandot in 1747. His name appears nowhere else in the official record. The word "matrikina," no doubt referring to matrilineal kin, appears nowhere else in Father Robert Toupin's collection of Potier's work. So,a8enda had violated a taboo. This act seems to have been socially punished accordingly, perhaps with some form of exile.

(4) Wyandot Clans Recruited

A fourth characteristic of the Wendat/Wyandot clans is that in certain social circumstances they appear to have recruited members. This was probably crucial to their survival during the diaspora of the second half of the seventeenth century, but may have been the case earlier when the different "tribes" or "nations" were being formed. Father Jérôme Lalemant wrote the following in 1639, suggesting the possibility of the recruitment of clans by the Bear and Cord, the most populous nations of the Huron, and the ones first in the Georgian Bay area homeland:

> They are the most populous through having, in the course of time, adopted more families; and as these adopted families always retain the names and memories of their founders, they are still distinct little Nations in those where they have been adopted,—preserving thereof the general name, and community of some minor special interests, together with dependence upon their two special Captains, one of war and the other of council, to whom the public affairs of their community are reported. (JR16:229)

There is one clear-cut case of this recruiting on a large scale. That occurred when the Turtle clan adopted the remnants of a small tribe, the Wenro, considered one of the Neutral people. Up until the late 1630s, the Wenro, who lived about thirty miles east of the Niagara River, were located precariously close to the Seneca, the westernmost of the Iroquois nations. The situation was fine for them as long as they had the support of other Neutral nations, which according to Father Jerome Lalemant they somehow lost at that time (JR17:25–27). It appears that their only recourse was to look to the Huron for support. In 1638, some six hundred refugees, most of them women and children, moved into the major Huron community of Ossossane (the main village of the Bear, located near the western extremity of Huronia) and some of the surrounding smaller villages. While *The Jesuit Relations* tell us only of the adoption by the Huron of this tribe, there is a short reference in clan lists in two Jesuit-written French–Wendat dictionaries that tell us of the Turtle clan's role in this adoption.

The Turtle Clan Recruited among the Neutral

In the entry for the Turtle clan was the phrase *tionnenria honnentre[a] hotienrotori*. The first two words can be translated unproblematically as "when a group is small"[27] for *tionnenria* and "they have them as maternal grandchildren"[28] for "honnentre[a]."

The third word is actually an incorrectly jumbled together combination of two words: "hotienro" and "otori." What is significant here is that the first word makes reference to the Neutral nation known in the literature as the Wenroronnon or simply Wenro. This people lived not far west of the Seneca, in what is now western New York State, so were in a precarious position. In 1638, they were forced to abandon their territory. The Huron meeting in council decided to adopt the people, and they were brought to Huronia.

The name Wenro appears to be formed from a combination of the noun root *-enr-* "moss" (Steckley 2007b, 276) and the verb root *-o-* "to be in water" (Steckley 2007b, 291–92), to get the meaning "it is wet moss." The usual way of writing the name Wenro is to add the populative suffix to this *-ronnon-* giving the meaning "people of" (Potier 1920, 66), to give us "people of the wet moss." With the masculine plural pronominal prefix -hoti- we get "they masculine," giving us "they (m) are wet moss."

The second component, based on the verb root *-ori-* "to cover" (Steckley 2007b, 306–7) signifies "it is covered."[29] Putting the two parts together we get "they (m) are covered with wet moss." A combination of *-8enr-* and *-ori-* in Wyandot in the late nineteenth and early twentieth centuries referred to the "moss-backed turtle" (Barbeau 1915, 72n2, 86n1). Significantly, it was the usual term at that time for the Large Turtle clan, the leading clan of the Turtle phratry of the Wyandot.

The Wenro were socially identifiable as Turtles, as the Bear and Deer nations of the Huron were also socially identified with a specific animal. The combined translation would then be: "When they were small in number, they had as maternal grandchildren those who are covered with moss" (i.e., the Wenro). The Turtle clan, then, had recruited fellow Turtles.

This may have significance for the Wyandot of the eighteenth century. We will be discussing the existence of phratries shortly. These are groupings of clans for certain social purposes. The Wyandot had three such phratries, the Deer, Turtle, and Wolf. Perhaps the recruitment of the Wenro was a source for the diversification of the Turtle phratry clans of the Wyandot. Maybe it began, or was stretched by the entry of, the Wenro into the clan world of the Wendat (Huron and Petun). I believe that the Huron had the same set of phratries with, as we will see, fewer members of the Turtle phratry.

There are three other Huron clans that may have connected with or even recruited from Neutral peoples. One was the Wolf clan. In the clan lists found in two dictionaries, the word *ahonrek* is found in the entry for the Wolf clan (FHO; FH67:96). This term is clearly cognate with *Atiaonrek*, a Neutral group whose name appears in the following list of nations defeated by the Iroquois, and recorded in *The Jesuit Relations* (42:197) of 1656 as part of the vision speech of an Iroquois spirit:

> I made you conquer the Hurons, the Tobacco Nation, the Ahondironons, Atiraguenrek, Atiaonrek, Tekoulguehronnons and Gentuetehronnons. (my emphasis)

The difference between the two terms exists only in the pronominal prefix, with *Ahonrek* apparently containing the feminine singular (,)a-, while *Atiaonrek* probably has the masculine plural -hati-, the same two pronominal prefix forms that appear with the root for wolf. I suspect that the people referred to lived in the Niagara region, as the terms "*Niagara*" and "*Ahonrek*" never appear in the same nation lists. Although no linguistic clues suggest this, it is possible that these people were identified with wolves, and that there was a special connection, perhaps involving adoption, between the two groups, the Wolf clan and the Wolf people. In our discussion of the name given to Father Chaumonot by the Neutral, and later shared with Potier, we will see another piece of evidence suggesting a connection.

In the entries in two dictionaries for the Hawk clan, we find the terms *hatiraenre* ("they (m) are…") and *Araenre* (possibly haraenre "he is…"). In the same list of nations presented above, we find the following:

> I made you conquer the Hurons, the Tobacco Nation, the Ahondironons, Atiraguenrek, Atiaonrek, Tekoulguehronnons and Gentuetehronnons. (JR42:197; my emphasis)

The term, which could be written as "hatira,enrek" (referring to a masculine plural pronoun) is clearly related, as is the ,era,enk recorded in the early 1670s in *De Religione* (Potier 1920, 662; Steckley 2004, 132–33, line 16). Both refer to a Neutral group. The term is close enough to the Oneida word for hawk *kalhakúha*[30] (Michelson and Doxtator 2002, 1035) to bear consideration that it too refers to hawks.

The evidence is not quite so clear with the name found in the Fox clan entry. In clan lists we find *Skanda,ona*, which does not resemble any clan name or term for "fox" that appears in the literature.[31]

We can speculate (without direct evidence) that clans also may have developed anew, be created out of split clans, or possibly developed through visions later honoured through practice and story.

Eight clans were reported among the Huron in the writings of the Jesuits in *The Jesuit Relations*. This is seen in the account of the ceremony held to console the French over the loss of young Jacques Douart, killed by some members of the Huron. In two places there are references in this to "eight nations" of the Huron:

> After that, eight Captains, from the eight nations that constitute the Huron country, brought each a present for the eight principal bones in the frame of the human body,—the feet, the thighs, the arms.... We also gave some [presents], in return, to all the eight nations individually. (JR33:243, 247)

In two Wendat dictionaries there are listings of eight Huron clans in the order: Bear, Deer, Turtle, Beaver, Wolf, Loon/Sturgeon, Hawk, and Fox (see Steckley 1982, 1988). However, the Wyandot had ten clans rather than eight, and some of the names of the clans were quite different in character, not referring directly to the totem animal, but to what appear to be place names.

(5) *Wyandot Clans Were Organized into Phratries*

The ten clans of the Wyandot were divided into three groupings or phratries: Deer, Turtle, and Wolf. A phratry, which is based on the Greek word for "brotherhood," is a grouping of a clan largely for ceremonial or ritual purposes.[32] In an early anthropological discussion of "The Iroquois Phratry" in *Ancient Society* (1877), Lewis H. Morgan defined a phratry as:

> a brotherhoood, as the term imports, and a natural growth from the organization into gentes [clans]. It is an organic union or association of two or more gents of the same tribe for certain common objects. (Morgan 1877)

In his study of the Six Nations of the Iroquois Confederacy, Morgan noted that the Seneca, Cayuga, Onondaga, and Tuscarora had eight clans divided into two phratries.[33] Phratries were expressed in various ways. They played lacrosse against each other; they sat on opposite sides of the longhouse in tribal council meetings; and they would play different roles in funerals (i.e., mourners and conductors of the ceremonies).

Phratries were found among some of the socio-politically complex Aboriginal groups, such as the Aztecs, the Hopi, and the Tlingit. They could, like clans, be exogamous (with marriage mandated outside the phratry). In fact, exogamy is often given in textbook definitions of phratry. Morgan noted that the Seneca would call fellow members of their phratry "brother" (probably "same-sex sibling") and members of the other phratry "cousin," and commented that this implied that the phratries had once been exogamous, but were no longer.

The term *hontaxen* or *hontaken* was put to the right of the three phratry groupings of the Wyandot in Potier's writing (Toupin 1996, 226, 259–60). This word means "they (masculine) are same-sexed siblings" (i.e., they are brothers or they are sisters), based on the verb root -,*en*- "to be same-sex siblings" (Steckley 2007b, 114). Despite that naming, the baptismal records show that phratries were not exogamous among the Wyandot. In the 1747 census, of the thirty-nine couples whose clan identities are both known, twenty-five married outside the phratry and fourteen married within the phratry. Similarly, of the eighty couples with known clan identities in the baptismal records, fifty-six were phratry exogamous, and twenty-four were phratry endogamous (involving marrying within the phratry). This is more or less what you would expect with no phratry exogamy rule in place. They would not have had the numbers to sustain a strict phratry exogamy. Perhaps such existed in their past, as is suggested by the fact that most of the marriages seem to be outside people's phratry.

Deer Phratry

The first-named phratry of the Wyandot was of the Deer. As you can see, phratries can contain clans with the same totem animal name as that borne by the phratry. It should be noted, however, that the name in Wyandot for the clan and for the phratry are different.

THE DEER CLAN The first clan listed among the Wyandot of 1747 was also of the Deer. Not surprisingly, it is largely because they were the clan that provided Sastaretsi, the grand chief of the Wyandot. The Deer clan was the first of three clans that comprised the Deer phratry (see below). There are two basic names used to refer to the Deer clan in the literature. One is the word for deer among Wendat speakers. *Oskennonton* (along with various cognate terms) refers to deer in several Iroquoian languages (Barbeau 1961, 168; Michelson and Doxtator 2002, 959 for Oneida; Woodbury 2003, 1074 for Onondaga; and Michelson 1973, 102 for Mohawk). Derived from the verb root *-sken-* "to be a manifestation of the dead" (Steckley 2007b, 240), it has the literal meaning of "one goes to or is in the land of the dead" (Potier 1920, 352). It refers in the Wyandot list to the Deer phratry as well. Perhaps that was its main use outside of the actual physical animal itself.

The term that makes specific reference to the clan appears in clan lists as *sontennonk* and *skiatennon*, among the Wyandot *es8tennonk*. These terms appear to be derived from a verb root *-ennon-* meaning "to take care of, keep" (Steckley 2007b, 275). This could be a reference to taking care of or keeping an important political office.

In the clan lists found in Wendat dictionaries, this clan appears as second behind the Bear clan. I long thought that this was because the Bear clan had prominence throughout the Huron. This may well be, but I recently have begun to speculate over whether this was true only among the Bear nation of the Huron. Recall from the discussion of the resuscitation of the Deer clan name Atironta that he was of the Rock nation and that he established first significant contact with the French. This might mean that the Deer clan might have been listed first if there had been a Wendat dictionary based on the dialect of and information from Rock informants, whose leader Hationta belonged to that clan. The Jesuits from 1635 onwards spent much more time with the Bear nation than with the others. This showed up in the dialects in which they wrote their dictionaries (Steckley 1991) and in which they wrote words in *The Jesuit Relations* (Steckley 1990b).

THE SNAKE CLAN The Snake clan is listed in the second position. This would seem to be because of its ultimate origin from the Deer clan (see below). The Snake clan of the Deer phratry had the name eangontr8nnon, meaning "people of the snake charm." The word is composed of the populative suffix *-ronnon-*, and the verb root *-ngont-* "to be a snake charm." This latter term, which curiously is not found in any of the Jesuit dictionaries, refers to a snake charm, as can be seen in the following quotation from *The Jesuit Relations* (33:217) written in 1648 by Father Paul Ragueneau:

> The Hurons believe that there is a kind of serpent which they call *Angont*, which brings with it disease, death and almost every misfortune in the world. They say that a monster lives in subterranean places, in caverns, under a rock, in the woods, or in the mountains, but generally in the Lakes and Rivers.
>
> They say that the Sorcerers use the flesh of that frightful serpent to cause the deaths of those upon whom they cast their spells. With that poisonous flesh they rub some object,—a blade of corn, a tuft of hair, a piece of leather or of wood, the claw of an animal or some similar thing. The objects thus rubbed with that ointment derive from it a malignant efficacy, that causes them to penetrate into a man's entrails, into his most vital parts, and into the very marrow of his bones, carrying with them disease and suffering, which consume and cause to perish those who are attacked by them, unless, through some contrary virtue, means are found to draw out those objects to which the spell is attached, as we have already stated.

The penetrating ability seems to be the key component of charms made from this snake. In 1915, French-Canadian anthropologist Marius Barbeau published the words of Wyandot elder Allen Johnson in the story, "The Ground-Squirrel and the Flying Lion [i.e., cougar]," when speaking about flying white lions that were beings that lived in the polar regions:

> From time to time, they alight here and there, making a kind of light when they come down. They are said to drop a round magical stone (*ya'gōncra'*),[34] when they want to break the solid ice and get into the water. Wherever this magical stone hits the earth, a thundering clash may be heard. (Barbeau 1915, 140n2)

In the origin myth of the Snake clan, we learn that a Deer clan woman is charmed by a snake, and she becomes the first female member of the Snake clan. In the recording of this story by Barbeau, published in 1960, we learn that: "The Snake gave to the people its own shining scales as charms to be used for their welfare" (Barbeau 1960, 12). While the word used to translate "charm" is not *-ngont-*, the connection between the charm and the clan appears well established.

Two Huron women, a mother and a daughter, living near Quebec in 1673, had names associated with the Snake clan among the Wyandot: Marguerite Egandarekoui ("she is present forever, she is eternal") (JR58:139) and Marie Anne Garihonnentha, her daughter (JR58:139). The Snake connection is through the latter. There is a ,Arihonnentha who is the sister's child of Tannenhochre, the Snake elder, and of a woman named A,angonta, after the snake charm, all living in the same house in Etionnont8t (Toupin 1996, 226, 259, E7).

Hondachiate,en "He has a burning tongue" The earliest undisputable written connection of a Wyandot bearing a Snake clan name is that of Hondachiate,en, "his tongue is burning" (see derivation below). One certain seventeenth-century appearance of the name was concerning three people representing the Wyandot in Montreal on 15 August 1682. One of those names was *Ondahiaste chen*, Burnt tongue (NYCD9:181).

There might be an earlier reference. In the writings of Champlain, we come across the name of Ochasteguin, a leader of the Arendaenronnon or Rock tribe, a name used occasionally to represent the entire people (i.e., the Huron). He was the trading partner of Iroquet, the Weskarini Algonquin leader, who invited him in 1609 to join in a raid on the Mohawk. Ochasteguin agreed. In the summer, some three hundred Algonquin and Montagnais led by Iroquet, along with about one hundred Wendat led by Ochasteguin, headed towards the spot where the Richelieu River meets the St. Lawrence from the south. They met with Champlain, and went up to the river and attacked the Mohawk. After the battle was over, a young French man, Etienne Brulé, went to Huronia. Brulé might have been adopted by Ochasteguin because of the near identity of the meaning of their names, both referring to burning. Ochasteguin's name is formed around the verb root *-te,en-* "to burn" (Steckley 2007b, 42). This element in his name is more clearly represented in Champlain's map of 1613, in which the Huron are referred to as "hochataigains" (Heidenreich 1971, map 2), and in the use of Ochasteguins elsewhere. The only questionable aspect about this being the later Snake clan leader's name is whether the *-ocha-* at the beginning of the name is short for *-ndachi-* "tongue" (Steckley 2007b, 134–35), or just

-*chi*- "mouth" (Steckley 2007b, 73), preceded by the pronominal prefix -*o*- ("she" or "it").

As we have seen in the discussion of the Deer clan, Atironta took over the main connection with the French. It is interesting to speculate whether a clash between the two leaders, Ochasteguin and Atironta, in this regard led to or encouraged the formation of a new clan, the Snake clan, that was not recorded by the Jesuits, as that clan only existed with the Rock nation, and not with the Bear with whom they lived. At this point, it can only be a matter of unsubstantiated speculation.

Several references in *The Jesuit Relations* might suggest that the Snake clan existed among the Huron, although not on their regular clan lists (which might be Bear-nation biased). One in particular stands out:

> Each family ["famille"] ... has its distinctive armourial bearing ["armoiries"], one having a deer, another a serpent, another a crow, another the thunder, which they consider a bird; and like objects. (JR15:181; additions from French on 180; emphasis mine)

THE BEAR CLAN   The Bear clan was named third in the Deer phratry list, different from its first place in the Huron clan lists. The name used for this clan is *hatinnion,en*, which means "they (masculine plural) are bears." The masculine plural is used in Wendat when a group is all male or mixed gender. The verb root is -*nnion,en*- "to be a bear" (Potier 1920, 451; Steckley 2007b, 194–95), a term of reference to the animal that is unique to Wendat speakers among the Iroquoian language family members. The same name is used for the animal and for the Bear clan. It is different from, although possibly cognate with, the name for the Wendat or Huron tribe or nation *hatinnia8enten* "they (masculine plural) are of bear country" (Steckley 2007b, 192), based on the root -*nnia8enten*- "to be of bear country" (HF65:124: c.f. HF59:114; Potier 1920, 450).

Turtle Phratry

The name given for the Turtle phratry in Potier's writing was endgia8ich,[35] meaning "they (indefinite) are turtle" (Steckley 2010b, 44). The clans of the Turtle phratry have names that can be quite confusing. The nineteenth- and early-twentieth-century information does not quite clear up the confusion. A good deal of the problem comes from the fact that the names do not seem to relate directly to a particular animal. They seem to relate more to place names. This is not unusual among Aboriginal clan names. For the Tlingit of Alaska, for example, "Clans were generally named for localities claimed as their place of origin or associated with the migrations of their ancestors"

(Campbell 1989, 120). Perhaps, at least in part, that is what was going on with the clan names of the Turtle phratry.

LARGE TURTLE CLAN The first-listed clan of the phratry is named by Potier "ennehensteeronnon" (Toupin 1996, 226, 228). In Connolly (1900), the name is presented as Yah'-nĕhs-tĕh'-rōh-nōh by Wyandot informant George Wright (Connolly 1900, 100), and as Gyowh'-wīhsh-yäh'-nĕh's-tĕh'-rōh-nōh by Mathias Splitlog, essentially the same word preceded by the word for turtle (Connolly 1900, 101). Both sources identify it as the name for the Mud Turtle, not the first-named turtle in either list. Breaking down the word is not easy. The -ronnon- is a populative suffix, translated as "people of" (Potier 1920, 66). The rest of the word could be based on the noun root -nnenst- meaning "seed, pit," typically referring to plums (Steckley 2010b, 157–58), but that does not seem to connect well with turtles. There was a place name, Pointe aux Pins (Pine Point) by the north shore of Lake Erie that has a similar name ",annenste," which might have been a place where the clan established or re-established itself, but that conjecture requires more evidence. I will be simply calling this clan "Large Turtle."

PORCUPINE CLAN The second name that appears on the Turtle phratry list is eronhisseeronnon (Toupin 1996, 226, 229). Wright presents the term as Porcupine: Yĕh-rĕh'-hĕhseh'-rōh-nōh. The people of the Porcupine, or the clan of the Quills (Connolly 1900, 100) and Splitlog gives "Yōōh-rēh[n]'-hĕh-sah'-roh-noh. The people of the Porcupine, or the clan of the Quills (Connolly 1900, 101). Barbeau (n.d., 438) uses the term "yaręheserunŏn." The word might involve the noun root -renh- "treetops, branches" (Steckley 2007b, 228), and the verb root -es- "to be long, tall" (Steckley 2007b, 279), with a metaphorical reference to quills, but I am not sure. At least this can be readily identified as the Porcupine clan.

While the dictionary lists do not say that the Huron had a Porcupine clan, in *The Jesuit Relations* (29:283) of 1646, there is reference to a Noelle Aouendous of the Rock tribe. This would seem to be a name shared with Marie-Joseph (A)8endous of the Porcupine clan of the Wyandot (Toupin 1996, 852, B597) daughter of ,Atera, a female Porcupine clan elder (Toupin 1996, 926, E107).

STRIPED TURTLE The next name is presented by Potier as "a'tïeeronnon" (Toupin 1996, 227–29). This would appear to connect with Barbeau's term ti'iyerųnŏ: "people of the small turtle." Wright presents a term for small turtle as "Tĕhn-yĕh'-rōh-nōh. The people of the Little Turtle" (Connolly

1900, 100). Splitlog used Gyowh'-wĭhsh-hoh[n]'-tēhn-yĕh'-roh-noh. The people of the Little Turtle (Connolly 1900, 101). The term appears to me to be possibly based on the verb root *-ati-* "to be basswood" (Steckley 2010b, 48), giving a possible meaning of "people at the basswood." What makes this name appealing is that when the Wyandot were first forming in the 1650s, they spent some time in the area of a Bois Blanc Island, the "bois blanc" referring to basswood, near where Lake Huron and Lake Michigan meet. This is a different place from the Bois Blanc Island they would be living on in 1747. The Wendat had a preference for using words for trees in their village names (Steckley 2007a, 132–38), so this is not too surprising. I have used the term "Striped Turtle" to refer to these people, although Small Turtle would serve just as well.

One Wyandot Striped Turtle name that appears in the early Wendat record (1642–44) is A,otiok8andoron, initially of the Deer tribe of the Huron association of nations (JR22:135, 139; 26:37, 295). There is another possible name with So8end8anne (JR37:109, 1652), which may connect with the name of a Striped Turtle elder of 1747 Sa8end8at.

PRAIRIE TURTLE   Finally, there is "entioronnon," "people of the great field" (Toupin 1996, 227, 229). George Wright uses the term Yĕh'tōh-zhōōh'-rōh-nōh. The people of the Prairie Turtle (Connolly 1900, 100). He also refers to it as Highland Turtle. So these people will be termed the Prairie Turtle clan. There is a possibility that the Huron name Ihanneusa (JR34:219, 1649) is actually the Prairie Turtle name Hannenhasa.

Wolf Phratry

The Wolf phratry bore the name *hannaarisk8a* "he is wolf." As with the Deer phratry and clan, both Wolf phratry and clan have the same identifying animal.

WOLF CLAN   The clan name was presented as *hatinnaarisk8a*, "they (m) are wolves" (FH1697:231). Among Iroquoian languages, this way of constructing a word for wolves is unique to the Wendat language. In his dictionary, Potier (1920, 450) claimed this word contained the noun root *-nna-* "bone" (FH1697:135; also *-nne-* Potier 1920, 450; Steckley 2007b, 182) as well as the verb root *-ri,-* "to bite, suck, chew" (Potier 1920, 346; Steckley 2007b, 233), thus giving the phratry and clan names the meanings "he chews bones" and "they (m) chew bones," respectively, certainly appropriate names for wolves.

HAWK CLAN   The next clan was named hatindesonk, meaning "they (m) are hawks" (Steckley 2007b, 154). This clan seems to have been on the decline. It did not have any elders in the council in 1747 and they had no clan houses in the communities in which Potier took census. There is in the baptismal record for 1729, the name Ondesonk, meaning "she, it is a hawk," but it is not found again in the official record of the Wyandot. This was a name that was held by a succession of Jesuit missionaries to the Mohawk (Fathers Isaac Jogues, Simon le Moyne, Thierry Beschefer, and Jacques de Lamberville; see Steckley 2007a, 240). The clan appears to have been dying out, or at least weakening midway through the eighteenth century.

STURGEON CLAN Another clan that had no elders in the council, and appears not to have had any houses in the villages of 1747, is the Sturgeon clan. There is a distinct dualistic nature to this clan that has baffled me for years. In the Wendat dictionaries the clan had two names. One was *h8enh8en* "loon" (FH1697:232). Also appearing in those lists are the words *hotiʿra,on* and *oʿra,on*, which mean "they (m) are sturgeon" and "it is a sturgeon," respectively (see FH1697:232). I do not know the nature of the loon and sturgeon connection. While sturgeon and loon clans exist among Algonquian peoples of the Great Lakes area (e.g., Ojibwa and Menominee), the clans have no special connection between them of which I am aware.

In the Wyandot listing for this clan there are also two names given. One is the aforementioned *hotiʿra,on*. The other name is *ti,ata,entsi*, which refers to the first woman on earth, ,Aata,entsik (see Brébeuf's "On the beliefs, manners and customs of the Hurons," JR10:124–57, 1636). Interestingly, Potier is careful to point out that it refers to only one clan (Toupin 1996, 227, 260). There is only one name associated with this clan and that is S8ndak8a, "eagle" (Steckley 2010b, 44). He was, interestingly, listed by Potier as one of the "considerés" or potential chiefs (Toupin 1996, 260).

Phratries among the Wendat (Huron and Wyandot)
There is evidence to support the idea that the Huron had the same three phratries. This is significant in that it demonstrates a kind of continuity of the nature of clans among the Wendat. This three-phratry structure may be old in Iroquoian culture, as the Wendat phratry threesome is not dissimilar from the Mohawk and Oneida three-clan structure: Bear, Turtle, and Wolf. Remember that the Bear is in the Deer phratry among the Wyandot. This is the grouping pattern I am suggesting for the phratries of the Huron.

A second kind of evidence comes from a comparison of the Huron clan list with that of the Wyandot in 1747. The latter is presented below along with the list of Huron clans. The names are presented in the order in which they appear in the two Jesuit Huron dictionaries. The Huron clans are spaced according to the phratries I believe they belonged to:

48 CHAPTER TWO

Wyandot Clan	**Wyandot Phratry**	**Huron Clan**
Deer	Deer	Bear
Snake		Deer
Bear		
Large Turtle	Turtle	Turtle
Porcupine	Beaver	
Striped Turtle		
Prairie Turtle		
Wolf	Wolf	Wolf
Hawk		Hawk
Sturgeon/Yaatayentsik		Sturgeon/Loon
Fox		Fox

Several points are worth noting. First, the Snake clan originated with the Deer clan (Barbeau 1915, 1960), so there is an even closer link than first appears between the first two Huron clans and the first three Wyandot clans. Second, with the beaver being a water animal like the turtle, an easy logic could connect the two in a phratry. Third, we see that the Sturgeon clan exists as a double-named clan in proximity to the Wolf in both instances. Further, it seems not surprising that a Fox clan would be linked conceptually to a Wolf clan.

There is a reference in *The Jesuit Relations* that suggests that the Huron may have had three phratries. In the 1648 condolence ceremony for the young Frenchman, Jacques Douart, who was allegedly killed by members of the Huron nation, there is a reference to "three presents given by the three principal Captains of the country" (JR33:247). There is a good chance that they were the leaders of the three Huron phratries.

INDIRECT EARLY EVIDENCE FOR THREE PHRATRIES AMONG THE WYANDOT
Twice in the late seventeenth century and early eighteenth century we find references to three leaders or spokesmen in intertribal meetings with the French. I suspect that each was representing his particular phratry. On 15 August 1682, representing the Wyandot at a meeting in Montreal were "*Soüaïti*, called the Rat, *Ondahiaste chen*, Burnt tongue…and *Oskoüendeti*, the Runner" (NYCD9:181). As has been discussed, the second is the name of a leader of the Snake clan of the Deer phratry. The first name appears to

be an alternative name for Kandiaronk, known as Rat (see next chapter). The clan of the third name is not known.

During the talks surrounding the Great Peace in Montreal in July and August of 1701, we have the name Houatsarant, a poorly written version of T'on8atsarandi, a member of the Porcupine clan of the Turtle phratry. Also there is Quarante Sols, a name I believe is associated with a leader of the Bear clan of the Deer phratry (see next chapter). Kandiaronk or Rat being the remainder, suggests to me that he was representing the Wolf phratry.

Another early form of evidence comes from when the Wyandot were at the mission of St. Ignace at Michilimackinac, in a chapter entitled "Of the Mission of St. Ignace at Missilimakinac" (JR61:95). The Wyandot community numbered about five hundred at that time, close to their population size in 1747. Jesuit missionary Father Philippe Pierson and the community were arranging a suitable ceremony to celebrate the birth of Jesus. According to Pierson:

> They desired, then, in execution of their design, to imitate what in other ages had been done by the three great stranger Captains, who came to confess and adore Jesus Christ in the Manger, and afterward went to preach him in their own country. All the hurons, Christians and non-Christians, divided themselves into three companies[36] according to the different nations [probably phratries] that constitute their village; and after choosing their Chiefs, one for each nation, they furnished them with porcelain, of which they were to make an offering to the infant Jesus. Every one adorned himself as handsomely as he could. The three Captains had each a scepter in his hand, to which was fastened the offering, and wore a gaudy head-dress in guise of a crown. Each company took up a different position. The signal for marching having been given them at the sound of the trumpet, they heeded the sound as that of a voice Inviting them to go to see and adore an infant God new-born. Just as the 1st company took up their march,–conducted by a star fastened to a large standard of the Color of Sky-blue, and having at the *rear*[37] their Captain, before whom was carried his banner,—The 2nd company, seeing the first marching, demanded of them [aloud] the object of their journey; and on learning it, they joined themselves to them, having in like manner their chief at their head with his banner. The 3rd company, more advanced on the Road, did as the second; and one after another, they continued their march, and entered our Church, the star remaining at the entrance. The 3 chiefs, having first prostrated themselves, and laid their Crowns and scepters at the feet of the infant Jesus in the Cradle, offered their Congratulations and presents to their savior. As they did so, they made a public protestation of the submission and obedience that they desired to render him; solicited faith for those who possessed it not, and protection for all their nation and for all that land. (JR61:115; emphasis mine)

In the following it is less clear that three groups are being referred to. It may be two, it may be three. In Cadillac's writing of 31 August 1703, we read:

> The Chief of the Hurons, who is very absolute over his tribe, has begged me to write to you that he would be very glad to proceed to France, to go and assure His Majesty of his fidelity, and of the ardent desire he has to enter into his service; and to that end he will form a company of fifty men of his tribe provided he is made captain of it, then he is given a lieutenant and an ensign, and that they are paid monthly, as well as their soldiers at the same rate as the officers and troops of the Navy are paid in this country. There is another chief of the same tribe who binds himself to do the same; they also beg you to have passages given them in the King's ships. I believe they intend to hunt for skins in order to present them to you, which is a token of their good will. The principal chief of the Hurons [i.e., Sastaretsi], who is one of the best-informed men I have yet seen among all these tribes, and is Frenchified, has requested me to write to you regarding the same matter, but, as his age does not allow of his making so long a voyage, he will send his nephew to you at the same time with another of his friends, in order to offer the King his services. (165–66)

SUMMARY

In this chapter we discussed the two main characters in this book: the Wyandot and their clans. We have seen that the Wyandot were formed out of related peoples, named by the French the Huron, the Petun, and more distantly the Neutral. Forced out of their southern Ontario homeland by the mid-seventeenth century, some of their number reformed in the centre of the Great Lakes during the rest of that century. More of that latter story will be told in the following chapter.

Essential to their social survival as a people were their clans. These were dynamic social groups that provided leadership and stability in the chaotic times that would follow. During this period they were and remained matrilineal while surrounded by patrilineal Algonquians and Europeans. They maintained their clan exogamy when regular marriage partners were dwindling. They owned names like aristocratic titles that provided a fountain of leadership from the diminished pool of people. They may well have developed new clans to deal with new challenges, and these clans, new and old, appeared to recruit membership from the general diaspora of the times. They gave coherence and unity to the people in troubling times.

Chapter Three

Five Wyandot Strategists of the Late Seventeenth Century

Sastaretsi, Kandiaronk, Sk8tache, the Baron, and Quarante Sols

In the previous chapter we looked briefly at who the founding peoples of the Wyandot were, and more extensively at the clan nature of their society. In this chapter we will look at the transitional period in the second half of the seventeenth century. The people were seeking out new lands that they could call home, and new configurations were being formed of two formerly separate peoples who spoke essentially the same language, and called themselves Wendat. I will be presenting this period through an investigation of the actions and strategies of five leading Wyandot figures, to all of whom we can put at least tentative clan identities. A leader persuades his clan members to go along with him, but he listens to what they have to say, so that he speaks for them as well. When French writers of the time spoke of individual Wyandot leaders acting or speaking in a particular way, these writers were also speaking of the individual's clan, and the clan's attempts to seek out some kind of stability—security in a seemingly unending series of unstable situations. One reason for thinking this way comes from the fact that we often find these individuals living somewhere apart from the other leaders, part of a "family group" that would most likely be a clan, or at least a significant section of a clan.

Four of the five names continued into the period of our main focus and were taken on by people who were significant figures in 1747. The one exception is a strange one, Kandiaronk. It is strange because of all the five individuals discussed here, he is the best known, and perhaps the most significant in terms of the history of the late seventeenth century.

SASTARETSI: DEER CLAN

Sastaretsi was the name of the person who could be called the Grand Chief of the Wyandot. He was the leader as well of the Deer clan and the Deer phratry. It was rather like he was a mayor, a provincial premier, and a prime minister all in one. As the name did not appear in the Jesuit literature about the Huron from the 1630s through the 1640s, it is reasonable to assume that it came from the Petun. Other evidence points to that as well, as will be seen shortly. If he were Huron, someone with his obvious significance would not have been ignored in *The Jesuit Relations* of that time. The French were always on the lookout for the "chief."

Unfortunately, the exact meaning of his name is not clear. The verb root is clearly -*es*- "to be long" (Steckley 2007b, 279), with the repetitive prefix -*s*- meaning "very." Both verb root and prefix were often used with Wendat names.[1] The name "Sastaretsi" has been translated as "long bark." This does not appear to be a valid translation, however. The noun root for "bark" is -*st*- (Steckley 2007b, 247), which leaves the -*ar*- unaccounted for in the translation. No Wendat noun root that takes the form -*star*- is readily apparent in the Wendat dictionaries.

How old the name was, and how long it had been the Petun leader's name are both open to question. The often imaginative Baron Lahontan talked about it being in existence some eight hundred years (see second chapter), but much of what he wrote about Aboriginal people was questionable. He liked to tell a good story more than he liked to adhere to tales for which he had actual evidence.

A story told by the Wyandot in the nineteenth century was that Sastaretsi was their leader from the time they lived by the St. Lawrence River (see Hale 1894, 6–8). This story may have had its origins in those St. Lawrence Iroquoians that moved west from their homeland by the river from roughly Quebec to Montreal to live with the Wendat between Georgian Bay and Lake Ontario during the sixteenth century (see Steckley 2010a, 5–30, 2012).[2]

The first written reference to someone bearing the name of Sastaretsi appears in a letter sent by Jesuit Father Rene Menard to his Superior in Quebec on 2 June 1661. He wrote of meeting with a "Huron who had started 11 days before from the Tobacco [Petun] nation" (JR46:143). When the same man left with three Frenchmen and three Potawatomi, Menard wrote: "They have a present to be given to Sastaretsi, on my behalf and on that of *dourach*"[3] (JR46:143). This gives us further evidence that Sastaretsi was a Petun name.

Sastaretsi's people were then living in the area of Black River, a tributary of the Mississippi, west of Lake Michigan, which meets the big river south of the westernmost point of Lake Superior. They would head northeast the next year to Chequamegon Bay (the mission of St. Ignace) about midway across the south side of Lake Superior.

In 1682, it was reported that some

> Hurons, or Tionnontatez [i.e., the name for the Petun] comprised under the name of their chief Sa[s]taretsi arrived at Montreal on the 13th of August, to the number of ten canoes, communicated their first word to the Count in the audience given them on the 15th of the said month. (NYCD9:178)

At this point the people had abandoned Chequamegon Bay. For some ten years they had been living at Michilimackinac near the spot where the three Great Lakes—Superior, Michigan, and Huron—meet. The "Count" referred to was Louis de Buade, Conte de Frontenac (1622–98), Governor of New France from 1672 to 1682, and again from 1689 to the time of his death in 1698.

The Wyandot speaker was Kandiaronk or "the Rat" (see below), and he spoke eloquently on Sastaretsi's behalf concerning his people's dealings with the Miami[4] and the Seneca. As these actions were personalized as being those of Sastaretsi, a number of scholars (Clifton 1983, 7; Curnoe 1996, 112; Havard 2001, 199) have wrongly interpreted the Rat as being Sastaretsi, which he definitely was not.

The published translated highlights of the speech teach us about the nature of the position of Sastaretsi among the people. Unfortunately, as is rife in the literature, the spelling of his name varies considerably. Each "word" referred to, in Wendat the noun root *-8end-*, which also means "voice" (Steckley 2007b, 216), is a message in itself in the presentation. The discourse of being "poor and miserable" and "having pity," possibly more accurately "having compassion," is part of the way in which the people addressed spirits and possibly trading partners with whom they wished to have a good relationship. The use of the word "father" is, I believe, a Wyandot bow of diplomatic politeness to French culture. Father had different connotations for the Wyandot than it did for the French. A Wendat father terminologically included father's brothers and they all belonged to a different clan than his children did (Steckley 1993a). Of greater clan significance were the mother's brothers of an individual, especially in the training of young boys. The term "father" was not used earlier in *The Jesuit Relations* when the Wendat were addressing the French. In *The Jesuit Relations* from 1635 to 1639 they used "nephew" (i.e., sister's son; JR8:93; 10:45; 13:171,181; 14:23; 15:25–29, 33, 57, 113; 17:209; see Steckley 1993a, 41–42).

This presentation, while recognizing the greater power of the French leader, would be more a discourse of equals than what appears in the more authoritarian expressions used in the French language, expressions rooted in the hierarchical nature of seventeenth-century French society. Keep in mind that in Wendat there are no words for command or obey. For the former, the closest equivalent was *-nnha-* "request, ask" (Steckley 2007b, 187). The closest expression in Wendat to "obey" is "being with someone's word," with *-8end-* and *-ra-* (Steckley 2007b, 221; see Potier 1920, 325) as in ehona8endra, "they (ind) will be with his word" (Appendix B1). There was no "will" that one could impose on another. There was *-ndi,onr-* "mind, thoughts" (Steckley 2007b, 163) that one could share. Finally, there were no masters. A person in charge of a particular situation was "being great in voice," with *-8end-* and *-io-* "to be great, large" (Steckley 2007b, 290) in the language that Sastaretsi spoke and in the social structure in which he was raised. A lot would be gained and lost in translation, from Wendat to French, as was also the case from French to English, especially with the Shakespearean English into which the translator of *The Jesuit Relations* often slipped:

> First Word. Speaking in the singular number the name of Sateretsi—they had come down at the request of Onontio [Frontenac, the French Governor] their father, who had told them by the Frenchmen to descend to Montreal, where they had come to hear his voice; that he saw them poor and miserable, because the young men amused themselves drinking; that they did not neglect coming at the command of their father, to learn his will and to request him to inform them of what was occurring; that they hear many rumors, and that the earth is turned upside down; that this causes them trouble, and they have recourse to Onontio to restore them their senses and to give them good advice.
>
> Second Word.... Onontio, thy son Satarsetsi hath just stated that he made an alliance with Ouiatanon, which means the Selugrue tribe,[5] who are Miamis and another tribe included in them. He entreats Onontio to receive and to protect them, as he does Sataretsi, who is no longer but one body and one spirit with Ouiatanon....
>
> Third Word. Onontio, thy son Saretsi styled himself formerly thy brother, but he has ceased to be such, for he is now thy son; and thou hast begotten him by the protection thou has afforded him against his enemies. Thou art his Father, and he acknowledgeth thee as such; he obeys thee as a child

obeyeth his father; he listeneth to thy voice; and doth only what is pleasing to thee, because he hath respect for his father and is obedient unto him....

Fourth Word. Onontio, thy son Sataretsi hath an upright mind; he is proud, and he defies any one to disgrace or reproach him with having acted ill, and having failed in anything towards his father. There are, notwithstanding, some among his brothers—both French and Indian—who have spoken evil of him, and accused him of creating disturbance; adding, he must be distrusted; he had been taken by the arm, to induce him to commit bad acts. But Sataretsi walks upright, and is subject to his father's will, who alone has the power to pull him by the arm, and to make him go wheresoever he listeth, because he is the master of the whole earth.[6]

Fifth Word. Sataretsi stands before the eyes of Onontio, his father, who behold him poor and miserable, whereafter he beseeches his father to have pity on him, to protect him, as he has always done, against his enemies; to permit him to trade off the peltries he has brought with him. (NYCD9:178-79)

Frontenac responded with some acknowledgment of what Sastaretsi said. However, he appears to have been concerned about Sastaretsi going to visit the Seneca, with wampum belts suggesting treaty, without telling him. Kandiaronk responded that:

> it was true that Sataretsi had been to Seneca; but he thought there was no harm in that, as the Kiskakons were aware of it, and that he went there only to arrange their unfortunate affairs, of which the Seneca accused them with Sataretsi. (NYCD9:179)

The Kiskakons were a band of the Ottawa who were accused of killing a Seneca.

In the Narrative of 1696-97, still at Michilimackinac, the Wyandot led by Sastaretsi presented three wampum belts to "Onnontio," the French Governor, "to assure him of the fidelity of Sataressy (that is, in the name of the whole nation in general)" (NYCD9:667).

In 1700, at a meeting of Charles le Moyne de Longueuil, the commandant at Detroit with four Native nations there, Sastaretsi was given a war belt of wampum:

> Sastarsedzy their King received it, placed it round his neck and told all the Nations that since they made him keeper of the Belt, he would take care to present it to them every time they would wish to follow him in an attack on the English. (NYCD9:707)

In sum, it can be said that Sastaretsi recognized and respected the authority of the French governor, was opposed to the English, but still wanted and needed to act with some independence from the French in his dealings with other Aboriginal groups. This can be called something of a consistent Deer clan strategy of the seventeenth and eighteenth centuries. Certainly, the close connection to French authority was such a strategy, as will be seen in later chapters.

KANDIARONK: WOLF CLAN (?)

To the French and English the best known Wyandot of the late eighteenth century was Kandiaronk (often mistakenly written as Kondiaronk).[7] In the Wendat language the word meant "Rat" (FH1697:169, 231). This was a new word in the language because rats first came to New France from Europe aboard ships. No other Wyandot is recorded as ever having that name, before or afterwards. The first apparent reference to Rat comes at a meeting in Montreal, on 15 August 1682. The Wyandot were at that meeting represented by three people: "*Soüaïti*, called the Rat, *Ondahiaste chen*, Burnt tongue...and *Oskoüendeti*, the Runner."[8] The first name is written in a number of different ways, not uncommon when the writer of Wendat was not a Jesuit: Soüoïas, Souaïa, Soüaïae. It appears that the word that the writer was attempting to reproduce here is Tsisk8aia,[9] the Huron word for "muskrat"[10] (FH1693:330; FH1697:232). This individual was the one identified as "their Orator, *Soüoïas*, in French The Rat" (NYCD9:178). As with the name Kandiaronk, this name did not appear to live on among the Wyandot of the mid-eighteenth century. While the last name seems to have been repeated among the Wyandot, more accurately written as Osk8indeti in 1775 (Toupin 1996, 899, B1305), there is no other reference to him that I can find. And his clan is not known.[11]

In 1701, there were again three leaders representing the Wyandot: Kandiaronk, Houatsaranti, and Quarante Sols (Havard 2001, 120; from La Potherie 1753, 4:225). The second name, more accurately written as "Ton8atsarandi" was the name of an elder in the mid-eighteenth century (Toupin 1996, 229) who belonged to the Porcupine clan, Turtle phratry. In 1747, as we will see later in this chapter, there were a sister and brother identified as Quarante Sols, who belonged to the Bear clan, Deer phratry. Taken with the previous representation of three, this suggests that Kandiaronk may have been Wolf phratry, probably the Wolf clan. The disappearance of his name after his death, and the diminished status of the Wolf phratry by the mid-eighteenth century lend a little support to this possibility. As we saw earlier, scholars have conflated Sastaretsi and Kandiaronk into one person. This is wrong as the latter was only acting as orator for the figurehead name Sastaretsi, when the Rat was said to be speaking "in the singular number under the name of Sa[s]teretsi."

Rat and Sastaretsi may have been brothers-in-law. In his *Nouveaux Voyages de M. Le Baron de Lahontan dans l'Amerique septentrionale* (translated as *New Voyages to North America*), Louis Armand de Lom d'Arce de Lahontan spoke of how the name/title was passed down over the centuries along the matrilineal or female line. In the example he presented, Lahontan (1970, 460) had Adario (his name for Rat) marrying the sister of Sastaretsi. While this may have been purely hypothetical, I suspect that it was not. If the Rat could marry the sister of Sastaretsi, he would have been of a different clan. As we have seen, the Wyandot married outside their clan. If Kandiaronk were Wolf clan, this would fit nicely in terms of clan exogamy rules with marrying a Deer clan woman.

Kandiaronk's next recorded entry onto this perilous political stage occurred during the late 1680s. At that time, the new Onnontio, Governor Jacques-René de Brisay de Denonville, was eager to persuade Kandiaronk, and all those Wyandot who might be persuaded by him to enter into battle, to make a definite commitment on the side of the French. In the summer of 1687, Denonville and his mixed regular soldiers, colonial militia and Aboriginal allies (in total slightly over twenty-one hundred strong) had struck deep into the home territory of the Seneca, the westernmost of the Iroquois nations. Although only a relatively small number of their several hundred warriors were killed or captured, the Seneca suffered much greater losses in other ways, as fields bearing crops, harvested food, houses, and sacred burial grounds were all destroyed (see Richter 1992, 158).

After this military mission of destruction, Denonville was still concerned about the threat the Iroquois and their English allies posed to French trade. Recently, their rival colonial power, through Iroquois intermediaries, had managed to complete a successful trading expedition to some of the various tribes living in the Michilimackinac area, near where the Wyandot lived. Governor Denonville wanted the Great Lakes Aboriginal nations to commit militarily to keeping the Iroquois away from the rich trade in beaver pelts that this area provided.

For his part, Kandiaronk seems to have been concerned about what strong public commitment to the French might mean to the relationship between his people and the Iroquois. They needed either flexibility or power to deal with the Iroquois confederacy. If an official French–Wyandot military alliance was not backed by a substantial French force, it would merely serve to alienate the Iroquois, without providing the might necessary to cope with the grim consequences of that alienation.

In the fall of 1687, Kandiaronk pledged his allegiance to the French cause on the condition that both nations were to make war on the Iroquois until the latter's ability to retaliate was effectively neutralized (see Lahontan 1970, 220).

Kandiaronk led a group of at least forty (see Lahontan 1970, 149, 220 and Parkman 1966, 174 for contrasting figures) warriors from Michilimackinac to Fort Cataraqui (now Kingston), where Lake Ontario flows into the St. Lawrence, in the late spring of 1688. They came intending to strike a telling blow in a joint French–Wyandot campaign against the Iroquois.

Kandiaronk and his men were in for a shock. Denonville had failed to receive the reinforcements from France he had hoped for and knew he needed. Not for the first or last time, the colony was cast adrift by the home country to fend for itself militarily. Kandiaronk was unaware of this lack of overseas reinforcement. The French liked to create an illusion of strength with its Aboriginal allies. What Kandiaronk did know was that he needed to act fast to improve this situation. An opportunity presented itself. Denonville had just arranged to have ambassadors from the Onondaga meet with him at Montreal to negotiate peace. They were to speak for the Oneida and the Cayuga, but significantly not for the recently raided Seneca, nor the experience-cautioned Mohawk, arguably the two most powerful of the Iroquois tribes, the guardians of the western and eastern doors, respectively, of the metaphoric house that was the Confederacy. To Kandiaronk this peace negotiation might well have looked like French faithlessness combined with an Iroquois ploy. For Kandiaronk knew only too well that the Iroquois were well schooled in the advantages of divide and conquer. Several times in the past the Iroquois had made peace with the French in order to be able to attack unhindered the Native allies of those seemingly inconsistent Europeans.

However, Kandiaronk had a plan. He pretended to accept the news passively, and to paddle back home peacefully. Once out of sight of the fort, he headed east toward a place he knew the Iroquois ambassadors would pass by.

After a wait of almost a week, Kandiaronk's plan and patience were rewarded. The ambassadors, travelling without the usual caution of a war party, were caught by surprise and easily defeated. When their leader, the Onondaga chief Teganissorens, protested that they had been on a mission of peace, Kandiaronk declared in seeming astonishment and anger that he had been deceived. He claimed that Denonville had informed him that a war party was to come that way, and had instructed him to ambush the Iroquois on that spot. He then released all his prisoners save one, saying:

> Go, my Brethren, though I am at War with you, yet I release you, and allow you to go home. 'Tis the Governour [sic] of the French that put me upon this

black Action, which I shall never be able to digest unless your Five Nations revenge themselves and make their just Reprisals. (Lahontan 1970, 222)

The Onondaga appear to have been convinced by Kandiaronk's clever charade, although Teganissorens (whose name was also recorded as Decanesora) would remain loyal to the French throughout the next two decades. It no doubt sounded a lot like what the Seneca and Mohawk had been telling them about not trusting the French. The Onondaga told Kandiaronk that if he should wish to make a separate peace, the Five Nations would be willing to negotiate.

It should be pointed out that the Iroquois themselves were playing a double game at this time, having Teganissorens and his party as a kind of red herring of peace, while they themselves were attacking the Illinois, Algonquian-speaking allies of the French.

Kandiaronk had not yet completely acted out his plan. The next step was his treatment of the prisoner kept in apparent accord with the long-established custom of replacing someone lost in combat, of adopting him into the nation. Kandiaronk took the prisoner back to Michilimackinac. There he presented him to the French commandant at the fort. Unaware of the peace negotiations, the commandant had the protesting Iroquois executed. The prisoner's pleading that he was an envoy of peace was to no avail. Kandiaronk had gone around saying that fear of death had driven the man crazy.

One more step was soon to follow. Kandiaronk released an old Iroquois who had been captured and subsequently adopted by the Wyandot many years before. He instructed the man to inform his people of what he had just witnessed, that an Iroquois invited by the French as a peace envoy had been shot and killed by a French commandant, despite his pleas of the nature of his mission.

We will pick up Kandiaronk's story a little later when he played a very different role—a peacemaker's role.

SK8TACHE: PORCUPINE CLAN

Other Wyandot leaders would arise with different strategies for the survival of their small-in-number people. One Porcupine clan name appears in the seventeenth-century literature as a "troublemaker" for the French. He was referred to as Scoutache and the misprinted Scoubache in the references that follow. In a summary of Governor Denonville's letters in 1685 to M. de Seignelay, we read, "A man named Scoutache, who is among the Outawas, has told them that he, Denonville, was preparing to attack them, which has alarmed them" (NYCD9:274).

In a letter of the next year, 12 June 1686, Denonville wrote the following:

> I have had again the honor of advising you this fall that a man named Scoubache, a native Huron, has been to the Iroquois to induce them to make war upon us. It has since been discovered that his principal design was to betray all the Hurons at Michilimakina and that Traitor did in fact, conjointly with others like himself, deliver up to the Iroquois seventy Huron who were dispersed a-hunting between Lake Erie and Lake Huron, in the country called Saquinaw. (NYCD9:293)

According to Denonville then, Sk8tache was attempting to get the Iroquois on his side by offering seventy Wyandot prisoners to them. It is unlikely that Sk8tache would betray his people. That he was in some way trying to lessen the pressure of the Iroquois on his people through some independent strategy that was unknown to the French, but not necessarily anti-French, and certainly not anti-Wyandot is more believable. He might even have been attempting to trap the Iroquois by promising them non-existent prisoners. Lacking Sk8tache's written voice in the matter, it is hard to know what his intent was. Sacrificing his people to obtain a stronger relationship with the Iroquois does not seem a likely goal.

We do not know when that Sk8tache died and when another took his place, thus reviving the name Sk8tache. We do know that the next recorded Sk8tache had the first name Louis. In 1747, Potier recorded that the Wyandot man was fifty-six years old (Toupin 1996, 241). He had some stature among his people at that time. His name was mentioned first in his house (PV2), a large one, in which the Porcupine clan and the Striped Turtle clan shared influence. His daughter Françoise was married to Tio8endata, who was a man of influence in the Porcupine clan, as was Nicholas Orontondi, who was also found in that house. Louis could not have been Striped Turtle, since the two wives he was recorded as having (not at the same time)—the 1747 elder Ts8ndehe and Christine Tok8ennon-ioti—belonged to that clan. Further, his niece Catiche Ts8chiaen, the child of a sister of his, was Porcupine clan.

While he was not then an elder of the Porcupine clan, this Sk8tache's influence at that time can be seen in the fact that he was involved in a Wyandot peace initiative after Nicholas Orontondi's abortive attack on Detroit. The Chevalier de Bertel or Berthet, French commandant among the Algonquian-speaking Illinois people at that time, wrote a letter that contained the following information concerning his peacemaking activities, partnered with Quarante Sols of the Bear clan:

> At the end of January, 14 Hurons of Sandosket, with Scotache and Quarante Sols at their head, come to Detroit to ask for the release of the three prisoners confined in irons, the remainder of the five who had been taken at Bois blanc Island, where they had been attacked by the French when Nicolas sued for peace. The deputation made such fair promises that Chevalier de Longueuil, though feeling great repugnance to the release of these three prisoners [consented to their discharge, on] the advice of the principal Frenchmen and Indians in the fort. (NYCD10:156–57)

He seems, then, to be continuing the independent style of political policy of his predecessor, speaking on behalf of his clan brother, Orontondi.

Louis must have died before 1763, as a testament and anniversary was held to honour his death that year (Toupin 1996, 197, TA25). His name was resuscitated by at least 1791, as two girls were baptized on 14 August of that year, and each was recorded as being a "fille de sCoutaChe"[12] (Toupin 1996, 939, B1539, B1540).

THE BARON: PRAIRIE TURTLE CLAN (?)—AN ALTERNATIVE TO KANDIARONK

Then there was Le Baron,[13] a Wyandot whose Aboriginal name is not presented in any source that I have seen. He would first clash publicly with Kandiaronk in May of 1695. It was at a meeting of the principal chiefs of the Wyandot and Ottawa with Antoine Laumet de la Mothe, sieur de Cadillac, then the commandant of Michilimackinac. Being discussed was an impending attack by the Iroquois against the Miami, allies of the Wyandot, the Ottawa, and the French. The Baron, relaying an Iroquois message, stated that the Iroquois meant no harm to the allies by this attack. Rather, they were "going to devour the Miami in order to unite the whole earth; inviting all the lake Tribes to repair with the French to the neighbourhood of Detroit when the leaves are red" (NYCD9:606).

Kandiaronk did not agree with this plan. His response was a call for unity of the Wyandot with their Miami brothers and sisters by acting against the Iroquois:

> We have but one cabin and one fire, and we ought to have one mind. Let us unite. The opportunity is favourable. There is corn in the village to feed the women and children; we have brave warriors. What hinders us to die like men defending our lives? Shall we remain passive whilst our brethren are being carried off? (NYCD9:606)

Although war plans were made, no action was taken. Something was holding them back. A major source of hesitation was revealed at a meeting held on 1 June. The Baron spoke of having encountered an ancient man and his wife, each supposed to be about one hundred years old.[14] According to the Baron, the old man had experienced a series of revelations from the "Master of Life," a term used to refer to the god of the missionaries.[15] One part of the alleged message, as related by the Baron, had seriously disturbed those intending to initiate action against the Iroquois. In the words of Cadillac:

> [T]he old man forbid them to be the first to strike the Iroquois, as he who should begin would be infallibly destroyed, and the Iroquois himself would be annihilated were he so bold as to be beforehand with them with his hatchet. (NYCD9:608)

The Baron seems to have had cards he was not showing, to the French at least. Even as he was travelling to Montreal to speak on behalf of the Wyandot to the French authorities, his son was part of a secret embassy sent to the Seneca (NYCD9:619).

For Kandiaronk the cost of the Baron's political manoeuvring was high. With the Baron's increasingly apparent close ties with the Iroquois, the neighbouring Algonkians were becoming more and more suspicious of the actions of the Wyandot. In 1696 an Ottawa raiding party of twenty went out looking for Iroquois (NYCD8:648). Along the way they encountered Kandiaronk's son and a single Wyandot canoe containing mostly women and children. It was not long before violence flared. All of the Wyandot were killed.

In 1697, at least thirty Wyandot (Havard 2001, 242n25), some of whom were from the Baron's family, had gone to New York, Iroquois territory, to see about being granted land there. The Baron went to the Miami, apparently continuing his role as Iroquois agent. There were plans afoot for a large Iroquois war party to join with a group led by the Baron to strike the unsuspecting Miami.

But this was not to be. Kandiaronk "notified the Miamis to be on their guard and not to trust the Baron" (NYCD9:672), and led a smaller intercepting force comprising about 150 Wyandot, Potawatomi, Ottawa, and Sauk. He learned from Iroquois scouts he had captured that there were about 250 in the Iroquois war party. They also informed him that the group had only canoes enough to carry about sixty people. Kandiaronk utilized this knowledge to devise a clever plan of attack. As Jesuit historian Charlevoix eloquently tells it:

> [Kandiaronk] advanced with his whole force towards the spot where he had been told the enemy was encamped; when he came within gun-shot, he feigned to be surprised and alarmed at their number, and pretended

flight. At once sixty Iroquois sprang to their canoes to give chase; the Rat pushed out from land, and plied his paddles till he was two leagues from shore. There he stopped and drew up, receiving with firing the first Iroquois volley, which killed only two of his men, then, without giving them time to reload, he dashed on them so furiously that all their canoes were riddled or stove in. Thirty-seven were killed, fourteen taken, the rest drowned. Among them were five of the highest chiefs in the nation. (Charlevoix 1900, 5:68)

Although we read nothing of Le Baron after 1697 in the usual sources, I suspect that he may have quietly returned to his people rather than go live with the Iroquois. For the name Le Baron lived on among the Wyandot, changed to "8aron," the -w- replacing the -b-, which does not exist in that language.[16] There is a man called 8aron who fathered baptized children with four women of the Deer, Snake, Large Turtle, and Striped Turtle clans. These children were baptized from 1729 to 1736 (see Toupin 1996, 826, 829, 832, 839). His wife, Dorothée Sk8atandi of the Striped Turtle clan, was referred to as "La8aron" (Toupin 1996, 186, 204, 208, 921). It is noteworthy that the godfathers for his first two baptized children bore Iroquois names: Osaetagenrat and Ganna8asiohar.[17] His namesake's ties with the Iroquois may have continued with this next possessor of the name.

We can say that he could not have been Deer, Snake, Large Turtle, or Striped Turtle because of clan exogamy and his marrying women of these clans. As the other leaders of the later years of the seventeenth century were Wolf, Porcupine, Bear, and Deer, we can at least propose that he might have been of the Prairie Turtle clan. That fits with his independence of action, which, as we will see, other leaders deemed Prairie Turtle definitely followed.

QUARANTE SOLS: BEAR CLAN

Quarante Sols (1659–1707) was the French name of the leader of one of the groups of the Wyandot that came together in the Windsor/Detroit area at the turn of the eighteenth century. It can be translated as meaning "Forty Cents." Andrew Sturtevant's likely hypothesis as to what it signified to the French was that it was "probably a reference to what the French perceived as the man's avarice" (Sturtevant 2011, 41n21). He belonged to the Bear clan (see below). Between Sastaretsi and Quarante Sols there appears to have been a clan-based division, which might even go back to a difference in national origin, the first being Petun, the latter Huron. While his Wyandot name is not known, Quarante Sols bore the Ottawa name of "Michipichy." This may be the same name as that of the mythical underwater cat, said to be responsible for the deaths of those who die mysteriously in lakes or rivers. Jesuit Father Sebastien Rasles, writing on 12 October 1723 about his experiences with the Ottawa at Michilimackinac, discussed the following element concerning their spiritual beliefs and rituals:

> They call the *Manitou* [spirit] of waters and fishes *Mishibichi* ["large cat," in the Ottawa language] and they offer him a somewhat similar sacrifice when they go to fish, or undertake a voyage. This sacrifice consists of throwing into the water tobacco, provisions, and kettles; and in asking him that the water of the river may flow more slowly, that the rocks may not break their canoes, and that he will grant them an abundant catch. (JR67:159–61)

The significance of this spirit figure will be picked up in the discussion about the Prairie Turtle clan in the next chapter. There seems to be an association between this underwater cat and spiritual resistance to the Jesuits.

In a rather cryptic reference, Kandiaronk stated his somewhat qualified faith in the words of Quarante Sols, in a speech in which he was instructing his allies to follow Onnontio. This speech is definitely in Wendat, as I can easily translate it back from English in my mind. Note the use of the term "ally" here, which does not exist in Wendat. Quarante Sols was not a clan or phratry brother, so may not have been called such a kin term for this reason. I suspect that the verb root *-atenro-* "to be friends" (Steckley 2007b, 45) was used here:

> We have but one cabin and one fire, and we ought to have but one mind. Let us unite. The opportunity is favorable. There is corn in the village to feed the women and children; we have brave warriors. What hinders us to die like men defending our lives? Shall we remain passive whilst our brethren are being carried off? I have confidence in the word of Quarante Sols, our ally, who, though a prisoner, exhorts us not to trust the word of the Iroquois. We ought to have no will [i.e., mind] but that of our father, and we cannot make peace without him. Let us adopt sure ground for our resolution. (NYCD9:606)

It is difficult to know exactly what Kandiaronk meant when he said that Quarante Sols was a prisoner. Did he mean that his fellow Wyandot was a prisoner of the Iroquois? Or was he being more subtle? The Wendat word for "prisoner," the noun root *-ndask8a-* (Potier 1920, 448; Steckley 2007b, 144–45), also referred to a domestic animal. He may have been chiding Quarante Sols for acting as a domestic animal or pet of the Iroquois, and not as an independent man or wild animal.

In 1697, the French governor Frontenac distrusted Quarante Sols as one he felt was encouraging the Iroquois to conquer his St. Joseph River neighbours, the Miami (Havard 2001, 207). The policies of Wyandot leaders towards the Miami seem often to be suspected of treachery by French governors. We will pick up the story of Quarante Sols later in this chapter.

KANDIARONK AS A PEACEMAKER

At the turn of the eighteenth century, ambitious plans were being laid to organize the most extensive set of negotiations for peace ever held in New France to that time. Never were representatives from so many First Nations to come together to speak in council. These talks were to involve not only the Wyandot, Iroquois, and French, but all the nations allied with the French, and those tribes on the upper Great Lakes, which still possessed a large measure of independence.

It was in contributing to this peacemaking process that Kandiaronk had his greatest impact on the history of New France. During the 1690s, the Iroquois were becoming desperately short of people (see Havard 2001, 62). They needed to have returned those of their people who had been captured.

This being the case, it is not difficult to understand that one of the main obstacles to peace in the Great Lakes area involved the return of prisoners. As Gilles Havard aptly puts it:

> In the Native societies of northeastern North America, releasing prisoners was equivalent to losing one's relatives. The chiefs, moreover, did not have the authority to oblige families to give up prisoners. (Havard 2001, 71)

It was not just resistance on the parts of those who had taken the prisoners into their families. Some of the captured Iroquois had doubtless become comfortable in their new lives, and would be unwilling to go back to their original people. They may have married and had children among their adoptive people (see chapter four for a discussion of how that happened with other former prisoners among the Wyandot).

In this area of negotiations Kandiaronk played a vital role. Many Aboriginal leaders and their people were far from eager to come to talk peace with the Iroquois. They were even more reluctant to return their hard-earned Iroquois prisoners as a strong statement of goodwill. It was largely through the respect that these people had for Kandiaronk that they all finally agreed to making promises of prisoner return as a precondition for negotiations. Without his encouragement, one wonders whether all the groups involved would have gone along with this idea.

In September 1694, Kandiaronk made the following speech in Montreal. He was stressing the importance of returning prisoners, trying in this speech to get the Cayuga and Seneca delegates to the conference to talk their fellow Confederation members into doing likewise:

> I have listened to your words, Goyogouen [Cayugas] and Tsonnontouan [Senecas], it is good that you have come to meet our Father Onontio...he is willing to see the Iroquois here again, provided that they bring him back

his nephews who are prisoners among them, French, Hurons, Outaouaks [Odawa], and his other Allies, so I exhort you with this [wampum] collar, you Goyogouen and Tsonnontouan, to give spirit to the three other Iroquois nations. (Havard 2001, 57)

Onanguicé, the leader of the Potawatomi, was particularly difficult to persuade to bring prisoners to foster the peace process. Kandiaronk spoke on 1 August 1701 about what he had to do to overcome this well-founded fear:

Onanguicé explained that we were moving too quickly to bring back all the Iroquois prisoners. The Nations felt strongly that this was so. I made him the present of a kettle and a gun [both valued trade items] to urge him to follow me to Montreal, assuring him that there was more reason to be content than he thought. He therefore decided to come. (Havard 2001, 104, 240n66)

Almost all of the First Nations involved in the meeting were tired of fighting and wanted peace. However, suspicions were running high, and first steps were difficult to make. Kandiaronk was a major force in clearing the path of obstacles so that these first hesitant and necessary steps could be taken. Invaluable were his efforts during the actual negotiations, particularly after it was discovered that the Iroquois had not brought all their prisoners with them.

In September 1700 there was a preliminary meeting in Montreal. Kandiaronk talked tough to the Iroquois delegates, reminding them that the Seneca:

had formerly violated the general peace... [and] were bent only on the complete destruction of the French, planning not even to spare their Father, whom they intended to be the first to be put into the Kettle, for an Iroquois threatened Monsieur de Frontenac that he would drink his blood from his skull... that their brother Corlard [Iroquoian name for the Governor of New York] treated them so harshly, they who had always been so loyal, that they had lost most of their warriors by supporting his side in that war, that he had not protected them from the burning of their villages and their forts... that their hands were bloody with the blood of our allies, that their flesh was even still between their teeth, and that their lips were all gory with it, that secret hearts were known... that they preferred to walk in the darkness of war... [but] today... the Sun dissipated all these clouds to reveal that beautiful Tree of Peace[18] which was already planted on the highest mountain of the earth. (Havard 2001, 201, 275n54)

The Great Peace of Montreal of 1701

The problem was the prisoner exchange was as unresolved as ever, so Kandiaronk had to work hard to keep the peace at the conference. In frustration, he spoke the following words to Louis-Hector de Callière (1648–1703), Governor of New France from 1698 to 1703, early in the conference. As I believe that the original translations from Wyandot to French to English are a bit misleading, I have injected some Wyandot meanings on the words:

> My Father, I come to say to you that I [follow]...your voice [i.e., -8end- "word, voice"]; remember that you told us last fall that you wanted absolutely that we bring you all the Iroquois Slaves [-ndask8- "prisoner, domestic animal"] who are among us. We [followed your word]...and we are [following your word]...since we bring them. Let us see at the same time if the Iroquois [follow your word]...and how many they have brought back of our nephews [young men] who were taken since the beginning of the war.... If they have done so, it is a mark of their sincerity; if they have not done so, they are dishonest. I know, however, that they have not brought any. I told you last year that it was better if they brought our Prisoners first, and now you see how it is, and how they have deceived us. (Havard 2001, 150)

Regrettably, the first days of the conference were Kandiaronk's last days on earth. Although articulated in what we would now term an exaggerated manner, as was the historical writing style of Europeans at that time, the words of Jesuit historian Father Charlevoix eloquently capture the double spirit of hopefulness and tragedy that took flight with Kandiaronk's death:

> [O]n the first day of August, the first public session was held, and while a Huron chief was speaking, the Rat fell sick. He was attended with all solicitude, inasmuch as on him the Governor-General built his main hope of successfully terminating his great work. He was almost exclusively indebted to him for this wonderful concert, and this assemblage, till then unexampled of so many nations for a general peace. When he came to, and recovered his strength, he was placed in an armchair in the midst of the assembly, and all drew around to hear him.
>
> He spoke at length, and being naturally eloquent...he was heard with boundless attention. He described with modesty, and yet with dignity, all the steps he had taken to secure a permanent peace among all the nations; he made them see the necessity of such a peace, and the advantages it would entail on the whole country in general and each tribe in particular, and with wonderful address showed distinctly the different interests of each....
>
> His voice failing, he ceased speaking, and received from all present, applause, to which he was too well accustomed to be affected by it, especially in his actual condition; in fact he never opened his lips in council without receiving such applause even from those who dislike him....

He felt worse at the close of the session, and was carried to the Hotel Dieu [hospital], where he died two hours after midnight....

His death caused a general affliction, and there was no one French or Indian who did not show that he felt it. (Charlevoix 1900, 5:145–48)

Standing for the first time in Kondiaronk Hall in Wendake in June 2012, I remembered those words, or at least the gist of them. The occasion was the first academic conference of the four remnant descendant groups of the Wendat and of those, like me, who were studying their language, culture, and history. All of us had been affected in some way by his life.

THE RETURN OF QUARANTE SOLS

In 1701, Quarante Sols claimed to have been helping the Miami get to Montreal by building them canoes and giving them gifts (Havard 2001, 276n91). Kandiaronk may have been successful in making Quarante Sols see the value of the Great Peace.

On 27 February 1702, Quarante Sols made the following speech after he returned from his journey visiting the Miami:

> Last summer, Onontio told me to go for the Hurons who were with the Miamis and bring them here, that we might make our fire quite near to yours. I have carried out his wishes, I bring them all, and we are going to join those who came from Missilimakinak in the place you have appointed for us [i.e., Detroit].
>
> I gave ten red coverlets, this autumn, to a chief of the Miamis to invite him to come here with all his tribe and light his fire here. He accepted the present and, during the last few days, after consulting on this matter, he asked their opinion and they decided that they would go and collect the bones of their dead and set them in order [i.e., have a Feast of the Dead] and that, next year, they would come and settle at Detroit. (Margry 5: 411–12)

He then spoke of the reply that the Miami gave to Aouendando (also written as Aouenano), a Seneca claiming to represent the Iroquois. He was actually representing a conciliatory faction within the Confederacy (see Havard 2001, 92, 94):

> Here is one of the largest calumets to be seen; Take it home with you, Aouendando; then bring it back to this village, bringing us our men whom you are keeping prisoners; then you will be welcome, and your two sons—whom we will not give up to you now—we will place in the palm of our hand and there shall be nothing to detain them.

Here is another calumet, which we beg you to take to your village; then send it to the other four villages of your tribe, in order that they may set our men at liberty. (Margry 5:412)

Quarante Sols then presented a wampum belt or necklace to Aouendando, scolding him lightly with the following words:

This necklace tells you that we think you very niggardly; your hands are always closed. All the tribes have obeyed Onontio by bringing him all the prisoners they could collect; he sent a Frenchman to you to unbind ours, who were to come to Detroit last autumn. Every day and every moment we turn our faces towards the village of the French which is at Detroit, and we blush to see that no one comes. (Margry 5:412-13)

Cadillac had convinced Quarante Sols to come south to Detroit. Jesuit Father Etienne de Carheil, the second Jesuit to bear the name Haondechete, "he bears the country," (Steckley 2007a, 241),[19] was very much opposed to the move, believing that the greater contact with French traders would mean that the Wyandot would be debauched by the alcohol. Carheil much preferred, like his fellow Jesuit Father Armand de la Richardie after him, to have the Wyandot under his personal influence and control. For him, Quarante Sols must have seemed to personify the "evil" influence of the traders, so he was quick to speak and write ill of him.

There is some small evidence that Cadillac was adopted by the Bear clan, which would have solidified the relationship between him and Quarante Sols and other members of Quarante Sols' clan. In the 1747 census, there was a young woman, Marguerite Oatonh8entsinde, who was a niece of Bear elder Marie Ts8endask8a, living in the Bear clan house PV16 (Toupin 1996, 214, 248). In brackets the name La la mothe was given. This would appear to be referring to the La Mothe in Cadillac's name.[20] This suggests an association between Cadillac and the Bear clan.

Quarante Sols led the people of his community to the new Detroit home of the Wyandot by 1703. Still the greater part of the Wyandot, headed by Sastaretsi, had not left Michilimackinac. In a council held on 2 June 1703 by the Wyandot at Detroit, which the Ottawa were attending, Quarante Sols said the following about his recent trip to Michilimackinac:

On my arrival, I told Sastaretsy at the council that I was doing the will of Onontio, who had told me to come see him and to hear him.

I told him that my fire had been with the Miamis, but that I had hearkened to the word of Onontio and had taken it to Detroit to obey him.

By a [wampum] necklace—I invite Sastaretsy to remove his fire from Missilimakinak and take it to Detroit, in order that all our tribe may be re-united. Onontio wishes this. He has good eyes; he has seen that the land at Missilimakinak is a poor land [e.g., for corn-based farming]. Once, it is true, our men were slain at Taronto;[21] but the reason was that there were no French people with us. There are some at Detroit, a big village. That had made us safe. He who commands there [i.e., Cadillac] has understanding; he watches night and day, he takes heed of everything.

By a second [wampum] necklace. Sastaretsy, look at this necklace. It is the same which you gave me, to invite me to join you at the village of Missilimakinak, for you said that was the command of the Governor. Think now of this necklace, it should bring you back to the place where the word of Onontio is. It is at Detroit where our tribe should be re-united, in a good land.

By two bracelets. A Great Iroquois chief from the Mountain of Montreal [Kahnesatake or Lake of Two Mountains Mohawk]...urges you to re-unite. (Margry [1888] 1974, 5: 430)

According to Quarante Sols, Sastaretsi disagreed with him, saying that the French governor wanted them to live in Saguinan where the Ottawa were. He said he had heard no such message:

Finally, after discussing it a long while, it was resolved that the old men [male elders] at Missilimakinak and those at Detroit should go down to Montreal in order to settle this dispute, and that we should do what Onontio wished. (Margry [1888] 1974, 5:430–31).

Cadillac was worried about what would happen if the Wyandot leaders went to Montreal. The Wyandot in Detroit had informed him of their position on 14 May, prior to Quarante Sols' return from Michilimackinac: "We come to tell you that we will not quit our village, and will not go to the English." In reply Cadillac probably disingenuously stated, "I had no such thought about you; I know that the Hurons have understanding, and will not start mischief" (Margry [1888] 1974, 5:426). Responding to this remark, the Wyandot half reassured him that:

When Michipichy [i.e., Quarante Sols], our Chief, has returned from Missilimakinak, it may be that a canoe or two will go to Montreal to take Onontio the news of what he has done. (Margry [1888] 1974, 5:426)

On 3 June, a council was held in Fort Pontchartrain (Detroit). A wampum necklace had been sent to the Wyandot from the Seneca in Quarante Sols' absence. The following exchange shows Cadillac's distrust. Quarante Sols' words in reply seem to be serving a variety of purposes. He lectured Cadillac on the etiquette of Aboriginal politics. As well, he seems to be communicating the traditional Aboriginal notion of not knowing as truth what you don't directly experience. Whether, as Cadillac no doubt believed,

Quarante Sols was also holding back what the elders may have said to him, cannot be determined. He also may be accusing the Ottawa of duplicity. Here is the exchange:

QUARANTE SOLS: "I come to tell you what I am to do at Montreal, where I am going. This is a necklace which was sent to us by the Iroquois and was brought to us by the Iroquois; we do not know what it signifies." (Margry [1888] 1974, 5:428)

CADILLAC: "How is it that you received this necklace without knowing for what purpose it was sent to you?"

QUARANTE SOLS: "It is a long time since we received it; I was not present, and our old men [elders] have forgotten what it said."

CADILLAC: "Your old men [elders] are not regarded as children, that their memory should be so short."

QUARANTE SOLS: "We do not accept this necklace [i.e., do not agree with or accept its purpose]; but we are going to take it back to the Sonnontouans [the Seneca], to learn what it signifies; for it is a serious matter not to reply to a necklace; that is the custom among us. The Outaouas will be able to tell you what it is, for our men [elders] have forgotten." (Margry [1888] 1974, 5:428–89)

CADILLAC: "The Outaouas will reply to me that, as you received it, you ought to remember. But, since this necklace is dumb and has lost its message, I can only be silent." (Margry [1888] 1974, 5:429)

Quarante Sols then tried to reassure Cadillac by saying what he will say through wampum both to Sastaretsi and to Louise-Hector de Callière, Governor of New France from 1698. He seems to be hinting that the French must be a constant support or the Wyandot will move elsewhere. First, what he was going to say to Sastaretsi was:

> We are in a good place at Detroit, and have large fields there; there is no need to seek others; now we must make but one and the same fire, and when our lands are old we will seek another place. (Margry [1888] 1974, 5:429)

The last part of this presentation seems to both refer to the practice of moving a community's location slightly when the fertility of the land is used up, and to issue a warning about a larger-scale move.

Second, to Callière Quarante Sols said the following. He appears to be saying in essence that as the French have invited them to a place where they are vulnerable to a number of different enemies, they should continue to protect them. The implicit warning appears to be that as the Wyandot had chosen to come there, so they could choose to leave and take others with them:

> It will very soon be two years that we have been at Detroit; we come to see you today and to tell you that we have been exposed on all sides there. The fire of Sastaretsy is a good fire; it is at Missilimakinak, with the Miamis and at Sonnontouan [with the Seneca]; it was he himself who took it to Detroit. It was not the French who put it there; and when the tribes go to Detroit and see the smoke, they will say: "That is the fire of Sastaretsy; and as long as that fire and the fire of the French remain at Detroit, we will warm ourselves there together." (Margry [1888] 1974, 5:429)

Cadillac responding, showing some displeasure:

> If this necklace were addressed to me, I should have my reply ready at once; but since you are taking it to Onontio, he will give you the answer himself, for he is wiser than I. (Margry [1888] 1974, 5:430)

Andrew Sturtevant (2011, 34–86, see esp. 44–55) hypothesizes in his doctoral dissertation that, in his last years, Quarante Sols, under the distorted Wendat name Cheanonvouzon,[22] set out to form a "Southern Alliance" between the Iroquois, the Miami, and the Wyandot to counteract the influence of the Ottawa and their fellow Anishinabe (including the Mississauga, Ojibwa, and Potawatomi). It is interesting in that regard, as we will see shortly, that Quarante Sols was Bear clan, and that in the first half of the eighteenth century there were two Seneca men, Joseph Sachiendoa and Michel Tierontaron, both baptized in the 1730s, who were married to Bear clan elders, one of whom was known as "la vielle 40 sols." Perhaps this reflects the connection between Quarante Sols as a Bear leader at the beginning of the eighteenth century and the Seneca.

On 27 April 1707, Quarante Sols was baptized, named Louis Antoine, and died. But the name Quarante Sols would stay on, as we will see shortly.

As Quarante Sols belonged to the Bear clan, what I have just presented suggests that the Bear clan may have come to Detroit before the Deer clan did. Further, there appear to be more Huron names found among the Bear clan than among other Wyandot clans. Perhaps this is because they had more of a Huron component to them than the Deer did. It could be that what was being witnessed here was a final reconciliation between two powerful clans, the Deer and the Bear, themselves possibly representing the remnants of the Petun and the Huron, respectively.

Quarante Sols Returns

Forty years later, Anastasie Ts8nde,en, a female Bear clan member of the Wyandot elders' council was termed "la vielle 40 sols" (Toupin 1996, 221). Interestingly, she was married to a Seneca man. Her brother, André Sohondinnonn, also a Bear clan elder, was likewise called "40 sols" (Toupin 1996, 222). Two other Bear clan members, 1747 male Bear elder Honarak and female Bear elder A8innonke's niece Ok8oindate, both had "40 sols" written after their names in the mortuary register in 1759 (Toupin 1996, 929). I believe this would appear to express a connection between the Quarante Sols just discussed and these figures from the mid-eighteenth century. This connection, I feel, is that of being Bear clan. It is reasonable to suspect, also, that as the Bear clan is overrepresented with Huron names, Quarante Sols was Huron and not Petun in origin.

Sohondinnon might have been a war chief. As with A,a8as, he, too, has comments written after his name that suggest a military role: "Sa[,] ohetsaron atrio,e," meaning "he encourages them in warfare, fighting." He seems to have been mistrusted by the French. His French "nickname" was "la borgne." This literally means "the one-eyed one," but also can refer to someone being "disreputable." There are no readily available clues as to which interpretation the French favoured.

His name appears in a separate entry that might be referring to a Huron of the time amongst the Wyandot. More information about him comes from one entry following his name: "sohendinnon v. ok8endissena v. hannionenhak hatatiaθa...le lorretain...jongleur" (Toupin 1996, 226).

This tells us that he spoke French, as "hannionenhak hatatiaθa" can be translated as "He is French,[23] he speaks in such a way"[24] (i.e., "He speaks French"). It also would appear that he is from the Huron community of Lorette or Wendake, a supposition reinforced both by his being able to speak French, and by the fact that his wife A8oindite had a name that is found in *The Jesuit Relations* (JR52:228–29; Steckley 1998a) and in the 1770s in Lorette (Steckley 1998b).

Finally, the term "jongleur" points to his being a shaman, something that would add to French Jesuit distrust of him.

In 1747, both people of his name were recorded as being separated from two wives: Sendak8oin, the Deer clan elder, and the aforementioned A8oindite.

The Wyandot elder Sohondinnon seems to have been able to play the part of both war chief (see chapter 4) and peace chief. Concerning the latter, we have just seen how he worked with Sk8tache to get prisoners returned in 1747. In 1759, Andre Sohondinnon died (E127, Toupin 1996, 929). Neither name, neither Sohondinnon nor 40 sols, was revived by the people.

SUMMARY

In this chapter I have examined the lives of five male Wyandot players in the dispersal times of the second half of the seventeenth century and early eighteenth century, before the people settled in the Detroit/Windsor area. It is my contention that they were of five different clans: Deer (Sastaretsi),

Bear (Quarante Sols), Porcupine (Sk8tache), Prairie Turtle (the Baron), and Wolf (Kandiaronk), representing the three phratries: Deer (Sastaretsi and Quarante Sols), Turtle (Sk8tache and the Baron), and Wolf (Kandiaronk). Their strategies would appear to be the group tactics of specific clans, for whom they were the speakers and primary actors. When the nations or tribes were shattered and scattered, the biggest starter pieces that led to putting the puzzle back together were the clans through their leaders.

Chapter Four

Other Nations and the Clans of the Wyandot

Missionaries and Other Strangers Enter Their Midst

THE JESUITS

A List of Requests Is Presented
For the first quarter century of their time in the Detroit area, the Wyandot did not have a missionary living with them. Some were happy with that, others were not. This situation would change shortly after the people sent a delegation in 1727 to Montreal to speak to the new (since 1726) French Governor Charles de la Boische, Marquis de Beauharnois (Michigan 1905, 34:49–51), bringing with them a short list of requests. Two of these requests related to greater Wyandot independence. One was for a freer system of trade at Detroit, enabling them to do a little "comparison shopping" at different trade houses. A recent set of circumstances had tended to narrowly restrict trade in the last few years (see Michigan 1905, 34:46–48). Another was to ask that the sometimes pushy, in the eyes of some Wyandot, Detroit commandant, Pierre Alphonse de Tonti, be dismissed from his post. Fearing the "resentment" of the Wyandot (see Sturtevant 2011, 36), this request was granted.

The third was to repeat a request made seven years before, by Jesuit Father Pierre François de Charlevoix, reiterated in 1726, that a missionary be sent to their community. This had been a contested issue among the people. As we will see in chapter 7, it seems that some leading women in the community were more in favour of this move than were some of the male leaders. A priest might challenge the independence and authority of these male leaders. At least potentially they could increase that of the female leaders.

The Wyandot threatened to move their village if their requests were not met. Worried about the possible consequences of the proposed threat, particularly as it might affect the plans then being made for the French and their Amerindian allies to fight the Fox nation, Beauharnois granted their requests (Michigan 1905, 34:51–53).

Beauharnois and the other French officials had a view of the role of missionary that the Wyandot male leadership would not be happy to have to deal with. This view is clearly reflected in Beauharnois' letter of 1 October 1728 to the Minister of Marine in which he wrote:

> The reverend Jesuit fathers have sent a missionary to the Hurons [Wyandot] of Detroit who appears well fitted to carry on this mission, and to curb the proud spirit of this tribe. (Michigan 1905, 34:63)

Further, it seems to me that the fact that since Charlevoix's seven-year-old request for a missionary was rather suddenly granted once, in French official eyes, the Wyandot had begun to stir up trouble. It is rather indicative that a good part of the missionary's perceived role was intended to be one of strong influence on, one might say interference with, Wyandot political decision-making.

Father Armand de la Richardie Comes to Live with the Wyandot

The missionary who eventually was sent was Jesuit Father Armand de la Richardie (1686–1758). He had left Paris three years earlier and had spent about two years living with the Huron of Lorette (Wendake). If he had expected the Wyandot to be the same "good docile Christians" that the Lorette Huron were usually described as being (see Charlevoix 1761, 2:22–26), he would have been severely disappointed, or at least challenged in what he found with the Wyandot. Shortly after his arrival with the people, he reported his religious disappointment in their community. To his way of thinking, there was no one who actively professed the Christian faith when he arrived. This would be something of an exaggerated judgement call on his point. A French official had declared in 1710 that the Wyandot were the "best catholics" of all the Aboriginal peoples in the area (Raudot and Silvy 1902, 175). His fellow Jesuit Father Pierre François de Charlevoix had written, based on his 1721 visit to the people, that they were all Christians, just lacking a missionary (in Lajeunesse 1960, 27). A number of Wyandot had

Christian first names, which strongly suggests that they had been baptized prior to coming to Detroit, and may well have been practising Christians during the time that they had no missionary living in their midst. Aboriginal people's tenacity in holding onto their version of Catholicism in the absence of a resident priest is well documented. Such was particularly the case among the Mi'kmaq of the Atlantic provinces during the latter half of the eighteenth century, when Catholic priests were forbidden by the British colonial powers to practise in the region (see Robinson 2005, 52).

Father Richardie received the name Ondechra8asti, which means "it is a beautiful or good country," with the noun stem -*ondech(r)*- "country" and -*8ast*- "to be beautiful, good" (Steckley 2007b, 296 and 214, respectively). It seems to have been unique to him. No other missionary or Wyandot is recorded as bearing this name. Perhaps it came from his description of heaven, for which the usual referent was -*ronhi*- "sky" (Steckley 2007b, 236). The word was used in an earlier written text as part of a description of heaven (Potier 1920, 609), talking about what the French console themselves with when they are dying:

A,8erhe | d'onn' aa,a8enhej | oeri-ichien n' | on,8aties | ex' |
We believe | when we die | it matters little | we are abandoning it | this, here
ondechen | itsondechachen | ondi | ondaie ichien | onnianni
a country lies | it is a very bad country | finally | it | it is a long time
etsa,8atondechen | ,aronhia,e | daat | ondecha8asti
we will be put in another country | in the sky | the very | it is a beautiful country
We believe that when we die it matters little, for we are leaving, abandoning a very bad country, that eventually we will be put in another country for a long time, a very beautiful country.

Linking with the Porcupine and the Deer Clans

Father Richardie developed a strong relationship with two clans in particular: the Deer and the Porcupine. It could, of course, be equally said that these two clans developed particularly strong relationships with him. Agency, or choice, would have operated on both sides.

Let's look at the Porcupine clan connection first. On 10 October 1728, he joined in an official church-sanctioned matrimony between Wyandot community leaders Marguerite Atsironde of the Porcupine clan, who would be that clan's leading female elder in 1747, and her husband Charles Tsoaisens (his name sometimes written as Hooisens), whom Richardie baptized on 10 October 1728, the day before their wedding. No other Wyandot couple would be granted that sacrament until 1746, when Father Pierre Potier came to the mission. It is not known how much a factor was a lack of desire by the Wyandot to go through the formal ceremony, and how much was Richardie's refusal to grant it. Both factors were probably an influence (see chapter 5).

Atsironde and Tsoaisens' thirteen-year-old son, named Armand after the priest, was baptized in June 1729 (Toupin 1996, 822, B19).[1] Two other children of theirs were baptized that year, one eleven (Toupin 1996, 822, B18) and another seven (Toupin 1996, 823, B26). The future Porcupine clan leader, Pierre Tiao8endata, Charles Tsoaisens' son, was baptized at twenty years old, on 18 June 1730 (Toupin 1996, 827, B112). Interestingly, no woman's name is given as the mother, but she must have been Porcupine clan because her son was.

Richardie was especially close to Deer clan members of authority. Marie Nendaentons, the first of four women listed as Deer elders in the 1747 council (see chapter 7), was recorded as being his sister: "soror patris" ("sister of the father"; Toupin 1996, 225) and "Soeur du P. La Richardie" ("sister of Father La Richardie"; Toupin 1996, 258). Her family (probably she) had adopted him. She had three children baptized in 1729: Joseph who was eight (Toupin 1996, 825, B59), Nicolaus who was seven (Toupin 1996, 825, B60), and Jacques who was five (Toupin 1996, 825, B61).

Deer clan, Deer phratry, and Wyandot nation leader Sastaretsi also had two children baptized that same year (Toupin 1996, 825, B74, B75). The Deer clan led all the other clans in baptisms from 1729 to 1732. It is quite likely that the conversion process was at least in part political on both Richardie's and the Deer clan's part.

What did Richardie feel about this family connection? In March 1746, he wrote the following, which I have translated from the original Wendat. It seems to indicate his acceptance of his familial connection with the Deer clan (although there is otherwise a lack of evidence of the clan of the person in question). I do not believe that he was speaking metaphorically of a young person as his grandchild:

> At Point Pelee, a fruit that would, should have been full, at the village, she died, Ondechonniaha, who used to be my granddaughter, a young girl. (Potier 1920, 685; translation mine; see Appendix C for full text)

Increasing Tension for the Wyandot under Father Richardie's Watch

During those early mission years of the late 1720s and most of the 1730s, the Wyandot proved to be useful allies to the French, particularly in their common struggle against the Fox. The Wyandot did not meekly toe the French line, however. They often fought when, where, and whom they chose. In the spring of 1738, the independent actions of the Wyandot stirred things up among the peoples of the area. At a council meeting of the neighbouring tribes, they declared peace with the "tettes plattes" (the Catawba; see below and Appendix B2) in a manner that the Algonquian-speaking peoples seemed to have perceived as being too high-handed and suspicious for them to bear.[2] For the Ottawa in particular, this was the proverbial straw that broke the camel's back, the beaver pelt that sunk the canoe. When this perceived affront was compounded by suspected Wyandot complicity in a Catawba defeat of a combined Ottawa–Potawatomi war party, the Wyandot and their Algonquian neighbours entered into a state of undeclared but ever-threatening warfare (Michigan 34, 151–54).

Father Richardie appears to have been a player in this move. The governor planned to have Wyandot warriors sent out to raid the Catawba, thus to diminish the suspicions of Wyandot collusion with that people. In one reference to the matter (Michigan 1905, 34:182), the plan was said to be upset by the message of a wampum belt "secretly given" by someone who Beauharnois did not name in his writing to the Minister of Marine back in France. This could well have been Richardie, for in another reference (which may have been about the same incident), there was talk about a split existing between the elders and the young men regarding whether or not the Catawba should be attacked. Richardie made it very clear that he favoured the peaceful stance of the elders and that Beauharnois and his "spiritual advisers" (a negative reference to the Sulpicians, see below) were supporting the warring stance of the young men (Michigan 1905, 34:189).

The situation in and around Detroit grew tense. The Wyandot were worried because they were significantly outnumbered by their Algonquian neighbours.[3] In order to even the odds somewhat, the Wyandot appealed to French Iroquoian solidarity, asking the mainly Mohawk communities of Kahnawake and Oka (Lake of Two Mountains or Kahnesatake) and the Lorette Huron to assist them in the expected conflict, and to perhaps provide for them a home, should such be needed in the future.

That autumn, the Wyandot abandoned their fields and village and wintered near Sandusky[4] Bay on the south shore of Lake Erie. But that was only a temporary solution. Something had to be done to put an end to this crisis situation. In these circumstances, Richardie arose as a political figure, influencing not only the future of the Wyandot, but, through them, also that of the entire Ohio Valley–Great Lakes region. As we will see, it was not just a simplistic, straight-line cause and effect type of influence, but a complex interweaving of factors in which action and result were not always readily predictable.

Many Wyandot felt that they should move to live closer to their Iroquoian brothers and sisters living amongst the French, settling somewhere not far from Montreal. There they could feel safer from the fluctuating tides of Algonquian opposition.

This plan was first articulated to the French early in 1739. In that year a Wyandot leader named Nicholas Orontondi, a prominent member of the Porcupine clan, who was reported to be the "great chief of that tribe" though he was not, came to Detroit in order to ask permission for his people to move to live closer to Onnontio, the governor of New France, whose home was by the St. Lawrence River (Michigan 1905, 34:164).

One must understand that the Wyandot were not making a humble plea for protection. While they made this and subsequent requests in the name of the fears of their women and children, this was in part traditional political rhetoric to save face, only in part reality. Further, they would not move unless they were invited with appropriate dignity and unless a place was prepared for them in advance. Only under these terms could the Wyandot leaders maintain their all-important sense of pride and independence. Anything less and they might have opted to stay where they were and take their chances (Michigan 1905, 34:197–98; Wisconsin Historical Collection 1906, 17:378–79).

Richardie, despite his living with the Wyandot for about ten years at that point, never seemed to understand or have sympathy for the diplomatic sensibilities of the Wyandot. He saw anything other than obedience on their part as expressing their "vanity" (Michigan 1905, 34:172). His actions at that time were not determined by a respectful appreciation of the politically precarious position of the Wyandot. The moves he made seemed to be primarily governed instead by his two great fears, two events that he wanted to prevent at all costs: (a) that the Wyandot would move east and join with the Iroquois of the Six Nations and the English (Michigan 1905, 34:195–97); and (b) that the Wyandot would be taken away from his religious jurisdiction and from that of the Jesuit order.

Because of this first fear, he initially supported the proposed move to the heartland of New France. However, he would change his mind and would end up in sharp opposition to an influential member of the Prairie Turtle clan—a clan with which he and his successor, Father Pierre Potier, would come to clash.

The Prairie Turtle Clan and Father Richardie

In the previous chapter, we talked about the possibility that the Baron, someone whom the French leaders did not trust, belonged to the Prairie Turtle clan. In the eighteenth century, this clan seemed to form among the Wyandot the primary locus of resistance to missionary and French control. The late-seventeenth-century Baron would fit neatly into that category.

The main individual that Richardie combatted with was ,Ang8irot. He was a very important person in Wyandot society. Not only was he the leader of the Prairie Turtle clan, but he also was the head of the Turtle phratry (Toupin 1996, 260), making him one of the three leading male political figures among the Wyandot.

Interestingly, during the first few years of Father Richardie's mission, the Prairie Turtle was one of the leading clans in terms of baptisms. By 1731, ten of their number had been baptized, sharing the lead in that category with the Deer clan.

Ang8irot was not a major participant in baptism. However, he was not hard-core anti-Christian either, as you might think, reading the writings of his antagonist Father Richardie. In 1741, a twelve-year-old adoptive son of his, named Jean-Baptiste was baptized (Toupin 1996, 849, B542). The next year his newborn son was "struck with water" (the Wendat expression for baptism) as well (Toupin 1996, 850, B568).

But Father Richardie was determined to vilify and isolate Ang8irot. This can be seen in a letter written in 1741 by the more subtly manipulative Governor Beauharnois advising Richardie against such obvious political actions:[5]

> my Reverend Father, I cannot omit to inform you that I know perfectly well that this chief is a most important man in his tribe, and has half the village at his disposal; he is therefore a man to be humoured. Many people have told me that you do not like him; that you did not admit him to any council; that his people had spoken and he had said nothing; and that, when he saw me, he would let me know that he has reason to complain, since you gave him out to be a dangerous and pernicious person. On an occasion like this it is advisable, rather, to appear to have confidence in him, so as not to disgust him, and thus to induce him not to thwart my purpose. (Michigan 34:203–4)

Ang8irot resisted the attempts of Richardie and other French leaders to downgrade his authority. This is clearly illustrated in a letter that Beauharnois' nephew wrote on 2 August 1742, when the latter apparently was trying to ply ,Ang8irot with alcohol. It should be kept in mind that in 1747 Potier used the pejorative Latin term "bibax" (i.e., drinker) to refer to the Prairie Turtle leader (Toupin 1996, 214). The French had identified what they thought was his weakness:

> Angouirot, a famous chief of the opposite party, that is of those who do not wish to go down, Angouirot, I say, more obstinate than ever, persists still in the same feelings. I have every reason to Fear that this man may spoil my success as he joins to a cunning and subtle mind, the ability of an accomplished politician. He listens to everything and never makes answer. Presents and other inducements—nothing is spared.... I invited him yesterday

to take supper with me. Invoked to speak frankly this sly rogue, fearing the wine might betray him, and lead him to disclose what was in his mind, took the precaution of eating and drinking only with the very greatest moderation. (Wisconsin 17:354)

Further, it is distinctly possible that the opposition between the two men was religious as well as political. The evidence for this is of a rather unconventional nature, coming from a story well known to the nineteenth-century Wyandot. In this story, entitled "The Origin of the Panther Fraternity" by anthropologist Marius Barbeau, a group of Wyandot received spiritual power from a white panther[6] living in a spring.[7] According to P.D. Clarke, who recorded the story:

> The principal portion of this association were of the Prairie Turtle Clan. And they were repeatedly warned by the Catholic priest, then at Detroit, what would be the consequence, if they did not renounce the evil spirit or strange god they worshiped. "Throw away the baneful substance, which came to you from the devil, by one of his emissaries in the shape of a panther," he said to them, "for just as certain as you continue to keep it among you, the time is not far distant when you will be ruined by it, both body and soul." (Barbeau 1915, 344)
>
> A few years after the white panther appeared to the Wyandott at the spring, the Wyandott who called it up and received its blood, turned traitor to his nation and joined their enemy, the Senecas, then inhabiting the banks of Niagara, and he, at one time led a war party of that tribe to a Wyandott village in Michigan, while the men were absent. The leader of this war party slew two young Wyandot women in a corn field near the village; then flew northward with his men, and crossed Detroit river at the next island, just above the French fort; thence marched through the woods towards Lake Erie.... The traitor and his party were overtaken while crossing a miry creek, at some distance from the lake. They slew the renegade and his followers, but spared the lives of two Senecas, to carry the news to their people. (Barbeau 1915, 343–44)

Two questions come to mind here. The first is whether this is the spirit figure of *Mishibichi* (see previous chapter) carried on into a later time. The second is can we say that this is in some ways the story of Ang8irot passed down over the generations? It is difficult to know for sure. No matter what the source of the animosity between the Prairie Turtle leader and the priest, it is important to note that that clan would over the years be less connected to Christian ceremonies and relationships than any other. Starting in 1729 and continuing into 1741 and 1742, they had the lowest participation rate in baptisms of any of the eight major clans. In the deathways ceremonies (see below), they were minor players.

The Rise of Nicholas Orontondi of the Porcupine Clan

At the same time as Ang8irot was being so vehemently opposed by Father Richardie, another member of a clan belonging to the Turtle phratry rose to prominence in the Wyandot's dealings with the French. This individual was the aforementioned Nicholas Orontondi of the Porcupine clan. It is important to note that at this time he was being represented as being one of the three Wyandot "chiefs," even though Ang8irot remained the head of the Turtle phratry.

Orontondi had been early active with baptism, being a godfather five times in 1730, 1731, and 1732 (Toupin 1996, 828 and 829 twice and 831, respectively, B122, B136, B143, B154, B196). One of those times was for his son Ndo,ente's child, a son who was also early involved with baptism. He would have looked good to Richardie.

Orontondi travelled to Quebec in the summer of 1740 to speak alone with the governor. I believe that in the nature of and circumstances surrounding this visit one can see the political hands of Father Richardie quietly and subtly at work in the shadows trying to pull strings.

In 1741, Beauharnois wrote of Nicholas Orontondi in the following way, clearly treating him as if he was one of the three phratry chiefs of the Wyandot:

> Orontony sent me sticks of porcelain [wampum] on behalf of the whole village, by which he asked for permission to come and settle near me, as he could no longer live in peace at the place, because, said he,—you would always be accused of taking part in every attack that might be made by the Flatheads [Catawba] upon the tribe at the post; and in order to avoid coming to cruel extremities some day, he repeated the request which you had made to me....
>
> You, Sastaretsy, with Tayetchatin [Ta,echiaten, the Wolf phratry chief] and Orontony, sent me a message to make known to me what your purpose was, in the hope that I would have compassion on your position; and you told me that if I had pity on the Hurons I would bring them near me; that your opinion was supported by two belts....
>
> Afterwards, you requested your Father the Commandant, and the three Black Robes [Jesuits],[8] to support your message to me with such energy that the request you made to me should not be refused; that your words were written down, and that Nicolas alone should be admitted to my chamber. I did so; you know it. (Michigan 1905, 34:192–94)

It is curious that this trip was to be made by Orontondi alone, and that the words of a Wyandot message preceding him stated emphatically that he and no one else was to be admitted to the office of the French governor. Further, it seems a little odd that the message he was to deliver (which was composed by Father Richardie) had more significance than that which Orontondi himself had to say. It was clearly stated that he was not to be listened to if he "should have allowed himself to be gained over to stop them from coming down" (Michigan 1905, 34:199). He could carry the message, but he could not speak.

It seems to me that these precautions were directed against the influence of Ang8irot, in fear that he might be allowed to speak to Beauharnois, in fear that he, as the leader of the Turtle phratry to which Orontondi belonged, might be able to sway the thoughts of the younger lower-status man. Such fears were primarily those of Father Richardie.

It is fair to state that in no small way Richardie contributed to Orontondi's rise to become an influential figure, even if that contribution was primarily limited to his cutting away at the power base of Ang8irot, Orontondi's potential "rival" (at least in Richardie's eyes). With his growing experience with the Wyandot, Richardie must have suspected that he would not be able to influence the Wyandot decisively, or hope to get them to agree with his political agenda, unless he could bank on the support of the leaders of all three of the Wyandot phratries. Such being the case, he needed to back a prominent figure in the Turtle phratry whose views were in accord with his own. Orontondi, as the head of one of the Turtle phratry clans, would be an ideal candidate.

This is not to say that Orontondi was Richardie's pawn; he wasn't. Nor is it to imply that he did not have the ability to rise to authority on his own; he did. It is just that Richardie's actions probably facilitated that rise by "creating an opening" at the top, which Orontondi was well positioned to fill.

Although, as earlier stated, Richardie was initially in favour of a Wyandot move away from the English and amongst the French, he changed his mind. This change would flow from his more self-focused fear that the Wyandot might then come under the influence of French priests of another order, potentially even depriving him of his position of influence over "his Indians." His concern in this regard is revealed in a letter he wrote to fellow Jesuit Father Jean-Baptiste St. Pe. In this letter, Richardie stated his belief that, although the Wyandot appeared to be pressing for the move so that they could live closer to the French governor, another agenda was at play:

> That is only what they pretend: in reality they wish that it would be the people from the Sault [Kahnawake] of the Lake [Lake of Two Mountains or Kahnesatake]. The latter are not in my good books, as you may think, hence, if the General will hear their prayers, the people from the Sault must be their envoys to them, and their deputations should arrive here next spring to use the gentle violence that they desire. (Michigan 1905, 34:172)

One major reason that the Mohawk of the Lake of Two Mountains were not in his "good books" was that their priest, newly arrived in 1739, Father François Picquet, was of the Sulpician religious order, not Jesuit. If the Wyandot moved in with the Mohawk there, then Richardie would lose his ecclesiastic power base. Members of the two orders would not share a mission. What complicated this situation further was the fact that Richardie's fears were fed by Governor Beauharnois' closeness to Picquet, and what seems to have been the governor's not too well concealed suspicions of Richardie, and of Jesuits in general. The above-quoted letter, which was intercepted by Beauharnois, proved to be one of the initial volleys fired in an ongoing paper conflict between the missionary and the governor, degenerating into a power struggle over the fate of the Wyandot (Michigan 1905, 34:189, 209–12, 412–15). That this was how Richardie envisioned the situation is seen in the following excerpt from a letter he wrote to Father Pierre-Luc du Jaunay, then Jesuit missionary to the Ottawa at Michilimackinac:

> It is easy to see that the Chevr. [de Beauharnois] wanted to take this mission away from us, that it might fall to his friend M. Piquet who has already begun to have clearings made and huts built for receiving them; but, happen what may, the Hurons would never have any missionaries but us. (Michigan 1905, 34:210)

Richardie gradually withdrew his support for the original plan and began to give his blessing to an alternative plan in which the Wyandot would be moved to Grosse Isle in the Detroit River. Despite Beauharnois having sent his nephew (said to have been adopted by the Iroquois living in French territory) with a group of Kahnawake and Lake of Two Mountains Mohawk in 1741, in order to present an invitation to the Wyandot, Richardie managed to sabotage that venture. The people remained under his mission care.

The Orontondi Movement

During the 1740s, the world around the Wyandot was beginning to change significantly. The English were moving increasingly closer towards them. In 1743, the trader George Croghan moved west of the Alleghenies, along the southern shore of Lake Erie, as far west as Sandusky Bay, pioneering a new trade route. The contact with the English that Richardie had dreaded and had fought so hard to prevent was becoming well established. A group of three Wyandot (possibly one from each phratry), led by Orontondi, went east to Albany on 30 July 1743. They took with them a wampum treaty belt said to have been given to the Wyandot forty years earlier by the Iroquois. They came to request trading privileges and were welcomed openly.

This desire to trade with the English accelerated in 1744 when war was declared between England and France. For the English were able to effectively blockade French ships bringing valued trade goods to New France. The French fur traders suffered from a shortage of goods; the goods they did have were priced high to their Aboriginal customers. Meanwhile, English traders, backed by gifts sent from British colonial governments, had much more to offer and could trade their goods at lower cost (Pennsylvania 5:350; Wisconsin 17:446–47).

In 1745, Orontondi, with a considerable number of Wyandot from both villages, set up a separate village near the banks of the Sandusky River. At about the same time, other traditional allies of the French, such as the Mississauga, were moving towards a closer relationship with the English.[9]

It is difficult to say for sure why Orontondi made this move. Perhaps having tasted power as "the" representative of the Wyandot, he found it difficult to return to being secondary in importance to the hereditary chief Sastaretsi and to the new Turtle phratry leader Sa,ents8a't (see chapter 6). Once Ang8irot died, Richardie had no more reason to support Orontondi as Ang8irot's rival. Perhaps Orontondi found that Richardie was backing more compliant leaders as the head of the Turtle phratry. This could have included Thomas Ts8nnonkanien, who became head of Ang8irot's clan. Another candidate is Babi, or Jean-Baptiste A,otiok8andoron, the head of the Striped Turtle clan, who just before the death of Orontondi (in 1750) was said to have reason to fear that he would be "demoted" if Orontondi returned to join with the other Wyandot (Ott 1936, 207; see below).

Orontondi himself and his allies gave perhaps the best reason for their move when, speaking to the English trader Conrad Weiser, they said that:

> their coming from the French was because of the hard Usage they received from them; That they would always get their Young Men to go to War against their Enemies, and wou'd use them as their own People, that is like Slaves. (Pennsylvania 1851, 5:350)

While there might be some exaggeration here, perceived ill treatment from the French probably was a factor. The split with the French, however, was not a complete one. They still were religiously served by Fathers Richardie and Potier. In addition, they did not initially seem to be too anxious to take up arms against the French. That was a big—potentially lethal—step.

The Wyandot and the Algonquians of the Great Lakes region were uncertain at this time as to which way the wind of victory between French and English would blow. They were receiving contradictory messages. The Iroquois had yet to declare themselves as being anything but neutral in the European-based squabble.

Worried about the loyalties of his Aboriginal allies in that region, Governor Beauharnois was anxious to have them fighting against the English. While, like General Louis-Joseph Montcalm, commander of the French forces from 1756 to 1759 after him, he did not assign much value to Aboriginal military effectiveness, he did feel that by keeping them engaged against the English, he would be discouraging the English from soliciting their aid (NYCD10:20). A few warriors (including some Wyandot) from the Detroit region went with the French to raid English settlements in the Carolinas. However, many more were standing back to wait and watch what was unfolding. The French needed a few solid military successes to discount the often repeated English claim that the French would soon be defeated.

Thus, when the French and some of their Aboriginal allies attacked and defeated the stockaded Dutch–English settlement of Saratoga on 28 and 29 November 1745, it was played up by the French as a major triumph. In a letter from Paul-Joseph Le Moyne de Longueuil, then governor of Detroit, written in Wyandot (and probably originally composed) by Richardie and read to the leaders or "Grand Council" of the Wyandot on 4 April 1746, the Wyandot were officially told of this victory (Potier 1920, 684–85; for the full text see Appendix B2). This letter is a cleverly written piece of propaganda. The role of the Kahnawake Mohawk is played up. The number of the enemy killed and taken prisoner appears to be exaggerated. The Wyandot are falsely reassured that the Iroquois of the Six Nations were not angry at the French and their Aboriginal allies for the defeat of Saratoga.

On 25 March 1746, Richardie suffered a paralytic stroke. He left for Montreal in July, thus removing his influence on the Wyandot of Orontondi's band, whom he had been visiting and serving. At about the same time (14 June) most of the leaders of the Ottawa, Potawatomi, and Saulteaux, who were either sympathetic to the French or did not want strife or trouble with the French, left for Montreal too. A few months later, the Iroquois had decided to end their neutrality and strike against the French and their Aboriginal allies.

The combined effect of these events made the time right for the English and those siding with them to make their move. It was not long afterwards that Orontondi began to act aggressively against the French and to link his envoys with those of the Iroquois to urge such heretofore indecisive groups as the Shawnee and the Miami to strike the French in their area. The fact that now, for the first time, a significant Wyandot leader, a member of a group long one of the most politically potent of the Aboriginal allies of the French, was saying to attack the French would probably be a significant factor in winning these and other tribes over.

In 1747, the seeds of dissention that Orontondi was sowing were beginning to show their contentious heads above the ground. Five French traders were killed coming back to Detroit from an outlying post on the Ohio River (NYCD10:114–15). This killing was attributed to Orontondi's Wyandot as they lived in that area. On 31 May, three more French traders were killed near the Saginaw River by the Ottawa (NYCD10:115, 119). Around that time the Saulteaux also claimed responsibility for the death of a French trader. Young men of the Ottawa, Potawatomi, Mississauga, and Saulteaux harassed the French with such acts as killing their livestock. The Miami captured the French fort in their area and made prisoners of the inhabitants (NYCD10:140).

Almost all of the Aboriginal nations of the Ohio valley–Great Lakes region were ready for action against the French (NYCD10:119, 128). The one major event needed to set off a chain reaction of effective raids against French posts was the capture of Detroit. It was what Orontondi had promised to do. It was what he had to deliver.

Orontondi had lost the crucial element of surprise after the killing of the five traders, and particularly after a Wyandot woman had informed a lay brother of the details of Orontondi's plans (NYCD10:115). He could still grab victory, however, if he would act decisively, and if he could get the support of the other Wyandot leaders.

He arrived at Bois Blanc with his warriors on 20 May 1747. This caused Potier to flee to the fort that night despite the fact that Orontondi claimed to have come there in peace. As Orontondi surveyed the situation around him, he encountered some stumbling blocks that he could not surmount.

At the end of March, a reinforcement contingent numbering thirty-two coming from Montreal had arrived. It included four Lorette Huron, four Kahnawake Mohawk, four Lake of Two Mountains Mohawk, four Abenaki, and two Malecite (Potier 1920, 157; see Appendix B2). These peoples had just declared war on the Mohawk in New York on 5 March, and were firmly committed to the side of the French against the English and their Iroquois allies. The presence of their French-speaking Catholic Iroquoian brethren, with whom they had exhibited such a close bond in the recent past, could be an effective agent in dissuading the Wyandot from attacking Detroit.

Religious influence too was strongly exerted to prevent the success of Orontondi's mission. A letter from Father Richardie had arrived with the contingent from Montreal (Potier 1920, 686–87; see Appendix B4). In this letter, the Jesuit assured the Wyandot who were not with Orontondi that he would not blame or excommunicate all Wyandot for what was done by one dissident section. He threatened, however, to judge those who chose to associate with them. He was, in other words, applying ecclesiastic "blackmail" on the Wyandot.[10] As well, a letter from Jesuit Father Daniel Richer (Potier 1920, 687; Appendix B5), missionary to the Huron of Lorette, stressed that if the English took control then Christianity could no longer exist in the country. Richardie's blackmail and Richer's letter would combine to act quite efficiently to divide the Wyandot, perhaps making those who were with Orontondi reconsider their current military stance. The Wyandot, including Orontondi, were quite religious and seemed to be attached to the Catholic faith. That this was apparently true for Orontondi is suggested by the fact that on 19 November 1747, Orontondi was married in the mission by Father Richardie (Shiels 1936, 38), one of very few marriages that the priest performed.

The two other leading figures in Wyandot society—Sastaretsi, head of the Deer phratry and of the Wyandot generally, and Ta,echiaten, head of the Wolf phratry—would not side with Orontondi. It seems that they had becoming increasingly close to Richardie as he had (among other things) tended to support their authority against the independent actions of young men anxious to prove themselves as warriors. With his people effectively divided, Orontondi was unsuccessful.

Nicholas Orontondi died on 20 May 1750 (Toupin 1996, 923, E52). Over the next two years, the Porcupine clan led all clans in the number of baptisms (where clan has been identified). The women of the clan seemed especially to want to reconnect with the mission. It is difficult to determine whether it was because Orontondi had been holding them back, or because they felt that the position of their clan was weakened, with a need for a stronger mission connection to give the clan strength. It is clear that the Porcupine clan had not separated from the others.

Father Richardie left the Detroit Wyandot mission for good in 1751 to "retire" in Quebec until his death in 1758.

Nicholas de Gonnor

In 1743, a new missionary arrived among the Wyandot, with the original intent of replacing, or at least assisting, a weary Father Richardie (Lajeunesse 1960, xlvii). His name was Father Nicolas de Gonnor. Although, owing to illness, he stayed only one year, he did receive a name: Sarenhes (Toupin 1996, 235, 261). The name means "he is tall treetops," with the noun root -*renh*- "treetops, branches," and the verb root -*es*- "to be long" (Steckley 2007b, 228, 279). This name had a Huron heritage, belonging to a prominent trader who died in 1636 (JR8:151). In 1747 this name (also written as Shorenhes) belonged to the Striped Turtle clan member Pierre Sarenhes. It would look, then, that Father de Gonnor was adopted by the Striped Turtle clan. In 1743 the Striped Turtle was second in clan participation in baptisms behind the Bear clan; in 1744 it was tied for first with the Large Turtle clan. That the Striped Turtle clan belonged to the Turtle phratry is significant here. He was the second missionary to live with the people, and he was adopted into the second phratry. Phratry order prevailed.

Pierre Potier

In a note written by Father Richardie, Father Pierre Potier introduced himself thus:

> Here I am, my children. I wished that I would greet respectfully as my own child those whom I would find. I intend to encourage them all so that their forces (of conviction) would stand, so that they would listen to and believe all the special "holy" matters which I will teach them. I will love them completely, all those who will follow the word of the great voice. (translation mine; see Appendix B1 for full text)

Father Pierre Potier was born in Blaindain, Belgium, 21 April 1708. After studying and teaching in his home country, he arrived in New France on 1 October 1743. His first work there, as was also true of Father Richardie, was with the Huron at Lorette, studying their language under the knowledgeable tutelage of Father Pierre-Daniel Richer, known as Hechon to the Wendat. He remained there for a little over eight months.

On 26 June 1744, he left Quebec for the Detroit mission, landing at Bois Blanc Island in September. He worked as assistant to Richardie, learning the language and the administrative routines from him, until July 1746 when his mentor left.

Potier was early linked to the Wolf clan. The initiative for the linking probably came from both sides. That he was the third missionary adopted and that this adoption was into the third phratry, that of the Wolf, suggests that the Wolf clan played a major role in forming the link. Both parties acted to their own benefit in forming the link. It served both of their needs.

Major evidence for the link can be seen in his Wyandot name Horonhia,ete, "He carries or bears the sky." This name had a complicated history. The first time it was recorded was as *Oronhiaguehre* (the *-r-* before the final *-e-* was a typographical error for *-t-*), presented as the Neutral name for Jesuit Father Pierre Chaumonot (JR18:41) in 1640.[11] Since Chaumonot gave up the name for the more significant *Hechon*[12] a short time after 1649 (when the first Hechon, Father Jean de Brébeuf died), *Horonhia,ete* may have gone without resuscitation from then until 1677, when the next known Jesuit bearer, Father Claude Chauchetiere, came to the Huron community of Lorette (FH1693:241; Jaenen 1969b, 139–40). He died in 1709.

In 1737, a Wolf clan man bearing that name, also possessing the French–Christian name Antoine, was the godfather for a baptism (Toupin 1996, 843, B441). Antoine took the name Tandarei8oin after the Wolf clan gave the name Horonhia,ete to Potier. Antoine's new name was first noted in the census of 1747 in the elders' council list (Toupin 1996, 229), with both names appearing in the entry for his house (Toupin 1996, 220).

It is interesting, that in the list of "François à L'ile aux bois blancs," there are two French men presented as bearing the name "horonhia,ete anien," Joseph (L'esperance) Rochelot and Regis (Toupin 1996, 261). The "anien" means "my child." Why this is used is unclear. Did Potier adopt these men into the Wolf clan? It is possible.

Another point linking Potier to the Wolf clan came about in 1746, when Potier took over baptismal duties from Richardie. His first baptism was "unofficial" (i.e., not one entered into the records) and took place on 2 December 1745, when he baptized "une Louve," a Wolf clan woman close to death at Etionnont8t (Toupin 1996, 323). On 15 August 1746, he baptized three adult Wolf clan members, all siblings: older brother (but second son) Jean Baptiste Toratati, Marie Tso,enron, and Marie Nengieton; this was followed on 7 October by their fifteen-year-old brother, Mathias Atioronhon (Toupin 1996, 856, B682, B683, B684, B689, respectively). Potier mentions having baptized a fifth sibling, probably a brother, in Etionnont8t (Toupin 1996, 221). Potier identified the clan of the two males, something he did not do for any other of his hundreds of baptisms. There was a link forged between Potier and his adopted Wolf clan members.

During that same first year of his mission work (1746), Potier performed one marriage. It was of Jean Baptiste Toratati to Marie Jeanne Ts8tsaondoaon, on 4 September, only the second marriage of a Wyandot in the records (Toupin 1996, 908, M2). One of the witnesses was Wolf clan member Tiendase, who had long been involved with baptisms.

Potier even identified a man as Wolf who died in August 1746, a day after being baptized. This baptism was not in the official record. Again, that clan identification would not be done for a member of any other clan.

Potier may well also have been trying to "court" the Prairie Turtle through members of that clan who were most amenable to missionary influence. The evidence of this comes from the relatively high number of ages (twenty-four)[13] he gives for Prairie clan members, from small children to adults such as Louise Ondechi8ri at forty and young elder Ta,enndrak at twenty-eight. He gives more ages for people of this clan than of any other. This suggests to me that he was trying to get to know them, and, of course, wanting to influence them as well, particularly with the earlier alienation of the leader of the clan in 1747 and recently dead. Interesting is the house

92   CHAPTER FOUR

in which he knew the ages of the highest number of people: PV11, with twenty-three ages of Prairie Turtle clan members given. In the two other Prairie Turtle houses—GV5, which was the house of Ang8irot's widow and their children, and GV2, which had two Prairie Turtle elders in it—there were no ages given. The leading male in that house was Tahatie, who (as we will see in chapter 6), would be opposed to Potier and the French in supporting the Pontiac movement. Potier seems to have been spending his time with the Prairie Turtle clan members whom he found easier to influence. This suggests to me that he had more contact with them than with comparable members of other clans.

Clans and Ages in the Census

Clan	House	Number	Total Number	Rank
Deer	PV6	3		
	PV11	2		
	PV13	13	18	3
Snake	PV4	2	2	7/8
Bear	PV1	2		
	PV16	3		
	PV18	4		
	GV13	6	15	4
Large Turtle	PV2	4		
	PV13	5		
	GV6	1		
	GV13	2	12	5
Porcupine	PV1	6		
	PV2	1		
	PV14	1	8	6
Striped Turtle	PV2	7		
	PV10	9		
	PV11	1		
	GV13	2	19	2
Prairie Turtle	PV10	3		
	PV11	23		
	GV12	1	27	1
Wolf	GV12	2	2	7/8

In terms of absolute numbers we have the following:[14]

Clan	Number	Rank
Prairie Turtle	24[15]	1
Striped Turtle	19	2
Deer	18	3
Bear	15	4
Large Turtle	12	5
Porcupine	8	6
Snake	2	7/8
Wolf	2	7/8
Total	84	

Jean-Baptiste de Salleneuve

Potier had some assistance in the Wyandot mission from Jesuit Father Jean-Baptiste de Salleneuve (1708–64; JR71:175) from 1755 to 1759, another priest adopted by a clan. He bore the name Otre8ati (Toupin 1996, 236), a Snake clan name, held by a Jacques Hatre8ati ("he is punished"), eldest son of Snake clan elder Susanne Sendanion, and married in a Christian ceremony in 1747 (Toupin 1996, 908, M5). Jacques is last recorded as bearing the name in 1752. It seems that after Father Salleneuve left the Wyandot, his name was passed on. In 1760 an Otre8ati was a participant in an anniversary service (see chapter 5 for a discussion of this ceremony; Toupin 1996, 948, SA14). In 1762 an Otre8ati was a godfather to a Pierre (probably Otre8ati's Christian name). In 1774 and 1777 Thomas Otre8ati was a godfather (Toupin 1996, 897, 903, B1285, B1378).

Again, we can see phratry order in the naming of a Jesuit missionary. He was named after a Wolf phratry name was applied to a missionary. He received a name from a clan that belonged to the Deer phratry, the next in order.

Jean-François Hubert

Another priest who had some contact with the Wyandot, and had a Wendat name, was the man who replaced Potier as officiator at baptisms: Father Jean-François Hubert (1739–99). He bore the name Harih8a8a,i "he holds matters of importance in his hand." This was a name that went with the position of bishop of New France since Laval (JR45:41–43; 49:89; FH1697:71). In 1747 it belonged to a young Bear clan member named François, son of prominent Bear clan woman Asenra,e-haon (Toupin 1996, 214). The latter name belonged to a Huron woman of particular significance in the 1640s to 1660s (see chapter 7), who may have adopted Laval after he landed in Quebec in 1659. One wonders what this connection meant to the two sides. Hubert's consistently poor spelling of Wyandot names demonstrates that learning the Wyandot language had not been a significant part of his training. He was not a Jesuit, so this is probably the case. Like bishops before him, when he received the French position, he acquired the Wendat name.

So we can see, then, that over the period in question five men worked as missionaries to the Wyandot. Each one was adopted by a different clan. Two points should be noted here. First is that the adoption followed Wyandot phratry order in terms of the first four missionaries: Deer, Turtle, Wolf, and then Deer again, with the second phratry adoption taking place after the first Deer phratry adoptee (Father Richardie) had left the people. Father Hubert, not being a Jesuit, and receiving a name because he was a bishop, is out of the loop of this pattern. Second is that it should be noted that none of the missionaries were adopted into the Prairie Turtle clan, which is not surprising considering their relative lack of connection with the missionaries.

Missionary Adoptions

Missionary	Clan Adopted Into	Phratry
Father Armand de Richardie	Deer	Deer
Father Nicholas de Gonnor	Striped Turtle	Turtle
Father Pierre Potier	Wolf	Wolf
Father Jean-Baptiste de Salleneuve	Snake	Deer
Father Jean-François Hubert	Bear	Deer

FRENCH COMMANDANTS OF FORT PONCHARTRAIN DU DETROIT: PHRATRY ALTERNATING ADOPTION

There may have been a similar phratry alternating pattern among the commandants of Fort Ponchartrain du Detroit. If, as was suggested in the previous chapter, the first commandant (1701–10), Antoine de la Mothe Cadillac, was Bear clan, and therefore Deer phratry, this would follow phratry order. The second commandant was François de la Fore(s)t, in temporarily during 1705, but officially commandant from 1712 to 1714. The name "la la foret" was attached to Marguerite Atsironde, Porcupine clan elder (Toupin 1996, 202, 240). Her son, Pierre Tio8endata (also known as le Manchot), was also a leading figure in the Porcupine clan, and he had the name "la Foret" associated with him (Toupin 1996, 249, 260). The Porcupine clan belonged to the Turtle phratry, so this fits with the potential phratry alternating pattern for French commandants.

For the third commandant, Jacques Charles Sabrevois, Sieur de Bleury (1714), no clan affiliation has been found. If we were to follow the alternating phratry pattern, it would be a Wolf phratry clan, and would be followed by a Deer phratry clan. The fourth was Pierre Alphonse de Tonty (or Tonti), commandant from 1717 to 1727. Deer clan members, and possible brother and sister, Onda8annhont and Ondechientonk, were referred to as "Tonti" and "la Tonti," respectively (Toupin 1996, 219). This suggests that Tonti was adopted by the Deer clan. Perhaps there was a clan reason why the list of requests included relieving him from duty. Had he alienated the clan that adopted him? Or was this an attempt by one of the Turtle phratry clans to reduce the influence of the Deer phratry?

For the next two commandants (who would be Turtle and Wolf phratry, following the proposed pattern), I have been unable to identify according to clan. For the seventh commandant, Ives Jacques Hugues Pean, Sieur de Livandiere (1733–36), we have the name osta8oinchront (Toupin 1996, 234, as the more poorly recorded Sta8oinchrons on 262), a name which appears in the 1747 census for a Wyandot as "osta8oinchrons" (Toupin 1996, 223). This would seem to be the word *osta8enchont*, meaning "it has rattles attached," the Wendat word for rattlesnake (FH1697:193)—a good bet would be a Snake clan, and therefore a Deer phratry name. Interestingly, that would have had all three Deer phratry clans have their "turn" at adopting the French commandant.

ETHNICITY: MEMBERS OF OTHER NATIONS IN THEIR MIDST

Not everyone living in the two villages was Wyandot by birth. Adoption of people of other nations was a long-standing characteristic of Aboriginal peoples in northeastern North America. This is an aspect of local culture that seems to me to have been downplayed or ignored in the traditional historical literature. The data compiled suggests that there were at least about forty-eight people in the two communities who were born as members of other nations, slightly less than 10 percent of the population. In order of larger to smaller numbers they are: fifteen Catawba, fourteen Fox, ten Seneca or Iroquois, three Ottawa, three Chickasaw, one Miami, one Abenaki, and one Potawatomi. The gender balance seems fairly even with twenty-four males, twenty-one females, and three unsure (as the words "Tet(t)e Platte" were given for Catawba, with no gender marker in the French). Of course, the numbers of those adopted into the Wyandot would be higher than that as people long ago adopted might no longer be spoken of in terms of a "foreign" origin by the Wyandot when Potier was taking the census. And there would have been people from generations past who had been adopted, or who had parents who had been adopted, into the Wyandot.

The Catawba

In 1738, at a council meeting of the neighbouring tribes, the Wyandot declared peace with the "tettes plattes." We have seen how badly received that decision was by their Algonquian speaking neighbours.

The term "Tettes Plattes" (Flatheads) was applied by the French to a variety of tribes living in what is now the southeastern United States: primarily the Catawba, Choctaw, Chickasaw, and Cherokee. The term referred to the practice of skull deformation of infants by attaching a board to their pliable young skulls. As the Wyandot had different terms for Cherokee, Chickasaw, Choctaw, and "tettes plattes," it appears that the Siouan-speaking, agricultural Catawba were the "tettes plattes" group with whom the Wyandot made peace. Additional evidence comes from the fact that other Iroquoian languages employed similar terms (e.g., Oyadagahrocne, Mooney 1894, 68; NYCD5:386).

Wyandot Names for the Catawba, Cherokee, Chickasaw, and Choctaw

8ata,enronnon	tetes-plattes (Toupin 1996, 231, 263)
entarironnon	cherakis (Toupin 1996, 231, 263)
chicachia	Les chicachia [Chickasaw; Toupin 1996, 231; see Toupin 1996, 264 for "Chikachia"]
tsacta	Les chactas [Choctaws] (Toupin 1996, 231)

In the census of 1747, we find that there were six houses in which Catawba lived. Two of them were what could be called Catawba houses, both found in the Petit Village (PV9 and PV12). These are headed by Sandatsa8at and Marie Magdalene 8,etenhaon, respectively.

In the ninth house of the Petit Village (PV9), all five people were Catawba (Toupin 1996, 207, 243–44). The head of the household was Sandatsa8a't, referred to also as Le bijou ("the jewel") in French. Also in that house were his unnamed oldest son; his youngest son, Martin Totondiasen; and his two sisters, Ts8ndaetia (named La busquette[16] in French) and Tienk8i (named "bibax" in Latin for "drunkard"). Potier might have been glad that these "bad influences" would have their own house, where they might be less likely to corrupt Wyandot by their "bad example." Perhaps Potier or Richardie forced this aspect of the issue, driving them out of "good" Christian houses.

Marie Magdalene 8,e'tenhaon was the head of the household in PV12 (Toupin 1996, 211, 245), a house in which there appears to have been seven people: herself, two sons (in the second census also the wife of the youngest), three daughters, and a Fox married to Hannenratendi of the Snake clan. She was very much involved as a godmother for baptisms. She was a godmother for at least one baptism each year from 1733 to 1737 (Toupin 1996, 834, 836, 838, 841, 844, B247, B255, B257, B291, B338, B374, B383, B450), and one in 1746 (Toupin 1996, 856, B685), for a total of nine. In three of those cases there was a Snake clan member involved as mother and daughter, making it possible that Marie Magdalene belonged to the Snake clan. Interestingly, she was the godmother of a Fox nation member who had been baptized, Maria Tsok8enderon

What is most significant about this woman for our story here is that she would marry Orontondi. The French opposition to this marriage can be seen in the following quotations from Father Robert Toupin:

> The name of Marie-Magdeleine 8entenhaon is tied to that of the Huron rebel Nicholas Orontondi, whose blow or raid, May 20, 1747, had put in peril the Huron nation and provoked the destruction of the village of Isle aux Boix-Blancs. It is, however, the same year, on November 20, that Father Armand de La Richardie blessed the marriage of Nicolas with Marie-Magdeleine, a misalliance in the speaking of the Baron de Longueuil, the sacrilege being even with a mortal sin. (Toupin 1996, 187; translation mine)

Other houses that had a Catawba member include PV8 (Toupin 1996, 207, 243), headed by Entaron8oin or Kinench8e of the Large Turtle clan. He married an Ottawa woman, and the house, with seven people in it, also had two Fox in it along with the Catawba. Most of the people in the house were not Wyandot by birth.

Another house in which there was a presumably adopted Catawba (an adult male) was PV14 (Toupin 1996, 213, 246–47), which is a mixed Porcupine and Large Turtle house.

There are two more houses that had Catawba members. These are the Prairie Turtle dominated house of GV2, and the Bear dominated house in that same village (GV13). Neither Catawba is named.

The Jesuit record does not have any Catawba being baptized until after 1747. Few of the Catawba living with the people in 1747 had Christian names. Later, however, baptisms took place: in 1751, a seven-year-old girl was baptized, with Deer clan elder Catharine Nond8annon as her godmother (Toupin 1996, 862, B766); in 1764, a five-year-old boy was baptized (Toupin 1996, 886, B1115); in 1768, a sixteen-year-old young man was baptized (Toupin 1996, 891, B1185); and in 1771, a fifteen-year-old young woman with a Large Turtle godmother (Toupin 1996, 894, B1241) and a sixteen-year-old young man were both baptized (Toupin 1996, 894, B1243). This may be one reason why most of the Catawba lived in separate houses. With the exception of Marie Magdalene 8,e'tenhaon, they might not have been Christians. That part of the assimilation into Wyandot society seemed to have taken time for the Catawba.

The Fox
The situation was different with the Fox. They did not live in separate houses, and most of them were baptized. The Fox people—an Algonquian-speaking people known to themselves as Mesquakie or "Red Earth people" and to the Wyandot as Skenchioronnon or "Fox nation or people" (Toupin 1996, 264)—were very resistant to the influence of the French, which eventuated in a kind of proxy war from 1710 up until 1740 with the more French-influenced Aboriginal nations leading the way in fighting the Fox. The Wyandot were part of that war effort.

In his insightful article, "Slavery, the Fox Wars, and the Limits of Alliance," Brett Rushforth (2006) informs us of the trade in hundreds of Fox slaves (mostly women and children) who ended up working for French families living along the St. Lawrence River valley, one of the well-kept secrets in the traditional historiography of New France. As with the Wyandot, at least some of them were baptized. It would be interesting to find out what their eventual fate was, a good potential doctoral dissertation, and good comparative material for what I am going to be writing about regarding the fate of the Fox who were adopted into Wyandot society.

In *The Fox Wars: The Mesquakie Challenge to New France*, historians R. David Edmunds and Joseph L. Peyser strived, reasonably successfully, towards presenting a Fox-eye view of the struggle. Unfortunately, it seems to me that in so doing, they were in effect perpetuating the Noble Savage versus Nasty Savage dichotomy of earlier historians. For they (1993, 75) appear to have taken on a little anti-Wyandot bias as well, as the following quotations would appear to demonstrate:

> Particularly vindictive, the Hurons amused themselves by torturing or shooting "four or five of them every day" until they had killed all their prisoners.

In February 1732, some one hundred Fox prisoners were escorted to Detroit. Edmunds and Peyser (1993, 168) stated the following concerning what happened to them:

Afraid that the Hurons, like the other tribes, might eventually weaken their resolve and relinquish the Fox prisoners, Jean-Charles d'Arnaud, an officer at Detroit, warned the Hurons that if they permitted the Fox captives to live, they would be "nourishing snakes in their bosom." Inspired by such advice, the Huron killed most of the remaining Fox prisoners.

There are several things wrong with this type of statement. First, it is misleading to think that the Wyandot would automatically do what the French told them to do. Second, and more serious in this case, this statement, and in fact the entire book, contains no telling of any other consequences that would happen to Fox taken prisoner by the Wyandot. The authors make no mention of Fox being adopted into Wyandot society, which is a mistake because adoption had long been the practice of the people. Baptism of people from the Fox nation, too, was not mentioned. Both adoption and baptism took place, with the latter more specifically documented, but implying the existence of the former.

In the mid- to late 1730s we find a small flurry of Fox referred to in the Wyandot baptismal record. In 1734, six Fox children were baptized, aged seven to fourteen (Toupin 1996, 835, 836, B262, B275, B276, B280, B292, B300). In 1735, four more Fox children were baptized, aged two to fourteen (Toupin 1996, 838, 841, 843, B324, B326, B384, B423). Seven of these ten children were boys. Of the ten children, we have two Porcupine women as godmothers (Toupin 1996, 835, B262, B276, the latter the elder Atsironde); two Bear elders as godfathers (Toupin 1996, 841, 843, A,a8as, B384 and Sohondinnon, B423); and one Deer woman as godmother (Toupin 1996, 836, B300).

On 24 June 1736, three adult Fox women underwent baptism: Agatha ,Ang8enta, Marie Tsok8enderon, and Catherine Nenniense. Curiously, at that point, none of them had skenchio,e "at the fox," a short form of the Wyandot word for the Fox, written after their names in the baptismal record. Perhaps they had been living with the Wyandot for awhile before being baptized. Their stories are presented below. In 1738, another adult Fox woman was baptized (Toupin 1996, 845, B474).

In the stories that follow you will see a few key points. The first is that adopted (and baptized) Fox could become prominent among the Wyandot. The story of Susanne Sendaniont, told in chapter seven, shows that to be true. She became literally a Snake that the people were glad to "nourish in their bosom." The second is that Fox incorporated into Wyandot society were not all adopted by one clan, but seem fairly spread out among the clans. We have individuals from the Deer, Snake, Bear, Large Turtle, Porcupine, and Striped Turtle clans among their number. Only the Prairie Turtle[17] and the Wolf seem outside of this pattern. The third is that those adopted would appear to be children (mostly boys) or adult women. The only apparent exception to that appears to be Jean E8atirhon, who lived in the Bear house of GV13, the same house as Agatha ,Ang8entak (there named A,eng8entak; see below). He is said to be a "viellard," that is, an old man (Toupin 1996, 223, GV13).

A Fox woman other than Sendaniont who appears to have been of significance was Marie Magdalene Ndatihaon of the Striped Turtle Clan. She was the adopted sister of Dorothée Sk8atandi, a Striped Turtle woman who was first named on her household resident list, and the mother of female elder Marie ,Aennench (see Toupin 1996, 208–9, PV9). She was probably adopted sometime after 1733, as another woman, with the first name Franciscus, held that name that year (Toupin 1996, 833, B223).

There was an adult Marie Magdalene, Fox woman, baptized in 1738 (Toupin 1996, 845, B474). With her husband Augustin Tsondechati, Marie Magdalene had three children baptized: Angelica in 1736 (Toupin 1996, 841, B389), Agnes in 1739 (Toupin 1996, 846, B498), and Therese in 1743 (Toupin 1996, 851, B595). Although she was listed as living in 1747 in the large Striped Turtle house led by Sk8atandi, she died in August 1746, while six months pregnant (Toupin 1996, 921, PV10). Her name was revived by 1753 (Toupin 1996, 865, B801).

Marie Tiok8enderon was in 1747 a widow, and adopted sister, probably,[18] of Porcupine clan elder Marguerite Atsironde, in whose house (Toupin 1996, 203, 241, PV1) she lived with her three children. She had children baptized in 1734 and 1737 (Toupin 1996, 835, 842, B264, B408). She was baptized as an adult in 1736 (Toupin 1996, 840, B374). She died in 1757 (Toupin 1996, 928, E116).

Louise 8tsia, sister of leading Deer clan elder Marie Nendaentons seems to have played a significant role in the processes of incorporating Fox into Wyandot society. She had Fox-born Ignace On,8etak (possibly the seven-year-old Ignace, who was baptized in 1734; Toupin 1996, 835, B280) as her adopted brother. They both lived in the Deer clan house PV6 in 1747. 8tsia was also the godmother of Louise ,Areendannon, when the latter was baptized on 16 August 1734, as a twelve-year-old girl. In 1747 ,Areendannon lived in PV10, a Striped Turtle house, with her husband Striped Turtle elder Martin Sa8end8at, and their two children, Antoine Hentaras (sixteen) and Marguerite 8achitaha. The entry for their family was right beside fellow Fox-born Marie Ndatiohaon's entry in the list for the house.

On 24 June 1736, Agatha ,Ang8enta, "Pouch," (Steckley 2007b, 180) was baptized as an adult, with Deer clan member Catherine Sk8atenre as her godmother (Toupin 1996, 840, B370). Her first child was baptized as Joseph in 1743 (Toupin 1996, 851, B591), with her husband Simon Osta8oinchrons or Osta8enchron, possibly of the Snake clan.[19] She lived in 1747 in the big Bear clan house GV13, with her husband and two sons (Toupin 1996, 223, 255). There is a good chance, then, that she had been adopted by the Bear clan.

Catharine Nenniense was baptized as an adult on 24 June 1736 (Toupin 1996, 840, B375), with Marie Tia8ennion of the Large Turtle clan as her godmother. In 1747, she lived in PV2, in what appears to have been the Large Turtle section of the house, right before Large Turtle elder Anne A8innonke (Toupin 1996, 205, 241). That makes it possible that she was Large Turtle clan herself. In 1751, she and her husband Ta,are8at, had their son Joseph baptized (Toupin 1996, 862, B764). In 1756, she was a godmother (Toupin 1996, 873, B920).

On 24 June 1734, a ten-year-old Fox boy was baptized, Francis Honatoka8i (B292, Toupin 1996, 836). By 1747, his own child Catherine was baptized, with his Bear clan wife Agnes ,Annondiasa (Toupin 1996, 857, B697); then their daughter Louise was baptized in 1749 (Toupin 1996, 859, B717); then three more children were baptized in 1752, 1755 and 1759 (Toupin 1996, 864, 870, 878, B787, B872, B1002). His name had various spellings, including On,8atoka8i. In the 1747 census, a man named On,8atoka8i was listed as living in PV16, married to a niece of Bear elder Marie Ts8endask8a (Toupin 1996, 214).

A Fox man, named Toonrok, is a bit of a conundrum. He lived in the Bear clan house PV18, and was presented as being "frere d'enons et du manchot," which means he was the brother of the Bear clan leader Enons and the Porcupine leader sometimes known as le manchot (Pierre Tio8oindata). This Toonrok is probably the individual, named Jean Baptiste Hoonr8t, that was baptized at fourteen in 1734 (Toupin 1996, 835, B276). This would not help to clear up the clan identity mystery, as his godmother was Marguerite Atsironde of the Porcupine clan.

Seneca and Other Iroquois
Five Seneca (recorded as Tsonnont8oin, a Wendat version of their own name meaning "very big hill or mountain") and other Iroquois were baptized as adults in 1735 (B341), 1736 (B359 and B368), and 1737 (Toupin 1996, 839, 840, 842, 844, B402, B451, B462). All but one (B451) were men. Three of them had Wyandot wives in 1747. No Seneca or Iroquois children were mentioned in the Wyandot baptismal record.

In the census of 1747, we have one Iroquois house, made up of Therese 8e8as,[20] her sister, and her sons, one with his wife (PV3). Then there is Joseph Sachiendoa (baptized as an adult in 1738; Toupin 1996, 844, B462), his Bear elder wife Onnond8, and their six children, two of whom were baptized the same year as he was (Toupin 1996, 844, B463 at age nine, and B457 a newborn). It is not certain where they lived in 1747, as both of them were listed for two houses (PV18 and GV15). Another Iroquois man (this time identified as Seneca; GV13) with a Bear elder wife is Michel Tierontaron, who was baptized in 1737 (Toupin 1996, 842, B402), and was married to the influential Ts8nde,en. Finally, there was François ,Andataès (baptized as an adult in 1736; Toupin 1996, 839, B359) with his Snake clan wife A8innnoni8oin.

The Ottawa
The Ottawa had been long-term neighbours of both Wendat groups, the Petun and the Huron, and later the Wyandot. Member bands of the Ottawa were in Michilimackinac when the Wyandot were there. And the Ottawa moved into the Detroit area at roughly the same time as the Wyandot did. The groups were usually allies, but the relationship had its rocky periods during the eighteenth century, as we have seen. In 1747, no Ottawa men were reported as living in the Wyandot community, but three Wyandot men had Ottawa wives in the Petit Village (PV3, PV8, PV15). In PV8, the man first named in the house list had an Ottawa wife, the other husband on the list had a Fox wife, and two Fox men and one Catawba (named simply as a tette platte) were also living there. There were no Ottawa husbands mentioned in the census.

There was only one Ottawa recorded as being baptized in the Wyandot mission, and that was in 1734 (Toupin 1996, 835, B268). That person was reportedly "morti proximus," in other words, near death. One girl with an Ottawa mother was baptized in 1735 (Toupin 1996, 838, B338). The godmother was the Catawba-born Marie Magdalene O,ennhenhaon. In 1752 (Toupin 1996, 863, B780, B781) and 1762 (Toupin 1996, 882, B1055) an Ottawa father had his children with an Iroquois mother baptized. In 1765 (Toupin 1996, 887, B1132) the same happened with an Ottawa mother.

The Chickasaw
The Chickasaw (who, like other Aboriginal nations of the American southeast, spoke a Muskogean language) fought during the 1730s alongside the British and their allies and against the French and their allies. This means that, like the Fox, they could be seen as enemies of the Wyandot as this time. As we have seen above, the Wyandot called them Chichachia, in imitation of their name.

The first of the three male Chickasaw reported as living with the Wyandot in 1747 was Oki8a, the adopted brother of Angelique Osk8ara, a Large Turtle elder, both of them living in PV2 (Toupin 1996, 205). In the same house, and adopted into the Porcupine clan, was the second Chickasaw,

Nicolas ,Annaotaha. He was given a name that was significant among the Huron of the seventeenth century (see Steckley 1992d, 27–39). The third Chickasaw was Mathias Ondok8a, who was the adopted brother of Deer clan elder Marie Nendeniont (Toupin 1996, 213, 246), and thus himself a Deer. She was a niece of Sastaretsi, making Ondok8a a nephew of the Wyandot leader, thus giving Ondok8a strong political Wyandot connections, especially with his living in the large Deer house of PV13. He was baptized in 1744 (Toupin 1996, 853, B617). No Chickasaw women appear to have been adopted into Wyandot society.

Miami

The Miami are an Algonquian-speaking people that had a long history of connection with the French. As we have seen, the Wyandot referred to them as Tochingootr8nnon "people of the Crane" (Toupin 1996, 231). In the 1747 census, the Miami adopted by the Wyandot was Marie Agnes i8ennonh8e, who lived in the Large Turtle house GV6 (Toupin 1996, 218, 252) and was married to Large Turtle elder Pierre 8en8oin. She was listed as a godmother as early as 1732 (Toupin 1996, 831, B185) and as the mother of a baptized son the same year (Toupin 1996, 832, B207).

Potawatomi

The Potawatomi are an Algonquian-speaking people closely connected with the Ojibwa and the Ottawa. The one Potawatomi identified as living with the Wyandot in the census of 1747 was Matthias Okia, who was married to the Deer elder Catherine Nond8annan, living in GV13. He was baptized in 1737 (Toupin 1996, 842, B415). Their children were also baptized.

Abenaki

The Abenaki are another Algonquian-speaking people, living in the eastern part of New France at the time. Although there was only one Abenaki recorded as living with the Wyandot in 1747, an adult male who was thirty-seven years old, living in PV6, a Deer clan house (see Appendix A), the baptismal record has a number of Abenaki living with them over the years, at least temporarily. A woman named Anna—whose Abenaki name was written variously as Aon8imoa, Am8im8a, and Aoinea—was married to a Prairie Turtle man named Tsita8is, and they had two children baptized in 1731 and 1732 (Toupin 1996, 829, 834, B147, B245). She possibly belonged to the Large Turtle clan, as Large Turtle elder Anna ,A8innonke was her godmother (Toupin 1996, 832, B220). An adult man who had taken a Wyandot name, Joseph Te hona,annra, was baptized in 1732 (Toupin 1996, 832, B218). Perhaps he was the thirty-seven-year-old man mentioned in 1747.[21]

Clans Relating to Other Nations

Six of the eight active Wyandot clans were involved with adopting or godparenting the newcomers to their society: Deer, Snake, Bear, Large Turtle, Porcupine, and Striped Turtle. The Prairie Turtle and the Wolf seem not to be involved, in the case of the former this shows part of their general lack of connection with Christian ceremonies. There seems in particular to be a lot of Deer clan involvement. Two significant adopters were Deer: Louise 8tsia and female elder Marie Nendeniont. Godparents include Wyandot grand chief Matthias Sastaretsi, elder Nond8annon, Louise 8tsia, and Catharine Sk8ate,enre, all of them important people in Wyandot society. And it should be noted from the chart presented below that the Catawba houses are positioned especially close to Deer clan houses.

Petit Village Housing Pattern: Clan, Ethnicity, and Positioning

The bolded identities are those of people of different ethnicities.

PV3 (Iroq.) PV2 (Po/S) PV1 (Po) central pathway   PV4 (Sn)
　　　　　　　　　　　　　　　　　　　　　　　　PV5 (abandoned)
　　　　　　　　　　　　　　　　　　　　　　　　PV6 (D) PV7 (Sn) PV8 (**mostly outsiders**)
　　　　　　　　　　　　　　　　　　　　　　　　PV9 (**Catawba**)
　　　　　　　　　　　　　　　　　　　　　　　　PV10 (S) PV11 (Pr)
　　　　　　　　　　　　　　　　　　　　　　　　PV12 (**Catawba**) PV13 (D)
　　　　　　　　　　　　　　　　　　　　　　　　PV14 (Po) PV15 (S)
　　　　　　　　　　　　　　　　　　　　　　　　PV16 (B)
　　　　　　　　　　　　　　　　　　　　　　　　PV17 (Pr – abandoned)
　　　　　　　　　　　　　　　　　　　　　　　　PV18 (B) PV19 (Po – abandoned)

Grand Village Housing Pattern: Location and Size

GV1 (?) GV2 (Pr)
GV3 (?) GV4 (L)
GV5 (?)
GV6 (L)
GV7 (Huron)
GV8 (D)
GV9 (D) GV10 (D – abandoned)
GV11 (Sn)
GV12 (W)
GV13 (B) GV14 (L – burned down)
GV15 (?)

Identity Key

Clans

B	Bear
D	Deer
L	Large Turtle
Po	Porcupine
Pr	Prairie Turtle
S	Striped Turtle
Sn	Snake
W	Wolf

Nations

C	Catawba
H	Huron of Lorette
I	Iroquois

SUMMARY

We have seen the actions of the missionaries, their connections with different clans, and the responses of the different clans in terms of rituals. Father Richardie was connected with the Deer (who adopted him) and Porcupine clans, but lost some of his connection with the latter through his withdrawal of support for one of their leading figures, Nicholas Orontondi. The Deer clan was an early starter in terms of Christian rituals. Father Potier was most closely linked with the Wolf clan. They adopted him, and gave him a Wolf clan name that seems to have originally come from a Neutral group identified with the Wolf. He also seems to have courted at least one house of the Prairie Turtle, whom he appears to have known very well.

The Wyandot themselves adopted peoples of a number of different nations, most prominently the Catawba and the Fox, both of whom they fought against at some time. It is important to mention these adoptions (implied by baptisms) to show an aspect of Wyandot and of traditional Aboriginal society generally, which seems to be generally under-reported in the historical literature. It is easier and more typical for historians to write of the Wyandot killing their enemies.

Chapter Five

Wyandot Participation in "Christian" Rituals

Father Pierre Potier had a detailed mind that liked to record many different sorts of information. That makes his writing a great ethnohistorical source of both French and Wyandot cultures of his time. His recording of the Wyandot participation in at least nominally "Christian" rituals can aid researchers immeasurably in understanding the Wyandot involvement in these rituals. The use to which it has been put here is just one way in which we can learn about the Wyandot from these records. There is much more that can be gleaned from this information.

BAPTISMS

Of all the Christian sacraments and ceremonies that the Wyandot participated in, none of them was more significant nor as frequently enacted as baptism.[1] This is to a large extent because baptism was by far the leading ritual goal of the Jesuits. In "The Warrior and the Lineage: Jesuit Use of Iroquoian Images to Communicate Christianity" (Steckley 1992a), I discussed how the Jesuits connected the idea of baptism with the important Wendat social entity of the matrilineal lineage (-*h8atsir*- Steckley 2007b, 100). Baptism was presented by the Jesuits to Iroquoian people as a form of adoption, of family or lineage building. In the Wendat text *De Religione*, written sometime in the 1670s by Jesuit Father Philippe Pierson who spent time with the Huron of Wendake and the Wyandot of Michilimackinac,

Pierson posed the question that the Jesuits undoubtedly had often put to them by their mission charges: "How do you profit, Jesuit, when you baptize them? What will it give you?" (Steckley 1992a, 499). Part of the answer was as follows:

> Would it be a trifling matter that I rejoice that one hundred people I baptized would arrive in the sky when they die? They would form a group[2] there, those I adopted as my children. I would thus form my lineage (-*h8atsir*-), my large lineage. (Steckley 1992a, 499)

It should not be surprising, then, that from 1728 to 1779, Jesuit missionaries performed 1,402 baptisms of Wyandot (including a few members of other Aboriginal groups, as we saw in the last chapter, as well as a very few Frenchmen). Compare that with the Christian marriage records of the Wyandot mission, in which forty-six marriages were recorded from 1728 to 1785 (see discussion below), and mortuary records or funerals, of which there were 175 from 1746 to 1784 (also see discussion below).

The baptismal records looked like this. These examples come from the first ten baptisms of 1732 (Toupin 1996, 831). Note the matching of the first name of the baptized and of the godparent.

Ten Samples from the Baptismal Record of 1732

Form: First or Christian Name...Father's Name...Mother's Name...Godparent's Name...Date

B185   agnes...P[ater]. Harachiara, M[ater]. Agnes gatonk...Ma[trina][3] agnes ,onan nonh8e 13 janu[uarii]

B186   Margarita...P. Martin sa8end8ann, M. Ma[ria] ,annend8k...Ma marg[uarita] ,entioha 2 feb

B187   Armandus. P onta,ennonti M. ,arendachie...Pa[trinus][4] Pater de la Richardie 11 feb.

B188   catharina...P. pet[rus] ha8endaraties, M. Cecilia te 8endik8ak8a Ma. Cat[harina] skannonta8a 12 feb.

B189   christina P. anie8endet, M. ,a8enion...Ma Christina ,arhonnens 17 feb.

B190   M. Joanna 7 an.[5] P. dechignonha, M christina ,arhonnens...17 feb.

B191   Catharina...P. incertus,[6] M. ,aarendi...Ma Cath[arina] aronissachien 17 feb

B192   Catharina ska8endandoa 20 an...Ma Catharina sk8atenre 2 martis

B193   Theresia 3 an...P ign. Tannenochre, M. Mar: nnendisen...Ma engatona 18 maij

B194   Monica...P hachiendase, M. lud: tsonnen...Ma agnes ondechienton 1 junij

Father Richardie's early success with the Wyandot can be seen in his baptism count. By 1735, he claimed that all of his Wyandot charges were baptized Christians, something of an exaggeration, but there had been 347 baptisms by the end of that year (Toupin 1996, 839). Andrew Sturtevant (2011, 25), using a variety of sources and employing the calculation of multiplying the number of warriors counted by four to get the total population, gives a Wyandot population of six hundred in 1730 and one thousand in 1737. If we split these figures down the middle, and use the eight-hundred figure that he used for both 1729 and 1761, then the number of people baptized during that period would be about half the Wyandot population. It should be pointed out that the vast number of baptisms during this period were of children. Only forty-four of the first 347 were adults (people fifteen or older): twenty-eight male and sixteen female (see Age of Baptism below for full figures). This number included two Abenaki, one Seneca, and one "Iroquois."

Sampling Bias

What Richardie and Potier did not mention, but is something we can track using their records, is clan participation in baptism. Much can be learned from how clans differed in their participation in the ceremony at a particular time, or overall. There are two caveats to be issued concerning the clan-identification process. The first, and most obvious, is that I could not identify the clan membership of all those living in the Wyandot communities in 1747. Of the 576 people listed in the two villages, 376 are clan identified, almost 64 percent. In eighteen of the twenty-nine houses, most of the members were clan identified (see Appendix A for the census and clan-identified numbers for each house).

The second and less obvious caveat deals with a fundamental bias in this clan-identification process. It is important to recognize that with these clan-participation "scores," and similar such figures, there will be something of a sampling bias in my findings. This comes from my main source for learning clan identity. In chapter 6, we will be looking at a part of the census that can be called the elders' council of 1747, an amazing research tool. Each of the eight main clans of the Wyandot had both male and female elders, and these are identified by Potier in the census. Significantly, the numbers of clan members on the council vary across the clans. In order of size, largest first, they are as follows:

Wyandot Clan Elders, 1747

Clan	Number	Ranking
Bear	13	1
Large Turtle	11	2
Striped Turtle	8	3
Snake	7	4
Deer	6	5/6
Prairie Turtle	6	5/6
Porcupine	5	7
Wolf	4	8

What I have termed baptism participation here includes not only the people being baptized but also their mothers, fathers, godmothers, and godfathers. All other factors being equal, you would expect that the clan-identified participation in baptisms would follow the same order of largest to smallest. Mothers of these clan-identified elders, children of the female elders, sisters and brothers, nephews and nieces of both male and female elders can be expected to be of the same clan as the elders. The more elders, the more such mothers, siblings, children, nieces, and nephews that I was able to identify as to clan membership. This generally held true, with some important exceptions.

Clan Participation in Baptisms (in rank order)

Clan	Clan Participation in Baptisms	Ranking	Compared to Sampling Bias
Bear	379	1	as predicted
Large Turtle	314	2	as predicted
Striped Turtle	244	3	as predicted
Snake	215	4	as predicted
Porcupine	213	5	up two places
Deer	170	6	as predicted
Prairie Turtle	158	7	down one to two places
Wolf	108	8	as predicted

As we can see, the clans rank pretty much as predicted by the sampling bias—with the exception of Porcupine being higher and Prairie Turtle being lower in the baptism ranking. In these cases other factors must be in play. We saw earlier that we should expect a low Prairie Turtle score for baptisms, as with other Christian rituals and roles. Their history, especially the antagonism between Richardie and ,Ang8irot, would have such an effect. Richardie and the Porcupine clan were much more closely linked, with predictable results in Christian-based ceremonies. Their close connection should lead to a higher participation in baptism.

The figures for clan-identified baptisms was a little different. There were 468 clan-identified baptisms, almost exactly one-third of the total number of baptisms.

Clan-Identified Baptisms (in rank order)

	Baptisms	Rank	Compared to Sampling Bias
Bear	94	1	as predicted
Large Turtle	78	2	as predicted
Striped Turtle	77	3	as predicted
Porcupine	62	4	up three places
Snake	52	5	down one place
Prairie Turtle	44	6	as predicted
Deer	29	7	down one to two places
Wolf	23	8	as predicted

The Deer fare worse here than in general baptism participation. Between 1640 and 1650 inclusive there were no Deer baptisms that I can identify. From 1744 to 1779 their clan-identified numbers stayed seventh overall. This might be because, having had their important leading figures baptized early on, and their connection with Richardie solidified with adoption, they did not need to have their younger members baptized as a symbolic statement of closeness. The death of a number of their leading figures in the mid-1740s may also have been a factor. The subtle pressure to baptize that came from the "top" in the Deer clan would have lessened.

With this sampling bias caveat being issued, we can now deal with the baptism figures and their implications. The following is a chart for 1729, the first full year in which Father Richardie baptized the Wyandot. The chart represents clan participation in baptism. The features counted are baptisms, mother and father of the baptized, and godfather and godmother of the baptized. There were ninety-nine that year, which was the highest of any year on record. Clan identities have been established for twenty-one baptisms, including twenty mothers of the baptized, thirty fathers of the baptized, but only three godfathers and three godmothers. The reason for the latter is that it was not until 1731 that the Wyandot participated significantly as godparents, owing in part, no doubt, to there not being sufficient among them that Richardie would feel were "Christian enough" to play that role. Looking at this from the Wyandot side, being a godparent was a new role for the Wyandot, one that would grow in importance as the people gave it meaning in terms of their own culture, and as the number of godparents grew.

The following is a chart of clan participation in different roles in baptism for the first full year, 1729. The clans are divided into their appropriate phratry.

Clan Participation in Baptism for the Year 1729 (in phratry order)

Roles	Baptism	Mother	Father	Godfather	Godmother	Total
Deer Phratry						
Deer	6	6	6	0	0	18
Snake	3	2	6	0	0	11
Bear	1	1	1	1	1	5
Total	10	9	13	1	1	34
Turtle Phratry						
Large Turtle	2	2	2	0	1	7
Porcupine	3	3	4	0	1	11
Striped Turtle	5	5	2	2	1	15
Prairie Turtle	1	1	3	0	0	5
Total	11	11	11	2	3	38
Wolf Phratry						
Wolf	1	1	7	0	0	9
Hawk	0	0	1	0	0	1
Sturgeon	0	0	0	0	0	0
Total	1	1	8	0	0	10
Totals	22	21	32	3	4	82
Grand Total	22	21	33	3	4	83

Clan Baptism Participation by Rank Order for 1729

Clan	Participation	Rank	Compared with Sampling Bias
Deer	18	1	up four/five places
Striped Turtle	15	2	up one place
Snake	11	3/4	up one place or as predicted
Porcupine	11	3/4	up three/four places
Wolf	9	5	up three places
Large Turtle	7	6	down four places
Bear	5	7/8	down six/seven places
Prairie Turtle	5	7/8	down two/three places

There are several interesting facts to note here. One is that the Deer clan had, for the year 1729, the highest number of baptisms, with six, and participation in baptism, with eighteen, overcoming the sampling bias significantly. As we have seen, Father Richardie's adoptive sister, Nendaentons, and his adoptive clan brother, Sastaretsi, were active participants in baptism that year. The Deer clan's involvement would later diminish, as commented on above. But their participation in the first year shows their desire to maintain what appears to be the Deer clan's traditional position of closeness to the French and their priests, as illustrated in chapter 2 with the Deer clan leader Ationta.

Also noteworthy is the pattern found for the Wolf clan. Generally speaking, over the period from 1728 to 1779, more mothers than fathers of the baptized are recorded. This should not be surprising as typically the clan of the baptized was identified by my first discovering the clan of the mother. Of the clan-identified parents of the baptized, there are 445 mothers and 378 fathers, a significant difference of sixty-seven. But here in 1729 we have Wolf clan fathers of the baptized, outnumbering mothers by seven to one, an unusual ratio for the baptismal record. The Wolf clan men who would be in 1747 the phratry leader (Ta,echiaten) and the clan leader (Hondatorenha) and their maternal cousin, whom they would consider their brother[7] (Jacob Atiendase), would be active in the first few years of baptism. The former would even have Father Richardie as godfather (one of only two times that happened with a Wyandot baptism) for his son Armand in 1732. As with the Deer clan, Wolf clan baptism participation would fall off. In fact, of the ninety clan-identified baptisms that took place from 1728 to 1735, only one would be of a Wolf clan member. But their baptisms would surge in 1746, when they adopted the next priest to live with them, Father Pierre Potier (see previous chapter).

Let's now move down to 1735, and see what the patterns are, having that number represent the "early period" somewhat arbitrarily.

Clan Baptism Participation by 1735 (in rank order)

Clan	Number	Ranking	Compared with Sampling Bias	Compared with 1729
Snake	77	1	up three places	up three/four
Deer	70	2	up three/four places	down one
Striped Turtle	52	3	as predicted	down one
Large Turtle	51	4	down two places	up two
Porcupine	49	5	as predicted	up two/three
Bear	33	6	down five places	up two/three
Prairie Turtle	32	7	down one/two places	up one/none
Wolf	18	8	as predicted	down three

From this you can say that the Snake and Deer clans, two closely related clans, both started off quickly in receiving baptism, but that the Large Turtle started somewhat slowly, the Bear clan very slowly, and the Prairie Turtle, as it would consistently, was scoring lower than the sampling bias would predict.

I am including one more chart, for the census year of 1747, as it is the main focus year of this study.

Clan Baptism Participation until 1747 (in rank order)

Clan	Number	Ranking	Compared with Sampling Bias	Compared with 1735
Bear	145	1	as predicted	up five places
Snake	144	2	up two/three places	down one place
Striped Turtle	133	3	as predicted	no change
Large Turtle	131	4	down two places	no change
Deer	111	5	as predicted	down three
Porcupine	96	6	as predicted	down one
Prairie Turtle	67	7	down one/two places	no change
Wolf	61	8	as predicted	no change

You can see that the system is more equal now, with the Snake clan a little high still, and with the Large Turtle clan a little low but climbing. The Wolf clan seems to have been benefitting a bit from what can be called the Potier baptisms (see previous chapter). The Prairie Turtle, as always, scored lower than the sampling bias would predict. The Bear have reached the level predicted by the sampling bias. They would never lose that position after that.

Age of Baptism
The Jesuits kept fairly rigorous track of the ages of those who were baptized. In the first full year of baptism, 1729, ninety-nine were baptized: sixty-seven children (ages one to fourteen), twenty-seven newborns, and five adults (fifteen and over). From 1728 to 1738 people of all ages were being baptized, not just newborns. This is to be expected, as adults were being converted and baptized at this time.

Adult (fifteen and over) baptisms tell a few small stories. There were ninety-one of these: seventy-eight from 1728 to 1738. The last recorded Wyandot adult baptisms were of the four adult Wolf clan members that Potier baptized in 1746. Those that followed were of different ethnicities. Adult baptism was more of a male event—roughly two-thirds of people baptized as adults were male. Leading Wyandot women, such as Anastasie Ts8nde,en (Bear clan), Christine ,Arhonnens (Large Turtle), Margaret Atsironde (Porcupine), Marie Ts8ndehe (Striped Turtle), Catherine Tsa8ointondi (Prairie Turtle), and Marie ,Aendi (Wolf), who were the first names listed as female elders in the elders' council (see next chapter) were already baptized and had Christian names before Richardie came to baptize the Wyandot.

In terms of adults whose clan has been identified, we have four Large Turtle (1731–34) baptisms; four Wolf (1746); three each for Bear (1734–37), Porcupine (1730–36), and Striped Turtle (1729–34); two each for Snake (1729–34); and one each for Deer (1738) and Prairie Turtle (1737). In terms of other groups, there were seven Seneca or Iroquois, six of them males. The same is true of the three Catawba, the one of the two Abenaki, and one Potawatomi, and one Chickasaw. This contrasts with the Fox, all four of whom were women.

Spiritual Kinship: Godparents and Clans
One particularly interesting aspect of the interaction between Wyandot clans and baptisms is that pertaining to godparents. The godparent–godchild relationship is referred to in the anthropological and religious studies

literature as "spiritual kinship" (see Frishkopf 2003, 4). It is not just a Christian relationship, but exists in some form in many cultures and their religions across the world. While I do not know whether some form of spiritual kinship existed in traditional Wyandot culture, the clan responding to most kinship needs, we can tell from Richardie's and Potier's records that they were very much involved with it in a Christian sense (with undoubtedly their own cultural features added). In the vast majority of the baptisms of the Wyandot there are listed the godfather or the godmother of the child or adult baptized. I use "or" here as usually there is only one—the godparent almost always being of the same gender as the person being baptized.

While there is no information I can garner with respect to the exact nature of the godparent relationship among the Wyandot, we do know a few things. The gender of the godparent and the godchild are almost always the same. As noted above, and following European practice, the Christian or first name of both are typically the same. And most Wyandot baptisms of the eighteenth century included the participation and initiation of the godparent–godchild relationship. It became the expected.

During the first three years of Wyandot baptisms, from 1728 to 1730, most of the godparents were French, often with the baptized individual having both godfather and godmother. By 1731, however, the great majority of the godparents were Wyandot, typically only one godparent per baptized person. French godparents were always there each year, but during most years up into the 1780s they were rare. The Wyandot community was spiritually self-sustaining in that way.

There seems to have been something of what I might call a patrilineal bias in the godparent–godchild relationship. Here is how I determined that there was this bias. There were seventy-nine baptisms in which I was able to determine the clan identity of the baptized, the two parents of the baptized and of the godparent. In forty-seven cases there was a matching of the clan of one of the parents and the godparent. In thirty-four of those cases the clan matching was between the father and the godparent (male or female), with only thirteen being with the mother and the godparent. That this might be true more generally was suggested with forty-six baptisms in which there was clan identification of only one parent, as well as the godparent. In thirty-two cases the match was with the father, only fourteen with the mother.

The evidence I have suggests that in the early years godparents for a baptized Wyandot child came from any clan that had a suitable Christian prospect for godparent. The Snake, Deer, and Porcupine clans seemed to be the most likely to provide that out-of-clan godparent. Gradually, however, it looks like sharing clan membership became another feature of the godparent relationship, especially with certain clans, most notably the Bear.

Godfathers

The Snake clan led the way in the number of godfathers up until 1749. You could say that the Snake were overrepresented in terms of godfathers. This was due largely to the fact that Snake clan member Matthias Ondachiate,en was recorded as godfather the greatest number of times: twelve. Another Snake man who frequently served as a godfather was the elder Stanislaus 8asanion with seven. Significantly, he was the first named of the male Snake clan elders. The Bear clan took over the lead from the Snake clan by 1759, and led up to 1779. This could reflect at least in part the sampling bias discussed earlier.

I have compiled a list of those who became godfathers most frequently, and placed the information on the chart below. Several points should be noted from this chart. One is that frequent godfathers are almost always (one exception) people who have high status otherwise—that is being a phratry leader (two), a clan leader (five), or elder (twelve). Four were "considerés," as we will see in the next chapter, these were males who were not yet chiefs, but were on a path to great positions of leadership. Another is that the Snake clan is overrepresented with four of the sixteen. Clearly under-represented is the Prairie Turtle clan, with none of the top sixteen, which is not surprising given their general low participation in Christian ceremonies. The only Prairie Turtle elder to participate in baptism as a godfather was Tahatie (three times).

Leading Godfathers in Rank Order: Their Clans and Statuses

Name	Number	Clan	Status
Matthias Ondachiate,en	12	Snake	male clan leader
Handatorenha	8	Wolf	male clan leader, elder
Taronhi8rens[8]	8	Large Turtle	male clan elder
Te,atak[9]	8	Large Turtle	leader after 1747
Te Horonhi8texa	8	Large Turtle	male clan elder
Otiok8andoron	7	Striped Turtle	male clan elder
8asanion	7	Snake	male clan elder, first named
Taretande	6	Bear	male clan elder
Sastaretsi	5	Deer	clan/phratry, nation leader, and male elder
Orontondi	5	Porcupine	male clan elder
Ta,echiaten	5	Wolf	male clan leader, phratry leader

118 CHAPTER FIVE

Name	Number	Clan	Status
Otre8ati	5	Snake	no formal status[10]
Taonchientonk8i (Enons)	4	Bear	male clan elder, clan leader
B. Annien8indet	4	Snake	male clan elder
8en8oin	4	Large Turtle	male clan elder
E. Annien8indet	4	Deer	male clan elder
Tio8endata	4	Porcupine	male clan leader

Godmothers

I have also compiled a list for godmothers. Again we see from the chart that godparents are individuals who are well placed in the community. We have four women who are the first named on the elders list, seven 1747 elders, and four who are what I am calling house leaders, the first ones named in their houses. Predictably, the Bear clan is overrepresented. And just as predictably, there are no Prairie Turtle women on the list.

Leading Godmothers in Rank Order: Their Clans and Statuses

Name	Number	Clan	Status
,Arhonnens	11	Large Turtle	female elder (first)[11]
Sk8ateenre	10	Deer	mother of female elder
Oennhenhaon	8	? (Catawba)	house leader
Agnes A8ennon	8	?	?
Atsironde	7	Porcupine	female elder (first), house leader
Ts8nde,en	7	Bear	female elder (first), house leader
,aendi	7	Wolf	female elder (first)
Tsondendora	6	Snake	house leader
Onnond8	5	Bear	female elder
te chiea8annen	5	?	?[12]
Onnond8annon	4	Deer	female elder
A8endii	4	Snake	house leader, mother of elder
Niendaharonk	4	Bear	female elder
Tsosk8a	4	Striped Turtle	?[13]
Tia8ennion	4	Large Turtle	eldest daughter of ,Arhonnens

The Deer clan led the way up in the number of godmothers until 1749, after which the Bear and Large Turtle clans pretty much shared the lead, as is statistically predictable. One reason for the Deer clan's early lead was the role of Catherine Sk8ateenre, who, as we can see above, was ten times a godmother.

CHRISTIAN MARRIAGES: A MISSIONARY–WYANDOT COMPROMISE

In the Wendat language there is a verb root *-ndia,-* "to marry" (Steckley 2007b, 156), as well as a verb root *-onda-* "to be a spouse" (Steckley 2007b, 295),[14] and another *-atennonha-* "to be spouse" (Steckley 2007b, 44), which always takes a plural form. *The Jesuit Relations* of the first half of the seventeenth century make no mention of there being a formal marriage ceremony among the Huron. As pointed out earlier, there were relatively few officially sanctioned and recorded Christian marriages among the Wyandot: only forty-six from 1728 to 1785 (Toupin 1996, 821, 908–10, 932), thirty-nine within the Richardie/Potier mission period. There were none recorded from 1729 to 1745, 1748 to 1752, 1754 to 1763, and 1769 to 1772. There were probably several reasons for this.

Traditional Wendat culture allowed for relatively easy divorce. As Bruce Trigger puts it concerning the Huron of the first half of the seventeenth century:

> Any marriage could be terminated at the wish of either partner. Prior to the birth of a child, infidelity and divorce seem to have been common and were matters of little concern. Afterwards, couples separated only infrequently, and if they quarrelled or became estranged, friends and relatives would intervene to save the marriage. In spite of the apparent stability of these mature marriages, even elderly couples continued to take the right of divorce seriously. One of the main reasons that middle-aged men gave for not becoming Roman Catholics was their fear that if their wives left them, they would be unable to marry. (Trigger 1976, 49–50)

Another reason for the low number of Christian marriages among the Wyandot during this period is that it does not seem to have been a Jesuit priority. In none of the Christian texts written in Wendat by the Jesuits, including the fifty-three-page *De Religione*, have I found a discussion of the necessity of being married by the church. There were few Huron–Christian marriages reported in *The Jesuit Relations*.

The missionaries opposed adultery, but would not refuse baptism to children born out of wedlock in that way. On 15 May 1746, for example, we have the following baptismal entry. It should be noted that this person was baptized by Father Richardie:

francisca nata ex adulterio cujus pater taotechaton haatsi
[Françoise born out of adultery whose father...he is called Taotechaton][15]
(Toupin 1996, 855, B664; translation mine from Latin and Wendat)

The man was Louis On,8atechraton, Bear clan nephew of elder Christine A8innonke, and husband of Snake elder Tiaondise8a. Interestingly, we learn a few names in that house (GV13) list were born of adultery, including the children of Christine A8innonke's niece, who had two children "genuit ex fornicatione [given birth to out of fornication, i.e., not in marriage]" (Toupin 1996, 223).

Perhaps there was a basic missionary practicality here, for which the Jesuits are well known. Putting too much pressure on conformity in marriage might mean fewer baptisms. And baptisms were the missionary bottom line, as we have seen.

In a passage entitled *Festin des Noces*, in Potier's collection of religious pieces written in Wendat, an anonymous author talks about why people should marry and stay married (see Appendix D). Compared to the Jesuit "hard line" on baptism—get baptized or go to hell—this is a soft sell. If you have a Christian or "sacred" marriage, Jesus and Mary will be there with you in the ceremony. Jesus will pray for you. The real "sins" appear to be adultery, separation, and divorce, rather than not having a Christian ceremony sanctify your marriage.

It could prove instructive to compare the Wyandot community with other mission communities. The French at Detroit had eighty-one marriages between 1768 and 1781, which appears to be a higher rate, but I do not know the population represented. It would be better, anyway, to compare the Wyandot with another Aboriginal group missioned to by the Jesuit. It is hoped that someone else engaged in similar research will use this study for comparative purposes.

Even with the low number of marriages, something of a clan pattern still emerges. This can be seen in the following chart. For a few of the first marriages, including the second, and fourth to sixth, there were Wyandot witnesses involved too. They have been included in the scoring of clan marriage participation. Later, there were either witnesses who were not listed or the formal status of witness was dropped.

Clan Marriage Participation in Ranked Order

Clan	Number	Rank	Relationship to Sampling Bias
Large Turtle	15	1	up one place
Porcupine	7	2	up five places

Wolf	4	3	up five places
Snake	3	4/5/6	as expected
Bear	3	4/5/6	down three to five places
Deer	3	4/5/6	up one to down one place
Striped Turtle	2	7	down four places
Sturgeon[16]	1	8	---
Prairie Turtle	0	9	down two places

The Large Turtle seems to be the clan that favoured this ceremony the most. Of the twenty-seven marriages in which clan has been identified for at least one of the partners, twelve have a Large Turtle bride or groom (with three witnesses in the early years). It seems to be more the choice of Large Turtle men, as they make up nine of those twelve. In fact, there are two Large Turtle male names, where being married with Christian ceremony appears to be a characteristic or responsibility of the name holder. The 1747 male elder name, Te ,atak, for example, appears three times with three different individuals bearing the name in 1765, 1775, and 1785 (Toupin 1996, 909, 910, 932, M20, M33, M45). Also repeating is the Large Turtle name Ochron,oti in 1747 and 1766 (Toupin 1996, 908, 909, M4, M24). Another male name, Ha8endanienton, was repeated in 1776 and 1775 (Toupin 1996, 909–10, M23, M31), but I do not know his clan identity. Large Turtle is strongly suspected, but evidence is lacking

On the other end of the scale, I have found no marriages in which a Prairie Turtle was one of the partners, consistent with their lack of participation in other Christian rituals. In addition, the Bear and Striped Turtle clans are definitely under-represented.

Potier soon learned that this sacrament had to be handled differently in Wyandot country than in his own. The first marriage ceremony that Potier performed, on 4 September 1746, did not exactly lead to a lasting marriage. From a Jesuit perspective it was a disaster. The groom was Wolf clan member Jean Baptiste Toratati and the bride was Marie Jeanne Ts8tsaondoaon. By the time Potier had recorded the census in the spring of 1747, Toratati was living with another woman, twenty-two-year-old Louise Arindetak, the daughter of Sastaretsi (PV13), no less, while he was also recorded as living with his bride of the previous year, in GV12 (the Wolf clan house). By 30 July 1747, Toratati and Arindetak had a child baptized at six months old (Toupin 1996, 856, B691). That child must have been born in January 1747, a little more than four months after the wedding ceremony. Marie Jeanne would have another husband at least by 1750 (Toupin 1996, 860, B735). On 13 June 1754, a seven-year-old daughter of hers would be baptized (Toupin

1996, 868, B842). Torotati, who had died in the meantime, was the father. A few others who received Christian marriage ceremony would marry others later, but not so quickly as in this case.

Ten times couples had children baptized some time prior to their Christian wedding (Toupin 1996, 821, 908–10, M1, M4, M9, M14, M15, M18, M20, M25, M28, M30). Two had children baptized the same day as the wedding (Toupin 1996, 909–10, M23, M27; Toupin 1996, 888, 890, with B1141 for the former and B1178 and B1179 for the latter); one baptized the day before (Toupin 1996, 910, M34; Toupin 1996, 889, B1314); and one baptized shortly afterwards (Toupin 1996, 909–10, M24, M37, with B1155). Strict adherence to sexual abstinence prior to marriage was an unrealistic goal for the Wyandot mission. The Jesuit missionaries obviously recognized that fact.

Christian Marriage Records of the Wyandot (1728–85)

	Year	Husband	Clan	Wife	Clan
M1	1728	Charles Tsoaisens	---	Marguerite Atsironde	Porcupine
M2	1746	Jean-Baptiste Toratati	Wolf	Marie-Jeanne Ts8tsaondoaon	---
M3	1747	French marriage			
M4	1747	Antoine Ochron,oti	Large Turtle	Marie ,aesk8a	---
M5	1747	Jacob Otre8ati	Snake	Agnes Annend8ach	Bear
M6	1747	,Atsi[s]taronka	---	Agnes Nentechien	Porcupine
M7	1747	Nicolaus Orontondi	Porcupine	,Etenhaon	---
M8	1753	Honnenra,enhiat	---	Rose Sk8at	---
M9	1753	Ts8kares	---	Te 8achinien	---
M10	1753	Te horonhiate	Striped Turtle	A8innon-8oin	Snake
M11	1753	,8en8ten (Traondi)	Porcupine	,Anda8a,ens	---
M12	1753	8en8en	Large Turtle	Tarih8aon	---
M13	1753	A8endandiniont	Large Turtle	Chi-8ate	---
M14	1764	Taontariai	---	Susanne Ts8ndendora	Snake
M15	1765	Harman Ndo,entet	---	Christine Hondehaon	---
M16	1765	Thomas Totkiak8araten[17]	---	Anastasia Dechronngiahak	---
M17	1765	Mathias Onda8atont	Deer	Maria D8oindata	---
M18	1765	Pierre Arontenta8i	---	Christine Tiesa	---
M19	1765	Tkiechena	---	Iemmea	---
M20	1765	Te,atak	Large Turtle	Sk8achiendo,at	Deer
M21	1766	Paul ,Arih8atkiondi (8tondi)	---	Catherine Chi-a8ointeha	---
M22	1766	Tkierontaronk	---	Marguerite ,Aandeton	Large Turtle

M23	1766	Ignace Ha8oindanienton	---	Marie ,Aronhiende	---
M24	1766	Harman Ochron,oti	Large Turtle	Catherine Otrenhaton	---
M25	1767	Jean-Baptiste Ts8(n)dats8t	---	Anna 8enda,on	---
M26	1767	Andre Otatkiondi	---	Anne Andatsaron	Porcupine
M27	1768	Pierre endetsarons	---	Louise ti-onnens	---
M28	1768	Toussaint 8ointaris	---	Therese te-8io	Large Turtle
M29	1773	Harman toron8tat	---	Agathe sk8atandi	Striped Turtle
M30	1774	Skaronhiati	---	Louise [Te 8asenta]	Large Turtle
M31	1775	J.B. Ho8oindanienton	---	Te-atia	---
M32	1775	Joseph ho8enda,ete	---	Marguereite Sindinde	---
M33	1775	J.B. Teata	Large Turtle	Christine Nentenion	Bear
M34	1775	Pierre Ts8nnonchies	---	Françoise eongontak	---
M35	1775	Mathias esten8is	---	Catherine A8oinnontask8i	---
M36	1775	Tkieronngiak	---	Susanne ,Arendachié	---
M37	1775	Jacqueau S'ondak8a	Sturgeon	tkiaronk8a	---
M38	1775	Joseph Tendiatkie	---	Terohi	---
M39	1775	Joseph Entaron8a	Large Turtle	Therese 8ende,annonk	---
		Marriages after Potier			
M40	1782	Jean Baptiste Narisk8a	Wolf	Marie Louise	---
M41	1782	Pierre Anoniakonk	---	Marie Ta 8inri8t	---
M42	1783	Joseph Ose,8ti	---	Suzanne [Tokiak8aratin]	---
M43	1785	Jean Baptiste Teata	Large Turtle	Marguerrite	---
M44	1785	Thomas	---	Marie	---
M45	1785	Francois Haronissa	Large Turtle	Francoise veuve [widow] Daillon	---
M46	1785	Thomas Tondasquaia	---	Therese Doguentette	---

WYANDOT DEATHWAYS: HYBRID PRACTICES

In *The Huron–Wendat Feast of the Dead*, religious historian Erik R. Seeman (2011, 2) speaks of the similarities in the "deathways" of the seventeenth-century French and Wendat, by which he meant "deathbed scenes, corpse preparation, burial practices, funerals, mourning, and commemoration of the dead." In discussing Jesuit Father Jean de Brébeuf's classic description of a Feast of the Dead in 1636, in which perhaps some seven hundred individuals were buried, Seeman (2011, 1–2) wrote:

Brébeuf's largely sympathetic portrayal of the Feast of the Dead drew on parallel Catholic and Wendat understandings of death and human remains. Both groups adhered to religions that focused on the mysteries of death and the afterlife. Both believed that careful corpse preparation and elaborate mortuary rituals helped ensure the safe transit of the soul to the supernatural realms. And both believed in the power of human bones.

This acceptance (or at least non-condemnation) of some of the religious and other cultural practices of the Wendat was not just a quirk of Brébeuf's, but was part of an often practised Jesuit policy of tolerance of cultural differences that did not directly violate the basic principles and tenets of Christianity. This policy eventually got them into trouble with the Vatican hierarchy and with other religious orders in the late eighteenth century for what were called the "Chinese rites." This Jesuit policy was termed *il modo soave* or "the gentle way" by Italian Jesuit Father Alessandro Valignano, who spelled out what this meant in his instructions in 1579 to Jesuits working in the East Asian missions of China and Japan:

> Do not attempt in any way to persuade these people to change their customs, their habits, and their behavior, as long as they are not evidently contrary to religion and morality. (Seeman 2011, 44)

These would lead to or enhance the possibility for what can be called "hybrid Christian ceremonies" or syncretic practices among the various peoples that the Jesuits missioned to, including, of course, the Wendat. The three principal deathway ceremonies of the Wendat were as follows. There was the Atsataion (lit. "one has a meal"; see Steckley 2007b, 64) or farewell feast conducted when someone was about to die or entering into a situation of great peril (e.g., going to war or on a long dangerous trade mission; see Steckley 2007a, 186). Then there was the Feast of the Dead. This ceremony, in which those who had died over a certain period of time, say ten to fifteen years (marking the move of a village once the nutrients of the corn fields and other resources in the immediate area had been used up), would be reburied (termed secondary burial in the literature) after their bones were specially prepared, placed on scaffolding, had presents given in their name, and then placed in a common pit (called an ossuary by archaeologists). Later there would be a condolence ceremony, discussed in the first chapter, in which a name was brought back to life.

In his earlier and more general work, *Death in the New World: Cross-Cultural Encounters, 1492–1800* (2010), including the Algonquian peoples of New England and their relationship to the English, Seeman looked at the contact period as one in which even those deathways considered traditional had changed significantly with European influences, such as the influx of new material culture, disease (and resultant large scale death), and Christian deathways. Grave goods and multiple burials increased, the former possibly being one major show of differentiation by rank of how people were buried, and Iroquois condolence rituals became more elaborate, at least during the Seven Years War through what Seeman terms the death diplomacy of the English and the French, who were both trying to stay on the good sides of the Iroquois populations to which they were most closely linked.

There was an Atsataion recorded among the Huron in 1648, with permission or at least acceptance of the Jesuits (JR34:113). The term would continue on into Wendat dictionaries of the late seventeenth century: "Repas...f[air]e un repas [to make or have a meal] Atsataion" (FH1697:178, cf. Potier 1920:204). The Feast of the Dead essentially died out among the Huron in the 1640s (although at the same time spreading to their Algonquian allies northeast and west of them over the next few decades; see Hickerson 1965), but elements would continue on, specifically the elaborate gift-giving. This can be seen in the following description of the final aspect of a funeral for a Wendat in 1675. Note that the author, Father Claude Dablon, refers to the gift-giving as a kind of Wendat innovation:

> When the hour for the funeral has come, the clergy usually go to the cabin to get the body of the deceased, which is dressed in his finest garments, and generally covered over with a fine red blanket, quite new. After that, **nothing is done beyond what is customary for the French, until the grave is reached.** Upon arriving there, the family of the deceased, who hitherto have only had to weep, display all their wealth, from which they give various presents. This is done through the captain, who after pronouncing a sort of funeral oration, which is usually rather short, offers the first present to the church,—generally, a fine large porcelain collar,—in order that prayers may be said for the repose of the dead person's soul. Then he gives, out of all the dead man's effects, three or four presents to those who bury him; then some to the most intimate friends of the deceased. The last of all these presents is that given to the relatives of the deceased, by those who bury him. (JR60:35; emphasis mine)

Not long afterwards, a condolence ceremony was held:

> Finally, some days after the burial, when the tears of the relatives have been dried to some extent, they give a feast to bring the deceased back to life,— that is, to give his name to another, whom they urge to imitate the dead man's[18] good actions while taking his name. (JR60:37)

The innovation of Wendat-style gift-giving is also noted in 1678, concerning the souls in Purgatory, a concern of the Catholic Jesuits:

> They have established a rather singular practice among themselves for the relief of the souls in Purgatory. In addition to their offerings in the Church for that object, and the alms that they give the poor; in addition to the devotion on the fourth Sunday of each month,—to which the indulgence for the souls in Purgatory is attached, and which devotion is so great that day resembles Easter-time,—as soon as a person dies, the relatives make a spiritual collection of communions in all the families, soliciting them to offer as many as they can for the repose of the soul of the deceased. (JR61:37)

It should be noted that particular Jesuits would be more inclined to the "gentle way" than others would. In my reading of *The Jesuit Relations*, Father Paul Ragueneau, Superior of the Jesuits at Sainte-Marie Among the Hurons in 1648 when the Atsataion ceremony was held, was a proponent, but a previous Superior, Father Paul le Jeune, was not. Likewise, I would argue that Father Pierre Potier was more inclined to the gentle way than was his predecessor, Father Richardie. His greater willingness to perform Christian marriage and his apparent initiation of a variety of deathway rituals strongly suggests that to me.

Unfortunately, we know little about what took place at the different rituals of mourning recorded by Potier. We can make a few generalizations. Most of the sponsors or hosts were clan members and a huge majority of them were women. Rituals of mourning were definitely women's work among the Wyandot of the eighteenth century. Also, it is important to say that gifts were given, an Aboriginal as well as a European Christian tradition in important religious ceremonies.

I like to think that there were many linkages to traditional Wendat practices. I would love to be able to link up resuscitation of names with the Christian deathways recorded by Richardie and Potier, since I suspect there was a link, but I cannot yet come up with any direct evidence.

Registre Mortuaire

We will begin with the "Registre mortuaire" (Toupin 1996, 801–15, 921–32). First, it is important to note that this does not record all the dead. There is a selection process involved here in some way. Many, probably most, Wyandot were buried without official Christian service. The numbers recorded for this service are too low. They represent a Christian funeral service that not all people opted for. Recording of these services began with Potier. There are 175 such services recorded for the years 1746–85 (the last four years being recorded by Potier's successor), or about 4.5 a year, which would represent too low a rate. And there are many names not included in this list, but who were the subject of other rituals of mourning that we will be discussing shortly.

Compare the annual baptism rate of roughly 26.5 per year (1,402 baptisms divided by fifty-three years) with that of the Christian funeral rate of 4.5 per year. If we subtract the adults (fifteen and older) who were baptized, then we would have roughly 24.8 born and baptized each year. That would result in a population growth rate of about twenty a year. Over fifty years, that would mean a gain of 1,000 people, around twice the size of the population in 1747. As the population seems to have stayed about the same over that period (Sturtevant gives eight hundred for the population in both 1729 and 1761), that might suggest that the percentage of Wyandot who had a formal Christian funeral might be something around 13.25 percent: not a lot.

All clans participated in this ritual, even the Prairie Turtle, who tended less to be involved in other such rituals. As you can see from the chart, the Wolf clan participated above their predicted numbers. This at least partially would reflect their close relationship with Potier, discussed above.

There was gift-giving involved as with other Christian–Wyandot rituals related to mourning, a product of the practices of both contributing cultures. Generosity was and is a primary Aboriginal value. Gifts included pots (ordinary size and large), blankets, and wampum beads of varying numbers, as well as strings of wampum.

Entries would give the name, often the date, sometimes the location, their age and, if they are young, who their mother, aunt, or grandmother (much less often a male relative, e.g., Sastaretsi) was, and sometimes the cause of death and a gift given in their honour. The following are examples:

Examples from the Registre Mortuaire

Christine hande't8-haon (tsaondis) fille d'ondechi8ri... 16 ans (Toupin 1996, 927, E113)
[Prairie Turtle]
Louise tia8oinnion (Niece de la mitasse) 24 ans. (Toupin 1996, 925, E96)
[Deer]
harman hang8ir8k, neveu de la la foret (ecrasé par un arbre à la riv[iere] aux ecorces)...
Couverte
[Porcupine]
(Toupin 1996, 925, E85)

128   CHAPTER FIVE

SERVICES

There were twenty-four mourning rituals named by Potier "Services" (Toupin 1996, 921, 924–25, 928–29, 942), extending from 1746 to 1760. Typically the entry was short, saying who was sponsoring the ritual, usually two or three people, who the ritual was for, and perhaps, what major gift was given. Usually, fellow clan members were the sponsors. The following is an example from 1760. I have added clan identities:

Example of a Mortuary "Service" Held in 1760

27 apr. tïea [Large Turtle] et a8oindara [Striped Turtle]...*Nic sa8oind8at ,eh[en]. [Striped Turtle]...,enk8[ara; cloth] (Toupin 1996, 929)

Anniversaires

There are thirty-one "anniversaires" (Toupin 1996, 926–29) recorded by Potier, incorporating the years, 1755–58 and 1760. Potier records usually one sponsor or host, the name of the dead, and the major gift given. To give you a sense of what the gifts were, I am presenting them as follows. I don't know who the gift is given to, whether it was the church or the family of the deceased.

Gifts Given in Anniversaires (Toupin 1996, 926–29)

A1	4 chats	skins of raccoons[19]
A2	12 chats	skins of raccoons
A3	,arich	leggings
A4	308 gr[aines] de porc[elain]	wampum beads
A5	,arich et onnonk	leggings and string of wampum[20]
A6	,arich	leggings
A7	2 peaux de ch[ats] passes	tanned raccoon hides
A8	1 peau de ch. Passée	one tanned hide
A9	249 gr[aines} de porc[elain]	wampum beads
A10	580 gr[aines] de porc[elain]	wampum beads
A11	129 gr[aines] de porc[elain]	wampum beads
A12	...	
A13	mitasse	leggings

A14	4 chats	skins of raccoons
A15	4 castors	beavers
A16	2 liv[res] et demi de Castors	beavers
A17	porcelaine	wampum beads
A18	2 liv[res] de Peau de ch:	skins of raccoons
A19	2 liv[res] de chev[reuil]	deer
A20	3 liv[res[et demi de Castor[s]	beaver
A21	2 peaux d'ours	bearskins
A22	près de 800 gr[aines[de porc[elaine]	wampum beads
A23-31	no gifts were listed…	

It should be noted that the gifts given were generally not those of European origin, but were the type of items that had been given prior to contact.

Services Anniversaires

Much more extensive in terms of the recording of names of participants/gift givers (see example below) are what Potier referred to as the Services Anniversaires (Toupin 1996, 942–55, 960–76). They extended initially from 1759 to 1760, were not practised from 1761 to 1767, and then returned for the time period of 1768 to 1771. The idea of a particular day of the year having an anniversary was initially foreign to the Wyandot, but we know that the Jesuits taught them that concept with respect to the anniversary of an individual's baptismal date. In an earlier text, *Instructions to a Dying Infidel*, probably written sometime in the mid- to late seventeenth century, we have a Jesuit writing the following:

> Do not let the day be lost when they strike you with water. Let it be that forever a day will be named, forever you will be put in the sky, happy, when this day reappears to you. You will think, "Great thanks to the day when I was struck with water, baptized." (Steckley 2013; translation mine)

Introduced to the practice, other anniversary dates could be established.

Example of the Recording of an Anniversary Service (Toupin 1996, 951–52, SA16)

20 aout [1760]…a8oindiandihi [Large Turtle female elder] t'a8oinnon…a,aronhie't [f]…,aronta,onra[f]

…

*M. Jean: ,aendeton [,ehen] [Large Turtle woman]

a,ihachientak[8oin]…an: enk[21]			
hotrendaentak8oin[22]			
hondak8onniak h8nda [her spouse][23] atsen	[plate]		
jaqueau hond8en [her son][24]	ok8istatarihata	[frying pan]	
Atsironde (f)	atsen	[plate]	[Porcupine elder]
Te ok8oinnonioti (f)	atsen	[plate]	
Aïa,e (f)	,anneno	[pot]	
Ts8nde,en (f)	,anneno	[pot]	[Bear elder]
Niendaharonk (f)	atsen	[plate]	[Bear elder]
,atera (f)	,anneno	(Couv[erte]) [pot cover]	[Porcupine elder]
A8innonke anne (f)	a,ah8a't	[large spoon]	[Large Turtle elder]
Te otkiêrachra (?)	hong8tsa	[provision bag]	
Nendask8a (f)	,aerat	[spoon]	
Nienditak (Schol[astique]) (f)	ong8atsa	[provision bag]	
O8oindara (f)	,aerat	[spoon]	[Striped Turtle elder]
Ka8oindi (f)	,ar: (B)	[stone][25]	[Striped Turtle elder]
,aenench (f)	,at:	[possibly plate][26]	[Striped Turtle elder]
Te ,achiatonta (f)	,ar	[stone]	
Onnond8annon (f)	kandechrak8a	<(rouge)> [?][27]	[Deer elder]
Onnond8 (f)	ka8atsa,eta	[meat bearer][28]	[Bear elder]
Nienditak agnes (f)	atatonchra	[willow basket]	
8atenhaon (f)	,annenh8oin	[corn sack, bag]	
Nonnonh8e (nendask8a h8ena) (f)	(kandechr:	[?]	
i,etenhaon (f)	,annenh8oin	[corn sack, bag]	
ota8ata (f)	hong8atsa	[provision bag]	[Large Turtle elder]
Ao8ase (?)	kandechrak8at (bleu)		[?]
,aendi (f)	,annenh8oin	[corn sack]…	
	.kandechr:	[?]	[Wolf elder]
Annenti (f)	,annenh8oin [corn sack] – ong8tsa [provision bag]		
Neniense 8oh8ia,ar<oin> (f)	,achran:	[pickaxe]	
Sk8achiendo,at (f)	achrann:	[pickaxe]	

Te 8oinngia (f)	atienda	[mat]	
Ora,ete	(m)	onn: (bleu)	[string of dark wampum beads]
Haonh8entsia,i (m)	onn: bleu	[string of dark wampum beads]	

*onnond8haon (f) ase8at {te hannenti8a ontati,ena anneno,
Andatsandiniontak ,achran: ato,en…enk8ario ,ar. , ,at: ,and8chra…,andera
[a hanging pot, pickaxe, axe, large piece of cloth, stone, plate, robe, and a strap for carrying things]
Achienk ,andera,e ,andorenchra ,annenh8oin…a8eti de sten i8at
[three straps with which women carry things in a sack, all that is inside it]

*tsok8oindaronk (f)	,at	[plate]
Toronngiahak (f)	,at	[plate]
Tsa8oin-innon (f)	achrannentati	[pickaxe]
,arendachien (f)	,at	[plate]

This is an anniversary service for a Large Turtle woman, Marie-Jeanne ,Aendeton. The first-named sponsor was a Large Turtle elder in 1747, possibly the leading one, as Christine ,Arhonnens, who had held that position, had died in 1754 (Toupin 1996, 925). All the other Large Turtle female elders contributed gifts in the ceremony. The other sponsors were women as well. There were the names of female elders from other clans as well: three from the Bear and Striped Turtle clans, two from the Porcupine clan, and one each from the Deer and Wolf clans. As well, almost everyone who contributed a gift was female. The only males were her father and her son, listed first and second, plus two more, of a list of thirty-two.

Generally, as with the participants in other anniversary services (see chapter 7 for another example), you find, as with the other mortuary services, that women are the leading figures.

Testaments et Anniversaires

In the interim period, when none of the anniversary services were held, from 1761 to 1767, there were the rituals referred to by Potier as "Testaments et Anniversaires" (Toupin 1996, 955–60, TA). There were seventy-six such rituals, and based on their recording, they were scaled down somewhat. The Large Turtle clan was most involved, with nineteen participants and eleven people for whom the ceremony was held. About equal was the Striped Turtle clan with twenty-one identified participants and two people for whom the ceremony was held.

Example of Testaments et Anniversaires (Toupin 1996, 955, TA2, 1761)

| 4 Sept. | tia8oinnion;...(susan) otronhia,enk [Large Turtle] [Large Turtle] | *Pi[erre]. 8en8oin ,ehen [Large turtle] |

Participation in the Rituals of Mourning

Clan	Number	Rank	Relating to Sampling Bias
Large Turtle	20	1	up one place
Bear	18	2	down one place
Deer	15	3	up two to three places
Striped Turtle	15	4	down one place
Porcupine	11	5	as predicted
Snake	6	7/8	down two to three places
Wolf	8	6	up two places
Prairie Turtle	6	7/8	down one to two places

Services Anniversaires in Rank Order

Striped Turtle	99	1	up two places
Large Turtle	98	2	as predicted
Bear	91	3	down two places
Porcupine	60	4	up three places
Wolf	57	5	up three places
Deer	46	6	as predicted
Snake	43	7	down three places
Prairie Turtle	20	8	down two to three places

Testaments et Anniversaires in Rank Order

Clan	Number	Rank	Relating to Sampling Bias
Large Turtle	31	1	up one place
Striped Turtle	27	2	up one place
Bear	24	3	down two places
Porcupine	19	4	up three places
Deer	11	5	as predicted to up one place
Snake	07	6	down two places
Wolf	06	7	up one place
Prairie Turtle	05	8	down two to three places

Services in Rank Order

Clan	Number	Rank	Relating to Sampling Bias
Large Turtle	12	1	up one place
Bear	10	2	down one place

Deer	7	3	up two to three places
Snake	4	4	as predicted
Striped Turtle	3	5/6	down two to three places
Prairie Turtle	3	5/6	as predicted
Porcupine	1	7	as predicted
Wolf	0	8	as predicted

Anniversaires in Rank Order

Clan	Number	Rank	Sampling Bias
Bear	12	1	as predicted
Deer	6	2	up three to four places
Porcupine	5	3/4	up three to four places
Striped Turtle	5	3/4	as predicted to down one place
Snake	4	5/6	down one to two places
Large Turtle	4	5/6	down three to four places
Prairie Turtle	2	7	down one to two places
Wolf	0	8	as predicted

Total Clan Participation in Rituals of Mourning in Rank Order

	Number	Rank	Relating to Sampling Bias
Large Turtle	165	1	up one place
Bear	155	2	down one place
Striped Turtle	149	3	as predicted
Porcupine	96	4	up three places
Deer	85	5	as predicted to up one place
Wolf	71	6	up two places
Snake	64	7	down three places
Prairie Turtle	36	8	down two to three places

We can see from this who were overachievers regarding the sampling bias and who were more underachievers. Among the former, we can list the Large Turtle, Porcupine, and Wolf clans. For the Porcupine clan, we can look to the death of Nicolas Orontondi in 1750 for their increased participation in Christian-based ceremonies. In 1751 and 1752, the Porcupine clan had the highest number of baptisms (four and five, respectively) and the highest participation in baptisms (eleven and twelve, respectively) of any clan. This could mean that they were seeking alternative sources of political power once their influential leader died, or that Orontondi had been holding some of them back from being connected with the church.

Rituals of mourning underachievers include the Snake and Bear clans of the Deer phratry, and the Prairie Turtle clan in the Turtle phratry. For the Snake clan, I think that we can look to the death of Matthew Ondachiate,en in 1747 (Toupin 1996, 922, E39) as lowering their participation in Christian-based ceremonies. During his lifetime, he single-handedly caused the amount of participation for his clan to rise significantly.

SUMMARY AND CONCLUSIONS

In this chapter, we have looked at three types of ceremonies and their clan participation. The three types of ceremony are baptism, marriage, and deathways or mortuary ceremonies. Concerning baptism, which was by far the most common Christian ceremony, we find that the Porcupine clan achieved a higher number than predicted by the sampling bias, and the Prairie Turtle had a lower number. This is not surprising considering the relative closeness of each to Father Richardie, the former having his support, the latter his opposition, at least with their clan leader ,Ang8irot.

With marriages, which were relatively uncommon, it is the Large Turtle clan that by far overachieved. They had a special connection with the missionaries in that way. The Porcupine and the Wolf clans were also higher ranked than predicted, the former probably owing to their connection with Richardie, the latter because of their connection with Potier. The Bear, the Deer, and the Striped Turtle were little involved, and the Prairie Turtle clan bottomed out with no Christian marriages whatsoever.

In the deathways or mortuary rituals, we find the Porcupine, Wolf, and Deer fairly consistently up from what we would expect, and the Snake and Prairie Turtle down, the latter not a surprise as this is consistent with their participation in the other Christian ceremonies.

In general then we see that having a connection or disconnection with missionaries seems to be key to a clan's participation in Christian ceremonies; the Deer and the Porcupine were connected with Father Richardie, although the former gradually disconnected; the Wolf were connected with Father Potier. The Prairie Turtle had no such connections as a clan unit.

Chapter Six

Wyandot Leadership
Male Political Roles

In this chapter we will be looking at the male-leadership structure of the Wyandot of the eighteenth century. With the highly detailed material available from Potier's writing, we have a unique opportunity to look at this subject in some depth. We also have the Wendat language to guide us concerning the nature of Wyandot male leadership.

THE NATURE OF WYANDOT LEADERSHIP

To get some sense of what the nature of Wyandot leadership was, you need to become familiar with one verb root that was used by Wendat speakers to describe positions of significant authority: *-nda,era-* "to copy, imitate" (Steckley 2007b, 136). In *The Jesuit Relations*, the writers often used the French word "capitaine" to refer to Wendat and other Aboriginal leaders. In what may be the oldest surviving Jesuit dictionary of the Wendat language, we have the following entry for "Capitaine" using this verb root:

| Capitaine auoir pour [to have for "Captain, leader"] | Enda,erati...honenda,erati il est capitaine <They (indefinite) choose to copy him.>[1] [He is "captain," leader.] (Steckley 2010b, 80) |

In a later Jesuit dictionary, we have the following, with the French word "chef":

Capitaine   Enda,erati...honenda,erati on l'a p[ou]r chef
[they, people have him for chief] (FH1697:30)

The -t- in the word translated here is the causative suffix, meaning typically "to cause something to be." It is the people who are doing the causing here, a statement of fundamental democracy. They have chosen a strong role model, to use a sociological term, a (very) significant other.

The eighteenth-century Jesuit historian Pierre François Xavier de Charlevoix (1682–1761), wrote in 1721 about the chiefs of the Wyandot and other Iroquoians, discussing the limits of their power:

> These chiefs generally have no great marks of outward respect paid them, and if they are never disobeyed, it is because they know how to set bounds to their authority. It is true that they request or propose, rather than command; and never exceed the boundaries of that small share of authority with which they are vested. Thus it is properly reason which governs and the government has so much the more influence, as obedience is founded in liberty; and they are free from any apprehension of its degenerating into tyranny. (Charlevoix 1761, 24)

Chiefs

"Chief" in English, "chef" in French, connotes more power than what most Aboriginal leaders had traditionally. The Wyandot did not form what anthropologists would call a "chiefdom." This involves a more complex socio-political structure than what they had, as well as more authority going to a leader, and typically the existence of large-scale economic redistribution in which the chief creates social debts among those to whom he has distributed goods. In traditional Aboriginal Canada, the term chiefdom would have only applied to some of the West Coast peoples, with the potlatch being the classic redistribution tool for chiefs. A good historical example of an influential chief of this kind was Maquina (ca. 1786–1825), a leader of the Nuu'chah'nulth or Nootka people of Vancouver Island. Roughly one-hundred people lived in his house, including about fifty "slaves." Here the translation is much more accurate than when used to refer to Wyandot "prisoners." For the West coast peoples, "slave" represented a long-term low-ranking status. Maquina's house was about forty-five metres long, about half the length of a football field (Steckley and Cummins 2007, 118). He can be called rich and his potlatches involved a great redistribution of goods:

> In his potlatch of 1803, he was reported to have given away 200 muskets, 200 yards of European-manufactured cloth, 100 shirts, 100 looking-glasses, and seven barrels of gunpowder. How much he gave away in Native goods

such as wooden carvings, Chilkat blankets, and salmon was not written down, possibly reflecting the bias of the non-Native writer as to what was important. (Steckley and Cummins 2007, 173)

Not all the items given away would have been his, as he would have drawn upon his clan members for such a gathering, but he would have controlled the redistribution. The Wyandot did not have such chiefly socio-economic or political means to have a giveaway on such a scale, although gift-giving was an important part of their culture.

The Sastaretsi

The Wyandot of the eighteenth century would be called a tribe by anthropologists, a political level in which leaders typically would answer quite well to Charlevoix's description: leaders who persuade and negotiate more than order people around. Still, the Wyandot did have a hereditary leader in Sastaretsi of the Deer clan and phratry, a man of some authority. Hereditary here does not mean someone automatically gains the position because of his or her lineage and birth order. In the case of Sastaretsi, we are looking at someone who was chosen from among the previous Sastaretsi's brothers and sisters' sons in the same sense as other inheritors of names were (see chapter 2). Like a European king, however, a young man or boy may have received the hereditary title with the death of his predecessor, but could not exercise authority because he was considered too young, too inexperienced for the role. He was subject to the guidance of an older person of authority or a regent much in the way a young contemporary French king would. Father Charlevoix spoke of the Sastaretsi of 1721 as being in such a position:

> Sastaretsi, whom we French call king of the Hurons, and who is in fact hereditary chief of the Tionnontatez, [Etionnontate] who are the true Hurons was also present on this occasion; but as he is still a minor he came only for form sake; his uncle who governs in his name, and who is called regent spoke in quality of orator of the nation. (Charlevoix 1761, 2:8–9)

He may have been considered a minor in Wyandot terms, but this Sastaretsi was not then a child. He had his first child baptized, a six-year-old boy, in 1729 (Toupin 1996, 825, B74), a child conceived in 1722 or 1723. In the Wendat language, *on,8entsentia* is reported in one dictionary as meaning a male between the ages of seven to seventeen (Steckley 2007b, 299; 2010b, 171). The next age group up is *on,8enienti*, referring to a young man from about twenty-five to forty (Steckley 2007b, 299; 2010b, 171).[2] In Appendix B2 the word honnon8enienti "they (m) are young men" is used in contrast to hati,8ennens "they (m) are elders." This Sastaretsi was probably high up in the *on,8entsentia* range in 1721 when he was still a minor.

Twenty-six years later, a then mature Sastaretsi of 1747 was leader of the Deer clan, the phratry, and the nation, a linking of roles that may have been of long-standing existence. He was the household head (first mentioned in his house, PV13, see Appendix A), one of the few males to be so (see chapter 7). His house was relatively large, having roughly thirty-nine residents. Near to it were two other large houses (PV10 and PV13). He played a major role during the 1740s as an intermediary with the French, travelling to Quebec and Montreal to represent his people and to listen to what Onnontio, the French governor, had to say. Unfortunately, he died that fall in Quebec (Toupin 1996, 922, E37), leaving the Wyandot temporarily without a Sastaretsi.

The name would have been resuscitated fairly soon after that. In 1758, we have a Sastaretsi opposing a French proposal presented in a wampum belt to their various allied Aboriginal nations, carrying with it the intention to attack the Iroquois. When it was his turn to speak, he said the following, articulating the interconnectedness through adoption and marriage between these nations and the Iroquois:

> I am surprised at your Conduct & Readiness to take up the French Hatchet, without considering the Consequence, especially as I gave you a Caution, before we entered the Fort or Council Room of the French. (Johnson 1922, 795)

He added to this:

> How can I who am the Flesh and Blood of the Six Nations and in whose Towns Numbers of our Friends & Children are living and settled, declare War against them. Where are there any of the Nations now present, that are not allied to the Six Nations also. To take up the Hatchet against them, would in my Opinion be wrong. Therefore I now declare before you all, that I will not comply with what is proposed by this Belt. (Johnson 1922, 795)

This man participated in the anniversary services six times in 1759 (Toupin 1996, 943, 944, SA2, SA3) and 1760 (Toupin 1996, 945, 947, 953, 955, SA4, SA9, SA18, SA20). This Sastaretsi died by 1765, as there was an anniversary testament for him on 2 July 1766 (Toupin 1996, 959, TA57). The next Sastaretsi died on 5 December 1783 (Toupin 1996, 931, E169). His name was recorded as Ignace Oatsenon[3] Sastaretsi. He was reckoned to be thirty years old at the time. A treaty signed that year[4] did not have his name on it. If he had become Sastaretsi in 1766, he would have been roughly thirteen at the time, an *on,8entsentia*, and probably would have had a regent to guide him. More specific information seems to be missing in that part of the Sastaretsi story.

A possible candidate for the role of regent would be Deer clan member Regis Onda8annhont. My admittedly slim reason for this suspicion is that when he died earlier in 1783 the mortuary record referred to him as the "Roy des hurons" or "King of the Wyandot" (Toupin 1996, 931, E163, with the name recorded as "Da8atont").

The last document of the political activities of the Wyandot that I have seen that has Sastaretsi's name on it is from 1790, a council held at Detroit on 19 May of that year (Curnoe 1996, 219).

Phratry Leaders

In the first census, under "3 grands chefs dans la nation huronne" we have the three names: "1...Sastaretsi...2 Sa,ents8a't...Ta,echiaten" (Toupin 1996, 227). In the second census we have "Sastaretsi, Ta,echiaten and ,ang8irot obit" (Toupin 1996, 260). I see this second list as kind of a negative comment against the missionary-disapproved man, putting him third when in the Wyandot order of precedence he should be second, as leader of the Turtle phratry. With Sa,ents8a't, his replacement, that more regular order was followed: Deer, Turtle, and Wolf.

Turtle Phratry

As we have seen, ,Ang8irot was the leader of the Turtle phratry before he died. He was Prairie Turtle clan. His replacement as Turtle Phratry leader, Sa,ents8a't, was Large Turtle clan. This suggests that no one clan "owned" the phratry leadership like the Deer clan owned the Deer phratry leadership. Perhaps it even points to the nature of the expansion of this phratry. The Huron Turtle phratry may have had only two clans in it, Turtle and Beaver (see chapter 2). The entry of the remnants of the Wenro "turtles" into the Turtle clan may have made for a larger Turtle phratry but, in addition, may have created a potential fault line of competition for leadership.

In 1747, Joseph Sa,ents8a't was more likely to have been graced with missionary approval. That may have helped to tip the balance in favour of the Large Turtle clan over the Prairie Turtle clan at that time. Sa,ents8a't was significantly involved with Christian ceremonies. He had daughters baptized in 1732, including a two-year-old (Toupin 1996, 832, B219); in 1733, an eight-year-old (Toupin 1996, 834, B255); and in 1734, a newborn (Toupin 1996, 836, B295). He was a godfather in 1731 (Toupin 1996, 830, B168) and in 1734 (Toupin 1996, 837, B307).

Strangely, the name Sa,ents8a't does not seem to be connected with any of the houses in the census. Father Toupin incorrectly identified him with Handechionionhak (Large Turtle elder ,Arhonnens's husband), as the latter person was named "le vieux sens8anne," the last word being probably an imperfect rendering of Joseph's Wyandot name. That man, who died that year at eighty (Toupin 1996, 922, E35), was possibly Joseph's father, ,Arhonnens. His mother was recorded as being "La vielle sens8anne" (Toupin 1996, 252). This appears to reflect French perception that the two individuals were the oldest of the line that owned that important name. That would be why "Le vieux" (the old one, male) and the "La vielle" (the old one, female) were affixed to their names.[5] In the summary of the main figures in the houses in one copy of the census, Potier wrote "sens8anne (fr[ere]: de mathias)" for that house (Toupin 1996, 239). "Mathias" was probably "Mathias Aron-issas," another Large Turtle clan elder. Sa,ents8a't may have been that man's brother, and the recording of names may have been jumbled, with the phratry leader belonging in that house (GV6). The number of differences between the two versions of the census regarding this house may point to this kind of mistake.

It is curious that Sa,ents8a't was listed as phratry leader, but not clan leader of the Large Turtle clan. And yet he was presented as the first name in the elders' council list for his clan. This could mean that he was the war chief to the peace chief that was Aron-issa, the one listed as the clan leader.

In 1759 and 1760, Sa,ents8a't, like Sastaretsi, his fellow phratry leader, was one of very few males involved with the anniversary services honouring the dead, participating seven times (Toupin 1996, 942–44, 947, 953, 955, SA1–3, 9, 17, 18, 20). In five instances both leaders acted to contribute in the same ceremony. The Wolf phratry leader did not follow suit. Once, Sa,ents8a't played the important role of *hotrendaentak8oin*, the one who publicly sings or prays for the dead (Toupin 1996, 947, SA9).

Sa,ents8a't opposed the Seneca in 1763, a people who had sided with Pontiac in his resistance movement (see below). As Howard Peckham notes in his *Pontiac and the Indian Uprising* (1970, 107):

> Another belt was sent to them [the Wyandot] directly from the Senecas early in 1763, according to an Ottawa named Notawas. The Huron chief at Sandusky, called Big Jaw, evidently saw one of the belts, for he later blamed the Senecas for starting the war.

Someone made an understandable translation error. There was no one among the Wyandot called "Big Jaw." The Wendat word for "jaw" is -,*oens*- (Steckley 2007b, 122), while the word for "forehead" was -,*ens*- (Steckley 2007b, 119). Sa,ents8a't's name should be translated as "he has a very big forehead,"[6] a name readily seen as potentially referring to a large turtle.

Sa,ents8a't had the anniversary of his death honoured in Christian ceremony on 26 June 1768 (Toupin 1996, 965, SA26), but his name would live on in stories of Wyandot victories in war over the Seneca and the Catawba.

In a story entitled, "The Wyandots at War with the Senecas," recorded in November 1911 by Marius Barbeau (1960, 52), and spoken in Wyandot by Smith Nichols, we have the following (as interpreted by Wyandot elders Eldredge Brown and Mary Kelley) with reference to Sa,ents8a't. The Wyandot were being pursued by the Seneca:

> Our people, finding out that their enemies were again after them, started in the direction of a creek. Now at their head was Sayentsuwat, the shrewdest of all in outwitting the enemy and escaping death, and the one who used to lead them against the Cherokees [i.e., the Catawba].

The story tells of the Wyandot winning battles, but the war continuing nonetheless. Fortunately Sayentsuwat was a shrewd and powerful leader, who had the ability to stop the sun when his people needed to return home and it was getting dark. Eventually the Seneca surrendered and declared themselves as brothers to the Wyandot (Barbeau 1960, 51–53; 1915, 271–75).

In another story, "War Between the Wyandots and the Cherokees [i.e., the Catawba]," told in Wyandot by Catherine Johnson and interpreted by Allen Johnson, the "great Wyandot chief Sayentuswat" (Barbeau 1960, 54) had organized a war party against the "Ground-Dwellers" (i.e., "people inside a cave").[7] The Wyandot were unable to completely defeat their foe as the Catawba would escape underground after being beaten. Sa,ents8a't had a vision of the spirit of the thunderers, Hinnon, who promised to help them. Hinnon destroyed the underground fortress of the Catawba, who then were forced to flee above ground, where they were defeated by the Wyandot (Barbeau 1960, 54; 1915, 282–83, 367).

"Good" Clan and "Bad" Clan: The Struggle for Phratry Leadership in the Turtle Phratry

While the people's historical traditions remember him in a positive light concerning this time, it appears that he and his clan did not have full phratry authority during the Pontiac resistance. There were two Turtle phratry factions at the time that took different stances. One was Large Turtle, with the leadership of Te,atak, another 1747 elder. Taking a different position was Tahatie, in 1747 a Prairie Turtle elder. Te,atak, and probably the other members of his clan, more connected to the church and more under the influence of Potier, took a relatively neutral stand. Tahatie and the Prairie Turtle clan, less connected to the church and the missionaries, as we have seen, not surprisingly sided more with Pontiac.

So far we have discussed Wyandot clans in terms of their integrative function. Here there would appear to be a significant division. I prefer to think of it as offering flexibility. If you at least appear to be offering support

142   CHAPTER SIX

for both sides, then whoever wins, you have connections with the winner. We saw in the third chapter how different leaders appeared to take different sides concerning the Miami and the Iroquois. Perhaps that gave them a form of insurance. The idea is worth entertaining. The Wyandot were on both sides of the War of 1812. Perhaps in the case of the Pontiac resistance, having leaders on both sides enabled the Turtle phratry, and perhaps the Wyandot in general, to be playing it safe. They certainly did not end up fighting each other, despite their appearing to take both sides.

Te,atak

At least three different people bore the name Te,ata(k) during the mid- to late eighteenth century. The first one was Antoine, the eldest son of the Large Turtle clan elder Sa8oindgiandij from her first marriage (Potier 1920, 150; Toupin 1996, 218–19, 251–52). The last written reference to his bearing the name was as a godfather in 1749 (Toupin 1996, 859, B722).

The Te,atak that resisted an alliance with Pontiac was named Mathias. He was the godfather at three baptisms, from 1753 to 1761 (1753, B809; 1755, B879; 1761, B1059; Toupin 1996, 865, 870, 882). The Large Turtle clan had a relatively high number of godfathers over the years, with forty-four. Te,atak participated in a Christian marriage, that rare occasion, in 1765 (P909, M20). In fact, as we saw in the previous chapter, that name and marriage became intertwined, with three people so named getting married in 1765, 1775, and 1785 (Toupin 1996, 909, 910, 932). The Deer woman he married then was the mother of his two previously baptized children (1758, B960; 1763, B1104; Toupin 1996, 876, 885). This Te,atak was dead by 1768, as can be seen by the fact that the anniversary of his death was honoured that year (Toupin 1996, 960, SA21).

The name was revived by a Jean-Baptiste, whose name first appears officially in 1771 as the godfather of a baptized boy who was to bear the same Christian name (Toupin 1996, 894, B1235), and a month later as the father of a girl named Catharine (Toupin 1996, 894, B1236). He was probably the one to sign the agreements of 1783 (as Tyachta, Curnoe 1996, 218), 1790 (as Ted-ya-ta, Curnoe 1996, 220), and 1795 (as Teyyaghtaw, www.wyandot.org/greenvil.htm), suggesting that the Large Turtle eventually won the struggle for phratry leadership.

Tahatie and Hannenhasa of the Prairie Turtle Clan

TAHATIE Tahatie was Jean Baptiste Tahatie of the Prairie Turtle clan. We have seen that an earlier Prairie Turtle leader, Ang8irot, was vilified by Father Richardie. Tahatie seems to have likewise been mistrusted by the

Jesuits. He was spoken of with suspicion by Father Potier in 1749. In a letter written on 29 September 1749, Father Potier writing to Longueuil, Tahatie's connections with the English and with Orontondi are stressed:

> Sieur Tahatie arrived lately from Orange [Albany] with a grand collar as a present for Nicolas [i.e., Orontondi] from the government of Boston in thanksgiving to him for having employed the hatchet of Onontio [the French governor]...against Onontio himself, and to invite him to betake himself to Boston or to Oswego with the promise that all the magazines will be open to him so that he may take freely from them whatever seems good to him. (Ott 1936, 205)

E.R. Ott (1936, 205n25), who included these words in his "Selections from the Diary and Gazette of Father Pierre Potier, S.J. (1708–1781)," misleadingly wrote in a footnote, "Tahatie was probably a renegade Huron who had married into one of the Iroquois families." The word "renegade" to me always prompts the question "renegade to whom." He appears to have done nothing that was treasonous to his people, and he did not marry into an Iroquois family.

What do we know about Tahatie? He was an elder in the council of 1747. He was the oldest son of Marie 8entïhaton. The Grand Village house in which he lived included his mother and his younger brothers—Taniendonien (Otreni8oin), who under the last name was also an elder, and Chonde'ta (Misting8ioin), who would be the executor to Orontondi's will.

HANNENHASA Also in that house was Hannenhasa ("He is little corn"),[8] who was the leading male name for the Prairie Turtle in the elders' council. His name is worth noting here as it appears that he may have been looking to the English to be good trading partners with the Wyandot.

One of the difficulties with looking at Wyandot names written both in French and in English is that the French is fairly regularly more accurate than the English. One reason for this, other than the linguistic training and expertise of the Jesuit missionaries, is the fact that French has a variety of nasal vowels (e.g., the -o- in bon, the -i- in vin, the -en- in chien, and the -a- in banque), while nasality is more limited in English. Wyandot is loaded with the nasal vowels to at least the same extent as French. English is not. So when English writers record Wyandot names, they sometimes miss the nasal vowels. I believe this to be the case with the name Ahannenhasa. The English leader William Johnston, who recorded the following on 10 September 1761, would appear to be an English-speaker missing a nasal vowel, with his use of the word Anáiása for what could be Hannenhasa.

The next day, Anáiása, a Wyandot chief, replied, expressing his pleasure at what Johnson had said. He added that if Johnston wanted more information about the recent activities of the Seneca, he should question one of those attending, pointing at Kiashuta, who was representing the Mingo [a Seneca group]. He then raised the question of trade and the need for "plenty of goods and that at a cheaper rate than we have hitherto been able to procure," on which many promises had been made. Finally Anáiása mentioned the matter of the white prisoners, saying that the Detroit nations had complied with the requests made two years earlier at Fort Duquesne [the English fort later to become Pittsburgh]. "But we must observe that they [the prisoners] are not slaves with us, being at their free liberty to go anywhere, or act as they please." (Johnson Detroit Journal, 17 Sept. 1761, Johnson Papers 3:483–87; as quoted in Middleton 2007, 41)

A short time later, he listened again to the Wyandot leader:

Here Anaiasa again expressed his pleasure at the proceedings, but raised his concern that the trade was "not at present on the best terms." He continued in the now familiar refrain. "We were always told before the reduction of this country that whenever you became masters of it we should…find the same treatment which we had met with from the French, and get from you such necessaries as we wanted, for which reason we now beg you will allow us a credit when the autumn comes in for what we shall want, as the French were used to do formerly." (Johnson Detroit Journal, 17 Sept. 1761, Johnson Papers 3:495–98; as quoted in Middleton 2007, 42)

It seems that there might have been another Prairie Turtle leader looking into new non-missionary-related solutions to the precarious situation of the Wyandot in the mid-eighteenth century.

It would be misleading to refer to Tahatie as a complete pagan or anti-Christian. Jean-Baptiste Tahatie had long been involved with baptism, even though there is no mention of his baptism in the records. The same was true of his two brothers. On 21 September 1733, two daughters of his and his wife Therese A8ennontak8i were baptized (Toupin 1996, 834, B249, B250). He was a godfather in 1734 (B309), 1758 (B990), and 1759 (B1012; Toupin 1996, 837, 878, 879). As noted earlier, he was the only Prairie Turtle who was a godparent to that extent. Only nineteen times were Prairie Turtle men named as godfathers from 1728 to 1779, a relatively low number.

His connection with Christianity was closer than that of his mother, who never appears in the baptismal record. Also not on that record or on another published church record were his younger brother Chondeta (Misting8oin) and the above-mentioned Hannenhasa.

Those Prairie Turtle who lived in PV11 bore Christian names, including the leading female elder Catherine Tsa8ointandi, her son (and also an elder) Mathias Ta,ennrak, and her other children, and as far as I can see all her grandchildren. We saw in chapter 4 that Potier was quite familiar with the ages of the people (and therefore with the people themselves) in that Prairie Turtle house (unlike the one in GV that held Tahatie and his brothers).

Still, there was low Prairie Turtle participation as godparents, in anniversary services, Christian marriages, and other Christian ceremonies. Generally speaking, it was the clan least connected to the missionaries.

Wyandot Clans of the Turtle Phratry and the Pontiac Movement:
The Storyline
The early 1760s were difficult times for the Wyandot. In 1760, the last year that Potier seems to have kept the mortuary record, that record tells a sad story of dysentery. In French it was written that people were dying "du flux" or "du flux sang," of the flux or the bloody flux, as it was known in English:

Date	Entry	Clan
9 August	le fils de skahonat, age de 5 ans, mort du flux [Skahonat's son, five years old, dead of the flux]	Large Turtle
10 August	M. Jeanne ,aendeton du flux venant du Niagara [Marie Jeanne ,aendeton of the flux, coming from Niagara]	?
11 August	un enfant chez hannenhasa (du flux) [a child at Hannenhasa's home (of the flux)]	possibly Prairie Turtle
15 August	susanne a8ointeha (du flux) venant de Niag. [Susanne A8ointeha (of the flux) coming from Niagara]	Deer
15 August	petit enfant, a8ointeha otrea [small child, A8ointeha's grandchild][9]	Deer
15 August	Marie Nendeniont (la mitasse) du flux sang [Marie Nendeniont ("the leggings") of the bloody flux]	Deer
21 August	petit enfant, ka8oindi otrea du flux [small child, Ka8oindi's grandchild of the flux]	Striped Turtle
29 August	petit enfant, t'ok8ennon,oti otrea...du flux [small child, t'ok8ennon,oti's grandchild...of the flux]	Striped Turtle

3 September	enf. de 6 ans, ,aenench otrea...du flux [child of six years, ,Aenench's grandchild, of the flux]	Striped Turtle
3 September	enf. de 2 ans, a8oindiandihi (otrea)...du flux [child of two years A8oindiandihi's grandchild of the flux]	Large Turtle
5 September	enf. de 18 mois, a8oindiandihi otrea...du flux [child of 18 months, A8oindiandihi's grandchild]	Large Turtle
19 September	enfant de nienteson de 2 ans...du flux [Nienteson's child of two years...of the flux]	Prairie Turtle
20 September	enfant au maillot a8oindg[10]iandihi otrea...du flux [child-in-arms, A8oingiandihi's grandchild] of the flux]	Large Turtle
21 September	enfant au maillot ,atera et a8oindiandihi otrea...du flux [child-in-arms, grandchild of ,Atera and of A8oindiandihi...of the flux] (Toupin 1996, 930)	Large Turtle

Along with killing disease, the Wyandot had to deal with the likewise potentially lethal effects of the fight between the French and the English for control of North America. This was a fight very much focused on the Great Lakes area where the Wyandot, their allies, and their foes lived. In the midst of this conflict another source of strife grew: an Aboriginal resistance or independence movement developed. One main focus is what is called the Pontiac movement, named after an Ottawa leader of the Detroit area. Neighbours and allies of the Ottawa, such as the Wyandot, the Ojibwa, and the Potawatomi were asked by Pontiac to join in the fight. The safe neutrality craved by many was made more difficult.

The Wyandot response, like the way they reacted to other conflicts along French and English, and later British and American, lines was twofold. Some would support one side, some the other. Remember how Tarhe took the American side, Bark-Carrier the British and Canadian, in the War of 1812. In this case, that included staying connected to the French primarily through their missionary, Father Pierre Potier, who threatened to deny them the sacrament of the Eucharist if they joined with Pontiac. Others joined with Pontiac, at least for a short time.

In the main primary source for the movement, originally written in French around that time, and whose title in English is "The Journal of Pontiac's Conspiracy: Of the Indians Against the English, and of the Siege of Fort Detroit by Four Different Nations Beginning May 7, 1763" (Quaife 1958), there is a clear contrast made between "good" and "bad," "Christian" and "pagan," in looking at the two positions taken by Wyandot Large Turtle phratry factions. We have the "good Huron band," and the "bad Huron band" (see Quaife 1958, 7). The leader identified for the "good Wyandot" was Te,atak. Tahatie (also written as Takay, Take, and Takee) was labelled "the chief of the bad Huron band" (Quaife 1958, 20).

The key scenes represented occurred in the spring of 1763, when Pontiac called with some success upon his allies to attack Detroit and other European forts and establishments. In "The Journal of Pontiac's Conspiracy," we get the following contrasting characterization:

> The two chiefs of [the Wyandot] nation were called the one Takay, who was like Pontiac in character, the other Teata, who was a very cautious and extremely prudent man. The last named, not of a disposition to do wrong, was not easily won over. (Quaife 1958, 6)

When Pontiac sent his messengers encouraging the Wyandot to join him:

> Takay, the chief of the bad Huron band...received them with enthusiasm and promised that he and his village were ready to obey the first demand of their great chief. (Quaife 1958, 20–21)

On 5 May 1763:

> When the appointed day had come all the Ottawas with Pontiac at their head, and the bad band of the Hurons in charge of Takay, repaired to the Potawatomi village where the expected council was to be held. (Quaife 1958, 21)

Tahatie and his small band of fifty, probably most of them of the Prairie Turtle clan, took part in an attack on Fort Detroit, then under English control.

On 11 May, Pontiac and his allies approached the Wyandot community in order to try to get Te,atak and his group to join with him. His group said that they needed to celebrate mass first, the next day, which was the "Feast of the Ascension of our Lord" (Quaife 1958, 62–63). Te,atak, along with "Baby"[11] ("Babi" or A,otiok8andoron of the Striped Turtle clan), told Pontiac that they would add their warriors (roughly sixty) to the force attacking Fort Detroit. Their speech (who was the speaker is not known), which they presented to their Wyandot faction, was reported as follows:

> My brothers, you see as well as we do the risks that we are running, and that in the present state of affairs we have nothing else to do but to side either with our brothers, the Ottawas and the Potawatomies, or else abandon our lands and flee with our wives and children—a rash thing to do. We would hardly get started to leave before the Ottawas and the Potawatomies,

and even those of our own nation, would fall upon us and kill our wives and children and then compel us to assist them. Instead of that, by co-operating now, we make sure that our families will be left in peace in our village. We do not know what the designs of the Master of Life towards us may be. Is it He who inspires our brothers, the Ottawas, to war? If it is not He who commands it He will well be able to make his desires known, and we shall yet be able to withdraw without being stained by the blood of the English. Let us do what our brothers demand of us, and spare not. (Quaife 1958, 64)

These two men were among the leading Christians in the Wyandot community. You can see in the previous chapter that both of them were among the leading Wyandot godfathers, with Te,atak assuming that role in eight baptisms, and Otiok8andoron in seven. It should not be surprising, then, that by 14 May Father Potier had:

by virtue of his calling and the power that he had over them [the Wyandot] had kept a part of them, especially the good band, within the bounds of neutrality by refusing them the sacrament. (Quaife 1958, 76–77)

When Tahatie and his small group of warriors decided to withdraw from the conflict later on in May that move too has been portrayed negatively (damned if you don't). Peckham (1947, 149–50) characterized Tahatie's band's decision to back away from Pontiac that May in misleading negative terms: defection, pagan, and treasonous:

the secret defection of the pagan Hurons under Také. They sent into the fort their interpreter, Jacques St. Martin, with a message to Gladwin. They complained that they had been forced into the war by Pontiac, but were willing to release the traders they had captured and pay them for their seized goods if the commandant would make peace with them. Gladwin replied that if they would carry out this offer, remain quiet, and try to separate Pontiac from his other followers, he would recommend them to the general. Pontiac appears to have remained unaware of this treason among the Hurons.

Understanding the clans involved and their leaders enables the portrayal to be much more complicated than the simplistic "good" and "bad," and "Christian" and "Pagan."

There is one further complication. On 25 May 1763, a testament and anniversary service was held for Tahatie. Did he die the year before, to be replaced by someone who would revive his name and take up the hatchet as his predecessor would have done? The sources do not tell us.

| TA19 May 25 | Marg. Te8oinngia | Cather. Sk8enderonk | *Tahatie ,ehen[12] |
| [?] | [Porcupine] | [Prairie Turtle] | |

(Toupin 1996, 956)

Wolf Phratry

Ta,echiaten was the leader of both the Wolf clan and the Wolf phratry. Strangely, he was not listed among the elders in 1747. He seems to have been disconnected from the other Wolf clan members, who lived in GV12, a Wolf house, not in PV4 or PV15, the houses he was recorded as living in, which were Snake and Striped Turtle (see Appendix A). His two wives were elders: first Sendanion, a Snake elder, and later Ts8ndehe, a Striped Turtle elder.

He had two children baptized, one in 1732 (Toupin 1996, 831, B201), and another in 1738 (Toupin 1996, 845, B473). Ta,echiaten was active as a godfather as well, five times between 1731 (B150, B225, 1733; B478, 1739; B618, 1744) and 1746 (B680; Toupin 1996, 829, 833, 845, 853, 856). Like Sastaretsi, he died in transit, representing his people in Montreal in 1747. His death so far from the eyes of his people was worrying to French officials, as can be seen in the following words from 6 September of that year:

> Mr. Michel writes of the death of Taychatin, second chief of the Hurons of Detroit, who had come down from Detroit with Mr. de Belestre. We fear that the death of this Indian and that of Sastaredzy, grand chief of that Nation, will create some unfavourable impression on the minds of the Huron of Detroit in the present conjuncture of affairs at that post. (NYCD10:123)

His name does not afterwards appear in the official church records, not in baptisms or in anniversary services. There is a good chance that this was because his name was not revived, and that the next phratry leader had another name. The most likely candidates would be one of the brothers Hondatorenha (clan leader and elder), Tandare-i8oin (leading elder in 1747), or Ts8ahea'ten. The best bet might be Tandare-i8oin. He had given his name to Potier. He participated in anniversary services four times in 1759 and 1760 (SA1, along with the Turtle phratry leader, SA14, SA18, SA20, the last two with both Deer and Turtle phratry leaders; Toupin 1996, 942, 949, 954) and had four children baptized between 1753 (B803, B888, 1755; B953, 1758) and 1760 (B1043; Toupin 1996, 865, 871, 875, 881). He was the most active male Wolf leader in Christian rituals.

Role of the Wolf Clan in the Nineteenth Century

In the latter half of the nineteenth century, the Wolf clan had a special role to play in the governance of the Wyandot. The Constitution of the Wyandot of Oklahoma, adopted on 23 September 1873, contained the following reference to the Wolf clan:

> The Wolf Tribe [i.e., clan] shall have the right to elect a Chief whose duty shall be that of Mediator. In case of misdemeanor on the part of any Chief, for the first offense the Council shall send the Mediator to warn the party; for the second offense the party offending shall be liable to removal by the Mediator, or Wolf of his Clan, from office. (quoted in Connelly 1900b, 29)

William E. Connelly (1900b, 29) added to this the line: "This has always been the position and office of the Wolf Clan." Earlier in that same text he (1900b, 27) wrote:

> The Mediator, Executive Power, and Umpire of the tribe was the Wolf Clan, which stood between the phratries, and bore a cousin relation to each.

John Wesley Powell (1881, 62) of the Bureau of American Ethnology wrote:

> The chief of the Wolf gens is the herald and the sheriff of the tribe. He superintends the erection of the council house and has the care of it. He calls the council together in a formal manner when directed by the sachem. He announces to the tribe all the decisions of the council, and executes the directions of the council and the sachem.

At meetings of the council:

> When all the persons are assembled, the chief of the Wolf gens calls them to order, fills and lights a pipe, sends one puff of smoke to the heavens and another to the earth. (Powell 1881, 62)

Concerning what Powell (1881, 67–68) terms "outlawry" (a wonderful nineteenth-century term), he states:

> When the person has been adjudged guilty and sentence of outlawry declared, it is the duty of the chief of the Wolf clan to make known the decision of the council. This he does by appearing before each clan in the order of its encampment, and declaring in terms the crime of the outlaw and the sentence of outlawry.

The Wolf clan of the Cherokee (termed "Aniwaya") provided the war chief for that people (Mooney 1900, 212). Was it a traditional Wolf clan association with Iroquoian peoples such as the Cherokee and Wendat? Did it relate to the natural association with wolves as warriors and protectors?

Was this a role played by the head of the Wolf phratry in the eighteenth century and even earlier? The earliest clear evidence for Wolf clan leader activity comes from a Huron bearing the Wolf clan name of Toratati, and described by the Jesuits as a "Captain" (JR38:51). In *The Jesuit Relations* written in 1653, we find the following:

> On the sixth of March of last year, 1652, the Hiroquois, who prowled around the French settlements all the Spring and all the Summer, defeated a Squad of Hurons who were going in search of them at a great distance, and found them very near, without expecting it. They were in ambush at the river of la Magdelaine, six leagues, or thereabout, above three Rivers. That Squad, commanded by a man named *Toratati*, fell into their hands and was entirely defeated. (JR38:49)

One of his warriors who survived told the Jesuits that:

> this Captain had been burnt [i.e., tortured with fire] and that those of his band that were left had been given their lives. It is thus that the Hiroquois swell their troops. (JR38:51)

If, as I speculated in the third chapter, Kandiaronk was of the Wolf phratry, that might have been when such a distinctive role for the Wolf phratry was developed, by one of the truly great men of the Wyandot.

Considerés

In the list of "Chefs" presented in Toupin's (1996, 260) invaluable collection of Potier's work we have, following the three phratry leaders of Sastaretsi, Ta,echiaten, and ,Ang8irot, the "considerés" that Toupin (1996, 178) interprets as follows:

Six hurons etaient candidats a la fonction de grand chef
[Six Huron that are candidates for the function of Grand Chief]

Nicolas
La foret
Tonti
Le brutal
bricon
Matthias

The "grand chef" is most likely each of the phratry leaders of the Wyandot, because, as will be seen shortly, there were representatives of all three phratries on this list. There appears to be no sense in anyone challenging the Sastaretsi role. They would be like assistant chiefs to the phratry chiefs. Writing in 1721, Jesuit historian Pierre Charlevoix (1761, 24) speaks of a rank above elders but beneath chiefs that he called "counsellors" or "assistants."

In the Wendat dictionaries I cannot find a Wendat word that is translated as considéré, but there are entries with "considerable," such as the following:

Te harihondache [he will not become a great matter]
il ne deviendra un hom[me] d'affaire, un considerable
[he will not become a man of affairs, one of considerable matter] ...
,achiend8annen [to have a great name]
avoir un grand nom, une grande reputation: etre d'une grande considerable
[to have a great name, a great reputation, to be of a great considerable one]
(Potier 1920, 254)

The list appears to be referring to the following significant figures among the Wyandot of this time. "Nicolas" is Nicolas Orontondi of the Porcupine clan, who is elsewhere referred to as the leader (along with le Manchot) of that clan (Toupin 1996, 226, PV2), and as an elder of the clan (Toupin 1996, 229). Interestingly, Orontondi has the French title "le regent" written after his name in the house list (Toupin 1996, 204, 241, PV2; see Appendix A). As Lucien Carr noted in 1884 regarding people chosen to be one of the fifty sachems of the Iroquois Confederacy:

> If the person chosen happened to be a child, as was sometimes the case, and incapable of acting for himself, it was customary to appoint a tutor or regent, whose duty it was to act for him, and to do everything that he might be called on to perform for the public good. This, in their figurative language, was termed "adding roots to the tree." (Spittal 1990, 31–32)

Did Potier see that Orontondi was acting as such a regent for someone chosen to be the elder for the Porcupine clan, or even, possibly, as the head of the phratry? It is hard to tell.

"La foret" seems to be Le Manchot or Pierre Tio8oindata (Toupin 1996, 204, 241, PV2), the other Porcupine clan leader. Reasons for associating the name La foret with this individual come from the reference to Pierre La foret as a godfather in a baptism of 1730 (Toupin 1996, 828, B119) and the significance of the individual, even though he was not an elder.

Tonti was Francois-Regis Onda8annhont of the Deer clan (Toupin 1996, 219, GV8), again not an elder. Le Brutal was S8ndak8a (v[13] Agnioton) of the Sturgeon clan (Toupin 1996, 224, GV15), listed as the leader of the Sturgeon clan, a clan that had no elders' council members.

The one known as "bricon" was Nicolas Taronhi8rens "he splits the sky in two,"[14] the leading individual in PV14 (Toupin 1996, 213; see Appendix A), and a Large Turtle elder.

His wife in 1731 was Porcupine elder ,Atera. He was listed as the head of his house (Toupin 1996, 213, 246). He was baptized as an adult in 1731, and had children baptized in 1731 (twice), 1736, and 1739 (Toupin 1996, 829, 830, 839, 846). He was a godfather for five individuals named Nicolas from 1736 to 1746, two of them adults.

In 1757, we find a Taronhi8rens with Ts8tses as his wife and a newly-baptized child (Toupin 1996, 874, P938). Then the next year the name appears with another baptized baby, but with a wife named ,Arenhatsi (Toupin 1996, 959, B959). The godmother was the new bearer of the important female Large Turtle name 8ata8ata. The old one died the year before. By 1760, there was a godfather with the Christian name of Jacques (Toupin 1996, 890, B1032), who would still have the Wyandot name in 1772 (Toupin 1996, 896, B1270). Whether he was the same as the Taronhi8rens in 1757 and/or 1758, I cannot tell for sure.

Mathias was Mathias Ondachiate,en of the Snake clan, a leading figure in his house (PV6, see Appendix A), the leader of his clan, but not (yet) an elder. Remember that his name was listed as a representative of what I believe was one of the phratries (the Turtle phratry) late in the seventeenth century. It was a name with a strong history.

You can see that the individuals share a number of characteristics. Four of them were clan leaders. Two of them were elders. Two of them were the first names mentioned in the census for their house, that is, they were household heads. And five of them were godfathers at least three times, with one, Mathias Ondachiate,en, leading the godfather pack with twelve.

Unfortunately for their people, three of them would not live long enough to fulfill their potential. Two died later in 1747, Ondachiate,en (Toupin 1996, 922, E39) and Onda8annhont (Toupin 1996, 922, E34), the latter one of three deaths that would weaken the leadership of the Deer clan. The other two were Sastaretsi and Nendaentons. Orontondi died in 1750 (Toupin 1996, 923, E52).

So our chart of "considerés" would now read as follows:

Name	Clan	Phratry
Nicolaus Orontondi	Porcupine	Turtle
Pierre Tiao8endata (le Manchot)	Porcupine	Turtle
Francois-Regis Ondannhont	Deer	Deer
S8ndak8a (agnioton) Le brutal	Sturgeon	Wolf
Nicolas Taronhi8rens (bricon)	Large Turtle	Turtle
Mathias Ondachiate,en	Snake	Deer

This seems like a reasonable distribution across the phratries, given that the Turtle phratry had the most clans, and that only one of the Wolf phratry clans contributed to the elders' council.

Clan Leaders

Also listed by Potier were the clan leaders, although sometimes he presented more than one. Sastaretsi was given as the Deer clan leader. For the Snake clan, Potier simply gave the name "Mathias" (Toupin 1996, 226, 259). This was fairly certainly the above-mentioned Mathias Ondachiate,en. He bore a name that, as we have seen, had long-term significance for the Snake clan. He can be seen as a great favourite of the missionaries and the French generally. Potier wrote on Hondachiate,en's death record on 23 October 1747, that he was a "bon chretien et tres fidel[e] francois" (Toupin 1996, 922, E39). He was a godfather seven times between 1731 and 1744 (Toupin 1996, 829, 832, 835,842, 843, 853, B156, B211, B212, B279, B419, B437, B617), and adopted an adult Chickasaw in 1736, a man with whose baptism he was involved (Toupin 1996, 840, B381). His name was revived by at least 1769, apparently for the father of a person baptized that year (Toupin 1996, 892, B1199). Strangely, however, his name is not mentioned in the elders' council list, and another individual, 8asanion, is listed first.

For the Bear clan, Potier gave the name A,a8as (Toupin 1996, 226) in the first census and Ennons in the second census (Toupin 1996, 259). It is not a case of one dying and the other replacing him, as they both died within about a month of each other in 1752 (Toupin 1996, 924, E68, E69). What may exist here is something of a distinction between "war chief" and "peace chief." When the former was listed in the elders' council (Toupin 1996, 228), there was the French word "(general)," which translates easily into English, followed by the Wendat phrase "ha8endio d'hotiskenra,et," which means "he is great in voice[15] [i.e., the one in charge] of those who are warriors." That would seem to be a good definition of a war chief. In *The Jesuit Relations* there was a discussion of how the Huron had both peace chiefs and war chiefs (JR13:59), with the war house having the name "Otsinontsiskiaj ondaon," "the house of cut-off heads" (lit. "head it is cut, it is a place")[16] versus "Endionra ondaon," "house of the council" (lit. "One's mind,[17] it is a place").

The main term for "warrior" in Wendat is *oskenra,e,te* (HF59, HF62:121, HF65:177, FH1693, FH1697:196; Potier 1920, 251), which also appears in Mohawk (Michelson 1973, 68). This involves the verb root -,ete- "to carry" (Steckley 2007b, 121), plus the noun root -skenr-,[18] translated by Potier as "guerre" or "war," although that translation might not be accurate (Potier 1920, 453; also see Steckley 2007b, 242).

It was noted in the previous chapter that the Bear clan was slow to be baptized at first. Perhaps one reason for this is that their leader was a war chief, more connected with traditional spirituality. A,a8as was not baptized, and didn't bear a Christian name. The death records show some of the hardship that A,a8as went through during this period. In 1746, he lost an eight-month-old grandson and a daughter (Toupin 1996, 921, E2, E3).

His wife was Prairie Turtle elder, Catherine Sa8ointondi. Their son, Ta,ann(d)rak, "Look at me," was also a Prairie Turtle elder. His daughter Tendioho had an eight-year-old child baptized in 1731 (Toupin 1996, 830); thus he was likely to be at least in his late fifties in 1747. A,a8as died in September 1752 (Toupin 2007b, 924, E69). His name does not appear to have been revived after that.

Enons lived in a Bear house (PV18), while A,a8as lived in a Prairie Turtle house, his wife being Prairie Turtle. I have noticed that there are more young men in the latter's house, but I cannot really say whether that is significant.

For the Large Turtle clan, the leader presented is Aron-issa(s) (Toupin 1996, 226, 260). He lived in PV2, a combined Large Turtle and Porcupine house. His wife was Ottawa. His name is second on the elders' council list for his clan, after Sa,ents8at, the phratry leader, with the name of Totarach given first with Aron-issa in brackets (Toupin 1996, 228). This was the way his name was presented in 1757 in his death notice (Toupin 1996, 928, E123). His name was revived in an English man, who was baptized at about twenty-five in 1782 (Toupin 1996, 906, B1411), but had been captured about twenty years earlier at five years old.

The fact that Sa,ents8at was listed first for this clan in the elders' council, combined with his later reputation as a great war leader, suggests that Aron-issa may have been a peace chief to Sa,ents8t's war chief.

For the Porcupine clan two names are listed as the clan leader: Orontondi and le Manchot (the one-armed one). The latter was more properly known as Pierre Tiao8endata (Toupin 1996, 226, 260). If you recall, both were deemed considerés. There is no clear indication, unlike with the two Bear clan leaders, that this was a war chief/peace chief distinction. Did they lead two factions within the clan, competing for leadership? Before addressing this question, I want to bring in another name: T'On8atsarandi. He was listed as the first name for this clan in the elders' council, with Orontondi as second. This seems bizarre given Orontondi's higher profile, but, to me, is not so strange if he were the war chief. Given his military role at this time, and given that the peace chief/war chief distinction seems to be at least hinted at in most of the clans, this interpretation has some credence.

By the time of the census, Orontondi had left the village and the house (PV2) that both he and T'On8atsarandi shared for Etionnont8t, and would soon attack Detroit, disbursing the community. Both died in the early 1750s: Orontondi in 1750 (Toupin 1996, 923, E52), and Tiao8endata died sometime before the baptism of a two-year-old child of his in 1752 (Toupin 1996, 863, B783),[19] with no recorded ceremony honouring his death.

For the Striped Turtle clan we have the name "babi" mentioned in the first census (Toupin 1996, 227) and "hokoindoron" in the second (Toupin 1996, 260). Both names refer to Otiok8andoron ("one is a valuable or difficult group"),[20] who was also the first-named elder of that clan. He must have been about fifty-five as an elder in 1747, as he was buried on 2 November 1782, when it was reckoned that he was ninety years old (Toupin 1996, 931, E162).

For the Prairie Turtle clan there are two names mentioned. One was ,Ang8irot, who had recently died, and the other was Ts8nnonkanien (Toupin 1996, 227, 260). Thomas Ts8nnonkanien was well placed in the Prairie Turtle clan (as his mother was Tsa8ointondi, the leading female elder) and in Wyandot society generally (his father was the Bear clan elder and possibly war chief A,a8as). Looking at the Christian ritual records, you can see that someone with his name was, unlike other Prairie Turtle clan members, a relatively active participant: five times being involved with the anniversary services from 1760 to 1771 (Toupin 1996, 945, 954–55, 965–67, 970, 974–75, SA4, SA20, SA28, SA35, SA41). The problem is that in 1781 someone with that name died (Toupin 1996, 930, E153), aged about forty. With the incomplete funeral records, it is hard to know exactly when the clan leader died.

With respect to the Wolf clan, again we have two names, Ta,echiaten and Hondatorenha (Toupin 1996, 227).[21] The first is the phratry leader; the second is one of two Wolf clan male elders, as well as being Ta,echiaten's cousin. There is no readily apparent differentiation of roles, as was possible to observe with the Bear clan. Yet there is the possibility that the peace chief/war chief distinction may have existed with this clan.

The remaining clan leader was Le brutal (Toupin 1996, 227) or S8nda'k8a (Toupin 1996, 260) of the Sturgeon clan, one of the considerés, as we have seen. Interestingly, his name appears to be the word for "eagle" (Steckley 2010b, 44). He was the only sign we have that the Sturgeon clan still had members. His house (GV14, see Appendix A) was a small one with his as the leading name, which included the two names, "S8ndak8a v. Agnioton" (Toupin 1996, 224).

Clan Leaders in 1747

Deer	Sastaretsi
Snake	Mathias Ondachiate,en
Bear	A,a8as, Ennons
Large Turtle	Aron-issa(s)
Porcupine	Nicolas Orontondi, Pierre Tiao8endata

Striped Turtle	Otiok8andoron
Prairie Turtle	Ang8irot (recently deceased), Thomas Ts8nnonkanien
Wolf	Ta,echiaten, Hondatorenha
Sturgeon	S8nda'k8a

Elders' Council

Councillors

In a list as unique and important as the whole census itself, Potier recorded what he termed "Les 3 Bandes huronnes avec Leurs anciens et Leur anciennes" (the three Huron bands with their male elders and their female elders) (Toupin 1996, 227). The three bands were the three phratries of the Wyandot: Deer, Turtle, and Wolf. The list comprises the sixty elders belonging to eight of the ten Wyandot clans.

You will notice that not every clan has the same number of elders, including female elders. This is similar to the fifty sachems of the original five nations of the Iroquois Confederacy (with the number of sachems in each nation ranging from eight to fourteen). Where there isn't a vote, but more of a discussion summarized by the ones in charge of reporting what the people say, precise equality of numbers is not too important. Consensus is key.

It is probably at this level that a term meaning "to be a tall tree" applies, as in the word in Appendix C2, *eeront8ten*, "they (ind) will be tall trees."

Table A: "Les 3 Bandes [Phratries] huronnes avec Leurs anciens et Leurs anciennes" (Toupin 1996, 227–29)

1° oskennonton ["it goes to the land of the dead"; Deer phratry]

hommes	femmes

1° es8tennonk ["they are keepers, guardians"; Deer clan][22]

hommes	femmes
Sastaretsi	nendaentons
eñie8indet etien[ne]	Sendak8an
	nendeñiont
	onnond8annon

2° eangontr8nnon ["people of the snake charm"; Snake clan]

hommes	femmes
8asañion	Sendañiont
hannenratendi	te ondise8a (soeur de

158 CHAPTER SIX

            ndikar[atase])   ndikaratase
            anien8indet Bar[nabe]
            tannenhochre

3° hatinñionen ["they are bears"; Bear clan]
            a,a8as (general)   ts8ndeιen
            ha8endio d'hotiskenra,et   niendaharonk
            Sohondinnon   onnond8
            Sa,ohetsaron atrio,e   te aïas
            ochiendaιete   tsa8oindask8a (Canerin
            Taretande   a8innonke (christ[ine])[23]
            ennons   asenraιe-haon
            honarak

2° endgia8ich ["they are turtles"; Turtle phratry]

1°ennehensteeronnon ["people where there are plum trees" (?); Large Turtle clan]
            Sa,ents8a't   ,arhonnens
            totarach: (aron-issa)   a8endgiandii
            hondechiaren8an   ota8ata (vielle pipon[ette])
            8en8oin   a8innonke (anne)
            te horonhi8teχa   Osk8arak (angel:)
            Taronhi8rens

2° eronhisseeronnon ["people…treetops"; Porcupine]
            t'on8atsarandi   atsironde
            gardien du tresor   ,atera
            orontondi   aronhiet

3° a'tïeeronnon ["people at the basswood"; Striped Turtle]
            otiok8andoron   ts8ndehe
            Sa8end8at   ,aennench
            harih8andiniontak   kaoindi
            tso,a8enda (general)   a8oindaara

4° entïhôronnon ["people where the prairie/field is large"; Prairie Turtle]
            hannenhasa   tsa8ointondi
            tahatie   La soeur d'hannenhasa
            ta,annrak   [tando,ares]
            otren-i8oin

3° hatinnaarisk8a ["they chew bones"; Wolf phratry and clan]
            tandere-i8oin   ,aendi
            handatorenha   nenditaχon

Male Elders

The verb root used to designate elders in the Wendat language was -,8annen-, meaning roughly "to be great, augmented, developed" (Potier 1920, 254; see also Steckley 2007b, 108). While it could refer merely to age, and to stature or size, it also referred to council member elders. In the entry in Potier's (1920, 254) dictionary, he presents the following:

> Les anciens, les viellards, les gens de conseil q[u]i deliberent des affaires, qui les decident et qui les reglent
> [the elders, the old ones, the people of the council who deliberate on affairs, who decide on them and rule on them.]
> hati8annens ehatirih8ichien
> [they (masculine plural) are elders, they (m) will conclude on a matter.].
> Les anciens determinerent cette affaire.
> [The elders will determine this affair, matter.]
> hotirih8ichia,i d'hati8annens
> [They (m) have concluded on a matter, those (m) who are elders.]
> Les anciens ont conclu, reglé l'affaire.
> [The elders have concluded, ruled on the matter.]

It should be noted here, and will be commented on in the next chapter, that although in presenting this verb form using all pronominal possibilities, including the feminine plural *ati8annens*, I have never seen in any of the Wendat dictionaries this verb used with the feminine plural to refer to women,[24] a bias of the Jesuit writers.

Deer Phratry

I have already written about Sastaretsi, so it is time to place Etienne Eñie8indet. The first point to make is that he shared a Wyandot name with Barnabe, a Snake clan elder. This, I think, may speak either to the Snake clan's origin within the Deer clan, or to the fact that the Snake clan seems to have been recruiting at that time.

The name could have been a Huron name, as in *The Jesuit Relations* of 1652, where there is reference to an "Annie8indet" being killed (JR37:110–11). That person could have been Petun; however, the Jesuits did not always make a clear distinction between the two during the years immediately following the dispersal. The reference to his death does not present sufficient context with which to distinguish his nation. What suggests that the name might have been Huron is the fact that in one of the copies of the census, in the list of "hurons de Lorette," there is reference to "anien8indet...ignace" (Toupin 1996, 236).

It is not easy to determine his age. We know from the baptismal record that one of his children was born in 1724, as the child was baptized at age six in 1730 (Toupin 1996, 828). If you put his age at being roughly twenty when this child was born, he would be at least in his early forties in 1747. His wife, Marie Tia8oinnion, belonged to the Large Turtle clan. Another one of his wives, Marguerite Ts8teses, was Bear clan.

He was involved with the anniversary services, at least three times. It is hard to tell, as the name appears with the -e- at the beginning, which was how his name was represented, and with an -a-, which was how the Snake clan elder's name was represented.

As an elder who was Sastaretsi's nephew, he would have been a good candidate to be the next Sastaretsi, although I have no evidence that he ever made that step up.

Snake Clan Male Elders

STANISLAUS 8ASANION The first Snake clan male elder was Stanislaus 8asanion. He lived in a Striped Turtle clan dominated house and, in 1729, had baptized children from two different wives: Onnondes, with the child being an eight-year-old named Franciscus (Toupin 1996, 824, B53); and seven-year-old Marie Catherine (Toupin 1996, 825, B73). Onnondes was his wife in 1747 (Toupin 1996, 208). The third baptism of a child of his was in 1740, with another woman, Catherine 8enonton8an (Toupin 1996, 847, B516). There is no reference to adultery in the baptismal record, and he otherwise seemed close to the church. He was a godfather five times from 1730 to 1742, a good indicator of his close connection with the church. He died in 1755, at sixty (Toupin 1996, 926, E104). The name was revived by 26 May 1771 at least (Toupin 1996, 973, SA38; see also Toupin 1996, 974, SA41).

MATHIAS HANNENRATENDI The first person named Hannenratendi who appears in the baptismal record was a seventy-five-year-old man baptized Franciscus on 16 June 1729. The second person named Snake clan elder, Mathias Hannenratendi, might possibly be the leader of the clan, the "Mathias" mentioned above. His first wife was Sk8ara, a Fox woman. He first appears in the baptismal record as the father of their child in 1744. After she died in 1748, he married Nennonh8e (after having children with two other women), a Large Turtle clan member, and the daughter of an elder. His French nickname was "L'etourneau," "the starling." That may or may not have been some kind of insult. He lived in a small house with a number of adopted people of other nations: Catawba and Fox. Children of his were baptized in 1744, 1753, and 1755. This would seem to make him relatively young for an elder. He died in on 18 June 1756. There is no record of his name being revived.

JEAN-BAPTISTE NDIKARATASE[25] He was the brother of Te Ondise8a, a woman who was also a Snake clan elder. One of the houses that his name is connected with was home to an adopted Fox and an Iroquois. While he was twice recorded as being a godfather (Toupin 1996, 854, 868, B658, 1745, B853, 1754), Potier does not record him as having any children living with him, or having any children baptized. He may have been relatively young for an elder. His wife was Ts8teharinnon, of the Striped Turtle clan. He lived in the same Striped Turtle dominated house as did his fellow Snake elder, Stanislaus 8asanion. His mother was A8endii. He did not participate in any anniversary services.

BARNABÉ ANIEN8INDET He is recorded as having the French designation "regent des nez" ("regent of the nose"), an expression whose significance, positive (as in being a regent) or negative is not clear. He was a godfather in baptisms of males called Barnabe in 1736, 1737, 1738, and 1739 (Toupin 1996, 841, 844, 847, B388, B399, B461, B501). His wife was the Bear clan elder Asenra,e haon, and they had a child baptized in 1739 (Toupin 1996, 846, B494). In 1747, they lived in a small house with four of their children. He participated in three anniversary services (Toupin 1996, 944–45, 947–48, SA3, 4 and 10), once in the special singing/praying role.

IGNATIUS TANNENHOCHRE He bore the French nickname of "coupe-jarret," literally "blow (to the) shank or back of the knee," figuratively in modern French a "setback,"[26] as with the English, "to be dealt a blow." He was living in Etionnont8t, with his sister A,angonta ("Snake charm") and her daughter when the census was taken in 1747. Their mother and sister lived in a Snake dominated house (GV11). His first baptized child, Pierre, was born in 1723 and baptized in 1735 (Toupin 1996, 838), so he must have at least been in his forties in the 1747 census. He had three children baptized. There appear to have been two people with his name in the baptismal records: this one, and a later one named Michael, who was involved with anniversary services. There was a French man with the last name of St. Pierre who also had this as one of the Wyandot names given to him (see Toupin 1996, 234, 262), possibly part of Snake clan's recruiting of new members.

Bear Clan Elders

ANDRÉ SOHONDINNON "QUARANTE SOLS" Like his clan leader A,a8as, Sohondinnon seems also to have been a war chief. As with a,a8as, he, too, has comments written after his name that suggest a military role: "Sa[,]ohetsaron atrio,e," meaning roughly, "he encourages them in warfare, fighting."[27]

Forty years after the first Quarante Sols died, Anastasie Ts8nde,en, a Bear clan member of the Wyandot elders' council, was termed "la vielle 40 sols" (Toupin 1996, 221). Her brother, André Sohondinnon, also a Bear clan elder, was also called "40 sols" (Toupin 1996, 222). This would appear to articulate a connection between the Quarante Sols discussed earlier and these figures from the mid-eighteenth century. This connection would seem to be that of belonging to the Bear clan. That the Bear clan is over-represented with Huron names suggests that Quarante Sols was Huron and not Petun in origin.

He seems to have been mistrusted by the French. His French "nickname" was "le borgne," which literally means "the one-eyed one" but also means "disreputable."

His name appears in a separate entry that might be referring to a Huron of the time amongst the Wyandot. More information about him comes from one entry following his name: "sohendinnon v. ok8endissena v. hannionenhak hatatiaθa...le lorretain...jongleur" (Toupin 1996, 226). This tells us that he spoke French, as "hannionenhak[28] hatatiaθa,"[29] which can be translated as, "He is French, he speaks in such a way" (i.e., "He speaks French"). It also would appear that he is from the Huron community of Lorette or Wendake, a supposition reinforced both by his being able to speak French, and by the fact that his wife A8oindite had a name that is found in *The Jesuit Relations* (JR52:228–29; Steckley 1998a) and in the 1770s in Lorette (Steckley 1998b).

Finally, the term "jongleur" points to his being a shaman, something that would add to French and Jesuit distrust of him.

In 1747, both people of his name were recorded as being separated from two wives: Sendak8oin, the Deer clan elder, and A8oindite.

PIERRE HOCHIENDA,ETE "HE BEARS OR CARRIES A NAME" We have seen that the elder Sohondinnon had a Huron connection. This was also true of his nephew, Bear elder's Ts8nde,en's son Pierre Hochienda,ete ("He bears a name"). He was the son of Ts8nde,en from her first marriage. He also appears to have been the half-brother of another one of her sons, Taretande, a child of Ts8nde,en's second marriage. His possible Lorette–Huron connection relates to the fact that the name "tachienda,e,te ... Romain" appears on the list of "hurons de Lorette" (Toupin 1996, 236).

Taretande was a son from the second marriage of Ts8nde,en, so would be a nephew of Sohondinnon. He was also known by the French term "Le bedeau" ("the beadle," a minor church official). This probably speaks about his position with respect to religious activities rather than being a metaphor for his position in the clan. He was a godfather five times between

1736 and 1760 (Toupin 1996, 840, 860, 867, 880, B361–62, B742, B828, B1028), which suggests it was the former.

His name has a Huron connection, being held by a leader at Ihonatiria in 1637 (JR13:214–17) and thereby a Northern Bear. The Northern Bear Taretande had a brother whose name, recorded as Sonnonkhiacon(c) (JR13:216–19, 222–23), was also held by Wyandot Bear clan member, Francois Sonnontkiaxon.[30] When the last named bore the name Harih8a8a, "He holds affairs of importance in his hands"[31] (Toupin 1996, 214), he was bearing the Wendat name given to those who, from the time of Laval, held the position of Bishop of New France (JR45:41–44; 49:89), the name Father Hubert would come to bear.

He lived in the big Bear house (GV13, see Appendix A) along with his mother and half-brother.

HONARAK Also living in that house, and also having an apparent Huron connection, was Honarak. Honarak appears to be the only Bear elder who did not have a Christian name. His son did not as well (Toupin 1996, 224), and his name does not appear in the baptismal record. We know that he was forty-three years old during the time of the census, as he died in 1754 at fifty (Toupin 1996, 925). He possibly shares a name with a Huron or Petun, Jacques Ondh8ara,k ("Door is on top"),[32] a man who was captured by the Iroquois in 1651 (JR36:122–23, 132–33). As his brother, Laurent Te hotronhiatase ("He is not a twisted sky"),[33] appears to share a name with a Lorette-Huron of 1768 (Steckley 1998b), it would seem to be more likely that both names were Huron rather than Petun in origin. He had the French appellation "40 sols" attached to him (Toupin 1996, 925), so he may have been a relative of Sohondinnon and Ts8nde,en.

PIERRE 8EN8OIN "PUTTING TOBACCO" He was the eldest son of Big Turtle elder, ,Arhonnens, the second child (Toupin 1996, 218, 252), possibly the brother of Sa,ents8at and Aron-issa. He lived in a Large Turtle dominated house (GV6; Toupin 1996, 218–19). His wife was Marie-Agnes I8ennonh8e, nicknamed "La mise," short for "La Miamise," meaning that she belonged to the Miami tribe. So, like fellow clan member Mathias Aron-issa, he had a Miami wife, possibly indicating a special relationship between that tribe and this clan. The first baptism of a child of his took place in 1736 (Toupin 1996, 841); the second in 1739 (Toupin 1996, 846); the third in 1741 (Toupin 1996, 849); so he would have been relatively young for an elder in 1747. He was a godfather in 1750, but in 1756 there was someone with the first name of Jean who was a godfather. This second person died, as there is a recorded death of a 8en8oin, but with the Latinized name Jano, in 1757. It was a bad year for the Large Turtle clan as two other elders, leading female 8ata8ata and male clan leader Aron-issa, died as well (Toupin 1996, 928).

If this is he, his name was quickly revived with a Pierre 8en8oin being recorded as a godfather in a baptism in 1758; a 8en8oin recorded as giving gifts in remembrance of a death in 1759, with the Large Turtle names Te horonhi8texa and Hondechiaren8oin surrounding his (Toupin 1996, 944); and then again in 1760 (Toupin 1996, 945).

JEAN BAPTISTE TE[34] HORONHI(8/O)TEχA "HE IS NOT A BURNING SKY"[35] Te horonhi8texa is the eldest son of Big Turtle elder 8ata8ata, both of whom had the French name Piponette associated with them, and was married to Nendaentons, a Deer clan elder. His name (without the negative prefix -te-) first appeared in the baptismal record when he was baptized as an adult on 6 June 1734, and appeared with a man named Martin as recently as 1739 (Toupin 1996, 846), as did his Christian name, Jean-Baptiste, that same year (Toupin 1996, 845). It was also a Lorette name (Steckley 1998b), so it had a Huron connection. Jean-Baptiste had a child baptized in 1741 (Toupin 1996, 849).

The house in which he lived in 1747 was dominated by the Large Turtle clan, with his mother heading up the listed names. He may have been related to Large Turtle clan member Te aondechoren, also found in this house, and also a Huron name. He was a participant in the anniversary services four times from 1759 to 1760 (Toupin 1996, 944–45, 947, 953–54, SA3, SA9, SA18, SA20).

Porcupine Clan Male Elders

N'ON8ATSARANDI The first male Porcupine clan name on the 1747 elders' clan list is T'on8atsarandi.[36] This was a name that had almost half a century earlier been associated with authority among the Wyandot.

The first reference to N'on8atsarandi was at the Great Peace talks in July and August 1701. His name, written as Houatsarant, was included with Kondiaronk or Rat, and the Bear leader Quarante Sols (La Potherie 4:222). It is conceivable that he was presented as the leader of the Turtle phratry, with Quarante Sols as the leader of the Deer phratry, and Kondiaronk as that of the Wolf phratry.

In the first house of the Petit Village (PV1, see Appendix A), in what I am calling the conservative or French faction house, right beside the house that held Sk8tache, N'on8atsarandi is listed as Joseph, the second-oldest son of Marguerite Atsironde, the first-named individual for the house, and the leading female Porcupine clan elder on the council. His father was Tsoaisens, a special favourite of Father Armand de la Richardie.

He was enigmatically referred to as the "gardian du tresor" (i.e., "guardian of the treasure") in the listing of the elders' council. I would love to know the nature of that "treasure."[37] He was a young man for an elder, particularly for the first one of his clan on the list, being about twenty-nine years old in 1747. He was eleven when he was baptized in 1729 (Toupin 1996, 822). That same year, and the next, a Baptiste On8atsarandi (spelled as ha8atsarandi) had a child baptized (Toupin 1996, 824). We do not know what Joseph's first Wyandot name was.

He had children of his baptized in 1749, 1752, 1755, and 1758 (Toupin 1996, 859, 863, 870, 877, B719, B778, B878, B977) with Anne 8enderes, and a godfather in 1753 (Toupin 1996, 865, B811). He died in 1759 (Toupin 1996, 929, E126). His death was honoured with gift-giving on 11 May 1760 (Toupin 1996, 929, 947, A28, SA7) by his children and a brother, but there is no evidence to show that his name was carried on beyond that time.

Striped Turtle Male Elders

MARTIN SA8END8AT (T)S(C)(A/O)8END8A(N/T)(N)(EN) Martin Sa8end8at was the second-listed male elder for this clan. He would change his name in 1747 to Tehatontaratase (Toupin 1996, 209),[38] as a man with that name who was about one hundred years old had died that year (Toupin 1996, 921), and Martin was chosen to resuscitate that name. His French name was La Calotte, or just Calotte. The first baptism of a child of his was in 1731 (Toupin 1996, 828), making him at least in his mid- to late thirties in 1747. There is a possible Huron connection with his name, as a similar name So8end8anne appears in *The Jesuit Relations* of 1652 (JR37:108–9). He was married to the adopted Fox woman Louise ,Areendaannon, both of them living in the large Striped Turtle house PV10 (see Appendix A) with their sixteen- and fifteen-year-old children.

His name must have been revived fairly quickly, as a Nicholas Sa8end8at had an anniversary service for his death in the spring of 1760 (Toupin 1996, 945, SA4).

PIERRE HARIH8ANDINIONTAK "HE HAS AN AFFAIR/MATTER HANGING"[39] Pierre Harih8andiniontak was the third-listed male elder of the Striped Turtle clan. His French nickname was "le glorieux," literally "the glorious one," but it is difficult to know whether or not that was sarcastic. His eldest baptized child was three in 1732 (Toupin 1996, 832), so he was at least in his thirties. He was married to the niece of Bear clan elder Marie Ts8endask8a, Torondiahak. They lived in the Bear house PV16. He had five children baptized from 1737 to 1749 (Toupin 1996, 843, 851, 855, 858, B443, B592, B670, B712, B713). He did not participate in the anniversary services.

JOSEPH TSO,A8ENDA Joseph, the fourth- and last-listed male elder of the Striped Turtle clan, may have played an important military role, as he is listed as the "général" (Toupin 1996, 229). Curiously, his name is not mentioned as connected with any house in the census (Toupin 1996, 179). This may relate to his apparently committing clan incest (see second chapter). He had a one-year-old child baptized in 1739 (Toupin 1996, 846, B497) with wife Tsondiochon, and another baptized in 1743 (Toupin 1996, 851, B578, no wife's name given), so he was probably at least in his thirties.

Prairie Turtle Male Elders

HANNENHASA "HE IS LITTLE CORN" OR "LE GROS JACOB" Hannenhasa, "he is little corn," nicknamed "Le gros Jacob" by the French, was recorded in 1747 as living in two houses: PV7 (Toupin 1996, 207, 243), a Snake clan house, and GV2 (Toupin 1996, 216), a Prairie Turtle clan house in the first census. He was listed as first of the Prairie Turtle clan elders.

There is confusion concerning his wife or wives. In the first census she is listed as "fem: du gros jacob" in the Snake clan house (Toupin 1996, 207). She may have been Snake clan elder Marie Margaret Te ondise8a, listed in PV9 (Toupin 1996, 208). My reason for saying that is that she is listed as having a seven-year-old child, Marie Ahiatonhon, and in October 1753 there was a death listing for "Marie hahiatonhonk fille du gros jacob, en mal d'enfant" (Toupin 1996, 925, B82).

In the mortuary record of 12 September 1760, there is the following reference: "andatoreta iroquoise age[e] de 50 ans, baptisee 24 h. Avant sa mort [baptized 24 hours before her death]. Olim mariee a [once married to] hannenhasa" (Toupin 1996, 930, E147).

On 29 June 1759, she was listed as the mother (with no father listed) of thirty-year-old Pierre Tsorih8a(t) "it is one matter," a Seneca (Toupin 1996, 879), who was elsewhere listed as twenty that same year (Toupin 1996, 977). There is a record of him being involved with an anniversary service in 1760, with a gift honouring the anniversary of two deaths (Toupin 1996, 947, 954, SA9, SA20). His general lack of presence in the baptismal record is telling, as we have seen, and not surprising for a Prairie Turtle leader.

TA,ENNRAK "LOOK AT ME!"[40] Ta,ennrak was the son of leading female Prairie Turtle clan elder (t)Sa8ointondi and leading male Bear clan elder A,a8as, and was recorded as living in their house PV11 (Toupin 1996, 210); in one census he was recorded as the leading figure in that house (Toupin 1996, 245). He was baptized at twelve in 1731 with Matthias Sastaretsi as his godfather (Toupin 1996, 829, B156). He was active in the baptismal record, with three children with Striped Turtle wife Tek8oina, baptized in 1740 (B530), 1744 (B607, as te ha,annra), and 1747 (B694, as ta,e,annrak) (Toupin 1996, 848, 852, 857). Two of the baptized were girls, with leading Deer clan women as godmothers, and Ta,ennrak was a godfather in 1747 (B689), 1752 (B768), and 1758 (B954) (Toupin 1996, 856, 862, 875). His participation in the baptismal record is atypical of his clan.

JEAN-BAPTISTE TANIENDONIEN "OTRENI8OIN"[41] Jean-Baptiste lived in the Prairie Turtle house GV2. He was the second son of Marie 8entihaton, after Tahatie. His name changed (see first chapter) from Taniendonien (see baptism B561 in 1742 as Hanniendo,en in Toupin 1996, 850) to Otreni8oin by this time (see baptism B716 in 1749 as Otronhi8oin in Toupin 1996, 858). He was a godfather once in 1753 (B807, as Otrenhi8oin in Toupin 1996, 865), and participated in three anniversary services in 1760 (Toupin 1996, 945, 946, 949, SA4, SA5, SA14).

Wolf Clan Elders

ANTOINE TANDERE-I8OIN "HORONHIA,ETE" We have seen before that he gave up his previous name, Horonhia,ete, to Potier, as an undoubted part of the adoption of the missionary, and that he might have risen to Wolf phratry leader.

SUMMARY AND CONCLUSIONS

We have looked at the male positions of authority among the Wyandot. From top to bottom this begins with the grand chief Sastaretsi. The next level is the phratry chief. Here we have Sastaretsi for the Deer clan. Second, there was ,Ang8irot (Prairie Turtle) followed by his successor Sa,ents8a't (Large Turtle) for the Turtle Phratry. This suggests that there might be some kind of divide or competition between the two clans for the leadership of this phratry, a fault line that appears to have been demonstrated with regards to the Pontiac movement. Third, we have Ta,echiaten (Wolf) of the Wolf phratry, possibly followed by Tandarei8oin. At the next level, there were the six men listed by Potier as consideres: two from the Deer phratry, Francois-Regis Ondannhont (Deer), and Mathias Ondachiate,en (Snake); three from the Turtle phratry, Nicolaus Orontondi and Pierre Tiao8endata, le Manchot (both Porcupine), and Nicolas Taronhi8rens, Bricon (Large Turtle); and one from the Wolf phratry,

S8ndak8a, Agnioton or Le brutal (Sturgeon). There is no description of what their positions entailed. Perhaps they were assistant chiefs of some type. It is curious that there is no representative in this group from the Bear clan, but it may be that with two possible "war chiefs" in their number, A,a8as and Sohondinnon, there might be equal status, but not of the peace-chief type. Perhaps this is also why there was no representative from the Striped Turtle clan, as Tsa,o8enda, an elder of that clan, had "general" listed after his name.

At the next level there are the leaders of the clan. Not surprisingly, Sastaretsi was the leader of the Deer clan. Mathias Ondachiate,en, equally unsurprisingly, was the leader of the Snake clan. The Bear clan had two names: A,a8as, who was presented in one census, and Enons, who was presented in another. There could have been a peace and war distinction here.

For the clans of the Turtle phratry, we begin with Aron-issa(s) of the Large Turtle clan. Then, for the Porcupine clan, we have Orontondi and Tiao8endata, who were just mentioned among the considerés. For the Striped Turtle, we have Otiok8andoron. The Prairie Turtle had Ang8irot, also the Turtle phratry leader, who had recently died, and his replacement for the clan leader position, Ts8nnonkanien.

For the Wolf phratry, we begin with having two names for the Wolf clan, Ta,echiaten, the phratry leader, and Hondatorenha, his cousin. Maybe the latter name was added after the death of the former in 1747. For the Sturgeon clan we have S8ndak8a, of the aforementioned considerés.

At the next level there are the male elders: the Deer clan having two, the Snake clan five, the Bear clan six, Large Turtle also six, Porcupine two, Striped Turtle four, Prairie Turtle four, and Wolf clan two. In terms of phratries, we have thirteen for the Deer phratry, sixteen for the Turtle phratry, and only two for the diminished Wolf phratry.

This can be illustrated in chart form as follows:

Male Wyandot Leadership Structure

Grand Chief
Phratry Chiefs
    Deer Phratry
    Turtle Phratry
    Wolf Phratry
Associate Chiefs (from each phratry)
Clan Leaders
Elders

In the concluding chapter, this chart will be filled in to illustrate the structure of male leadership among the Wyandot as it stood in 1747. Although all the names presented here are male, as we will see in the next chapter, this does not mean that all the power or authority rested with males—far from it. The women provided important leadership too.

Chapter Seven

The Political Roles of Wyandot Women

So far, only men's positions of authority, male Wyandot political roles, have been discussed. These are more clearly articulated in the primary documents and in the historical literature generally than are the political roles of women. In most of the writings of the Jesuits there are few reasons to believe that Wendat (or any other Aboriginal) women had any strong social or political influence in their societies. However, in Potier's detailed recording of the people, we have evidence to the contrary, although not much is spelled out for the historical interpreter as to the areas of authority possessed by these women. As we have seen already, Potier recorded the names of the people who, early in 1747, were members of what can be called the elders' council of the Wyandot. What is key to the discussion in this chapter was that he listed not only who the "anciens" (male elders) were, as did his Jesuit colleagues, but also who the "anciennes" (female elders) were. In addition to this, Potier presents a great deal about the participation of Wyandot women in the Christian-based rituals he recorded. This tells us a lot about their role in Wyandot society and gives us some social content to add to their names.

The words "matriarchy" and "matriarch" will not be used here, which is unfortunately not always the case with discussions of the roles of Iroquoian women. The technical anthropological meaning of these words relates to a political order in which females rule. That was not the case for the Wendat peoples. Women had significant influence (and still do) in Wendat cultures, but they did and do not rule. You likewise certainly cannot call Wendat societies patriarchies, where males rule, are all powerful, because they were not and they are not. The roles of women were and are too important to ignore. Men were the chiefs, but the leading women also had significant influence.

In all my reading of the seventy-three volumes of *The Jesuit Relations*, the annual reports of the Jesuits to their superiors back in France, and in my work with the Huron dictionaries that they wrote, I had never read the word "anciennes" before seeing it in Potier's elders' council list. It was always "anciens," talking about the male elders (see, for example, JR8:144; 10:27, 200, 212, 248, 304, 306; JR28:88).

This is typical of Jesuit treatment of the subject of women in Aboriginal culture. As an all-male society, spending most of its time with males in a patriarchal culture, the Jesuits knew little of female authority, of female culture, even in their own society. Of course, the Jesuits were not unique as European male writers in their neglect of female culture in their descriptions of seventeenth- or eighteenth-century Aboriginal people. In the previously mentioned work by historian Erik R. Seeman (2010, 154), *Death in the New World*, he notes that English writer Roger Williams (1603–83) was "blithely unconcerned with Narragansett[1] women and children" in his book, *A Key into the Language of America* (1643). Williams was a minister, an advocate of religious freedom, and one of the writers who can be considered relatively "sympathetic" or "understanding" of Aboriginal peoples; in his case, the Algonquian-speaking Narragansett in the area of his Rhode Island settlement of Providence. However, as a male coming from a patriarchal culture, he could not "see" women with authority. And, as Karen Anderson rightly informs us in the beautifully titled work *Chain Her by One Foot: The Subjugation of Women in Seventeenth-Century New France* (1991), when they saw socially strong women among the Montagnais (Innu) and Wendat during the seventeenth century, the Jesuits often did what they could to lessen female social strength.

In the case of the Jesuits, we can see this neglect of women and female culture in such aspects as the names presented in *The Jesuit Relations*. There appear to be about 268 Wendat names that they recorded, only thirty-nine of which are female names, or about 15 percent. When the expression for elders is used in their Wendat dictionaries, I have only found "hati,8annens," meaning "they (masculine) are elders,"[2] and "anciens," meaning "male elders" (see FH1697:13), as in the following:

> Capitaines, chefs de Conseil [captains, chiefs of council], des Anciens hati-8annens (FH1697:30)
> ga,8annen...les Anciens hati,8annens (HF59:72)

Typical of the treatment of councils and women in *The Jesuit Relations* is the following 1636 entry from Father Jean de Brébeuf (JR10:251):

> [T]hey [the Wendat women] make the fires, but do not warm themselves thereat, going outside to give place to Messieurs the Councilors.

Probably the women elders had already met, had their own council meeting, or were just about to do so. The male Jesuits would not have been invited to, did not know about, and would not have been expected to attend such meetings. Fortunately, there was more to Jesuit writing than the somewhat censored public-relations style writing of *The Jesuit Relations*. Jesuit historian Father Pierre François de Charlevoix (1923, 2:25) wrote in 1721 about the political practices of the Wyandot he had encountered:

> I have been assured, that they [the women] always deliberate first on whatever is proposed in council; and that they afterwards give the result of their deliberation to the chiefs, who made the report of it to the general council, composed of the elders.

While he felt this part of Wyandot democratic practice was more for "form's sake" than it was indicative of women having any real impact on the political process, Charlevoix still recognized that there were women's councils and elders. Less sceptical of women's political influence was another Jesuit historian of the period, Father Joseph François Lafitau (1681–1746), who came to New France in 1711 and from which time until his leaving in 1717, spent some time with the Mohawk of Kahnawake, near Montreal. In a scholarly work he published in 1724, entitled in English translation *Customs of the American Indians Compared with the Customs of Primitive Times*, Lafitau went to the opposite extreme of that of his Jesuit brethren who wrote *The Jesuit Relations*. After commenting on the distortion of *The Jesuit Relations* regarding the political and social influence of women in Iroquois society, Lafitau (1974, 69) wrote:

> Nothing is more real, however, than the women's superiority. It is they who really maintain the tribe, the nobility of blood, the genealogical tree, the order of generations and conservation of the families. In them resides all the real authority: the lands, fields and all their harvest belong to them; they are the soul of the councils, the arbiters of peace and war; they hold the taxes and the public treasure; it's to them that the slaves are entrusted; they arranged the marriages; the children are under their authority; and the order of succession is founded on their blood.

Regarding the elders' council Lafitau (1974, 69) wrote:

> And, although the chiefs are chosen among them [i.e., men], they are purely honorary. The Council of Elders which transects all the business does not work for itself. It seems that they serve only to represent and aid the women in the matters in which decorum does not permit the latter to appear or act.

And, concerning the choosing of who would become the male leaders of the people, Lafitau (1974, 70) said:

> The women choose their chiefs among their maternal brothers or their own children and it is the latter's brothers or their nephews who succeed them in the mother's household.

Charlevoix (1923, 23–24) said something very similar when he was writing about the Wyandot (generally then called Huron by French writers) in 1721:

> Amongst the Hurons, where this dignity is hereditary, the succession is continued through the women, so that at the death of a chief, it is not his own, but his sister's son who succeeds him; or in default of which, his nearest relation in the female line. When the whole branch happens to be extinct, the noblest matron of the tribe or in the nation chuses [sic] him chief.

In the French–Wendat and Wendat–French dictionaries there are no specific references to "clan matrons," the women who were leaders in the women's councils. I have only once read a Wendat phrase for "matrône," "oa'tandoron d'onnhetien"[3] (FH1697:116), which can be translated as "She is valuable, she is a woman." The dictionary entry does not indicate in what situations that phrase held.

What Charlevoix wrote is consistent with what was reported late in the nineteenth century with respect to Wyandot women. It does help us realize that even without being chiefs, women's political roles were still important. And there is some support in the Wyandot data Potier provided for this position, as you will read shortly.

Speaking of the Wyandot, J.W. Powell (1881, 61–62) wrote "Wyandot Government," in which he pointed out:

> In each gens [i.e., clan] there is a council, composed of four women, called *Yu-wai-yu-wá-na*.[4] These four women councillors select a chief of the gens from its male members—that is, from their brothers and sons. This gentile[5] chief is the head of the gentile council.
>
> The council of the tribe is composed of the aggregated gentile councils. The tribal council, therefore, is composed of one-fifth of men and four-fifths of women. The sachem[6] of the tribe or tribal chief, is chosen by the chiefs of the gentes....

The four women councillors of the gens are chosen by the heads of households, themselves being women. There is no formal election, but frequent discussion is had over the matter from time to time, in which a sentiment grows up within the gens and throughout the tribe that, in the event of the death of any councillor, a certain person will take her place.

In this manner there is usually one, two or more potential councillors in each gens who are expected to attend all the meetings of the council, though they take no part in the deliberations and have no vote.

When a woman is installed as councillor a feast is prepared by the gens to which she belongs, and to this feast all the members of the tribe are invited. The woman is painted and dressed in her best attire and the sachem of the tribe places upon her head the gentile chaplet of feathers, and announces in a formal manner to the assembled guests that the woman has been chosen a councillor....

The gentile chief is chosen by the council women after consultation with the other women and men of the gens.... At his installation, the council women invest him with an elaborately ornamented tunic, place upon his head a chaplet of feathers, and paint the gentle totem on his face.

Powell then is talking about two different political positions in nineteenth-century Wyandot society: household heads (the ones who chose female councillors), and female councillors themselves. These do not seem to be mutually exclusive positions. One woman could be both.

EVIDENCE FOR WOMEN'S POLITICAL INFLUENCE AND IMPORTANCE IN EIGHTEENTH-CENTURY WYANDOT SOCIETY

Responsibility for Prisoners

Lafitau spoke of women being responsible for prisoners. We are using here a more accurate term than his "slaves."[7] In terms of adoption of people from other nations, whether as the "prisoners" that Lafitau mentions, or as in furthering alliances, as in the adoption of Richardie by the Deer clan and Potier by the Wolf clan, our evidence suggests (although with admittedly limited numbers) that women may have had a leading role. Of eight adoptive relationships referenced in the 1747 census, six of them were given with respect to Wyandot women of significance, three of them from the Deer clan:

Female-Referenced Adoptive Relationships
1. Porcupine elder Atsironde having a Fox woman adopted as a sister
2. Deer elder Nendaentons having Father Richardie as a brother

3. Striped Turtle elder Sk8âra having a Chickasaw adopted as a brother
4. Striped Turtle Sk8atandi (mother of two female elders) having a Fox adopted as a sister. She may also have been the one that adopted Jesuit Father Nicholas de Gonnor in 1743.[8]
5. Deer elder Nendeniont having a Chickasaw adopted as a brother
6. Deer 8tsia (sister of elder Nendaentons) having a Fox adopted as a brother

Male-Referenced Adoptive Relationships
1. Porcupine elder Tiao8endata having a Chickasaw adopted as a brother
2. Both Bear elder Enons and Porcupine elder Tiao8endata having a Fox adopted as a brother.

Household Heads and Gender
Speaking about house and household property ownership among the Wyandot, Powell (1881, 65) wrote that:

> The wigwam or lodge and all articles of the household belong to the woman—the head of the household—and at her death are inherited by her eldest daughter, or nearest of female kin. The matter is settled by the council women. If the husband dies his property is inherited by his brother or his sister's son, except such portion as may be buried with him. His property consists of his clothing, hunting and fishing implements, and such articles as are used personally by himself.

This suggests that, when you see an older Wyandot woman named first on the list of residents in a particular house, you are looking at the name of the household head. The dictionaries are not very helpful here, as they seem to only recognize male household heads. An explanation is necessary here. The verb root -io- "to be large, great" (as in Ontario, "it is a large lake"; Steckley 2007b, 290) could be used with various nouns to indicate that someone was great or important in a particular social sphere (i.e., had influence there; e.g., -rih8- "matter, affair," -,entiok8- "clan, group," and -ondech- "country"; Steckley 2007b, 233, 286, 296). Unfortunately, when that verb root appears with the noun root -nnonchi- "house" (Steckley 2007b, 198), as with the other nouns mentioned, dictionary reference is made only to men:

> Cabane...honnonchio [he is great in a house] le m[aistr]e de la cab[ane] [the master of the house] (FH1697:29; see also Steckley 1987, 21)

> Chef csilii [councils] horih8io [he is great in a matter], belli [warfare] hotiok8io [he is great in a group, clan] (FH1697:35)

In no dictionary does there appear the word "mai(s)tress" or "mistress," but that would appear to reflect male Jesuit bias, not the absence of women of authority.

In the thirty occupied houses of the two villages, eighteen had an older woman mentioned first on the list of residents. The two villages follow a somewhat different pattern in this way. With the Petit Village, only seven of the sixteen active houses were "headed," in terms of being named first, by women. However, in five of the nine cases where the male name came first, it was the man's wife's clan that dominated the house. Perhaps in those cases Potier was influenced by the fact that these five were significant male leaders, including Ta,echiaten, the Wolf clan leader; Ondachiate,en, the Snake clan leader; A,a8as, the Bear clan leader; Taronhi8rens, a Large Turtle leader and one of the considerés; and Barnabe Enien8indet, a Snake clan elder. This might have led him to writing their names down first. The only cases in this village in which the male mentioned first had his clan dominate or make up a significant number were with grand chief Sastaretsi, and with Louis Sk8tache, whose Porcupine clan made up a roughly equal number with the Large Turtle clan in his house.

With the Grand Village, eleven of the thirteen occupied houses had an older woman mentioned first. In the two cases in which a man's name came first, the clan dominating the house has not yet been identified, but it would be the man's wife's clan. In the other two houses, the wife of the male listed first has her clan numerically dominate in the house.

Chart 1: First-Named Individual, Gender, and Clan in the Petit Village

House	Name	Gender, Clan/Nation	Status	Dominant Clan
PV1	Atsironde	female Porcupine	elder	Porcupine
PV2	Sk88tache	male Porcupine	---	Porcupine, Striped Turtle: wife's clan
PV3	8e8as	female Iroquois	---	her unidentified clan
PV4	Ta,echiaten	male Wolf	phratry head	Snake (wife's clan)
PV5	empty	---	---	---
PV6	Ondachiate,en	male Snake	clan head	Deer (wife's clan)
PV7	A8endii	female Snake	---	Snake
PV8	Entaron8oin	male Large Turtle	---	no clan[9]
PV9	Sandatsa8a't	male Catawba	---	no clan
PV10	Sk8atandi	female Striped Turtle	---	Striped Turtle

PV11	A,a8as	male Bear	clan head	Prairie Turtle (wife's clan)
PV12	8,e'tenhaon	female Catawba	---	her unidentified clan
PV13	Sastaretsi	male Deer	nation head	Deer
		phratry head		
		clan head		
		elder		
PV14	Taronhi8rens	male Large Turtle	elder	Porcupine (wife's clan)
PV15	Te 8arachiarande	female Striped Turtle	---	Striped Turtle
PV16	Ts8endask8a	female Bear female	elder	Bear
PV17	empty	---	---	---
PV18	Enien8indet	male Snake	elder	Bear (wife's clan)
PV19	empty	---	---	---

Chart 2: First-Named Individual, Gender, and Clan in the Grand Village

GV1	none	female	---	her unidentified clan	
GV2	8entïhaton	female Prairie Turtle	---	Prairie Turtle	
GV3	Aonchroni,en	male	---	no clan	
GV4	8ata8ata	female Large Turtle	elder	Large Turtle	
GV5	Te otiorachra	female	---	her unidentified clan	
GV6	Sa8oindgiandii	female Large Turtle	elder	Large Turtle	
GV7	Arhata	female Huron	---	her unidentified clan	
GV8	Ondechientonk	female Deer	---	Deer	
GV9	8ndaenton	female Deer	---	Deer	
GV10	---	abandoned	---	---	
GV11	Ts8ndendora	female	Snake	---	Snake
GV12	Nondeaon	female	Wolf	---	Wolf
GV13	Ts8nde,en	female	Bear	elder	Bear
GV14	---	burned down	---	---	
GV15	S8ndak8a	male Sturgeon	clan head	his wife's unidentified clan	

Wyandot Female Elders

We have twenty-nine female elders among the Wyandot. What can we say about the characteristics of these women? What social elements can we find that relate to their position of authority? First, there is their age. In the chapter on male political structure there was reference to a series of distinctions with one being males seven to seventeen, the next eighteen to twenty-five, and then twenty-five to forty. The series of terms used for female age groups is different. There is ,a8itsinnonha, which refers to a girl before she reaches puberty. The age was referred to as twelve in Wendat dictionaries (HF59:129 "Ga8itsinnonha jeune fille au dessous de 12 ans"). The next stage up is ,a8innon (upon which the elder name ,A8innonke may be constructed), which refers to a young woman of an age to be married (Steckley 2007b, 219). There appears to be no term for a mature woman, although a feminine pronominal prefix with the verb root -,8annen- was probably used.

The female elders of 1747 usually appear to be between at least their early thirties to fifties, with only one woman who can be considered "old." She was eighty. In a number of cases female elders were not the oldest women in their lineage. We can see that with the Striped Turtle elder Marie ,Aennench, who was a daughter of Dorothee Sk8atandi, first-named in the house in which they both lived (PV10). Similar to that are two other Striped Turtle elders, Ts8ndehe and Ka8oindi, both of whom lived in the same house with their mother Te 8arachiarande, who was the first listed in their common house (PV15).

We can also certainly say that the female elders of 1747 were deeply engaged in the ritual life of their community. Unfortunately, we cannot speak of the aspects of the community's ritual life that owe their origins more to traditional Aboriginal than to European culture, as Potier did not record that aspect of their lives. However, we do have this aspect of their roles well documented for Christian rituals, in which we can say they were leading figures. Two things should be kept in mind here. One is that the people's Christianity was maintained for decades without it being overseen by priests. Like with the Mi'kmaq of the Canadian Atlantic coast, who similarly went for long stretches of time as a Christian society with Christian-based rituals (see Robinson 2005), they would have chances to develop practices that would combine the Aboriginal with the European, to form unique rituals, led by the women.

When Jesuit historian and priest Father Pierre François de Charlevoix wrote in his *Journal d'un voyage fait par order du Roi dans l'Amérique septentrionale* (in Lajeunesse 1960, 27) concerning his visit with the Wyandot in 1721, he stated that they:

are all Christians, but have no missionaries. It is said they will admit of none; but is only true of a few of their principal men who have not much religion, and who do not suffer the others to be heard, who have been a long time desirous of having missionaries sent them.

Charlevoix (in Lajeunesse 1960, 27; 1923, 2:11) later gave a strong indication of who those "others" might be:

> I visited the two Indian villages near the fort. I began with the Hurons where I found all the matrons, amongst them the grandmother of Sasteratsi, in much affliction for being so long deprived of every spiritual succour.

He later (1923, 2:25) gave this as an example of the limitations of female authority. It is too bad that he did not name Sastaretsi's grandmother, as bearers of that name would doubtless provide counter examples illustrating the existence of "real" authority of women.

As Sastaretsi was the head of the Deer clan and hereditary grand chief of the Wyandot, it is not unlikely that his grandmother might be the leading female elder of that clan, and a significant person in her own right in terms of the whole nation. It is probable that there was a strong desire on the part of some of the significant female leaders for their people to have a missionary among them. When the leaders of the Wyandot made a request for a missionary six years after Charlevoix wrote the above, this may have been due to their influence.

On a more individual level we can see this with the Porcupine clan elder Marguerite Atsironde. She and her husband Charles Tsoaisens were the first Wyandot couple to be married in Christian ceremony. The ceremony was performed on 11 October 1728 (Toupin 1996, 821, M1). This was the day after Tsoaisens was baptized, suggesting that the push for Christian ceremony came from Atsironde, his wife but not yet his Christian bride. She might have been one of the clan "matrons" who Charlevoix spoke about, her husband one of the "principal men" who were resistant. Father Armand de la Richardie (in Lajeunesse 1960, 28) wrote in 1741:

> One Hoosiens [Tsoaisens], having embraced the christian faith after much delay, was such an example to all his kinsmen, that of his whole family not even one resisted the Holy Spirit.

There would not be another Christian marriage recorded until 1746, when the new missionary Father Pierre Potier arrived.

Godparents

In chapter 3, the topic of the spiritual kinship of godparents to godchildren was introduced. There were 265 instances of baptisms for which I could establish the clan identity of the godmother. This is compared with 234 such instances for the clan identity of godfathers, about 12 percent less. The top fifteen godmothers, in terms of the frequency with which they entered the relationship, ranged from between four and ten times. Of these women, seven were elders, two others were the mother (Sk8ateenre of the Deer clan and A8endii of the Snake clan), and one was the daughter of a female elder (Tia8ennion, daughter of Large Turtle elder ,Arhonnens). Four of the seven were listed first in their clan list of female elders: ,Arhonnens (11) of the Large Turtle clan, Atsironde (7) of the Porcupine clan, Ts8nde,en (7) of the Bear clan, and ,Aendi (7) of the Wolf clan. Five of the top fifteen were household heads, women named first in the list of house residents. Clearly, one common aspect of being a woman of standing in the Wyandot community was being a godmother. Parents would seek out such women to give status and learning to their children.

Leading Godmothers

Name	Number	Clan	Status
,Arhonnens	11	Large Turtle	female elder (1st)
Sk8ateenre	10	Deer	mother of female elder
Agnes A8ennon[10]	9	?	?
Oennhenhaon	8	? (Catawba)	house leader
Atsironde	7	Porcupine	female elder (1st), house leader
Ts8nde,en	7	Bear	female elder (1st), house leader
,Aendi	7	Wolf	female elder (1st)
Tsondendora	6	Snake	house leader
Onnond8	5	Bear	female elder
Te chiea8annen	5	?	?[11]
Onnond8annon	4	Deer	female elder
A8endii	4	Snake	house leader, mother of elder
Niendaharonk	4	Bear	female elder
Tsosk8a	4	Striped Turtle	?[12]
Tia8ennion	4	Large Turtle	eldest daughter of ,Arhonnens

Women Involved in Religious Ceremony

The literature of the nineteenth and twentieth century frequently discusses the role of Iroquois women in religion. Of particular note is the position of Keeper of the Faith (see Morgan 1904, 177–79), here described by Lucien Carr (in Spittal 1990, 32–33) in 1884:

> there was in every gens [clan] a certain class of persons styled Keepers of the Faith, who designated the times for holding the periodical festivals, made

the necessary arrangements for their celebration and conducted the ceremonies. In a general way too, they exercised a sort of supervision over the morals of the people, remonstrating with the evil-doers, and when necessary, reporting them to the council for exposure, which seems to have been their only mode of punishment. They also delivered religious discourses whenever such things were deemed advisable; and as they were a systematically organized body with well-defined duties, it is difficult to understand why they should not be styled a priesthood. To this order women were admitted in about equal numbers with the men.

There would be elements of this type of authority, and perhaps of a less formal, but nonetheless still recognized group, in the Wyandot context occurring much more frequently with women than with men, who held a similar position with respect to missionary-approved ceremonies, such as those described in the following section.

Rituals of Mourning: Anniversary Services, Testament Anniversaries, and Anniversaries

Traditionally, as we saw in chapter 5, the Wendat people put a great deal of time, energy, and ritual focus on the treatment of the dead. Their Feast of the Dead—in which people who had died over a ten-to-fifteen-year period (the lifespan of a village and its nutrition-depleted cornfields) were buried or reburied in one spot—was the greatest ceremony of the Huron in the first half of the seventeenth century.

Potier recorded several rituals that involved mourning for the honoured dead. While they would have been missionary-approved Christian-based ceremonies, they would probably have included traditional Wyandot elements. This would include a major role being taken by women, especially those in positions of authority. While little remains of what may have taken place in these rituals, looking at the participants involved tells us of the significance of women in these rituals.

There were twenty-four mourning rituals named by Potier simply "Services," extending from 1746 to 1758. In every case in which the sponsor of the ritual was mentioned the person was a woman. Included were nine female elders, three Bear, and two each of the Large Turtle and Porcupine clans, and one each from the Deer and Striped Turtle clans: ,Arhonnens (Large Turtle; S9, Toupin 1996, 924), Onnond8annon (Deer; S12, S19, S23, Toupin 1996, 928–29), Onnond8 (Bear; S14, Toupin 1996, 928), A8endara (Striped Turtle; S15), ,Atera (Porcupine; S16), Ts8nde,en (Bear; S17, S22), Niendaharonk (Bear; S17), Sa8oindgiandi (Large Turtle; S20) and A,aronhiet (Porcupine; S20) (Toupin 1996, 929). No female elders of the Snake, Prairie Turtle, or Wolf clans were mentioned.

The most often recorded Christian-based ritual of mourning practised by the Wyandot was termed by Potier "Services et Anniversaires," which I call the anniversary services, honouring the individual dead at a commemorative service at least a year after the person died. The honouring involves a sharing of gifts (see example to follow and the example in chapter 5). The services that were recorded by Potier took place from 1759 to 1771. The vast majority of the participants, the gift-givers, were women in each ceremony. Only two males were involved to any significant extent in this ritual. They were men of great social stature: the grand chief Sastaretsi of the Deer clan, and the Striped Turtle clan leader and elder Otiok8andoron. There were forty-two recorded ceremonies. Thirteen of the most frequent participants, including the top six, were female elders: ,Aendi (29), Ts8nde,en (25), Niendaharonk (20), ,Aenench (19), Onnond8 (19), and Onnond8annon (16). Three of them were from the Bear clan (Ts8nde,en, Niendaharonk, and Onnond8). Four of the thirteen were the first named on their clan's female elder list: ,Aendi, Ts8nde,en, Atsironde, and Ts8ndehe.

Each ceremony had what can be called sponsors or initiators, usually two or three people, for each one. Only three were male. The rest were women. Leading sponsors were Bear clan elders Ts8nde,en and Onnond8, with five sponsorships each.

There was also a key role named in Wyandot ehotrendaentak8oin—"She or he will sing or pray for him."[13] This would probably involve praying or singing for the dead at some designated point during the ritual. Of the twenty-one times in which the individual performing this role was identified, fourteen times the person was female, only seven times male. Noteworthy is the number of times the Wolf clan elder ,Aendi performed this role: ten times (SA21–25, 27–28, 30, 41–42; Toupin 1996, 960–67, 974–75). She was a major ritual leader among the Wyandot of her time.

Example of the Recording of an Anniversary Service[14]
The following is an example of an Anniversary Service held on 3 June 1768. Note that both of the sponsors are women, and that of the thirty-one people listed as offering gifts, only eight are identified as men. It is interesting to observe as well that even though this ceremony was held twenty-one years after the elders list, that nine of the female elders named in 1747 are involved here, five of the first six mentioned. No doubt women who had been named to the elders' council in the intervening years, the names that we do not know, would make that number higher.

The ,ehen after the name of deceased means "used to be," and functions something like the English expression "the late." The * indicates that a person was an elder in 1747.

...ts8k8oinderon Cather[ine]: toronngiahak (f)...Pierre taontaria,i ,ehen

ehehach[ientak8oin...I will say a mass (lit. "put a flame")[15] for him] ,agnion,en [bear] tendi [two]
ehot[rendaentak8oin – She will put orenda, sing or pray for him]...,aendi*. (f; Wolf elder)...,at[o,en – axe]

Atsironde (f)*..............,ar[ich]	[leggings]	(Porcupine elder)
Niendaharonk(f)*......,at[to,en	[axe]	(Bear elder)
ts8nde,en(f)*..............,at:	[axe]	(Bear elder)
t'ok8oinnonïoti(f).......,at:	[axe]	
ota8ata(f)*..................,at:	[axe]	(Large Turtle elder)
onnond8(f)*................,ar:	[leggings]	(Bear elder)
Nendask8a(f)..............,at:	[axe]	
8atenhaon(f)................ar:	[axe]	
tsa8oinse(f)................,ar:	[leggings]	
oton8a8oin(f)............ondinien[at]tsia [white blanket lit. "it is called snow"][16]		
kandoaretsi (?)..........ondinientsia	[white blanket]	
otienha (f).................ondinientsia	[white blanket]	
toronniahak h8ena[17] (f)	[shared the white blanket]	
Nend8tkies (f)............,ar: (?)	[leggings]	
Nierindetak(f)............,at: (f)	[axe]	
o8oindara (f).*............,at: (f)	[axe]	(Striped Turtle elder)
tsondak8aïa(m)...........a8ichra	[cincture, belt][18]	
,ari8tate hat (m)..........,enkara	[cloth, fabric][19]	
ts8kares(m)................a8ointa	[tobacco pouch][20]	
Sotrioskon (m).............a8inta	[tobacco pouch]	
ts8aha,eten (m)............,enkara	[cloth, fabric]	
harih8andeton(m).......,ar:	[leggings]	
ha8oindandiniont(m)..,enkara	[cloth, fabric]	
ndiraentkia(m)...........a8ointa	[tobacco pouch]	
toto8ïsen(?)...............,enkara	[cloth, fabric]	
ts8nnonchies h8ena(m)..,arachi8	[shoes][21]	
k8araotrea(f)[22]...........,arachi8	[shoes]	
akonniakotrea(f)......,arachi8	[shoes]	
asenra,e-haon(f)*........ondinientatsia [white blanket]		(Bear elder)
h8endenngiandi(?).....i8ennenchra	[bracelet][23]	

ts8ndehe(f – Striped Turtle elder)* hatinnonchia8eti ,enk8ario...,ar:,at: te ,aiachiont[24]...ohonra8ointa...ato,en...,anneno, ,annenh8oin a8eti i8at
[All of (the people of) Ts8ndehe's house presented a large cloth, leggings, an axe, a cross, a gun, an axe, a pot, a large bag, and all that was inside it] (Toupin 1996, 961–62)

It was typical for the Testaments et Anniversaires to have two women as sponsors. Sometimes there were three, sometimes one. Familiar ritual-participating female elders' names are found with, for example, Onnond8 of the Bear clan, Atsironde of the Porcupine clan, and ,Ainench of the Striped Turtle clan participating in four each. Only five male names were mentioned, with the Striped Turtle elder Te hatontaratase mentioned twice (Toupin 1996, 958, TA46, TA48). Again, sponsoring these rituals was definitely a female role.

What was simply called "anniversaires" by Potier, related it seems to those who died the year before, were recorded from 1755 to 1760. Usually only one person was involved as a participant. Males were only mentioned three times. This ceremony seems very clan based. Of the eleven cases in which both the one holding the ceremony, and the one for whom the ceremony was held can be clan identified, nine have matching clans.

Exceptions to this participation in these missionary-approved rituals are the Prairie Turtle female elders Tsa8ointondi (who sponsored one anniversary service for a Prairie Turtle in 1768 (Toupin 1996, 968–69, SA32) and Tando,ares.[25] Perhaps this is one reason why the latter was only referenced by Potier not by name, but as "La Soeur d'hannenhasa."[26] Generally, as we have seen, the Prairie Turtle can be said to participate little in Christian rituals, and to be in opposition to the missionaries. As was discussed in the fourth chapter, there was conflict between their male clan leader ,Ang8irot during the years leading up to 1747. And in the Pontiac resistance of 1763, Tahatie, an elder in 1747, led the group of fifty warriors that sided with the Ottawa leader.

Participation in these Christian rituals does not, of course, mean that they were not involved in Wyandot rituals of a more traditional sort as well. Unfortunately, the Jesuits did not document these.

Relationships between Female and Male Elders

There were close family ties, both by marriage and by blood, shared between the male and the female elders. For example, nine of the female elders were married to male elders in 1747. We do not know to whom the older elders who had outlived their husbands had been married (for example, eighty-year-old Therese 8ata8ata).

Six of the female elders had their sons as male elders. No mother-and-daughter pairings of elders were found, perhaps because daughters would tend to revive their mother's names and elder statuses. Unfortunately, this cannot be adequately documented.

It is noteworthy that four of the six women who had sons on the elders' council were first on their clan list of elders. Ts8nde,en had two sons who were elders. In every case but perhaps one[27] the younger men lived in the house of their mother. This was particularly true of the Large Turtle clan, where three women, the first three on the female clan elder list, had their sons on the elders' council. That would have given them added influence in that clan:

Mother	Son	Clan in Which They Were Elders
,Arhonnens	8en8oin	Large Turtle
A8endgiandii	Ondechiaron8a	Large Turtle
8ata8ata	Te horonhi8texa	Large Turtle
Atsironde	T'on8atsarandi	Porcupine
Sa8ointondi	Ta,ennrak	Prairie Turtle
Ts8nde,en	Hochienda,ete	Bear
Ts8nde,en	Taretande	Bear

Four pairs of brothers and sisters were on the council: Nendeniont and Etienne Anien8indet of the Deer clan; Te ondise8a and Ndikaratase of the Snake clan; Ts8nde,en and Sohondinnon of the Bear clan; Tando,ares and Hannenhasa of the Prairie Turtle clan. There was only one instance of sisters being fellow elders: Ts8ndehe and Ka8oindi of the Striped Turtle clan. To me, these female–male family contacts helped these women to have an influence on those issues that might be considered "male territory."

INDIVIDUAL STORIES OF WYANDOT WOMEN OF SIGNIFICANCE

We saw in the previous chapter that there were differences in ranking between the male elders on the list—some of them were clan leaders or phratry leaders and, of course, one of them was Sastaretsi. Of the eight men who led (were listed first in their clan's list), four clearly had the highest ranking. There was Sastaretsi (a clan, phratry, and nation leader), a second phratry leader in Sa,ents8a‛t, and two more clan leaders A,a8as and Otiok8andoron.

It seems to me reasonable to suggest that we can say there were probably similar ranking differences between the first women in their elder listing. Three of them—Nendaentons, Ts8nde,en, and Atsironde—were the first names mentioned in the houses in which they lived. A fourth, Ts8ndehe, was second only to her mother (not an elder). With Tsa8ointondi, the Prairie Turtle elder, her name is second to her likewise high-ranking husband A,a8as, but the house was overwhelmingly Prairie Turtle. Being placed first on the elders list of a clan reflected, I believe, a woman's ranking among women, and in Wyandot society generally. I have noticed that they usually are a little older than the others. If you combined several factors—being listed first on the elders list for her clan, being listed first in the house list, and living in a house with a lot of people living in it—you would be a woman of definite influence. Take, for example, the homes in which Ts8nde,en (GV13, the house with the largest number of listed residents) and Atsironde (the house with the third-largest number of listed residents) lived. These were influential women in 1747 Wyandot society, as we have seen from their roles in rituals.

Deer Clan

Marie Nendaentons
Marie Nendaentons, the first listed of the Deer clan female elders, was doubtless one of the leading Wyandot women of her time. She seems to have been very well connected in the community. Her lineage had strong marital links with the Large Turtle lineage that included Ota8ata, a Large Turtle female elder. Her second husband was Large Turtle elder Te Horonhi8texa, 8ata8ata's son. A daughter of hers was married to a nephew of her husband, and a son of hers was married to his niece (the nephew's sister). It seems to me that these marriages may have been, at least in part, strategic. Further, her sister, Louise 8tsia, was married to Mathias Ondachiate,en, the leader of the Snake clan.

Her lineage was closely linked with the Jesuits. She (or some member of her lineage) had adopted the Jesuit missionary Father Armand de la Richardie, as she was recorded as being his sister (Toupin 1996, 225, 258). Sastaretsi would not have that connection, although he would have been a clan brother after that adoption. Her nephew, Atironta, bore the name of the first Wendat leader to visit the French at Quebec early in the seventeenth century. People bearing that important name included Jesuit martyr and saint, Father Gabriel Lalemant, who was given the name just prior to being killed in the spring of 1649. He may have been the first Jesuit adopted by this lineage.

Marie Nendaentons had three of her children baptized in 1729 (ages eight, seven, and five; Toupin 1996, 825, B59, B60, B61), the first full year in which baptism was available in her community. This would have made her at least in her early forties in 1747. She was a godmother five times from 1737 to 1747.

Unfortunately for the community, she died on 20 August 1747 (Toupin 1996, 922), the same month as Sastaretsi, male leader of the clan, phratry, and nation. The Deer were certainly diminished that month as they lost two of their key political figures.

Jeanne Sendak8oin

Part of understanding who Jeanne Sendak8oin was comes from knowing who her mother was, and thus her lineage. Her mother's name, Catherine Sk8ateenre, was one of the few Huron women mentioned by Jesuits in *The Jesuit Relations* (see below).

Jeanne Sendak8oin was Sk8ateenre's eldest daughter. Like her clan sister Marie Nendaentons, she had her child (two-year-old Jacob) baptized in 1729 (Toupin 1996, 823). Also like Nendaentons, she was married to a clan elder, Andre Sohondinnon of the Bear clan. She would have been at least in her late thirties in 1747.

After 1729, she was not an active participant in Christian ceremonies. She was never a godmother, nor did she participate in any anniversary services.

Marie Nendeñiont

Marie Nendeñiont, known also by the French nickname of "La mitasse violette" (lit. purple leggings), was the sister of male Deer clan elder Etienne Anien8indet and the niece of clan, phratry, and nation leader Sastaretsi, and she lived in the same house with them (PV13, see Appendix A). It was one of the larger houses, with thirty-nine people listed as living there. Although she was not recorded as having a husband, she had a married son, Skahonat,[28] so she must have been at least in her early forties in 1747. She had an adopted brother who was Chickasaw in origin. She did not become a godmother, but she did participate in four anniversary services before her death in 1760 (Toupin 1996, 930, E141).

Catherine Onnond8annon

Catherine Onnond8annon was the daughter of 8ndaenton, whom Potier enigmatically called "la vielle reine." She was a frequent participant in Christian ceremonies. She was nine times a godmother (Toupin 1996, 852, 862, 871, 873, 879, 881), from 1739 to 1760, but was not recorded as having any children of her own. Further, she was active in anniversary services, participating sixteen times from 1759 to 1771. Her husband was Te o8ent8t, the son of female Bear clan elder Niendaharonk. Her name was shared with a woman of Lorette in 1776, Marie-Joseph Annd8annen (Steckley 1998b).

Other Deer Women of Significance

Louise 8tsia

Louise 8tsia was Nendaentons' sister, and Atironta's aunt (whom he would also call mother). Although the first-named individual in the house that she lived in (PV5) was her husband Mathias Ondechiate,en, a Snake clan elder, the house was filled with Deer clan members. So she could be termed the head of the household as the first-named female Deer clan member. Even her sister's name is mentioned, although she had moved to Etionnont8t. The couple were serious Christians; she was a godmother at six baptisms, he was a godfather at twelve. She died in October 1747, three months after Sastaretsi and Nendaentons.

Catherine Sk8ateenre

Catherine Sk8ateenre, nicknamed "la vielle Catherine," appears to have been dedicated to Christianity and/or the French as she was a major participant at baptisms. She was ten times a godmother from 1730 to 1740, almost all of those times for girls with the shared name Catherine. She lived in Sastaretsi's house, was the mother of elder Jeanne Sendak8oin, and the grandmother of Sendak8oin's unnamed nieces and of her married son Jacob Etioronhon—probably the reason why "achi8ta" meaning "to be a maternal grandparent" (Steckley 2007b, 79) was put after her name in one of the census entries for the house (Toupin 1996, 246). This name has a Huron connection and character similarities with an earlier person with the exact same name, as can be seen in the following quotation from Father Simon le Moine's relation (JR41:104–5) of 1654:

> I had orders to ascertain what had become of a young Huron woman, a Christian, named Caterine Skouatenhré, whom we used to call "the Nun," because of her great piety and a modesty as exquisite as can be desired in a girl given wholly to God. Her sister told me that she had died while praying to God, having never forgotten him in the whole course of her illness, which had been long. Shortly before her death she said to her: "I am going to heaven, my sister, for Jesus is good and will show me mercy. As for thee, if thou desire to follow me, so that we may meet again in heaven, cherish thy faith more than life. Shun sin as thou wouldst death; and if, by mischance, thou fallest into it, remember that Jesus is good, ask his forgiveness, and tell him that thou wishest to love him." These last words have remained so deeply graven on the surviving sister's heart, that she cannot lose the remembrance of them. The good Soul could not see me often enough, in order to hear about God, and comfort herself, in my company, with hopes of Paradise.

Christine 8ndaenton

She was the first-named person in a relatively small Deer house (GV9) with her married sons (one of whom married Ts8ndehe, the Striped Turtle elder) and daughter and their spouses. One other reason to name her as significant was her French nickname of "la vielle reine"—the old queen. Unfortunately, there is little information about her. She died in 1751 (Toupin 1996, 923, E65). An anniversary was held for her in 1756 by Deer clan elder Catherine Onnond8annon. I believe that Catherine was her daughter, as one of her daughters (unnamed in the list for GV9) was married to a Te8ent8i (Toupin 1996, 219), and Ond8annan (as nond8annan) was reported as being married to Pierre Te 8ent8t in GV13 (Toupin 1996, 222), whom she was also honoring with an anniversary on the same day.

Snake Clan

Susanne Sendaniont: First-Named Elder

Susanne Sendaniont can be called a success story. She was born a Fox, an Algonquian-speaking nation with whom the Wyandot fought during the 1730s (see chapter 4). In the mid-1730s a good number of Fox prisoners were baptized by Father Richardie. In 1734, that included six Fox children aged seven to fourteen. From 1735 to 1737, four more children were baptized. On 24 June 1736, three adult Fox women underwent the ceremony. The stories of those three women are presented below. In 1738 an adult Fox woman was baptized. I cannot find out when Susanne Sendaniont was baptized.[29]

She became the Fox adoptee on record as becoming an elder, and she was named first of the two female Snake elders. She married well, her second husband being Jacques Ta,echiaten, the leader of both the Wolf clan and the Wolf phratry, a figure highly regarded in the Wyandot and French communities. She had four children baptized, three from her first husband, and one from her second. Her first baptized child was born in 1727 and was baptized in 1734; the last in 1738, so she would have been relatively young for a female elder in 1747, perhaps in her late thirties or early forties, not long out of her childbearing years. She was a godmother once. She was not involved with anniversary services. In 1747 she lived in a small house that held her, Ta,echiaten, and their children, including those from both of their previous marriages.

Te Ondise8a "She is not delayed, she doesn't delay"

There appear to be two women that bear this name: one who is a Snake clan elder, the sister of Ndikarase, a male Snake clan elder, and one who is the sister-in-law of Ndikarase. He married her sister Ts8teharinnon. There is another name that the Snake clan shares with another clan, the elder name Anien8indet (Barnabe is the Snake clan elder and Etienne is the Deer clan elder). I feel that perhaps the Snake clan had been what I call "recruiting" names and people. Perhaps that was one reason why a Fox woman was able to become a Snake elder. Because of the potential for mix-up in the sources, not a lot can be said definitively about this woman. She was married to Louis On,8atechraton, the nephew of Christine A8innonke, a Bear clan elder. They had no children.

Other Snake Women of Significance

Susanne Ts8ndendora
She is the first-named person (female household head) in GV11, a Snake clan house, which houses one of her daughters and four of her grandchildren. She was a godmother four times between 1730 and 1745 (Toupin 1996, 828, 840, 850, 854, B132, B376, B562, B652). Her name was revived by 1760, by someone who took the same first name, who took on the godmother role twice (Toupin 1996, 893–94, B1219, B1233), who even got married with Christian ceremony in 1764 (Toupin 1996, 909, M14), and who participated in anniversary services in 1769 (SA28) and 1771 (SA36, SA37, SA42, Toupin 1996, 965, 971–73, 975–76). She could not have been the Ts8ndendora of 1747, as this one gave birth in 1768 (Toupin 1996, 890, B1175). She set a Christian ritual standard.

Bear Clan

Anastasie Ts8ndeıen: First-Named Elder
Hers was the first name mentioned in a large Bear clan house (GV13). It has roughly seventy-four people affiliated with it, the most of any Wyandot house of the time. Even allowing for some repeats from other houses (i.e., people whose names are listed with respect to more than one house), that still makes this a very important house at the time. There are nine elders associated with it, including seven Bear clan members: herself; female elders Françoise Niendaharonk and Christine A8innonke; Sohondinnon and Honarak; and her sons Ochienda,ete and Taretande. Other members of the house included Françoise's daughter-in-law, Deer clan elder Onnond8annon; Sohondinnon and his Deer clan elder wife Jeanne Sendak8oin; Christine A8innonke; Honarak; and Snake clan elder Te ondise8a. She was probably at least in her fifties in 1747.

Françoise Niendaharonk

Françoise Niendaharonk can be called prolific. She and her husband, a Potawatomi man named Mathias Okia, had seven children baptized from 1735 to 1743, the oldest one born in 1726. Her husband was baptized the same year as was an eight-year-old child of theirs, so you can probably say that she was the predominant Christian influence in her family. The fact that she participated in twenty anniversary services and was a godmother four times support that claim. She was the mother-in-law of Catherine Onnond8annon, a Deer clan elder.

Marie Onnond8

Like Niendaharonk, she married outside the Wyandot (genetically but not socially), having an "Iroquois" husband Sachiend8a (with various spellings). They had five children baptized from 1737 (a five-year-old) to 1746. She was probably then at least in her thirties. She was a godmother five times from 1739 to 1776 (if the last named is her). Like her clan sister, she was very active in anniversary services, doing so nineteen times.

Marie Teaïas

The data on her is not very clear because of what may be a great variety of ways to write her name as it appeared in the official record. In 1747, she is not recorded as having either husband or children. We can say that she was a godmother four times from 1735 to 1739, including once for her clan sister and fellow elder Onnond8's child (1735; Toupin 1996, 837, B317); and twice for the children of her likewise connected Asenra,e-haon's children (1739, as Ti ,ahes and Te ,a,as,; Toupin 1996, 846, B494–95). She was probably in her mid-thirties at least. Both of these women lived in the same house (PV18) with her in 1747.

Marie Ts8endask8a (Canerin)

Little is recorded about her; nothing in the baptisms or in the anniversary services. Her niece Taronniahak was married to Striped Turtle elder Pierre Harih8andiniontak (Toupin 1996, 214), putting her probably in her fifties in 1747. Hers was the first name recorded of a small longhouse (fourteen names; Toupin 1996, 214, 248, PV16) dominated by Bear clan members, particularly her nieces, two of whom were married.

Christine A8innonke

Christine A8innonke, another Bear elder, was forty-eight in 1747. We know that as she died at fifty-five in 1754 (Toupin 1996, 925). She was the wife of Onda8annonhont, the Deer clan son of Prairie Turtle elder Ts8nnonkanien. Her name had a definite Huron connection. In *La Nation Huronne*, Marguerite Vincent writes of two women, Marguerite Rossidet with the Huron name of "L'aawinonke" (Vincent 1984, 73), and Marguerite Vincent, with the name spelled "La8inonke," whose meaning she gives as "belle fille huronne" (Vincent 1984, 165). Interestingly, she was married to Paul Picard, whose Huron name was Onda8annhont. Further, to this Huron connection, Ok8oindate, one of her nieces, had a daughter by the name of A,aris (Toupin 1996, 223), which would appear to be the same name as that of "Aia,ris," a Southern Bear woman who was killed in 1651 (JR36:122–23).

Asenra,e-haon
Clan elder Franciscus Asenra,e-haon ("She comes from the south") has deep Bear tribe and Huron roots in her family. Her Wendat name is the same as that of a devoutly Christian Huron woman talked about by Jesuit writers in 1669 (JR52:164–65); in 1674 (JR58:136–37); and in 1676, in the last case written as Jeanne Assenragenhaon (JR60:297). She hosted Jesuit Fathers Le Mercier, Ragueneau, Chastelain, and Chaumonot in Huronia in the 1640s.

She was the first woman named in a Bear household (PV18; P214—although in the second census she is just listed as "uxor"). She was never a godmother, and she only participated in two anniversary services.

Large Turtle Clan

Arhonnens: First-Named Elder
Christine ,Arhonnens was the leading female elder of the Large Turtle clan. As we have seen, she was godmother to nine different people. She accepted this role during the years 1732 (B189), 1733 (B226), 1734 (B299), 1735 (B347), 1736 (B366, B382, B397), 1747 (B701), and 1748 (B707), to girls and to one adult woman, almost all of them called "Christine," from the Large Turtle, Striped Turtle, Porcupine, and Bear clans. Her two eldest children seemed to have inherited this role. Her eldest daughter Marie Tia8ennion was four times a godmother, and her eldest son Pierre 8en8oin (as we have seen an elder himself) was four times a godfather. She had a daughter of hers baptized as an adult in 1733 (Toupin 1996, 834), so she was probably at least in her late fifties when she was an elder in 1747. Curiously, her Wyandot name was given as having a newborn baptized in 1743 (Toupin 1996, 851). It could be that someone else had her name. There was a Marguerite Aarhonnens who died in 1750 (Toupin 1996, 923), while Christine died in 1754 (Toupin 1996, 925). Her name was also a Huron name, as Marie Louise Arhonnens was married in the community of Wendake in August 1769 (Steckley 1998b).

194　CHAPTER SEVEN

Anne A8endgiandii ((S)a8(e/oi)n(d/g)iandii)
Hers was the first name recorded in GV6, a Large Turtle house with a significant number of people living in it. Her French nickname was "la Babillarde," which refers to a chatterbox or talkative person. In the 1747 census there were three children recorded from her first marriage, including the elder Hondechiaren8anor Te,ata(k); two from her second marriage, including Paul A8endandiniont, who was a baptized newborn on 26 July 1732; and a daughter and a son from her third marriage. Four of her children had died in 1746 (Toupin 1996, 921) near the White River, where two of her sisters lived in 1747 (Toupin 1996, 259).

She was a major participant in the anniversary services. She was involved eleven times in 1759 and 1760 (SA1–5, SA10, SA15–18, SA20, Toupin 1996, 942–48, 950–55). She died by 1762, as there was an anniversary testament for her that year (Toupin 1996, 956, TA8). Her name was revived within a few years, as someone with her Wyandot name was involved three times in 1771 (Toupin 1996, 973–76, SA38, SA41, SA42), carrying on her ritual practice.

Therese 8ata8ata
Therese 8ata8ata was eighty in 1747, as we know that she was ninety when she died in 1757 (Toupin 1996, 928, E122). This makes her by far the oldest of the female elders in the council. The name appears to have been revived by 1760 (Toupin 1996, 951 "ota8ata"), by someone who was quite involved with anniversary services (Toupin 1996, 951, 961, 963, 966, 967, SA16, SA21, SA22, SA24, SA28, SA29). Her French nickname was "la vielle piponette." Her son, Te Horonhiateχa, was also an elder. In her large longhouse, hers was the first name of twenty-four listed (GV3), and it was a Large Turtle house, containing, among others, her children and nieces and their children. Her niece's children would be called in Wyandot her grandchildren using the verb root -*atrea*- "to have as maternal grandchild" (Steckley 2007b, 61).

Anne A8innonke
She shared a Wyandot name with Christine of the Bear clan. Perhaps it was an age or status marker in some way. The verb root -*8innon*- means "to be a young woman" (Steckley 2007b, 219). However, after her Wyandot name came the French name "La vielle kinench8e" (Toupin 1996, 241). Angelique Osk8arak's nephew Entaron8oin was also called kinenche, so perhaps they were mother and son or aunt and nephew. This would make her older than a young woman. The fact that her name came before Osk8arak, and the latter was forty-nine, suggests that she was at least that age. There is no husband on record. She was a godmother in baptisms in 1732, 1742, and 1749, the first

two times to adults, and she honoured the dead with gifts in 1760 (Toupin 1996, 950–52, 954–55, SA15, SA16, and possibly SA20).

A new person by the name of Francoise A8innonke appears in the religious records from 1770 to 1779. As noted above, Christine died in 1754, but there is no record of Anne's death, so it is difficult to determine to which clan Francoise belonged.

Angelique Osk8arak
She was forty-nine in 1747 (Toupin 1996, 241). There is some confusion over who her husband was and what the state of their marriage was. The information presented for PV2, headed by Sk88tache, has her mentioned twice: the first just prior to her daughter Angelique Annentenion, who was twenty (Toupin 1996, 205), the second has her paired with A,otiok8andoron or Babi, the Striped Turtle elder (Toupin 1996, 205), with the words "separe...reuni" ("separated...reunited"). In the material for the Striped Turtle dominated house PV10, she is listed as his wife (Toupin 1996, 209) in the first census, but as "separee" in the second (Toupin 1996, 244). Given the close connection between A,otiok8andoron and Potier, I think there would have been significant pressure brought to bear to reunite them.

Toupin speculated that she was wife to the Snake clan elder hannenratendi (Toupin 1996, 185), as there is an "osk8ara" listed as his wife for a baptism in 1744 (Toupin 1996, 853, B621), but she would have been forty-six then, unusually old for giving birth. A "sk8aara" was listed as his wife in PV8 (Toupin 1996, 207). I suspect that might have been the Marguerite Sk8arak, the eleven-year-old Fox-fathered girl baptized in 1734 (Toupin 1996, 835, B262). There were two Fox listed as living in PV8. Support for my hypothesis that Angelique was only wife to A,otiok8andoron and not Hannenratendi comes from the fact that Angelique Sk8aara was the godmother for Sk88tache's ten-year-old daughter Angelique in 1729 (Toupin 1996, 824, B44). She was not involved with anniversary services.

Porcupine Clan

Marguerite Atsironde "She goes on all fours": First-Named Elder
Porcupine elder Marguerite Atsironde and her husband Charles Tsoaisens were the first Wyandot couple to be married in Christian ceremony. The ceremony was performed on 11 October 1728 (Toupin 1996, 821, M1). This was the day after Tsoaisens was baptized, leading me to believe that the push for Christian ceremony came from Atsironde. She might have been one of the clan "matrons" who Charlevoix spoke about; her husband one of the "principal men" who were resistant. When Father Armand de la Richardie

wrote in 1741 about "Hoosiens" "having embraced the [C]hristian faith after much delay" (see quotation above), the probable primary influence working on him was Marguerite Atsironde.

There would not be another marriage recorded until 1746, when the new missionary Father Pierre Potier arrived.

The Christian couple had three children baptized in 1729, ages eleven, thirteen, and seven (Toupin 1996, 822–23, B18, B19, B26), one of them (they had two children called Joseph), no doubt, the Joseph who became the elder T'on8atsarandi. Her eldest was christened "Armandus" in the Latinized form in the baptismal record, named after the missionary who had married her and her husband the year before.

Hers was the first name in a Porcupine clan dominated house with thirty-eight names attached to it, one of the larger houses in the Petit Village. It was recorded (Toupin 1996, 932) that she died in 1785 at age seventy-four, but she would probably have been older than that. If the son was hers who was baptized at thirteen in 1729, she would have given birth in 1716. She was probably in her late eighties when she died and in her late forties when she was an elder in 1747.

Marie ,Atera "Tree root"[30]

The first baptism of a child of hers was in 1731 (Toupin 1996, 829) and a daughter of hers had a child baptized in 1743 (Toupin 1996, 852), so she must have been at least in her late thirties in 1747. Her husband was the Large Turtle elder, Nicolas Taronhi8rens.

Her family seems to have had Huron connections. Her sister Marie had the name "8endo,ench" (Toupin 1996, 924), which seems to be the same name as the "Aoendoens" who appears in *The Jesuit Relations* of 1657 (JR43:122–23). Her daughter Marie had the name "8end8s" (Toupin 1996, 926) or ",A8end8s" (Toupin 1996, 853), which is the same name as the "Aouendous" who appears in *The Jesuit Relations* of 1646 (JR29:282–83), possibly as a Rock nation name.

She participated in the anniversary service six times in 1759 and 1760, once as a main figure (SA1–2, SA5, SA14, SA16, SA17, Toupin 1996, 942–46, 948–52). Three of her grandchildren also participated (SA14, SA18, Toupin 1996, 948–50, 953–54).

Aronhiet

The data surrounding this name is confusing. She did not seem to be living in any of the village houses. There is reference to a Marie-Jeanne ,Aronhiet in 1755 (Toupin 1996, 926), giving a gift of leggings and some wampum to honour the death of Christine ,Arhonnens of the Large Turtle clan. She also had children baptized in 1751 (Toupin 1996, 860, B739), 1755 (Toupin 1996, 869, B866), and 1759 (Toupin 1996, 878, B1000). In addition, she participated in three anniversary services in 1760 (Toupin 1996, 929, SA16, 17, 20). However, there is a six-year-old girl, Marie-Joseph, daughter of Snake clan elder Susanne Sendañiont (Toupin 1996, 206), who went by this name in 1747 (Toupin 1996, 206), and who had her first child baptized in 1751 (Toupin 1996, 860). Perhaps the name was shared by both clans, which is possible considering my hypothesis that the Snake clan may have been "recruiting" names and people.

Striped Turtle

Marie Ts8ndehe and Te 8arachiande
Marie Ts8ndehe was the leading female elder of the Striped Turtle clan, even though her mother Te 8arachiarande, who was not an elder, was the first person mentioned in her house (PV15). Ts8ndehe was her eldest daughter, while Ka8oindi, another clan elder, was her youngest.

My suspicions are that one reason her mother was not named an elder was that she was not able to blend Christianity with the traditions of her people, as the female elders tended to do. She was not baptized, nor was she ever a godmother. Interestingly, a new woman bearing the name Te 8arachiarande would shift the positioning of those two names, having children of hers baptized in 1756, 1759, 1766 (Toupin 1996, 872, 879, 888, B910, B1017, B1143), and 1768, the last-named instance with Ts8ndehe as the godmother (Toupin 1996, 891, B1193). She was also, with the first name Christine, a godmother in 1767 and 1774 (Toupin 1996, 890, 897, B1172, B1287).

Ts8ndehe's first child was baptized in 1735 (Toupin 1996, 837), which suggests that Marie was at least in her late forties in 1747 when she was an elder. Ts8ndehe's first husband was Jacques Ta,echiaten, leader of the wolf clan and the wolf phratry. Her second husband was Hondechonti, of the Deer clan.

She bore the French nickname "goitre," so may have had some kind of a neck disorder. Still, that possible deformity did not prevent her from being named and considered an elder.

Marie ,Aennench
She was married to Bear elder Honarak, and had her first child baptized in 1731 (Toupin 1996, 829, B143), so she must at least have been in her early thirties as an elder. Her last child was baptized in 1752 (Toupin 1996, 864), so we know that she was still in her child-bearing years in 1747. Interestingly, the father of her first two baptized children was Ndo,entet, Orontondi's son, and the first child's godfather was Orontondi (Toupin 1996, 829, B143).

She was a leading participant in the anniversary services, being involved nineteen times between 1759 and 1771 (Toupin 1996, 943–44, 949–52, 954, 960–62, 964, 966, 970–71, 973, 975), three times as a major sponsor (Toupin 1996, 967, 969, SA30, SA33, SA34).

Marie Ka8oindi

She was the youngest daughter of Striped Turtle elder Ts8ndehe, and lived in a small house (PV15) with her. The first baptism of a child of hers was in 1735 (Toupin 1996, 837), and the last was in 1746 (Toupin 1996, 856), making her at least about thirty and still in her child-bearing years in 1747. Her husband, Antoine Te,atak, was an elder of the Large Turtle clan. As with her fellow clan elders of the Striped Turtle, she was an important participant in the anniversary services, her name being recorded seven times from 1759 to 1760.

Marie A8oindaara

Her first child was baptized in 1729 (Toupin 1996, 824). At that time she was married to Porcupine clan elder, Joseph t'on8atsandi's predecessor, Baptiste. Her last child was baptized in 1739 (Toupin 1996, 846), when she was married to Bear clan elder Taretande. She was probably at least in her mid-thirties in 1747. Her husband Taretande was thirty-two.

Consistent within her position as a female elder of this clan was her extensive participation in the anniversary services, fifteen times, from 1759 to 1771. She also participated in an anniversary in 1755, and two testament anniversaries in 1764 and 1765 (Toupin 1996, 957, 958).

Other Striped Turtle Women of Significance

Dorothée Sk8atandi

Dorothée Sk8atandi was the first person named in the Striped Turtle dominated house PV10. She was the mother of two Striped Turtle elders, Marie ,Aenench and Marie Marguerite Te ondise8a. She was godmother of an adult Abenaki man in 1732 (B2180), and also was a godmother in 1734 (B308) and 1743 (B592, Toupin 1996, 837, 851). She died on 28 September 1746 (Toupin 1996, 921, E9). Her name was revived by at least 1775 (Toupin 1996, 900, B1325).

Prairie Turtle Clan

Catherine Sa8ointondi

Catherine Sa8ointondi (also written as Sa8entondi), the first-listed female elder of the Prairie Turtle clan, was clearly a woman of influence among the Wyandot. The Prairie Turtle clan leader Ts8nnonkanien and elder Ta,ennrak were both sons of hers. Her husband was Bear clan leader and first-listed elder Aıa8as. Although her husband's name was listed first by Potier, just before hers, the dwelling in which they lived was a Prairie Turtle house (PV11). It appears to have been a house of some significance as there were forty-nine people recorded as living there, although some of them were written as being in two different houses (one of the persistent problems of the census, see Appendix A). That was the largest number for any house in the Petit Village.

On 16 September 1731, she had three of her children baptized: twelve-year-old Mathias Ta,ennrak (Toupin 1996, 829, B156), who at twenty-eight would be an elder; ten-year-old Louise Ondichi8ri (Toupin 1996, 829, B160); and newborn Stanislaus Tondat8at (Toupin 1996, 829, B162). She was probably at least in her late forties when she was an elder in 1747. In 1736, she was a godmother of an adult woman (Toupin 1996, 840, B371). She died in 1752 (Toupin 1996, 924, E67). There is no official evidence of her name being revived.

Tando,ares

Hannenhasa's sister Tando,ares was also in the elders' council, and she lived in the Prairie Turtle house GV2 as well (Toupin 1996, 216). She was Bear elder Ennons' third wife, but they were separated (Toupin 1996, 215). It is noteworthy that both Tando,ares and Tsa8ointondi married prominent members of the Bear clan, pointing perhaps to a special link between the two clans.

Her name does not appear in the baptismal record. This record is made a little confusing by the fact that there was a Striped Turtle female called Agnes Tando,ares, who was seven years old in 1747 (Toupin 1996, 208, PV9), and who had a child baptized in 1761 (Toupin 1996, 882, B1050).

Wolf Clan

Marie Jeanne ,Aendi: First-Named Elder

Marie-Jeanne ,Aendi was a major player of religious roles. She was the leading participant in the anniversary services, as we saw above. She participated not just in gift-giving (which she did for twenty services), but also in a more distinctive role. The Wyandot term used for this role is ehotrendaentak8an (also spelled ehotrendaentak8oin), which means "(s)he will pray for him for such a reason or purpose." As we have seen, she performed this sacred Wyandot Christian role in ten of the forty-two ceremonies, from 29 May 1768 to 28 May 1769 (Toupin 1996, 960–75). No one else, male or female, did so nearly this often. She participated in the Testament Anniversary three times.

She was seven times a godmother, in 1742 (B556), 1751 (B739, B753), 1754 (B829, B857), 1758 (B958), and 1768 (B1174, Toupin 1996, 850, 860–61, 867, 869, 876, 890). The only recorded baptism of a child of hers was in 1749 (Toupin 1996, 858, B714), so she was young for an elder in 1747. Perhaps that was because Nondeaon, the mother or the mother's sister (still called mother by her nephews in Wyandot kinship), of the male clan leader Hondatorenha, and thus a possible elder, died in 1746. Perhaps the two older Wolf clan women, whose Wyandot names were not presented by Potier, just called "La vielle Marie" and "La vielle Louve," were not connected enough with the church and the missionary to be given an elder's role.

Marie-Joseph Nenditaxon

She had nine children baptized from 1737 to 1756 (Toupin 1996, 844, 846, 849, 851, 854, 859, 862, 866, 873), so she was probably somewhere from her late twenties to mid-thirties in 1747. Her husband was Atironta, the nephew of Deer clan elder Marie Nendaentons. She was a godmother once (Toupin 1996, 851, B585), and participated in an anniversary service (Toupin 1996, 950–51, SA15).

Other Significant Wolf Women
Nondeaon

Nondeaon was the mother of Hondatorenha, and the mother's sister (who would be termed "mother" by the Wyandot, but aunt for Potier) of Ta,echiaten. She was also the head of the one house dominated by the Wolf (GV12). Nondeaon may have been the woman named Marie, who was a godmother in 1736 (as ondaiehaon; Toupin 1996, 839, B354), 1739 (as ondaiehaon; Toupin 1996, 846, B487), and 1745 (as nondaiehaon; Toupin 1996, 854, B641).

SUMMARY

We have seen in this chapter that there is information from Potier's writing about women of influence among the eighteenth-century Wyandot. Primarily, we have looked at those women who were members of the elders' council. These were women who were generally middle-aged, early thirties to mid-fifties. There were older women who were not included in their number, although they may have been when they were younger. Here I am speaking primarily about those who were mothers of female elders—

prominent women such as Deer clan member Catherine Sk8ateenre, Striped Turtle Dorothée Sk8atandi, and Snake A8endii. The last two were also the first-named individuals in their houses. Sk8ateenre wasn't, but then, she lived in the house of the grand chief Sastaretsi, who was first named in their house. Perhaps we can say that they had "retired" from the role of active participants in politics, but still were highly regarded. They were well-connected in the community. Many had husbands who were also elders. Some had brothers, sons, or daughters who were also on the council. We can say that there was something of a ranking system with these women, with the women who were listed first having more authority, possibly being what can be called a "clan matron," although such a term was unused by Jesuit recorders, even Potier. These women were quite likely to be godparents. We can also say that these women were quite involved with religious rituals, particularly baptism and also the various ways in which the dead were honoured. These rituals, while approved by the missionaries, probably contained significant traditional Wyandot components as well, particularly the rituals of mourning. It is strongly suspected that they were the keepers of such traditions, as leading participants in the Christian rituals.

Chapter Eight

A Summary

We have been looking at the history of the Wyandot people, from their formation from two Wendat peoples (called by the French Petun and Huron), or possibly three (including the Neutre or Neutral), in the mid-seventeenth century, into the eighteenth century, with some references to the people in the nineteenth and early twentieth centuries. The main focus has been on 1747, when the new missionary Jesuit Father Pierre Potier compiled two similar censuses that, along with his church records of baptisms, marriages, and death memorials, comprise one of the best collections of data on an Aboriginal people in North America for the time period. As I tried to demonstrate in terms of the interests and aims of this book, much can be done with these primary documents. I have taken one path, there are doubtless others as well.

Special emphasis has been on the clan nature of the Wyandot, demonstrating how the clan system can become a way for people to socially survive and politically struggle against the challenges facing them in the swirling waters of a dramatically changing social landscape. When the larger social unit breaks up or faces possible destruction, the clans are foundations, flexible but strong, upon which such a people can depend.

The ancestral peoples founding the Wyandot were scattered west and east midway through the seventeenth century and, through clan leaders and their fellow clan members, acted out strategies that insured the survival of the people. Once the people came back together in the Detroit/Windsor area, the clans regrouped. When the Jesuit missionaries came to live with them, different clans pursued strategies that gave the Wyandot flexibility and strength to survive the dangerous times in which they lived.

They also actively recruited members from other peoples, perpetuating a strategy that had long served them well.

CLAN STRUCTURE OF THE WYANDOT

To review from earlier chapters, the Wyandot had ten clans, bundled into three phratries or collections of clans. These clans were as follows:

Deer Phratry
Deer clan
Snake clan
Bear clan

Turtle Phratry
Large Turtle clan
Porcupine clan
Striped Turtle clan
Prairie Turtle clan

Wolf Phratry
Wolf clan
Hawk clan
Sturgeon/Aataensik clan

The elders' council of these people suggests that only eight of these clans (excluding the Hawk and the Sturgeon/Aataensik clans of the Wolf phratry) were of significance in 1747, as only these eight contributed elders to the council.

During the latter half of the seventeenth century, the formative period for the Wyandot as a distinct people, several leaders emerged as significant. They were as follows, proceeding in the same clan order as above, with the clan I believe that each may have represented:

Late-Seventeenth-Century Wyandot Male Leaders

Deer Phratry
Sastaretsi	Deer clan
Quarante Sols	Bear clan

Turtle Phratry
Sk88tache   Porcupine clan
Baron   Prairie Turtle clan

Wolf Phratry
Kandiaronk   Wolf clan

Significantly, all three phratries—Deer, Turtle, and Wolf—are represented by these individuals, with the two more influential phratries having two of these figures each, as would be expected.

Eventually, the results of their strategies would be that the people would come together in related migrations to the Windsor/Detroit area during the early 1700s, their primary home during the eighteenth century.

Starting in the late 1720s, the Wyandot would be missioned to by first Jesuit Father Armand de la Richardie (1728–51), then later and longer by Father Pierre Potier (1746–81). Each of these missionaries would have different relationships with the clans. Father Richardie would be adopted by the Deer clan, who were following what can be called a "typical" Deer clan strategy of being close to the French, particularly the missionaries. Father Potier would be adopted by the Wolf clan, taking on a name that was first given to a missionary (Father Pierre Joseph-Marie Chaumonot) in the 1640s by what I suspect were a Wolf-identified clan or nation of the Neutral, the least documented of the three foundational nations of the Wyandot.

Father Richardie also early on had a good relationship with the Porcupine clan, which would be disturbed by the rise and the military tactics of Porcupine clan leader Nicholas Orontondi in the mid-1740s. Richardie had supported Orontondi against Prairie Turtle clan leader ,Ang8irot, but once ,Ang8irot died, and Orontondi showed some independence, that support seems to have been withdrawn.

Father Richardie's relationship with the Prairie Turtle clan was quite different. He opposed, with both fair means and foul, their leader Ang8irot, who was also the Turtle phratry leader, and therefore one of the three most influential men in Wyandot society. Their connection with Christian ceremonies was less than that of any other Wyandot clan. This would appear to reflect, at least in part, the nature of their relationship with Richardie. Potier seemed to have at least tried to reconnect that clan with the French and Christian mission, paying special attention to them in 1747, as seen by his demonstrated knowledge of their ages. He spent time with them, but it does not seem to have paid off in terms of their coming under his influence, at least for the clan as a whole.

THE CENSUSES OF 1747

Potier's two censuses of 1747 of the two villages that made up the main communities of the Wyandot are very informative sources to work with, despite some flaws such as contradictions in the two censuses and people being mentioned more than once (see Appendix A). Still, we can say that there were about five hundred people living in these communities, also that the number of people in any given house could vary, but could be quite large, along the traditional lines of the first half of the seventeenth century, rather than the smaller dwellings of their Algonquian-speaking neighbours (from one of whose languages came the English word "wigwam"), or the European-influenced nuclear family based on single-family dwellings. Further, where clan identity of the individuals can be determined, clan dominance in houses can be clearly demonstrated. This can be seen for most houses. The Deer and Snake clan houses seem to show a kind of phratry connection as they were typically located beside each other. It might also relate to the fact that the Deer clan was said to have given birth to the Snake clan. They had some sort of special connection.

The censuses also reveal that clan exogamy, marrying outside the clan, was still maintained at this time, but that the same did not exist for phratry exogamy, which may or may not have been a traditional practice. Most marriages where clan was identified showed that there appears to have been a slight statistical preference for partners of the same phratry.

An amazing and very informative feature of the census is Potier's recording of the elders' council. It helped in the identification of the clan membership of a good number of the Wyandot of 1747. It also helped in the compilation of the male leadership structure of the Wyandot of the time:

Male Political Leader Chart for 1747

Leadership Position	Name	Clan
Grand Chief	Mathias Sastaretsi	Deer
Phratry Chiefs		
Deer Phratry	Mathias Sastaretsi	Deer
Turtle Phratry	,Ang8irot	Prairie Turtle
	Sa,ents8at (after ,Ang8irot died)	Large Turtle
Wolf Phratry	Jacques Ta,echiaten	Wolf
Assistant Phratry Chiefs		
	Nicolas Orontondi	Porcupine
	Pierre Tiao8endata (le Manchot)	Porcupine

	Francois-Regis Ondannhont	Deer
	S8ndak8a (agnioton) Le brutal	Sturgeon
	Nicolas Taronhi8rens (bricon)	Large Turtle
	Mathias Ondachiate,en	Snake
Clan Leaders		
	Mathias Sastaretsi	Deer
	Mathias Ondachiate,en	Snake
	A,a8as	Bear
	Ennons	Bear
	Aron-issa(s)	Large Turtle
	Nicolas Orontondi	Porcupine
	Pierre Tiao8endata	Porcupine
	Jean-Baptiste Otiok8andoron	Striped Turtle
	,Ang8irot (recently died)	Prairie Turtle
	Thomas Ts8nnonkanien	Prairie Turtle
	Jacques Ta,echiaten	Wolf
	Jacques Hondatorenha	Wolf
Elders' Council Members		
Leading Figure	Mathias Sastaretsi	Deer
	Etienne Eñie8indet	Deer
Leading Figure	Stanislaus 8asañion	Snake
	Mathias Hannenratendi	Snake
	Jean-Baptiste Ndikaratase	Snake
	Barnabe Anien8indet	Snake
	Tannenhochre	Snake
Leading Figure	A,a8as	Bear
	André Sohondinnon	Bear
	Pierre Ochienda,ete	Bear
	Nicolas Taretande	Bear
	Ennons	Bear
	Honarak	Bear
Leading Figure	Sa,ents8at	Large Turtle
	Aron-issa	Large Turtle
	Antoine Hondechiaren8an[1]	Large Turtle
	Pierre 8en8oin	Large Turtle
	Jean-Baptiste Te horonhi8texa	Large Turtle
	Nicolas Taronhi8rens	Large Turtle
Leading Figure	Joseph T'on8atsarandi	Porcupine
	Nicolas Orontondi	Porcupine

Leading Figure	Jean-Baptiste Otiok8andoron	Striped Turtle
	Martin Sa8end8at	Striped Turtle
	Pierre Harih8andiniontak	Striped Turtle
	Joseph Tso,a8enda	Striped Turtle
Leading Figure	Hannenhasa	Prairie Turtle
	Tahatie	Prairie Turtle
	Mathias Ta,annrak	Prairie Turtle
	Otren-i8oin	Prairie Turtle
Leading Figure	Tandere-i8oin	Wolf
	Jacques Handatorenha	Wolf

PEACE CHIEF AND WAR CHIEF

In chapter 6, we discussed the idea that there were war chiefs among the Wyandot of this time. Three names stick out right away because of war references presented right after their names: A,a8as and Sohondinnon of the Bear clan, and Tso,a8enda of the Striped Turtle clan. It was further suggested that perhaps Sa,ents8at of the Large Turtle clan, and Orontondi of the Porcupine clan, were similarly war chiefs. It should be noted that the elders' council does not include four clan leaders: Ondachiate,en of the Snake clan, Pierre Tiao8endata of the Porcupine clan, Ts8nnonkanien of the Prairie Turtle clan, and Ta,echiaten of the Wolf clan. Perhaps they were peace chiefs in opposition to war chiefs presented in the elders' council: 8asanion (Snake), T'on8atsarandi (Porcupine), Hannenhasa (Prairie Turtle), and/or Tandere-i8oin (Wolf). Or did it work the other way? It is hard to know. What we can say is that a group of war chiefs existed, and may have had members representing every clan. And some war chiefs, like the peace chiefs, played more significant roles than the others.

FEMALE LEADERSHIP

The details of female leadership are much more difficult to establish because of the male biases of the two main recorders of data, Father Armand de Richardie and Father Pierre Potier. Yet, there is material that is presented that can help us try to determine who the most influential women in the community were. Perhaps the most distinctly useful aspect of Potier's recording of the elders' council was his references to the rarely mentioned "anciennes" or female elders. This enabled me to discuss the female leaders of the Wyandot, not just the usual male members. Altogether, we have four basic factors of significance to operate with when discussing female leadership among the Wyandot: first named in houses, first named in the elders list, membership in the elders list, and significant participation in Christian-based religious ceremonies or rituals. We can use these factors to form the following chart:

Female Leadership Chart

Phratry	Clan	Name	1st in House	List Number	Ritual Participation
Deer	Deer	Marie Nendaentons	Yes	1st	Yes
Deer	Deer	Jeanne Sendak8an	No[2]	2nd	No
Deer	Deer	Marie Nendeñiont	No	3rd	Yes
Deer	Deer	Catherine Onnond8annon	No	4th	No
Deer	Deer	Louise 8tsia	Yes	---	Yes
Deer	Deer	Catherine Sk8ateenre	No	---	Yes
Deer	Deer	Christine 8ndaenton	Yes	---	No
Deer	Snake	Susanne Sendaniont	No[3]	1st	Yes
Deer	Snake	Te Ondise8a	No	---	No
Deer	Snake	Susanne Ts8ndendora	Yes	---	Yes
Deer	Bear	Anastasie Ts8nde,en	Yes	1st	Yes
Deer	Bear	Françoise Niendaharonk	No	2nd	Yes
Deer	Bear	Onnond8	No	3rd	Yes
Deer	Bear	Teaias	No	4th	No
Deer	Bear	Marie Tsa8endask8aen	Yes	5th	No
Deer	Bear	Christine A8innonke	No	6th	No
Deer	Bear	Franciscus Asenra,e-haon	Yes[4]	7th	No
Turtle	Large Turtle	Christine ,Arhonnens	No	1st	Yes
Turtle	Large Turtle	Anne Sa8oindiandii	Yes	2nd	Yes
Turtle	Large Turtle	8ta8ata	Yes	3rd	No
Turtle	Large Turtle	Anne A8innonke	No	4th	Yes
Turtle	Large Turtle	Angelique Osk8ara	No	5th	No
Turtle	Porcupine	Marguerite Atsironde	Yes	1st	Yes
Turtle	Porcupine	Marie ,Atera	Yes[5]	2nd	Yes
Turtle	Porcupine	Aronhiet	No	3rd	No
Turtle	Striped Turtle	Marie Ts8ndehe	No	1st	Yes
Turtle	Striped Turtle	Marie ,Aennench	No	2nd	Yes
Turtle	Striped Turtle	Marie Kaoindi	No	3rd	Yes
Turtle	Striped Turtle	Marie A8oindaara	No	4th	Yes
Turtle	Striped Turtle	Dorothée Sk8atandi	Yes	---	Yes
Turtle	Striped Turtle	Te 8arachiarande	Yes	---	No

Turtle	Prairie Turtle	Catherine Tsa8ointondi	Yes[6]	1st	Yes
Turtle	Prairie Turtle	Tando,ares	No	2nd	No
Wolf	Wolf	Marie-Jeanne ,Aendi	No	1st	Yes
Wolf	Wolf	Marie-Joseph NenditaXon	No	2nd	Yes
Wolf	Wolf	Nondeaon	Yes	---	Yes

Looked at in this way we can see that the four women who were first in their houses, first in their clan's elder list, and major participants in Christian-based rituals—Marie Nendaentons of the Deer clan, Anastasie Ts8nde,en of the Bear clan, Marguerite Atsironde of the Porcupine clan, and Catherine Tsa8ointondi of the Prairie Turtle clan—were all leading women among the Wyandot of the mid-eighteenth century. The first three named also exhibited other signs of authority. Marie Nendaentons had the French missionary Father Armand de la Richardie as her adopted brother. Anastasie Ts8nde,en had two sons and a brother as fellow elders, and Marguerite Atsironde had a son as an elder, himself, like her, the first-named elder of his gender for his clan.

It should be noted that all the elders of the Striped Turtle clan were called Marie, and all of them were involved with Christian-based rituals. There could be a connection there.

We can see that all these women were active in the ritual life of the people especially in the deathways, or in nominally Christian ceremonies honouring the dead.

CLANS AND VILLAGES

One of the largely unresolved questions concerning Wendat and other Iroquoian peoples of the first two centuries of contact is the relationship between clans and villages. Did one clan dominate each village? Were all clans equally represented in each village? With our admittedly small sample here, plus the intervening factor of the Jesuits and the French generally, we can at least suggest that perhaps villages had uneven representation of each clan, with some clans tending to be stronger than others, but with no one clan overwhelmingly dominant.

With the two Wyandot communities of Petit Village (which had a population around 300 hundred with nineteen houses) and Grand Village (which had a population of around 230 with fifteen houses), we can see that the clans were represented differently in the two villages. In terms of the number of people identified by clan and the number of houses dominated by a particular clan we can see a pattern. Thirteen of the sixteen populated houses in the Petit Village and eight of the thirteen populated houses in the Grand Village have such clan dominance. In the chart of "Clan-Identified Individuals and Houses" we can see that in the Petit Village, three of the Turtle Phratry clans, Porcupine, Striped Turtle, and Prairie Turtle, as well as the Wolf clan, have a clear majority of their clan-identified members and houses. For the Grand Village, the Large Turtle clan has twice as many members and all of their clan houses. For the Deer phratry clans, there is a fairly even balance between the two villages, both in clan-identified members and in clan houses.

Clan Nature of the Two Villages

Clan-Identified Individuals and Houses

	Le Petit Village Clan Count		Le Grand Village Clan Count		
	Number Identified	Clan Houses Identified	Number Identified	Clan Houses Identified	Total Houses
Deer	29	2	26	2	4
Snake	19	2	10	1	3
Bear	32	2	32	1	3
Large Turtle	20	0	41	2	2
Porcupine	36	3	5	0	3
Striped Turtle	50	3	5	0	3
Prairie Turtle	35	1	10	1	2
Wolf	6	0	21	1	1
Sturgeon	0	0	1	0	0
Total	227	13	151	8	21

Now, looking at leadership, we see that the Petit Village has a greater score in terms of both male and female elders, even considering that there are seven (two Deer, one Bear, two Striped Turtle, one Prairie Turtle, and one Wolf) recorded as living in both communities. For male elders the numbers are twenty-one to twelve, for female elders twenty-two to seventeen, for a significant total difference of forty-three to twenty-nine.

Clan Elders and Their Communities

Le Petit Village				Le Grand Village Clan Count		
	Elders Male	Female	Total	Elders Male	Female	Total
Deer	2	3	5	0	3	3
Snake	4	1	5	0	1	1
Bear	3	7	10	6	5	11
Large Turtle	4	3	7	2	3	5
Porcupine	2	3	5	0	0	0
Striped Turtle	3	2	5	0	3	3
Prairie Turtle	2	2	4	3	1	4
Wolf	1	1	2	1	1	2
Elders Total	21	22	43	12	17	29

If we look at the recorded male clan leaders, we can see further that authority rested more in the Petit Village than in the Grand Village. Every clan leader was recorded as living either just in the Petit Village (nine) or in both villages (two). All the phratry leaders lived either in the Petit Village (three) or in both (one).

Male Clan Leaders (Men Named as Leaders of Their Clans)

			Phratry Leader
Deer	Sastaretsi	PV	1
Snake	Mathias Ondachiate,en	PV	0
Bear	A,a8as	PV	0
Large Turtle	Aron-issa	PV	0
Porcupine	Orontondi	PV	0
	le Manchot	PV	0
Striped Turtle	A,otiok8andoron	PV	0
Prairie Turtle	,Ang8irot	PV	1
	Ts8nnonkanien	both villages	1
Wolf	Ta,echiaten	PV	1
	Hondatorenha	both villages	0

There is a similar imbalance with the female clan leaders, those who were first named in the elders' council list. Five were recorded as living only in the PV, two in both villages, and only one in the GV.

Female Clan Leaders (First-Named in Elder List)

Deer	Nendaentons	both villages
Snake	Sendaniont	PV
Bear	Ts8nde,en	GV
Large Turtle	,Arhonnens	PV
Porcupine	Atsironde	PV
Striped Turtle	Ts8ndehe	both villages
Prairie Turtle	Tsa8ointondi	PV
Wolf	,Aendi	PV

CONCLUSIONS

The anonymous are victims of the history process, as you cannot even contest prior telling of their story, even to say that they are important, too much so to be ignored. What I have tried to do in this book is to take away the anonymity and casual mention of people who matter in the history of the Wyandot and of the Great Lakes in the eighteenth century. I have tried to both bring new information to light and to interpret that information. It is hoped that other scholars can put their own unique insights into this new information, so their interpretations go beyond and improve upon what I have thought and written here.

For scholars studying similar peoples, with similar records to draw on, this book can serve as a comparative work that could bring understanding to their own analyses. I often wished I had such a comparative work when I was trying to put this book together.

Appendices

APPENDIX A: THE CENSUS

Jesuit Father Pierre Potier compiled his census sometime early in 1747, before the 20 May raid by Orontondi's war party. It incorporates two villages, which Potier terms "Le petit village" and "Le grand village" (hereafter referred to as PV and GV, respectively), as well as two outlying settlements of Etionnont8t and A,aa,e. As we have seen, this naming of the two communities is a little strange in that the "little" village was somewhat larger than the "big" village. The census lists not just the names of a vast majority of the people, but also outlines the kinship and marriage relationships between most of them, as well as identifying the ethnic origin of some of the people who have been adopted by the Wyandot. There is hierarchy involved too, with the first named for each house being the most senior both in age and generally in status.

Unfortunately, Potier did not include the clan identity of the people in the houses. That does not mean, however, that they cannot be known. As discussed in chapter 5, through the clan identities that he provided for the members of the elders' council, and the clan identities provided through a few other less numerically significant means, I have been able to include the clan identities of many of the people in the houses, and will be including them in this outline of the inhabitants of the houses. In addition, we can also determine fairly reliably the clan dominance patterns of almost all of the houses.

While having this census material is a great gift to the researcher, trying to come up with an accurate picture can be an exercise in frustration. Absolute precision is not possible with this data, but getting a strong general sense of the two communities is achievable, and enlightening.

Two Main Difficulties with the Census

People Mentioned More Than Once
One of the more challenging aspects of dealing with Potier's census is his practice of repeating names in different houses. There are several potential

reasons for this double recording that I can see. One is that people did not confine their living to just one house, but, over time, could stay at one or another location possibly deriving from a number of social and seasonal factors. The Wyandot of the eighteenth century did not need a "permanent address" such as we have today in order to fill out governmental forms. They did engage in hunting and trading away from the community, so families might have moved out at various times, and then moved back to a new house if the old one had become filled in the interim. Or this could be an artifact of Potier wanting to write down lineage lists as well as who is actually in the house. While I am leaning towards the first possibility, I cannot be sure at this point. Perhaps both are in play.

There were forty-nine people who were recorded as dwelling in more than one house: eighteen twice in the Petit Village (PV); six twice in the Grand Village (GV); twenty-one in both; one in two PV houses and one GV house; one in two GV houses and one PV house; one in a PV house and in Etionnont8t; and one in both villages and in Etionnont8t.

Calculating the population of the Petit Village, we have 337 people listed. If you subtract the eighteen repeats plus ten from those in both villages, we get a rough population total of 309. For the Grand Village, we have 249 people listed minus the six repeats, ten from the two village dwellers and one from both this village and Etionnont8t, we get a rough estimate of 232 people. So we can talk about the population of the Wyandot at this time as being a little over 500 people.

House Lists That Don't Match
There actually was not one census list but two (Toupin 1996, 200–37 for the first census and add-ons, and 237–66 for the second). There is no explanation why. This is useful in terms of one providing further information that the other lacks, but can be confounding in that often the lists from the two censuses do not contain an identical set of people. In compiling my list, I have tended to err on the side of including everyone mentioned. Usually, the people listed are in the same order, but not always. And the first census tends to be the most complete of the two in terms of whom it includes in each house.

Again, in my reproduction of the census, I have tried to convey a general picture, not an absolutely precise one. The main points relate to such facts as:

a) a particular individual is mentioned first in a house list, showing her or his significance;
b) a house has a large population or a small one;
c) a house is dominated by a particular clan;

d) a house has a significant number of elders in it;
e) certain clans are linked.

These kinds of statements can be made with a reasonable degree of accuracy as they do not require a high degree of precision.

The Census: House Residents, Relationships, and Key Figures
Recognizing that with the flaws mentioned above, there can be no such thing as complete accuracy of the census; what I am presenting below is an educated guess, with some repeats of who is living in what house, what their relationships are, and who are the major figures (indicated with bolding). Where there is a clear clan dominance of a house, this is indicated in the heading, as is the ethnicity of the inhabitants where it differs from being Wyandot. The estimated number of people in the house, and the number of elders in the house, are presented at the end of each house list. Ages, where given by Potier, are included in each house list.

PV1: Porcupine (Toupin 1996, 182-83, 202-3, 240-41)
Atsironde (leading Porcupine elder)
her eldest daughter
her daughter's husband and their four daughters and two sons (the first four aged thirteen, twelve, seven, and three)
her eldest son (thirty-one)
her second-eldest son (**Joseph T'on8atsarandi** (twenty-nine)—Porcupine elder)
his wife and their two daughters and one son (the eldest two aged four and two)
a man, his wife, and their daughter
Atsironde's two nephews
Atsironde's niece and her husband
Atsironde's niece
Atsironde's adopted Fox sister
her three daughters
someone's daughter
five children of Makons
seven others (anonymous)
Estimated Population   45: 20 Porcupine, 4 Bear, 2 Wolf, 1 Striped Turtle, and 1 Snake
Number of Elders   2
Number of Ages   8

PV2: Striped Turtle, Porcupine, and Large Turtle (Toupin 1996, 183, 204–5, 241–42)
Louis Sk8tache (fifty-six) Porcupine
Sk8tache's daughter (Striped Turtle), her husband (Porcupine elder **Tio-8endata**), their two daughters and two sons (the eldest being ten, four, and three)
Sk8tache's daughter
Sk8tache's niece
Tio8endata's adopted Chickasaw man
Sk8tache's wife
three daughters and two sons (eighteen, thirteen, eight, five, and three-months old)
Nicolas Orontondi (Porcupine elder)
Sk8tache's eldest son and his wife
his second son
his daughter
adopted Fox woman
Anne A8innonke (Large Turtle female elder)
Angelique Sk8âra (her daughter and Large Turtle female elder; forty-nine)
her daughter (twenty), her husband, and their daughter (two) and son (one)
Sk8ara's adopted Chickasaw brother
Sk8âra's husband (Striped Turtle elder—**Baptiste Otiok8endoron**)
Mathias Aron-issas (Large Turtle elder) and his Ottawa wife
Estimated Population 31: 13 Striped Turtle, 7 Large Turtle, 5 Porcupine, and 1 Bear
Number of Elders   5
Number of Ages   12

PV3: Iroquois
Therese 8e8as
her eldest son and his wife
three more sons
her sister
Estimated Population   7: 1 Snake
Number of Elders   0
Number of Ages   0

PV4: Snake (Toupin 1996, 184, 206, 242, Snake Clan)
Jacques Ta,echiaten (Wolf phratry leader)
two sons (with former wife **Ts8ndehe**—Striped Turtle elder)
his second wife (**Susanne Sendanion**—Snake elder)
their daughter
Sendanion's three sons (the first two aged twenty and eighteen) from a previous marriage
Estimated Population 9: 7 Snake, 1 Wolf, and 1 Striped Turtle
Number of Elders 2
Number of Ages 0

PV6: Deer (Toupin 1996, 185, 206, 242–43)
Mathias Ondachiate,en (Snake clan leader)
his wife (**Louise 8tsïa**—Deer)
their son
8tsia's adopted Fox brother and his wife
Abenaki man (thirty-seven)
8tsia's two nieces (twenty and nine) and one nephew (eight)
8tsia's sister (Deer elder **Marie Nendaentons**)
her husband (Large Turtle elder **Baptiste Te horonhiotexa**)
Estimated Population 11: 2 Snake, 7 Deer and 1 Large Turtle
Number of Elders 2
Number of Ages 4

PV7 (Toupin 1996, 185, 207, 243)
A8endii Snake
her eldest son (**Ndikaratase**—Snake elder) and his wife
A8endii's eldest daughter and her husband (Prairie Turtle elder—**Hannenhasa**)
second daughter and her Iroquois husband
third daughter and her Fox husband
Fox (m)
Estimated Population 10: 5 Snake, 1 Striped Turtle, 1 Prairie Turtle, and 1 Deer
Number of Elders 2
Number of Ages 0

PV8
Entaron8oin (nephew of **8ata8ata**, female Large Turtle elder or of **Te haronhiatexa**, her son)
Ottawa wife
Hannenratendi (Snake elder) and his Fox wife
Catawba
male Fox
male Fox
Estimated Population   7: 1 Large Turtle and 1Snake
Number of Elders   1
Number of Ages   0

PV9
Sandatsa8a't (Catawba)[1]
his wife
his two sons
his two sisters
Estimated Population   6
Number of Elders   0
Number of Ages   0

PV10: Striped Turtle
Dorothee Sk8atandi[2] (Striped Turtle)
her eldest son
her eldest daughter (Striped Turtle elder **Marie ,Aenench**), her husband, their two sons, and three daughters (aged fifteen, eleven, nine, seven, and one)
her second daughter, her husband, their two daughters, and two sons (aged eleven, nine, seven, and three or four)
her second son and his wife (Large Turtle elder **,Arhonnens**)
her third son and his wife
her third daughter and her husband
her fourth daughter and her husband (Prairie Turtle elder, **Mathias Ta,enndrak**)
her fourth son
Stanislas 8asanion (Snake elder) and his wife
his widowed eldest son (thirty-one), his two sons, and one daughter (aged eleven, eight, and five)
his second son and his wife
Striped Turtle man (one hundred)

Baptiste Otiok8endoron (Striped Turtle elder)
his daughter from his first wife and her husband
elder's second wife (Large Turtle elder **Angelique Sk8âra**)
Striped Turtle elder (**Martin Sa8end8at**), his Fox wife, and their son and daughter
Sk8atandi's adopted Fox sister
Estimated Population   42: 22 Striped Turtle, 2 Large Turtle, 2 Snake, and 4 Prairie Turtle   **Number of Elders**   7
Number of Ages   14

PV11: Prairie Turtle (Toupin 1996, 187, 209–11, 245)

Michel a,a8as (Bear elder)
wife (Prairie Turtle elder **Sa8ointondi**)
their eldest daughter (Tendiho) and her husband
possible Prairie Turtle female (possibly Tendiho's daughter; thirty)
her two sons and two daughters (first three aged eight, six, and four)
    possible Prairie Turtle man (possibly Tendiho's son; twenty-eight), his wife, and their two sons (one aged two)
possibly Tendiho's second daughter (nineteen) and her daughter (one)
possible Prairie Turtle woman (twenty) and her husband
three Prairie Turtle females (aged eighteen, nine, and six)
A,a8as and Sa8ointondi's son (**Ta,enndrak**—Prairie Turtle elder), his wife, their two sons, and one daughter
A,a8as and Sa8ointondi's eldest daughter and her husband (**Hondatorenha**—Wolf elder)
their two daughters and one son (oldest two aged ten and seven)
A,a8as and Sa8ointondi's second-eldest son
Sa8ointondi's three grandsons and two granddaughters (aged ten, nine, seven, five, and three)
Sa8ointondi's son from first marriage (Prairie Turtle leader **Ts8nnonkanien**)
his wife (**Agnes Ondechientonk**)
Ondechientonk's daughter from previous marriage
Ondechientonk's son from previous marriage and his wife
young girl (two)
A woman, her husband, and their son
four young males (first three aged sixteen, twelve, and ten)
Estimated Population   49: 27 Prairie Turtle, 5 Deer, 1 Bear, 4 Striped Turtle, and 1 Wolf
Number of Elders   4
Number of Ages   23

PV12: Catawba
Marie Magdalene 8,e'tenhaon (Catawba)
her eldest son
her youngest son and his wife
her three daughters
Fox woman
Ennenratendi (Snake elder)
Estimated Population   9: 1 Snake
Number of Elders   1
Number of Ages   0

PV13: Deer
Mathias Sastaretsi (widowed; Deer elder)
his eldest daughter and her husband
his second daughter (twenty-two), her husband, and their two daughters (aged two and six months)
his second daughter (twenty)
her daughter
his eldest son (seventeen)
his second son (twelve)
his niece (fourteen)
Catherine Sk8ateenre (Deer)
her eldest daughter (**Sendak8oin**—Deer elder) and her husband (**Sohondin-non**—Bear elder)
her son and his wife
her two nieces
Sastaretsi's nephew (**Etienne Anien8indet**—Deer elder) and his wife
their son (twenty), his wife, and their daughter (three)
three young males and one young female (aged eighteen, eighteen, thirteen, and eight)
Marie Nendeniont (Sastaretsi's niece and sister of Anien8indet)
her son, his wife, and their son and daughter
two boys
a girl
Nendeniont's adopted Chickasaw brother
her daughter[3] and her husband
Estimated Population: 39: 15 Deer, 1 Wolf, 1 Bear, 2 Prairie Turtle, 7 Large Turtle, and 3 Porcupine
Number of Elders   4
Number of Ages   13

APPENDIX A   225

PV14
Nicolas Taronhi8rens (Large Turtle elder)
his wife (**Marie ,Atera**—Porcupine elder)
their two married daughters and their husbands
their son
male Catawba and his wife
man and his wife
their son and his wife
their daughter and her husband
woman and her second husband
Estimated Population   17: 7 Porcupine and 1 Large Turtle
Number of Elders   2
Number of Ages   0

PV15: Striped Turtle
Te 8arachiarande (Striped Turtle)
her eldest daughter (**Ts8ndehe**—Striped Turtle elder)
her husband (**Ta,echiaten**—Wolf phratry leader) and their two sons
Ts8endehe's second husband
Te 8arachiarande's youngest daughter and her husband (**Te,atak**—Large Turtle elder)
man and his Ottawa wife
Estimated Population   10: 5 Striped Turtle, 1 Wolf, 1 Deer, and 1 Large Turtle
Number of Elders   2
Number of Ages   0

PV16: Bear
Marie Ts8endask8a—Bear elder
her niece (**Taronngiahak**)
her husband (Striped Turtle elder—**Hari8andiniontak**)
woman and her husband (Fox)
possibly Hari8andiontak's daughter from a previous marriage (fifteen)
Taronngiahak's nephew, a niece, and one of either (six)
Ts8endask8a's niece and her husband (Fox)
Ts8endask8a's niece
man and his wife
Estimated Population   14: 8 Bear and 1 Striped Turtle
Number of Elders   2
Number of Ages   2

PV17
Ang8irot (Janus Quirinus)
bibax (Prairie Turtle), not existing at this time (Toupin 1996, 248, 214)

PV18: Bear
Barnabé Enien8indet—Snake elder
his wife (**Francoise Asenra,e-haon**—Bear elder)
their three daughters and one son
Te aïas (Bear elder—widow)
her two daughters
woman
woman
Aenons (Bear elder)[4]
his eldest daughter from first marriage and her husband
his youngest daughter from first marriage
his Adopted Fox brother[5]
Aenon's stepsister
her daughter and her husband (**Joseph T'on8atsarandi**—Porcupine elder—twenty-eight)
their three sons and one daughter (aged thirteen, eleven, four, and one)
Iroquois man
his wife (**Onnond8**—Bear elder) and their six children
Estimated Population 31: 17 Bear, 1 Snake, 1 Porcupine, and 1 Prairie Turtle
Number of Elders   6
Number of Ages   5

GV1: Les filles d'anne
widowed eldest sister
her younger sister and her husband
their eldest brother and his wife
their youngest brother
Estimated Population   6
Number of Elders   0
Number of Ages   0

GV2: Prairie Turtle
Marie 8entïhaton—Prairie Turtle
her eldest son (**Tahatie**—Prairie Turtle elder)

her second son (**Taniendonien**—Prairie Turtle elder)
her third son and his wife
Hannenhasa (Prairie Turtle elder)
his sister (**Tando,ares**—Prairie Turtle elder)
1 Catawba
Estimated Population   8: 6 Prairie Turtle and 1 Deer
Number of Elders   4
Number of Ages   0

GV3: *Healer's House*
Aonchron(i),en (a healer) and his wife
their son and his wife
their daughter and her husband
his nephew and his wife
Estimated Population   8
Number of Elders   0
Number of Ages   0

GV4: *Large Turtle*
Therese 8ata8ata (Large Turtle elder)
her eldest daughter
her son, his wife, and their five or six children
her daughter, her husband, and their four children
Te ondechoren (Large Turtle male, possibly their son), his wife and their
    two children
8ata8ata's eldest son (**Te horonhi8texa**—Large Turtle elder)
and his wife (**Nendaentons**—Deer elder)
their son
his nephew and his wife
his nephew
male
his sister
two nieces of Te ondechoren
two nieces of 8ata8ata
their children
Estimated Population   30+: 18 Large Turtle, 9 Deer, and 3 Bear
Number of Elders   3
Number of Ages   0

GV5
Te otiorachra (widow of Large Turtle phratry leader)
her eldest daughter
Baptiste Toratati (Wolf) (her husband)
her eldest son another daughter and son
Estimated Population 6: 1 Wolf
Number of Elders   0
Number of Ages   0

GV6: Large Turtle
Anne Sa8oindgiandii (Large Turtle elder)
her eldest son from first marriage (**Antoine D'ate,atak**—Large Turtle elder)
his wife (**Ka8oindi**—Striped Turtle elder)
her second son from first marriage and his wife
her third son from first marriage
her daughter from first marriage
her son from second marriage
her daughter from second marriage
her third husband
her son from third marriage
her daughter from third marriage and her husband
Christine ,Arhonnens (Large Turtle elder) and her husband
her eldest daughter and her husband (**Etienne Annien8indet**—Deer elder)
her eldest son (**Pierre 8en8oin**—Large Turtle elder)
his Miami wife, their two sons, and one daughter (the oldest two aged twelve and ten)
her second daughter and her husband (**Taniendonien**—Prairie Turtle elder)
her second son
her third daughter, her husband, and their son
Estimated Population 28: 17 Large Turtle, 1 Striped Turtle, 1 Prairie Turtle, and 1 Deer
Number of Elders   6
Number of Ages   2

GV7: Daughters of a Huron Man Named Toussaint
,Arhata—Huron widow
her younger sister—widow
her daughter and her husband

the third sister
the fourth sister
Estimated Population   6–7: 1 Porcupine
Number of Elders   0
Number of Ages   0

GV8: Deer
Agnes Ondechientonk—Deer[6]
her husband (**Ts8nnonkanien**—Prairie Turtle leader)
their eldest son, his wife, and their son
their eldest daughter and her husband
their youngest daughter and her husband
Ondechientonk's brother (?) and his wife (**Christine A8innonke**—Bear elder)
old Seneca widow
her son and his wife
her daughter and her husband
Estimated Population   16: 6 Deer, 1 Bear, and 1 Prairie Turtle
Number of Elders   1
Number of Ages   0

GV9: Deer
Christine 8ndaenton (la vielle reine—Deer)
her eldest son and his wife (**Ts8ndehe**—Striped Turtle elder)
8ndaenton's eldest daughter
her second son and his wife
Catherine Nond8annan (Deer elder)
8ndaenton's youngest daughter and her husband
a Fox widow
Estimated Population   10: 5 Deer, 1 Striped Turtle, 1 Bear, and 1 Large Turtle
Number of Elders   2
Number of Ages   0

GV10: Nendaentons (Deer elder) to Etionnont8t

GV11: Snake
Susanne Ts8ndendora Snake
her eldest daughter
her daughter's eldest son from her first marriage and his wife
her daughter's youngest son from her first marriage
her daughter's eldest daughter and her husband
her daughter's youngest daughter and her husband
her second son
her daughter's second husband
two daughters of Ts8ndendora (to Belle River)
Estimated Population   15: 9 Snake
Number of Elders   0
Number of Ages   0

GV12: Wolf (Toupin 1996, 94–95, 220–21, 254–55; Potier 1920, 151)
Nondeaon—Wolf
her eldest son (**Jacques hondatorenha**—Wolf elder) and his wife
her eldest daughter
her husband (separated?), a son, and either a son or a daughter (aged ten and eight)
her second son, his wife, a son, and a daughter
her third son (**Andareï8oin**—Wolf elder)
an old Wolf woman and her husband
their eldest daughter (**Nenditaxon**—wolf elder) and her husband
her youngest daughter and her husband
Fox man
an old Wolf woman
her eldest son and his wife
her second son and his wife
her eldest daughter
her second daughter
her youngest daughter
her youngest son
Estimated Population   29: 18 Wolf, 3 Porcupine, 1 Deer, 1 large Turtle, and 1 Prairie Turtle
Number of Elders   3
Number of Ages   2

GV13: Bear (Toupin 1996, 195–96, 221, 255)
Anastasie Ts8nde,en—Bear elder
her eldest son from her first marriage (**Pierre Ochienda,ete**—Bear elder)
three sons (aged twelve, ten, and five) and one daughter (aged three)
her second son (**Taretande**—Bear elder; thirty-two)
his wife (**A8endaara**—Striped Turtle elder)
their two daughters (the eldest aged ten)
Ts8nde,en's second husband
their eldest son, his wife, and their two sons (two and three months)
their eldest daughter and her husband
Francoise Niendaharonk—Bear elder
her son from her first marriage and his wife (**Nond8annan**—Deer elder)
her Potawatomi husband
their eldest son, his wife, and their child
their second son, his wife, their daughter and son
their next five sons
Sohondinnon (Bear elder—Tsonde,en's brother)
his wife (**Sendak8oin**—Deer elder)
Christine A8innonke—Bear elder and her husband
her nephew
her nephew
his wife (**Tiaondise8a**—Snake elder)
her niece
her husband and their two daughters
her niece
her daughter and son
her niece
Fox woman
her husband and their two sons
woman separated
her son (aged ten) and daughter
Old Fox man
Laurent T'atronhiatase, his wife, their three daughters and one son
Onh8arak (Bear elder and T'atronhiatase's brother) and his wife
one son
four girls and two boys (aged twelve, nine, seven, six, five, and two)
Catawba
Estimated Population   74: 26 Bear, 3 Striped Turtle, 2 Snake, 4 Large Turtle, 3 Deer, and 2 Wolf
Number of Elders   11
Number of Ages   15

GV15
S8ndak8a—Sturgeon
his wife
their eldest son and his wife
their youngest son and his wife
their daughter and her husband
a small boy
a man
his son
Iroquois
Onnond8 (Bear elder) his wife
son and his wife
Estimated Population   13: 1 Sturgeon, 1 Wolf, and 1 Bear
Number of Elders   1
Number of Ages   0

Etionnont8t
There are eight houses in Etionnont8t, but they are small houses, not what would be called a longhouse, each having only a few residents.

E1 – Porcupine
E2 – Sturgeon
E3 – Deer
E4 – ?
E5 – Bear
E6 – ?
E7 – Snake
E8 – Bear

E1
Nicolas Orontondi   Porcupine elder
There is no statement of who is with him in this house.

E2
S8ndak8a...Le Brutal Sturgeon
There is no statement of who is with him in this house.

E3
Nendaentons   Deer elder
Jaques Atironta   Deer

APPENDIX A 233

(nephew of Nendaentons)
Marie Joseph Nenditaxon
wife of Atironta   Wolf elder
niece   Deer
her three sons and one daughter   Four Deer
Catawba man   probably Deer
Estimated Population   9: 7 Deer and 1 Wolf
Number of Elders   2

E4
Atatiahak. La vielle coin   ?
(mother-in-law of Sastaretsi)   ?
her married son (le soldat)
Estimated Population   2

E5
[Alexis] Ta8ita   Seneca
[Elizabeth] nnendask8a   Bear
their eldest (Bear) son and his wife
their second son   Bear
Estimated Population 5: 3 Bear

E6
Sandetes   Fox
his Fox wife
Estimated Population: 2

E7
A,angonta (La Caliere)   Snake
her daughter
Tannenhochre (her brother)   Snake elder
Estimated Population: 3: 3
Number of Elders   1

E8
Sohendinnon   Bear
his separated wife (?)   ?
Estimated Population   2: 1 Bear
Total Estimated Population 25 (there were probably more)
Number of Elders   4

Aa,e *(Toupin 1996, 256–59)*

The cluster of small houses that was ,Aa,e or Hayagué, known otherwise as la riviere Blanche or White River, included four reported households:

A1 – Porcupine (possibly)

This includes five children of Makon's, four sons and one daughter. They may be of the Porcupine clan since in the first census they are recorded as being both in the Porcupine clan PV1 and in this house. The second census does not include them.

A2 – Snake

This place houses two daughters of the Snake clan woman Ts8ndendora, whose name is mentioned first in GV11. Again the people are mentioned in the first but not in the second census.

A3 – Large Turtle

This place houses two sisters of la babillarde, known as Sa8oindiandii in Wyandot, a Large Turtle elder.

A4 – Bear

This household would appear to only consist of la kannerin (la Canerin), known in Wyandot as Marie Ts8endask8a, a Bear elder associated as well with PV16.

Total Estimated Population   10 (there were probably more people than this)
Number of Elders   2

APPENDIX B: WYANDOT CORRESPONDENCE

Appendix B1: Father Richardie's Introduction to Father Potier

A series of letters written in Wyandot were exchanged during the years 1744 to 1747. They will be presented here in chronological order. A number of short forms are being used here with respect to pronominal prefixes. They are:

inc   first-person inclusive—a plural form that includes the listener
exc   first-person exclusive—a plural form that excludes the listener
ind   third-person indefinite—a plural form that can be translated as "they, people, one"
m   third-person masculine
f   third-person feminine
d   dual
pl   plural
s   singular

("compliment que le p. de la richardie me donna pour l'aller faire dans toutes les cabanes des hurons, le 7, sept. 1744")

[Introduction that Father de la Richardie gave me (Potier) to go to present to all the houses of the Wyandot] (Potier 1920, 684)

x' | i,e | [,]8aena | a,enrhon |
here | I go, am | I have you (pl) as children, my children | I wished, thought |
t'axennonronk8annionk | | d' |
I would grease their scalps many times, greet them (ind) with great respect | those, that |
aniena | d' | axeatorenha | a8eti | xehetsaronde |
my child | those | I would find them (ind) | all | I intend to encourage them (ind) |

d' | a,onk8ichoton | d' | aonxiatrihotat |
those | their (ind) force would stand | those | they (ind) would listen to us |

de sten taoten | de | [e]xerih8aniensten |
all kinds of things | which | I will teach them (ind) |

d' | orih8ato,eti | haoten |
that which | it is a straight, certain, holy matter | of such a nature |

Here I am, my children. I wished that I would greet respectfully as my own child those whom I would find. I intend to encourage them all so that their forces (of conviction) would stand, so that they would listen to and believe all the special "holy" matters which I will teach them.

Exennonh8eha | atiaondi | d' | ehona8endra |
I will love them (ind) | completely, perfectly| those who | they (ind) will be with his word|

d' ha8endio[1]
who he is great in voice

I will love them completely, all those who will be with the word of the Great Voice.

Long Translation

Here I am, my children. I wished that I would greet respectfully as my own child those whom I would find. I intend to encourage them all so that their forces (of conviction) would stand, so that they would listen to and believe all the special "holy" matters which I will teach them. I will love them completely, all those who will be with the word of the Great Voice.

Appendix B2: Governor Longueuil

This correspondence comprises a letter from Paul-Joseph Le Moyne de Longueuil, then governor at Detroit, written by Father Richardie, followed by a short note from Richardie himself. It should be kept in mind that Longueuil probably had little idea what was being said in the letter as he did not speak Wyandot. Richardie had a lot of opportunity to communicate what he wanted to here, with little fear that secular authorities would know what he was saying.

"Lettre de Mr de Longueuil aux hurons en hivernment ecrite par le p. de la Richardie le 20 mars 1746. Je la recu a ondietsi, et la lu aux hurons"

[Letter from Mr. De Longueuil (governor at Detroit) among the Huron in their wintering place, written by Father de la Richardie on March 20, 1746. I (Potier) received it at Ondietsi ("it is a long point of land") and read it there to the Huron] (Potier 1920, 684–85)

Tatak8isere[1] | sa,ohiatondihatie | d' | hati8annens |
Longueuil | he is going about writing to them (ind) | who | they (m) are elders |

Longueuil is going about writing to those who are (male) elders.

i8a,ennen | ,8aena | ,annendae | 8enchtra |
I said (in the past) | I have you (pl) as my children | it is autumn | perhaps |
d' | (e)ionchrontie | d' | ek8arih[8]aronj | daat
when | they (ind) will abandon the axe | when | we (inc) will listen | the very
,andoron
it is valuable, difficult

I said, "My children, perhaps when they abandon the axe (i.e., quit war)[2] we will listen. It is very difficult, valuable."

238   APPENDICES

d' | aiontatie | θo | axennhaha³ |
when/if | they (ind) would abandon it | there, that, then | I would request of them (ind) |
d' a,etsirih8enhasenniha⁴
   you should, would go to bear the matter to them (ind)

If they would abandon it, then I would request of them, "You should go bear, carry the matter to them."

onne a,ate8endaeritihatie | i,erhe |
behold I am going about fulfilling the word | I wish, think |
ahotindi,onrato,enk | de | xeena |
they (m) would be certain, sure | those | I have them (ind) as children |
t'aa8enk | onh8a ochre | ex' | ondechen |
if it happened | now next winter | this, here | it is a lying country |

Behold, I am fulfilling the word. I wish, "They should be sure in their minds, those who are my children, if it happened next winter in this country."

stan | de skahonat⁵ | te a,oraennen |
not | it is one canoe | they (ind) did not land |
te ,[i]atontari,e | Michel ha8enta8ennen | x |
at (where) a body of water is two (i.e., Quebec) | Michel it was his day | this, here |
ondaie entatek | ahannenrinde | onnontio, |
it it was a day | he led a group, army | it is a great hill i.e., French governor⁶

They did not land just one canoe at Quebec on St Michael's Day (29 September), on the day the French governor led an army.

ndae | sa,onditiok8enh8a | ek8a[,]ennhe,e⁷ | de |
truly | he brings them (ind) as a group | in summer, next summer | who |
sa,okaratatinnen | [a]tochingotronnon |
he took care of them (ind) | people of the crane, Miami⁸|

Truly, he brings the Miami whom he took care of in the summer.

,aro i8aia skandetati |
before, earlier it is (too) little on the other side of the pine, the Dutch |
ahoti[h[eratie,⁹ |
they (m) went directly
t'ek8atenraent | Sarastoge | ,aatsi |
where a palisade was thrown aside, knocked over | Saratoga¹⁰ | it is called, named |

Earlier, a few Dutchmen went directly to a placed where a palisade had been knocked down. Saratoga it is called.

,anda8a,eronnon | hotiskenra,eta(k) |
people of the rapid, river, Kahnawake[11] | they (m) bear war, are warriors |
ontahonkon'ten | ahontaenraraha |
they (m) commence to do something | they (m) attacked the palisade |
a8esk8ek | hatinnion,enhak | ok8e'tak8i |
afterwards | they (m) are French | lastly |
hatichra8aθa | din | (h)ondasa,annen |
they (m) are Algonquin | and | they (m) speak a strange language, are Abenaki |

The warriors of Kahnawake commenced the attack on the palisade, and afterwards (they were joined by) the French, the Algonquin, and the Abenaki.

ahontandat8ta8a | otenra,on | hatierontak |
they (m) knocked over his village | in the palisade | they (m) damaged, harmed it |
8ahia | onnonta,eronnon[12] | a8eti de | goig8oinronnon |
six | people at the hill, Onondaga | all | Cayuga

They knocked over the village. In their palisade they harmed six Onondaga and all the Cayuga.

enniot | i8asen | ts8tare |
standing fingers (10) | such a number of tens | seven |
isk8[a]senchare | daat | endiahaon | d' |
such a number of tens added to that | the very | they (ind) are males, men | who |
etiorhench[t]ronnon | ahonsen |
people of where the day comes | the English they (m) were finished|
otenra,on |
killed inside the palisade |
d' | otinnhetien | d'in | d' | echiaha | te 8arati |
those| they (f) are female, women| and | those | children (ind) | it is not counted |
n' honatindask8aen
they (m) have them (m) as prisoners

There were 170 Englishmen killed in the palisade, and an uncounted number of women and children taken as prisoners.

θo ichien | i8a | n' | (h)ondasa,i |
there | it is such a number | those | they (m) are finished, killed, dead |

240   APPENDICES

d' | hotiskenra,eta | hondatenro | 8ahia | ,anda8a,eronnon |
those | they (m) are warriors| they (m) are friends | six | people of Kahnawake |
asen | hatinnion,enhak | shaatat | hatichra8ata |
ten | they (m) are French | he is one person | they (m) Algonquin |
(h)ondasa,annen | ,entron[13] |
they (m) are Abenaki | nine |

The number of allied warriors who died are as follows: six Kahnawake people, ten Frenchmen, one Algonquin, and nine Abenaki.

achia θo | aharinientaha | onnontio |
as soon as | he put the matter to rest, pacified it | Large Hill (the French governor) |
a,ok8ate,atannon | t' | hotinnonchiaenton |
they (ind) set fire to many things, in many places | as, of | they (m) have many houses |
hotiskenra,eθa | [,]enta,e | etiendaronnion | d' |
they (m) are warriors | in a field, meadow | many places where they (ind) live | those |
etiorhenc[h]tr8nnon[14]| chia | te otia,i |
English | at the same time | it is split in two, Montreal |
shonde'ti
they (m) returned to such a place

As soon as the French governor laid the matter to rest, they set fire to the many houses and to the fields where the English were residing, and then returned to Montreal.

,ato,en | onne n'onh8a | 8a,enra | [e]tiorhenchtronnon |
it is true | behold now | spring | English |
hon[h]8entsa8eti | handat8ta8ahe |
all over his world | he goes destroying villages |
te [i,]iatontari,e | ekandataen |
at (where) a body of water is two (i.e., Quebec)[15] | where a village, community lies |
stan | i8aia | te hoatandik | onnontio |
not | it is a little, too little | he is not afraid | Great Hill, French governor |

It is true, now that it is spring the English intend to destroy the community of Quebec, and the French governor is not even a little bit afraid.

800 | n' | on8e | Taontoora,i[16] | ehonditiok8ichien |
(expletive (?)) |the | humans | Michilimackinac | they (m) will investigate it as a group |
d' | eeront8ten, | ehonkenseha |
those who | they (ind) will be standing trees (councillors) | they (m) will consider it |

te ,iatontari,e | t' | eoata8enk | d' | onnontio; |
Quebec | as, if | it will happen to someone | the | French governor |

The people of Michilimakinac, they will investigate it, their councillors will look at what will happen to the French governor in Quebec.

a te hon[h]8entsa,e | dex' | endaronnion |
all over his world, country | this, here | they (ind) live, reside in many places |
ontaxennonh8e | ehonkenseha | iθondi: |
where I love them (ind) | they (m) will consider it | also |

All over his country, where those live whom I love, they will consider it also.

ondaie ara | hati8annens, | stan | honnon8enienti | t'e,en |
it, they only | they (m) are elders | not | they (m) are young men | it is not |
ahonk8ichoton | ichien de xeena de | 8endat
they (m) should have standing force | I have them (ind) as children | Wendat
hati8annens | d' | aia,enrhon |
they (m) are elders | that which | they (ind) would wish, think |
ahek8akatanda |
we (inc) should visit him |
son,8a,ena | onnontio, | ek8atrihotata |
he has us as children | French governor | we (inc) will go to pay attention, go to council |
ti | ha8end8ten | de | son,8annh8aesti[17] | etio,enrake._ |
as | his word is such | that which | he knocked at our door | in spring |

Only the elders should consider it, not the young men for they should not have much force. My children, the Wendat elders should wish, "We should go to visit our father, the French governor. We will go to council, as he called us to council in the spring."

te xerih8asetandi | d' hati8annens, | ti | 8a,eren |
I don't hide a matter from them (ind) those | they (m) who are elders | of | I have done it |
onh8a | 8a,enra. |
now | spring . |

I do not hide anything from the elders of what I have done, now it is spring.

Te o,enron | t' | aoata8e[nk] de | [a]nniena | cha8annonronnon:
it is not trivial, unimportant | as | it happened | (my child) | Shawnee[18]

It is not unimportant, that which happened to my child, the Shawnee.

te o,enron | tsonnont8oinronnon, tiorhenchtronnon | horih8a8asennik |
it is not unimportant | Seneca, English | he seized his affair |
te sa,onnonhianditi | sonnioto[19] | etiendare; |
he caused their (ind) scalps to move, scared them | Sonnioto | where they (ind) live |

It is not unimportant, the Seneca seized the English matter and intimidated those who live in Sonnioto.

iha8en | ati, | a,iataxen | onn' | achi[h]ej: |
he said | then | we two (exc) are same sex siblings | when | you (s) die |

He said, then, "We two are brothers when you die."

a8eti | ontaxen | n'on8e | karontaen[20]|
all | they (f) are same sex siblings | those who are humans | at Detroit |
etiendare | hotirih8ichia,i, |
where they (ind) live, reside | they (m) had their matter finished, they were condemned to die
henderhe | ahenhej | atiaondi | de | k8ataxen |
they (m) wish, think | he would die | completely | who | we (inc.) are brothers |
cha8annonronnon;
Shawnee

He said then "When you die brothers, all the brothers (of those who live, living) at Detroit are condemned to die." Our brothers, the Shawnee wish that he would die completely.

daat | i,acharetsi | aha8ennentaha |
the very | it is a long string of wampum | he finished, concluded his speech |
ahenhaon | cha8annonronnon: | ti | aia8enk | a,iataxen |
he said | Shawnee | as | it would happen | we (exc) two are brothers |
de skitenrha; | onh8a θ'aat | axennhaha[21] de |
you have pity, compassion on me | as soon as | I would suggest to them (ind) |
erih8ichiaxa | karontaen | ona'ti | θo |
they (ind) go to investigate a matter | Detroit | on this side | there |
i,a8endi |ti | hoeren; |
it is the whole word | of | he did, said it |

The Shawnee finished his long string of wampum saying: "You have pity on me as soon as I suggest to them to investigate the matter at Detroit." That is the whole word of what he said.

ok8a,antnh(e) | sa,onnhandi, | din |
Ottawa | he commanded, requested of them (ind) | and |
d'haonh8a | 8ata,enronnon,e | harih8ichiaxon: |
he who alone | in Catawba country | he goes, has gone to investigate a matter |
ahenhaon | 8ata,enronnon | sakak8a | d' | honnonchiondi | ha8enda |
he said | Catawba | look at it | the | Iroquois | his word |

The Ottawa requested something of them, and he alone in Catawba country goes about investigating a matter. He said, "Catawba, look at the Iroquois' word."

ahenhaon | 8ata,enronnon, x' ire | tioskenia | de cha8annonronnon, |
he said | Catawba here he goes | near | who Shawnee |
hochandihati[e] | oïo | exandaontie, |
he goes up a river | Great River (Ohio River) | where a river continues |
θo | tsitrontaj | d' | erendi, | setaia | andiare,[22]
there | be in such a place | that which | he will pass | have a smoke | before
(eh)echiendi8at | ehechi,en, | ehechiennenrent, | ehechrio |
you will surprise him | you will see him | you will strike his army | you will kill him |

His word says, "My brother Catawba, the Shawnee are coming close, travelling up the length of the Ohio river. Be there when he passes by. Have a smoke (i.e., possibly a council meeting) and afterwards you will surprise him, see him, strike his army and kill him."

te hatierontak | ex' | ,itron | 8endat |
they (m) did not do any damage in such a place | here | I reside | Wendat |
hati,8annens | xeenditinnen | i8a,ennen | [,]8aena |
elders (m) | I asked for, prayer for them (ind) | I said | my children |
tsindi,onrachronnianna | de | sk8ataxen |
go prepare their thoughts, make peace with them (ind) | who | you (pl) are brother(s) |
daat | hondi,onr8ta8an | honnonchiondi |
the very | his mind is knocked over, upset | he is Iroquois |

The Wendat elders here where I live did not do any damage, trick anyone, as I asked a favour of them saying: "My children, go make peace with your brothers, the Iroquois, for he is (i.e., they are) very upset."

d' | axeatae[h]8aha | axennhaha |
when | I missed, needed them (ind) | I made assembled them (ind) |
honk8a,annha | i8atonk ichien de | ,e8enda
they (m) speak a strange tongue, are Ottawa | it says the | my word

anien | saka de | (e)hechiatrihotat²³ | tiorhenchtronnon
my child | quit, stop it | you will listen to him (in a matter) | English
a8eti | d' | honnonchiondi | sehahient | de | hiasten |
all | the | Iroquois | follow a path | who | he is father to you |
honnontio²⁴ | hiahahichia,indi | 8enchtra |
he is the French governor | he made the path for you | perhaps |
de ,ato,en de sakerons | ,aro ahontiatarest |
it is true you are afraid of it | before they (m) came, come here (for a reason) |
esenda,eratis |
they (ind) choose to copy you, choose you to lead |
exendi,onrachronnia |
I will prepare their (ind) minds, make peace with them|
θo | ,arih8etsi | de cha8annonronnon eatata,e |
that, there | matter is of such a length | Shawnee they (ind) number such |

I missed those Ottawa I assembled. My word says: "My child, stop listening to all the English and Iroquois. Follow the path created for you by your father, the French governor. Perhaps it is true that you are afraid. Before we choose you to lead, I will make peace with them." That is the length of the speech of the Shawnee.

Tsonnont8oinronnon | hati,8annens | a8eti | onnonta,eronnon | achia |
Seneca | they (m) are elders | all | Onondaga | beginning |
θo |ahonronj | t' | [a8]a,ota8enk | hondatenro |
there |they listened | of, if | it happened to them (ind) | they (m) are friends |
hotinnonchiondi | Sarastoge | hatieronton | d'onn' |
they (m) are Iroquois | Saratoga | they (m) are assembled | when |
(a8)a,8andat8ta8a
we (exc) destroyed, knocked over villages

All the Seneca and Onondaga elders are beginning to listen to what happened to their Iroquois friends at Saratoga when we destroyed villages.

Onnontio,e | honde'ti | andiske | ahendihon | achie |
at the French governor's | they (m) went there | at...(?) | they (m) said | truly |
a,isten | a,orih8a8an | de [a]xinnonhonk | kehen |
my father | they (ind) had a matter, agreement | we are related to them (ind) | used to be |
de stan | chi sentak8i | t'e,en | d' ache,e [end of line] | sarastoge |
not | you do it deliberately | it is not | you (?) them (ind) | Saratoga |

They went to xxx²⁵ at the French governor's place where they said: "My father, our dead relatives had an agreement, you did not deliberately xxx them at Saratoga."

Te 8astaθo | orih8a | e8aton | d' etiorhenchtronnon d |
prohibitive | a matter | it will become | English the |
hati8e,innen | axinnonhonk kehen | on,8annonchia8eti |
they (m) were all together | our relatives used to be | all our houses, nations |
on,8andi,onrachiens | t' | hotieren[26] | sasandi,onrhenk |
our minds are bad, we are angry | as | they did | let your mind fall, forget, forgive it |
atiaondi
completely, entirely

Do not let it become an affair of the English, they are together with our deceased relatives. All our nations are angry about what they did. Forget, forgive it entirely.

θo | [,]8aena | i,e8endetsi | d' a,8atendotonnion |
there | my children | my word is of such a length | I have told you (pl) many things |

There, my children, my words are of such a length. I have told you many things.

Te o,enron | te ,8annonronk8annion | a8eti d' i,erhe | ,aro,e |
it is not unimportant | I greet you (pl) with great respect | all I wish, think | soon |
sen | onsahontate,en ontatiena | Tatak8isere|
let it be | they (m) see each other again they (f) are parents and children | Longueuil |

It is no trifling matter that I greet you with great respect. All I wish is that soon they will see each other, those who are parents and children...Longueuil

Long Translation
Longueil is going about writing to those who are elders. I said, "My children, perhaps when they abandon the axe we will listen. It is very difficult, valuable." If they would abandon it, then I would request of them, "You should go bear the matter to them." Behold, I am fulfilling the word. I wish, "They should be sure in their minds, those who are my children, if it happened now, next winter in this country."

They did not land just one canoe at Quebec on St. Michael's Day (29 September), on the day the French governor led an army. Truly, he brings the Miami whom he took care of in the summer. Earlier, a few Dutchmen went directly to a place where a palisade had been knocked down. Saratoga it is called. The warriors of Kahnawake commenced the attack on the palisade, and afterwards (they were joined by) the French, the Algonquin, and the Abenaki. They knocked over the village and in their palisade they damaged six Onondaga and all of the Cayuga. There were 170 Englishmen killed in the palisade, and an uncounted number of women and children taken as prisoners. The number of allied warriors who died are as follows: six Kahnawake people, ten Frenchmen, one Algonquin, and nine Abenaki. As soon as the French governor laid the matter to rest, they set fire to the many houses and to the fields where the English were residing, and then returned to Montreal. It is true, now that it is spring the English intend to destroy the community of Quebec, and the French governor is not even a little bit afraid. Oh, the people of Michilimakinac, they will investigate it, their councillors will look at what will happen to the French governor in Quebec. All over his country, where those live whom I love, they will consider it also.

Only the elders should consider it, not the young men for they should not have much force. My children, the Wendat elders should wish, "We should go to visit our father, the French governor. We will go to council, as he called us to council in the spring. It is not unimportant, that which happened to my child, the Shawnee. It is not unimportant, the Seneca seized the English matter and intimidated those who live in Sonnioto. He said, then, "We two are brothers when you die." The Shawnee finished his long string of wampum saying: "You have pity on me as soon as I suggest to them to investigate the matter at Detroit." That is the whole word of what he said.

The Ottawa commanded and he alone in Catawba country, he goes about investigating a matter. He said, "Catawba, look at the Iroquois' word." His word says, "My brother Catawba, the Shawnee are coming close, travelling up the length of the Ohio river. Be there when he passes by. Have a smoke (i.e., possibly a council meeting) and afterwards you will surprise him, see him, strike his army and kill him."

The Wendat elders here where I live did not do any damage, trick anyone, as I asked a favour of them saying: "My children, go make peace with your brothers, the Iroquois, for they are very upset."

I missed those Ottawa I assembled. My word says: "My child, stop listening to all the English and Iroquois. Follow the path created for you by your father, the French governor. Perhaps it is true that you are afraid. Before we chose you to lead, I will make peace with them." That is the length of the speech of the Shawnee.

They went to xxx at the French governor's place where they said: "My father, our dead relatives had an agreement, you did not deliberately xxx them at Saratoga."

Do not let it become an affair of the English, they are together with our deceased relatives. All our nations are angry about what they did. Forget, forgive it entirely. There, my children, my words are of such a length. I have told you many things. It is no trifling matter that I greet you with great respect. All I wish is that soon they will see each other, those who are parents and children... Longueuil

Appendix B3: The Wendat Response

This letter was composed by the Wyandot in their wintering place. The person who wrote down this letter is not known. Neither is it known whether the person was French or Wyandot. One of the clan leaders may have been the original speaker, the one who composed the letter.

"Response des hurons a la lettre precedente le 5 avril 1746"

[Response of the Huron (Wyandot) to the preceeding letter, 5 April 1746] (Potier 1920, 685)

ihatonk | a,isten: | ichiatonk | innen tia8enk |
he says | my father | you say | greatly thank you |
[,]8aena | atiaondi | [h]orih8a8eti, | atiaondi |
my children | entirely, completely | it is all his affair | entirely |
hesk8atendoton(di) | de sk8aena | ti |
you (pl) told him [or he told you (pl)] | you have us as children | as |
,arih8ten;
it is such an affair

He says, my father, "You greatly say thank you, my children that it would be entirely his affair, completely he told you that you are parent to us, it is such an affair."

eθorih8ichiati | nonh8a | endixa | [h]esk8atendotondi|
he finished some affair at such a time/place | now | (?) | he told you (pl) |
ti | 8a | [h]orih8aron,en | dexa | ,ochrate. |
as | other(s) | he listened to a matter | this | it is winter |

He finished it, now he told you as others listened to a matter this winter (?).

,8aena | onne | a,atate8enda,erit | ti | 8a,eren |
my children | now, behold | I completed my word in such a way | as, of | I did, said |

247

,annenda,e | 8a,en | innen | stan | te e,onrih8ase't |
(in) autumn | I said | greatly, intensely | not | I will not hide news from you (s) |
de sten | ,arih8tas | eontat(iat)ie | θo |
all kinds of things | news arrives | (they ind) will go about talking) | that, there |
e,rih8aronj | v e,rih8are |
I will hear a matter, matters | I will push, have a matter |

My children, behold, I completed my word in such a way, I said in autumn, "Greatly, intensely, I will not hide news from you that I hear."

tia8enk | d' | a(i)ontatie | θo |
thank you | those who | they (ind) went about quitting it (?) | that, there | (they went about talking)
te tsitron | ti | 8aende,aronj |
I no longer reside | as, of | they (ind) would raise, rise, separate |
achierhon | ahotind[,]onrato,enk | de |
they wished | they (m) would be sure in their thoughts, mind | those who |
xeena | d' | hati[,]8annens |
I have them (ind) as children | those who | they (m) are elders |

Thank you to those who went about (?). They wished, "They would be sure in their thoughts, mind, those who I have as children," those who are elders.

onne ati | n'onh8a | a,8atonnhara | d' | a,8a,8annens |
behold then | now | we (exc) are on top of life, rejoice | who | we (exc) are elders |
onh8a θ(o) aat a,ondi,onrato,en | ti | 8a | de |
soon they (ind) are sure in their thoughts | as, of | others | who |

cheena | onh8a θ(o) aat | ets[o]nditiok8ichien[1] |
you have them (ind) as children | soon | they (ind) will again form a group |
a8eti | ehontonnharen | d'onne | ehonronj |
all | they (m) will be on top of life, rejoice | when | they (m) will hear it |
aia,enrhon ,ato,en isen | ti | h8eren d' |
they (ind) would think it is true you said it | as | he did, said it that which |
iha8en | a8eti | e,8atendoton |
he said it | all | I will recount to you (pl) |

Now, then, we who are elders rejoice that soon those others who are your children are sure. Soon they will all form a group, they will rejoice when they hear it, they would think, "It is true, that which you said that he said all that I will recount to you."

Tia8enk | a,isten | ondechra8asti, | onne | n'onh8a |
thank you | my father | Beautiful Country (Richardie) | when | now |
aesa8endaronj | de sk8aena | d' |
we listen, have listened to your word who | you who are our parent | that which |
ichiatonk | innen | [,]8aena | stan stena[2] tsinnionka |
you say | greatly, strongly, often | my children | not anything |
te ,arih8andare | de | ,arih8achien | dexa |
no matter exists | that which | it is a bad matter, affair | this, here |
ondechen | de | kaarontaen[3] |
it is a country | the | Detroit |

Thanks, my father Beautiful Country, now that we have heard you who have us as children, that you strongly say, "My children, there is no bad news, no bad affair here in Detroit."

Long Translation

My father says, "You greatly say thank you, my children that it would be entirely his affair, completely he told you that you are parent to us, it is such an affair." He finished it, now he told you as others listened to a matter this winter (?). My children, behold, I completed my word in such a way, I said in autumn, "Greatly, intensely, I will not hide news from you that I hear."

Thank you to those who went about (?). They wished, "They would be sure in their thoughts, those elders whom I have as children."

Now, then, we who are elders rejoice that soon those others who are your children are sure. Soon they will all form a group, they will rejoice when they hear it, they would think, "It is true, that which you said that he said all that I will recount to you."

Thanks, my father Beautiful Country, now that we have heard you who have us as children, that you strongly say, "My children, there is no bad news here in Detroit."

Appendix B4: Father Richardie to the Huron of Wendake

"Lettre du pere de la Richardie aux hurons a quebec 29 dec: 1746...recu le 1 avril 1747...

[A letter from Father Richardie to the Huron at Quebec, 29 December 1746 and received 1 April 1747] (Potier 1920, 686–87)

Ondechra8asti[1] | te sa,onnonronk8annionk |
It is a beautiful country, Father Richardie | he greets them (ind) with great respect |
,andata8eti | de | 8endat | etiore,endi | etiendare |
all the villages | the | Wendat | at the mouth of the river | they (ind) live there |

Father Richardie greets the Wyandot of all the villages at the mouth of the river.

te o,enron | [,]8aena |
It is not unimportant | I have you (p) as children, my children |
d' a,8aatichias |
we (exc) search for people |

It is not unimportant, my children, our searching for people.

Ak8eti | sk8a,atatre8ati | d' | i,erhonhonk |
Scarcely, hardly | I had stopped myself | that which | I used to think |
enn[a]endae | axennontratia | d' |
they (ind) are vain, braggarts | I went about following them (ind) | those |
etsirha,ensennihatie
they (ind) go about coming out of the woods, ambushing you
etsinniena[2] | hotinnontio[3] | a8eti | de |
they (ind) have you as children | they (m) are large hills, French governors | all | those |
sk8ataxenchrenton
[you pl. are brothers (?), they are your hanging brothers (?)]

251

Scarcely had I stopped myself, I used to think, "They are vain, those I went about following who go about ambushing your parents." Those who are French governors are your brothers.

Stan | θo | te ,a8endi | ti | 8a,endi,onr8tennen |
Not | there, that | it is not the whole word | as, of | my mind was such |
k8e de t' | akendianditen |
in order that | I strengthened their (ind) fingers, hand |

It is not the whole word story (?), my thoughts were such in order that I strengthen their hand.

θo | ichien [,]8aena | iskarih8ten | ti | ,arih8tennen |
that, there | my children | it is again such a matter | as | a matter was such |
etio,enrake | d' a,echiatorha | i8enchtra d' |
in the spring | when I felt pain[4] | perhaps |
i8aia | eo,enronha | d' a,ontatie | eskarask8a |
it is little | it will diminish, become smaller | forever | I will again leave |

My children, it is again as it was in the spring when I felt pain, perhaps it will diminish, when I will return forever.

Ata,8aka[ta]nda | andiare | a8eti | de |
come see us | afterwards | all | those |
sk8aena | onnontio | [o]ndaie |
we have you as children, our children | French governor | it, that |
esk8a8endaronj | etisk8andare |
you (pl) will listen to our words | you (pl) are located in such a place |
ta,8atrihotat | atiaondi | te 8asta θo |
listen to us (exc) | completely, entirely | prohibitive |
esk8atrihotat | de | sten taoten | d' |
you (pl) will listen to someone | that which | all kinds of things | that which |
i8achien | d' | esk8andi,onra8ensk8a |
it is bad, worthless | that which | thoughts you (pl) will have had |

In the meantime come see us, for we are all the children of the governor, and listen to our word where (we) live. Listen to us completely. Do not listen to the bad thoughts that you have had.

Stan | atiaondi | i8aia | te ,arih8ate | d' |
Not | completely | it is little | it is not possible, feasible | that which |

isk8erhonhonk | ,ato,en | atiaondi: |
you (pl) used to think | it is true | completely |
te k8a,enh8i | d' a,8atsihensta⁵ | d' |
we (inc) do not put it outside | who we (exc) charcoal, Jesuits | those |
axendi,onrhaten | d' axiniena | hotirih8iosti |
I doubted them (ind) | those | we have them (ind) as children | they (m) are Christians |

It is not even a little possible that which you used to think was entirely true. We who are Jesuits (i.e., are called charcoal) did not cause those of our children who are Christians to doubt.

Ondaie | ati | e8a,endi,onrato,enk | d' atrondi | i8aia
It, that | then | I will be sure about it | enough, sufficiently | it is little
sk8annonh8e | d' | e,akak8a |
you (pl) love me | when | I will look at, regard it |
hotinniontatie | de | xeena |
they (m) go about hanging from, being attached to it | those | I have them (ind) as children |

That, then I will be sure that you will love us (at least) a little enough when I will look at those who are attached to my children.

8enchtra | stan | d' aerat | t'e,en
Perhaps | not | they (ind) were not with, disposed to it | it is not
n' (e)onxiatorenha,
they (ind) will find us

Perhaps they are not disposed to finding us.

e,ihon | a,endi,onra,e hatirihonniannon⁶ |
I will say | in my mind they (m) say many things without reason |
de | xeena te ,ato,en | d' onnonh8e |
those who | I have them (ind) as children | it is not true | they (ind) love me |

Perhaps they are not disposed to wishing they will find us. I will say in my mind, "Those who are my children say many things without reason. They do not love me."

irerhe | onnontio | ahonteniennonnia |
he wishes, thinks | French governor | they (m) would be skillfully made |
t' | [ai]a,oata8enk | n' ontatiena |
as | it would happen to them (ind) those who | they (ind) are parents and children |

The French governor wishes, "It would happen to them, that they would be skillfully made as parents and children."

A8eti | esk8aronj | ti | ,arih8ten | dexa | ondechen; |
All | you (pl) will listen | as | it is a matter of such a nature| this | a country is, lies |

You will all listen as it is a matter of this country.

Sk8ataxen | hatindia8ointen⁷ |
you (pl) are brothers | they (m) are of the country of Bears, of Wendake |
hotindi,onrato,en
they (m) are sure

Your brothers, those of Wendake, are sure about it.

Sterhon | ati | stan | 8atsek | te honkonta |
Wish for it, think it (2d) | then | not | outside, outsiders | they (m) do not lie (?) |
daat | hotirih8iosti |
the very | they (m) are Christians |

Think it, then, you two, "They are not lying outsiders, they are great Christians."

,arih8a8eti | hatirihieriaθa |
It is all a matter | they (m) go straight to the matter |
din | n'endi [,]8aena | ta,8andachiondat |
and | we, us my children | make your tongue large to, lie to us! |
anniaten haon,e | d' esk8erhon | te son,8andi,onkennion |
afterwards | you (pl) will wish, think | he tricks, fools us |
daat | son,8aena | n' ondaie |
the very | he has us as children | that which |
son,8ak8eton | ioti | d' ason[,]8aationt |
he gave birth to, produced us | it is like| he introduced us to, caused us to enter |
otiok8ato,eti,e | d' | hotirih8iosti |
in a special, chosen clan, group | those who | they (m) are Christians |

They go straight to the whole matter. Lie to us, my children, and you will think, "Our father fools us that he has us as children, that he gave birth to us, that is such that he caused us to enter into the special group or clan of Christians."

Estennia,on⁸ | ati | tsatatontechohare | dˤ | i8achien |
Have courage | then | wash, cleanse your heart | that which | it is bad, corrupt |

oatorinnen
it was covered

Have courage, then. Cleanse your heart from the corruption that covered it.

Stan | isk8aia | 8kaot | te,en |
Not | it is very little | it is bad, corrupt | it is not |
ti | hotontechr8ten | onnontio | sk8enterha |
of, as | his heart is of such a nature | French governor | you (pl) have pity on us |
okendiati | de sten | d' hotindi,ongon |
extraordinary | all kinds of things | they (m) told a legend, story |
n'[h]onentachiasen(ni) | stan | echstra,e | te,en |
they (m) disapproved of his conduct | not | on their (ind) lips | it is not |
sk8annonh8e | anda,on | atiaondi |
we love you | inside | completely |

It is not even a little bit bad, the heart of the French governor. You have an extraordinary amount of pity on us. You listen to us in all sorts of things. They tell stories, those who disapprove of his conduct. "We love you" is completely not on their lips.

a8entenhaon | onsaharih8andandeta | d' |
continually | he redoubles, repeats the message | that which |
ihatonk | taot | ichien (a)a,a8enk | d' | 8kaot |
he says | wh-q | it happened to them(ind) | the | it is bad |
a,endi,onr8ten [a,o (?)] | Sastaretsi | eatata,e[9] |
their (ind) minds, thoughts are such | Sastaretsi | they (ind) are such a number |

He continually repeats the same question, "What happened to the bad thoughts of Sastaretsi?"

te ,ienteri | d' [h]orih8andera,i |
I do not know, have not experienced it | he makes mistakes, his mistake making |
hennonh8e | atiaondi | chia a te 8a,ont | ehennonh8eha |
I love him | completely | forever | I will love him |

"I don't have knowledge of his ever mistake-making. I love him completely. I will love him forever."

Te hosk8ahat | ,8aena | son,8annontio[10] |
he will not be hateful | my people | he is governor to us |
irerhonhonk | θo | a,a8enk | ti |
he used to wish, think | that, there | it happened | as, of |

hondi,onr8ten | honnon[c]hiondi d'
his thoughts, inclinations are, were of such a nature | he made a house, Iroquois
irerhe | askenonnia | θo | a,onh8entsate | din | n'onh8a |
he wishes, thinks | in peace | that, there | my world, country | and | now |
d' achienk | atonθa | son,8aio | annienronnon |
three | it makes such a number in a series | he killed us | Mohawk |

He who is our governor is not hateful my children, he used to think, "the Iroquois' wish was for peace in my country" and now it is the third time he killed us, the Mohawk.

Stan | te ha8eri | onnontio | d' a,ontatie | θo |
not | he does not wish, think | French governor | continually | that, there |
t'estrih8achra8a | arerhon | eshatatre8a't |
you (p) will make recompense | he wished, thought | he will stop, punish himself |
indecha
perhaps

He did not wish for you to make recompense forever, he thought that, "He will perhaps stop himself."

,ato,en | hiatendi,onrask8ahens | onnontio | de |
It is true | they two[11] (m) hate each other's minds, thoughts | French governor | the |
a8eti | Kora[12] |
all | English governor(s) of New York |

It is true that they hate each other's minds very much, the French governor and all the English governors of New York.

Ara iθochien irerhonhonk | onnontio | te 8astaθo |
Only he used to think | French governor | prohibitive |
ehonaatichiaxa | engen | ona'ti, | xa |
they (m) will search for him | seemingly, outwardly, in appearance | on this side | here |
tioskenia | ahatindi,onroianda | de xeena |
near, close by | they (m) came to amuse, distract, entertain | my children (ind) |
a8eti | d' [h]a,ih8atena | hotiskenra,e'ta |
all | I have them (m) as nephews | they (m) are warriors |

He used to think only, the French governor, "They (should) not search after him, outwardly, on this side, nearby they come to amuse themselves with (i.e., torture) my warrior children and nephews."

Stan | 8a | te ,arih8ten | n'onh8a | d' erehon |
Not | other(s) | it is not a matter of such a nature | now | he will think |
[e]tiorhenchtronnon | aha'ka |
people where day will come (English) | he quit, abandoned it |
hon(h)8entsachiatandesonk | dexa ondechen |
he goes about killing all over the country | this country |

It is not someone else's matter now. He will wish, "He will cease going about killing all over the countryside in this country."

8a θo onsa,ihon | tsi8endrak8a | ,8aena | sastehiaraha |
again I say it again | be with their (ind) word | my children | remember them, their (m) |
t' [as θ] | [h]otindi,onr8tennen | d' hati8annensk8a |
as | their (m) thoughts, intentions were such | they (m) were the elders |

Again, I say, "Follow their words, my children. Remember the thoughts, intentions of those who were the ancestor elders."

d'a8entenhaon | n' [h]ontatehetsarondesonhonk |
continually | they (m) went about all over exhorting one another |
ihontondenn | t [as θ] | hi,ondesa |
they (m) went about saying | as, of | (?) be country |
eon,ionh8entsandirha | ehek8atiatannentata |
our country will be firm | we (inc) will attach ourselves to him at some place |
onnontio | haeron,e |
French governor | at his body |

They continually went about encouraging each other saying... our country will be strong, we will attach ourselves to the body of the governor.

tsa'ka | n'ondaie d' | 8atsek | sk8atendi,onrenha8i |
quit | that which, it | outside | your (pl) mind, thoughts are carried |
tsarask8a | hati8annens | [,]8aena | tsarask8a | iθondi |
leave it | they (m) are elders | my children | leave it | also |
hotiskenra,eta | [,]8aena | tsakaratat[13] |
they (m) are warriors | my children | take care of it |
d8a d' | a,onnhetien | a8eti | echiaaha |
others those who | they (ind) are women |all | they (ind) (are) children |

Stop that which carries your thoughts elsewhere. Depart from the elders, my children. Depart from the warriors also, my children. Take care of those who are women and all children.

te o,enron | d' ehatonnharen | onnontio |
It is not unimportant | he will be on top of life, rejoice | French governor |
d'ehakak8a | [,]entiok8annen | de xeena |
he will look at it | it is a large clan, group (?) | I have them (ind) as children |
on,akatanda | ti | 8a,iata8enk |
I went visiting | as, of | it happened to me |

It is not a trifling matter that the French governor will rejoice when he looks at it, "A great group of my children I went about looking at, visiting, as it happened to me."

Te ,8annonronk8annionk | sk8andata8eti |
I greet you (pl) with great respect | all your (pl) villages |
e,ihej | aθo stan te a,aka | d' e,8annonh8eha |
I will die | if only not I will not quit | I will love you (pl) |

"I greet all of your villages with great respect, if only I will die without leaving my love for you."

Tsak8ichennia | d' esk8akaratat | orih8ato,eʻti |
Do it with all your force | you (pl) will take care of it | it is a special, true matter |
a8eti d' | (e)hesk8atrihotat | de sk8arih8anienstandik de |
all that which | he will listen to you (pl) | you (pl) teach us those |
sk8aena
you will have us as children

Take care of this special matter with all of your force. He will listen to you instruct us, you who are our parents (?).

θo | i,e8endetsi | ondechra8asti ,iatsi |
There, then | it is the length of my word | Richardie I am called |

That is the end of the words of I who am called Beautiful Country.

Long Translation
Father Richardie (Beautiful Country) greets the Wendat of all the villages at the mouth of the river. Scarcely had I stopped myself, I used to think, "They are vain, those I went about following who go about ambushing your parents." Those who are French governors are your brothers. It is not the whole word story (?), my thoughts were such in order that I strengthen their hands.

My children, it is again as it was in the spring when I felt pain, perhaps it will diminish, when I will return forever. In the meantime come see us, for we are all the children of the governor, and listen to our word where (we) live. Listen to us completely. Do not listen to the bad thoughts that you have had. It is not even a little possible that which you used to think was entirely true. We who are Jesuits (they are called charcoal, black) did not cause those of our children who are Christians to doubt. That, then I will be sure that you will love us (at least) a little enough when I will look at those who are attached to my children. Perhaps they are not disposed to finding us. I will say in my mind, "Those who are my children say many things without reason. They do not love me." The French governor wishes, "It would happen to them, that they would be skillfully made as parents and children." You will all listen as it is a matter of this country.

Your brothers, those of Wendake (the Huron), are sure about it. Think it, then, you two "They are not lying outsiders, they are great Christians." They go straight to the whole matter. Lie to us, my children, and you will think, "Our father fools us that he has us as children, that he gave birth to us, that is such that he caused us to enter into the special group or clan of Christians."

Have courage, then. Cleanse your heart from the corruption that covered it. It is not even a little bit bad, the heart of the French governor. You have an extraordinary amount of pity on us. You listen to us in all sorts of things. They tell stories, those who disapprove of his conduct. "We love you" is completely not on their lips. He continually repeats the same question: "What happened to the bad thoughts of Sastaretsi? I don't have knowledge of his ever mistake-making. I love him completely. I will love him forever." He who is our governor is not hateful my children, he used to think, "the Iroquois' wish was for peace in my country" and now it is the third time he killed us, the Mohawk. He did not wish for you to make recompense forever, he thought that, "He will perhaps stop himself."

It is true that they hate each other's minds very much, the French governor and all the English governors of New York. He used to think only, the French governor, "They (should) not search after him, outwardly, on this side, nearby they come to amuse themselves with (i.e., torture) my warrior children and nephews." It is not someone else's matter now. He will wish, "He will cease going about killing all over the countryside in this country."

Again, I say, "Follow their words, my children. Remember the thoughts, intentions of those who were the ancestor elders." They continually went about encouraging each other saying… our country will be strong, we will attach ourselves to the body of the governor. Stop that which carries your thoughts elsewhere. Depart from the elders, my children. Depart from the warriors also, my children. Take care of those who are women and all children. It is not a trifling matter that the French governor will rejoice when he looks at it, "A great group of my children I went about looking at, visiting, as it happened to me." "I greet all of your villages with great respect, if only I will die without leaving my love for you." Take care of this special matter with all of your force. He will listen to you instruct us, you who are our parents (?). That is the end of the words of I who am called Beautiful Country.

Appendix B5: Father Richer to Father Potier

Father Daniel Richer worked with the Huron at Wendake from 1715 to 1760. He, along with the people of Wendake, taught the Wendat language to both his fellow Jesuits Richardie and Potier. His ability in the language was such that he was given the name Hechon, previously given to Father Jean de Brébeuf and Father Pierre Chaumonot, two missionaries with exceptional abilities in Wendat who wrote dictionaries in Wendat.

P. Richer mihi[1] et aux hurons de lorette venus ici en ambassade du 26 dec: 1746 recu le 4 avril 1747

[Father Richer to me[2] (Potier?) and to the Huron of Lorette who came here in an embassy on 26 December 1746, received 4 April 1747] (Potier 1920, 687)

a,isten | (ae)k8a8e,ik | asken de | di8 |
my father | we (inc) should be together | let it be | God |

My father, we should be together with God.

te hesk8annonronk8annionk de | hechon | hesk8annonh8e |
he oils your (pl) scalp many times, greets you with respect | Richer | he loves you (pl) |

Hechon greets you with great respect. He loves you.

Estennia,on | ,8aena
Have courage | my children

Have courage, my children!

Onne | a,8atendoton | ti | hondi,onr8ten |
Behold | I tell you a story | of | his thoughts are of such a nature |

d' | onnontio | daat | hesk8andoronk8a | irerhe |
who | French governor | the very | he values you (pl) in such a way | he thinks |
daat | hotindi,onr8annens | hotindi,onra8astis |
the very | they (m) have great minds | they (m) have beautiful, peaceful minds |
hatinnion,enhak | daat | hotirih8iosti |
they (m) are French | the very | they (m) make the matter great, are Christians |

Behold, I tell you a story of the thoughts of the French governor. You are valuable, dear to him. He thinks that the French have very great, peaceful minds, and are very good Christians.

Irerhe | ati | otase'ti,e | ahotindi,onraiannonton |
He thinks | then | in hiding, in private | they (m) examined their minds, thoughts for holes |
annen | daat | hati8endandoronk8a | onnontio |
where | the very | they (m) value the words, their words are valued (?) French governor |
chia | d' | ahonk8ichoton | ahonatihetsaron |
at the same time the | their (m) forces would stand | they (m) would encourage them (m) |
n' (h)ontaxen d' | ahona8endrak8a |
they (m) are brothers | they (m) would follow his word |

He wishes that in private they examine their thoughts where they greatly value the words of the French governor. At the same time they who would have great force exhort, encourage their brothers to follow his word.

stihon | etiorhen'tronnon | ason,8andask8entaj de |
say it | English | he would have us as prisoners |
haonh8a | ha8endio | ahaton | dex' | ondechen |
himself | he is a great in voice | he would become | this | country is lying |
atiaondi | aonsa8atron8a | de ,arih8iosti |
completely | it would disappear | one makes a matter great, is a Christian, Christianity |

Say it, "The English would have us as prisoners and he alone would become great in voice, master of this country, and Christianity would disappear."

Onne | ti | ,arih8etsi | d' | hatatiak |
Behold | as, of | it is a matter of such a length | that which | he talks, his talking |
Hechon | ho8ennonh8a | n'onh8a | d' onnontio |
Richer | he carries, brings his word | now | French governor |

Behold, it is the length of the talking of Hechon. He now brings the words of the French governor.

Ndio¹ | ,8aena | ,8atrendaentandihatie | ,8annonh8e |
Come on! | I have you (pl) as children | I go about praying for you (pl) | I love you (pl) |
e,ak8ichoton | de | ,arih8a8eti | ,aatata,e |
I will have force | that which | it is all a matter | it is such a number of bodies |
de sk8ah8atsira | askennonnia | a8aton |
your (pl) lineage | in peace | it became |

"Come, my children. I go about praying for you. I love you. I will have the force for your whole lineage to live in peace."

Onne | a,isten | ta,atrendaenhas | de ,e,otsindachia |
Behold | my father | pray for me | I (an) old person |
8a θo | hechon ,iatsi |
Again | Hechon I am called. |

Behold, my father, pray for me, an old person.³ Again, Richer, I am called.

Long Translation

My father, we should be together with God. Richer greets you with great respect. He loves you. Have courage, my children! Behold, I tell you a story of the thoughts of the French governor. You are valuable, dear to him. He thinks that the French have very great, peaceful minds, and are very good Christians. He wishes that in private they examine their thoughts where they greatly value the words of the French governor. At the same time they who would have great force exhort, encourage their brothers to follow his word. Say it, "The English would have us as prisoners and he alone would become master of this country, and Christianity would disappear."

Behold, it is the length of the talking of Hechon. He now brings the words of the French governor. "Come, my children. I go about praying for you. I love you. I will have the force for your whole lineage to live in peace."

Behold, my father, pray for me, an old person. Again, Richer, I am called.

APPENDIX C: N'ENDI

N'endi #1 (Potier 1920, 687–88)

Located just after the correspondence are two passages named simply "n'endi," which means "we, us" (also "I" as it is a first-person particle). It matches the particle pronouns of *sa* for second person and *ondaie* for third person. It might have been some kind of in-house newsletter in Wendat written by Richardie and or Potier. It would be interesting to try to discover whether more of these exist. We would learn a lot.

Otrih8atontandi | ,8aena!... |
it is frightening | I have you (pl) as children, my children |

It is frightening, my children!

Atiaondi | otrih8atontand | ti | otieren | d8a | d' |
entirely | it is frightening | as, of | they (f) do it | others | those who |
otinnhetien | θoia | onne | i8enta,e |
they (f) are women | several, many | behold, when | such a number of days |
otirih8andera,i[1] | isen-chien, | otirih8andera,i | daat | orih8io! |
they (f) are mistaken | certainly | they (f) are mistaken | the very | it is a great matter |

It is completely frightening, that which other women do many days. They make mistakes, certainly they make great mistakes.

Taoten | otirih8andera,i[2]? |
wh-q | they (f) make mistakes |

What are their mistakes?

Ondaie | otirih8andera,i | d' ai8chra8endihatie[3] | d' |
it, they | they (f) make mistakes | she, one goes about full of grape(s) | that which |
a8e,atsi8a,en | ai8nnonratont, |
it is a bad tasting liquid[4] | she, one would cause someone to lose one's scalp |

They are mistaken in going around full of bad-tasting grape liquid, causing one to lose one's scalp (mind?).

Achienk | i8ennon | d' | otirih8andera,i, |
three | they (f) are such a number together | the | they (f) make mistakes |
tendi | [,]aenx8ake | skat | atiaondi | ,andata,e: |
they (f) are two | in a field | it is one | completely | in a village |

There are three (kinds of) mistake making, two in a field, and one completely in a village.

8enchtra | de | θo | onsa8enk | d'a8ask8ak |
Perhaps | (if) | there, that | it happened again | afterwards |
exeatingenk | onnonchiato,eti,e, | aste |
I will put them (ind) out | at a straight, true, holy house | outside |
e,ontrendaen | n'ondaie: |
they (f) will put orenda, pray | they |

If it happens again, I will put them outside the true house; they will pray outside.

ehotinn[g]iann[d]ik | stan | te e8ationde |
it will be a long time for them (m)[5] | not | they (f) will not enter |
onnonchiato,eti,e, |
in a true, straight, holy house|
θo | atiaondi | ea8enk | i,e8endetsi |
there | completely | it will happen | such is the length of my word |

It will be a long time they will not enter a true house, that entirely will happen. That is the length, end of my word.

Long Translation

It is frightening, my children! It is completely frightening, that which other women do many days. They make mistakes, certainly they make great mistakes. What are their mistakes? They are mistaken in going around full of bad-tasting grape liquid, causing one to lose one's scalp. There are three (kinds of) mistake making, two in a field, and one completely in a village. If it happens again, I will put them outside the true house; they will pray outside. It will be a long time they will not enter a true, straight, holy house, that entirely will happen. That is the length, end of my word.

N'endi #2 (Potier 1920, 688)

onne | (e)sk8endit[k]iok8ichien⁶ | sk8a,i8annens, |
behold | they (f) will again form a group | you (pl) are elders |
sk8annhetien, | a8eti | de | sk8askenra,etak, |
you (pl) are women, | all | those who | you (pl) are warriors |

Behold, they again form a group, you who are elders, you who are women and all you who are warriors.⁷

Tsatrihotat, | onne | ârih8ten | n'onh8a | ex' | entate: |
pay attention | behold | my news, matter is such | now | this | day exists |

Pay attention, behold my matter is such this day.

Otiok8andoron⁸ | chia | ,entiok8a8eti |
it is their (f) valuable group | at the same time | all a group together |

d' | hotiskenra,etak | d' | hondariskonnen |
those who | they (m) are warriors | those who | they (m) ventured together |
,ondastak8andinnen ichien de | Marie | d' | ason | ndeheren |
they (m) promised her | Marie, Mary | when | still | far |
a te ontre | ahendihon: |
they (ind) are distant | they (m) said |

Otiok8andoron and all the warriors who ventured together promised Marie, when still they were far away, they said:

ta8entenr | Marie d'ies8s | hechiena, |
have pity, compassion on us | Marie of Jesus | you have him as child |
ta,8aatannonstat | d' etsa,8ahaon d' |
preserve us | we (exc) return (it) |
etiendare | d' a,8ataken | n' |
where they (i) live | we (exc) are brothers, our brothers | those who |
onxiatrendaentandi | d' | hotirih8iosti |
they (ind) cause prayers for us | those who | they (m) make the matter great, are Christians |

Have pity on us, Mary, who has Jesus as her child, preserve we who return to where our brothers live, those who cause prayers to be said for us, those who are believers, Christians.

Exechiensta, | a,8erhe | n'ondaie |
I will fete them, hold a feast for them (ind) | we wish, think | those who |
axinnonronk8annion[9]._ |
we greet them (ind) with great respect |

I (Otiok8andoron?) will hold a feast for them, we think, those whom we greet with great respect.

Ha,onatrihotati | de Marie ha,o(n)atannonstatihatie |
she pays attention to them (m) | Marie she goes about preserving them (m) |
stan | ichien skat etioton. |
not | one one is lost |

She pays attention to them, Marie, she goes about preserving them. Not one is lost.

Sa,otenri (v. Ha,ontenri)[10] | iθondi | son,8a8endio[11] |
he has pity, compassion on them (ind) | also | he is great in voice to us |
θo ichien | ia8endi | ti | hotindi,onr8ten._ |
there, then | it happened | as | their (m) minds, thoughts are such |

He has compassion on them also, he who is great in voice to us. It happens as their minds are such.

Ahati8endaierit | ichien onh8a | ex['] entate | de |
they (m) cause her word to be completed | now | this day | those who |
sa,ochiensθa | (h)ontaxen | d' |
he fetes them, causes a feast for them (ind) | they (m) are brothers | those who |
hotirih8iosti | n' | onxiatrendaentandihik |
they (m) are Christians | those who | they (ind) prayed for us, caused prayer for us |
ondaie de | sa,ochienstak8a a8e,aa8i d' |
they | he feted them (ind) with such a thing it is good tasting water, liquid |
oskennonton, | a8eti | endiahaia[12] | d'oskennonton | x' ondaie_. |
deer | all | a little food | that which is deer | this it |

They cause her word to be completed, those who this day he fetes. They are siblings, those believers who prayed for us. They he feted with good-tasting water and deer, all the food is deer.

Long Translation
Behold, they again form a group, you who are elders, you who are women and all you who are warriors. Pay attention, behold my matter is such this day. Otiok8andoron and all the warriors who ventured together promised Marie, when still they were far away, they said: "Have pity on us, Mary, who has Jesus as her child, preserve we who return to where our brothers live, those who cause prayers to be said for us, those who are believers, Christians. I will hold a feast for them, we think, those whom we greet with great respect." She pays attention to them, Marie, she goes about preserving them. Not one is lost. He has compassion on them also, he who is great in voice to us. It happens as their minds are such. They cause her word to be completed, those who this day he fetes. They are siblings, those believers who prayed for us. He (presumably the Striped Turtle leader Otiok8andoron) feted them with good-tasting water and deer, all the food is deer.

APPENDIX D: FESTIN DES NOCES

In Potier's collection of religious writings in the Wendat language, there is a passage entitled *Festin des Noces*, or Wedding Ceremony (Potier 1920, 570–71). It is an important passage in relating what I would call the Jesuits' soft-sell approach to this sacrament. It begins with a reference to the seven sacraments. Then we have the following:

I am about to tell a story about marriage, as it is told in the holy writing. They are inviting Jesus to their marriage. Jesus and Marie together, parent and child, they invited them. It is like Jesus commences to be present at their ceremony. He thought, "It would be valuable, getting married." He thought also, "It would be valuable to humans when they marry." Would it be unimportant, then, that it is valuable, that which is called being married? As he himself made a matter, he who is great in voice, that they would marry, it would be a sacred marriage, he made that when they get married they pray.

They made mistakes in great matters, those who do not keep the matters of he who is great in voice. Others going about destroying what Jesus, he is great in voice, made. Having compassion, he made a matter for us, Jesus. He thought, "I will pray for them. It is good that I will make for them that which will make them do good, that they will go to marry." One thing he thought:

> It will strengthen marriage. They will no longer divorce, when I pray for them. They will become one in their bodies when they take each other. They are of one mind, also, they will become two together. They two will love each other, they two are together in that they will help each other with such an instrument.

Would it be unimportant that those who make mistakes would not help each other, and not love each other, those who are spouses? Would they not have made mistakes, those who would commit adultery? They corrupt marriage, those who marry, commit adultery, and divorce. They break in many places, marriage, that which he who is great in voice made. They are again separated, from he who is great in voice, also when they divorce, those who are spouses. It has no power, when they are married, when they pray, wishing, "She should divorce me, she who is my spouse. It is not possible. You two are separated, you and he who is great in voice, when you wish, "I would be separated (again) my spouse and I."

Give thanks, you who are married, by praying. He who is great in voice did good for you. Do good, then, take care of sacred marriage, that which Jesus who is great in voice made, since he wished, "They should do good, those who would go to marry. It is true that they will profit from it, that matter which I made for them."

It is one thing that he wished, he who is great in voice, as he made marriage, "It would cure them in vain, they would make marriage, peacefully place. Do not have sex with others." Do not make mistakes in sex. This one that he wished for, he who is great in voice, "When they go to marry," he wished, thought, "A human would be born. It is true that they will teach each other, those who will give birth. It is true that they will take care of each other, those who would do good."

Notes

NOTES TO CHAPTER 1

1 There are several alternatives available for naming these people. I have chosen to call them "Wyandot" as they were ancestral to the peoples of Michigan, Kansas, and Oklahoma who so name themselves now. Contemporary writers referred to them as "Huron," as do several modern writers. I do not so name them as they were linguistically distinct from their Huron cousins, as well as having a somewhat different clan system, which is a major part of this work. The language itself I tend to refer to as Wendat, which has dialects including Wyandot, which I suspect is based in one of the dialects of the Petun, and was most similar to the Wendat dialect spoken among the Southern Bear (see Steckley 2007a, 45), long-term neighbours of the Petun (see chapter 2).
2 Jacques Charles Sabrevois, Sieur de Bleury, commenting in 1718, wrote: "They build their cabins all of bark and make them very substantial, High and rounded like arbors, and very long" ("Wisconsin Historical Collections" 1902, 16:368).
3 For example, Raymond Firth's classic *We, the Tikopia* (1957), based on the New Zealand anthropologist's five months of fieldwork in 1928–29 on the small Pacific island of Tikopia, presents the four-clan social structure of the people in a way that presumes little European or other contact and that assumes there had previously been no change for an extensive time period. While elegant in its functionalist description, we get no sense of how the clan structure came to be.
4 This is based on the noun root *-h8end-* "island" (Steckley 2007b, 100–101). The basic problem with this as a potential meaning is that there would be no pronominal prefixes in this word. Wendat verbs require pronominal prefixes. For example, with the Wendat name for Christian Island, by the southern

shores of Georgian Bay, we have ,ah8endo,e, meaning "it is an island in water." The verb root involved is -o- "to be in water" (Steckley 2007b, 291–92). The pronominal prefix is -,a- (ya) meaning here "it."

5 Charles Garrad, the foremost archaeologist working on Petun sites, often remarks on the fact that the ethnohistorical literature makes it seem that the Petun grew this tobacco, even though there is no evidence for this and there is a long history of tobacco growing in southwestern Ontario, by the Neutral, by the settlers that followed, and by the tobacco industry until fairly recently.

6 I wonder whether the Huron ever adopted Champlain, giving him a name and a clan. They probably would not have tried to pronounce his name, the -m- and -l- in Samuel, and the -p- and -l- in Champlain being too alien to them (none of these sounds were in their language).

7 Sagard several times made some cultural commentary in the lines of his dictionary, telling people not to oil themselves with sunflower oil (Steckley 2010, 269) and such. One of my favourite translations from one of the lines in Sagard's dictionary is (from the French, the Huron is awkward but close) "Do not fart here. Go fart outside" (Steckley 2010, 359).

8 Here we find such features as a -g- after an -n- and before an -i-. This is written as a superscript above the -d- that appears in other Wendat dialects. Then there's another -g-, this time written above the second of two -n's- written before an -i-. Another prominent feature is a -k- written over a -t- that appears before an -i-.

9 By 1718 they were growing French peas and wheat ("Wisconsin Historical Collections" 1902, 16:368).

NOTES TO CHAPTER 2

1 One could argue that this could be expanded to five peoples, if you consider the St. Lawrence Iroquoians and the Wenro, who joined the Huron before the dispersal.

2 In the early 1700s, the Tuscarora, who lived in the North Carolina area, were being harassed by American settlers, which eventually led to the Tuscarora War of 1711 and 1713. They moved west and were invited to join the Confederacy. They were sponsored in 1722 by the Oneida and given land in Confederacy territory.

3 Masculine will hereafter be represented in translation as (m). Iroquoian peoples' names involve the masculine plural as it is used when there are both females and at least one male involved. The use of the feminine plural indicates a group that is purely female. The indefinite is another, more generalized, third-person form, meaning "they, people, one."

4 The word is developed from the noun root -nnont- "hill, mountain" (Steckley 2007b, 207), and the verb root -te- "to be present, exist" (Steckley 2007b, 253) with the populative suffix -ronnon- meaning "people of."

5 I suspect that they might have termed the Huron some version of the Bear nation's name (see below).
6 The -8- was a Jesuit convention for writing a -u- over an -o-. It represents a -u- before a consonant and a -w- before a vowel.
7 Excluded here are the *Ataronchronon*, "people of the clay or mud in water" as there were only two references to them in *The Jesuit Relations* (1637, JR13:61; and 1640, JR19:125).
8 The noun root here is -*ngeend*- "fishing line, cord for a net" (Steckley 2007b, 176), and the verb root is -*ondi*- "to make" (Steckley 2007b, 296).
9 The noun root is -'*rend*- "rock, stone" (Steckley 2007b, 227–28). The verb root is -*en*- "to put, lie" (Steckley 2007b, 83).
10 The comma -,- here represents a similar symbol employed by the Jesuits to represent a -y- like sound. The noun root is -*ahont*- "ear" (Steckley 2007b, 17), and the verb root is -,*enrat*- "to be white" (Steckley 2007b, 118).
11 See Hunt (1940) for the "beaver war" hypothesis and Trigger (1976) and Brandão (2000) for different hypotheses, more convincing in nature than Hunt's.
12 One aspect of this involves the nasal vowels written in Wendat and French as -an-, -en-, -in-, and -on-, for which the English language has no direct equivalents.
13 An alternative explanation that is often given was presented by historical geographer Conrad Heidenreich with it coming from "Old French meaning a 'ruffian,' 'unkempt person,' 'knave' or 'lout'" (Heidenreich 1971, 21).
14 This might indicate that this entry was composed when Brébeuf was working with the Huron Christian, Joseph Chihoatenhwa, who was of the Turtle clan (see Steckley 2007a, 52).
15 A noun stem is distinct from a noun root in that it includes a verb root plus a suffix, usually the nominalizer -ch(r)-, but sometimes the instrumental suffix.
16 The instrumental is a root suffix that typically adds a "by such a means" or "to or at such a place." With a very few roots, the instrumental transforms a verb root into a noun stem:
  k8atoioannonχ8a we were moved by such a means
  aioɴ8atientak we would be put in such a place
17 While other Northern Iroquoian languages have the form with the instrumental suffix, in modern dictionaries the resultant noun stem does not refer to clans, but to any group (see Steckley 2007b, 286). They do not still have the verb root from which it came. Long-term contact with English speakers probably was the reason for the loss.
18 Father Jean de Brébeuf used the noun stem to refer to "church," in the general sense of the Christian church (see Steckley 1978).
19 In a minority of the dictionaries a -g- was used initially where others sources use the -,-.
20 This quotation alone should have informed scholars that Rat and Sastaretsi were not the same person.

21 For accounts of the Condolence Ceremony, see William Fenton's *The Great Law and the Longhouse* (1998), and chapters 4 and 5 in Horatio Hale's *The Iroquois Book of Rites* (1883).
22 The Wendat noun root -8end- refers to "voice, word" (Steckley 2007b, 216).
23 The French recorders of Wendat words often missed the initial 'h,' which was unfortunate as that could change the pronominal gender of a Wendat word, the -h- coming with the masculine form typically. Without that initial -h- the verb or noun would usually be considered female or as 'it.' That could mean that the Jesuits, when they were first learning the Wendat language, might often be referring to females, when a male reference was intended.
24 Interestingly, this name was in the St. Lawrence Iroquoian language.
25 In presenting these baptisms, I am following Father Toupin's convention of using a B plus a number standing for the number of the baptism on the list.
26 Marguerite Vincent gives the meaning of this name at Wendake as signifying la8inonke, "c'est-à-dire 'la belle fille huronne'" (Vincent 1984, 165).
27 The word *tionnenria* has been broken down as follows:

-ti-	cislocative prefix	"when, where"
-o-	pronominal prefix	"she, it"
-nnenr-	noun root	"group, armed force" (Steckley 2007b, 184)
-ia-	verb root plus diminutive	"it is small" (see Potier 1920, 161)

28 The word *honnentre[a]* has been broken down as follows:

| -honnen- | pronominal prefix | "they–them" |
| -atrea- | verb root | "to have as maternal grandchild" (Steckley 2007b, 61) |

29 The -o- is a pronominal prefix translated as "she, it," and the -t- is the semi-reflexive.
30 The -l- in Oneida corresponds to an -r- in Wendat.
31 In Sagard's dictionary we find the usual term for fox -ndatse- "fox" (FH1697:231), which is used to refer to the clan (see Steckley 2007a, 49, 54), given as referring to "Renard gris" or gray fox, and probably referring to the red fox, a form of otsinnentonk (FH1697:231), referring to what appears to be the cross fox phase of the red fox, and "Hahyuha," which I have yet to decipher, possibly referring to the silver fox (Steckley 2010, 84). The Wyandot referred to the Fox nation as Skenchioronnon (Toupin 1996, 231), a term coming from another Iroquoian language.
32 In Steckley (2007a, 55–60), I suggested that the Aiheonde or inter-clan burial relationship might have been just such a ritual purpose.
33 In the anthropological literature such a division into two is called moiety, from the French word for "half."

34 This is ‚angonchra, which appears to be the noun form of the verb.
35 The -d- and the -g- each are dialect alternatives. The -d- appeared in the Huron word, while Potier had written a -g- as a superscript because that is what he heard among the Wyandot.
36 The word "bandes" was used in the French (JR61:114).
37 I do not know why the word "rear" was used here as the French word was "tete," meaning "head" (JR61:114).

NOTES TO CHAPTER 3

1 Six of the names of the female elders of the Wyandot in 1747 had the repetitive prefix at the beginning of their names. Including Sastaretsi, four of the names of the male elders did so too. The name Sarenhes, "he is long branches, tall treetops," contains the verb root -es-.
2 Archaeological evidence concerning pottery informs us that St. Lawrence women (the makers of the pottery) lived with the Huron, the Petun, the Mohawk, Oneida, and Abenaki (see Chapdelaine 2004 and Petersen et al. 2004).
3 This appears to be the name *oracha* given to Jesuit Father Charles Garnier before his death in 1649 (JR16:239; 22:151; 33:111). One problem is that I cannot find a successor to that name that would have been there in 1661.
4 The Miami are an Algonquian-speaking group then living by the western shores of Lake Michigan. Their Wendat name was Aθochingotronnon, "Crane people," named after the sandhill crane, traditionally sacred to the Miami. The name of this people has nothing to do with that of the city in Florida.
5 This may be a miscopy of the French "de la grue" meaning "of the crane," referring to the sacred animal of the Miami (Callender 1978, 689).
6 This would be written in Wendat as "a8eti haondechio or haonh8entsio," meaning "all, he is great or large in the country, in the world" (Steckley 2007b, 215, 296, 298).
7 I say inaccurately here as the -k- would represent a -y- (or -‚-) combining with a -t-. That would happen with the feminine form -‚a- (-ya-), but there is no form -‚o- that fits any pronominal prefix.
8 The name is derived from the verb root *-sk8in-* "to go or come running, in a hurry" (Steckley 2007b, 246). With the -t- causative suffix, it could add the meaning "for some reason, by some cause."
9 This could mean "it is a very small chest or trunk of the body," with the noun *-sk8-* "chest, trunk of the body" (Steckley 2007b, 243) incorporated into the verb *-a-* "to be such a size, quantity" (Steckley 2007b, 13).
10 This differs from the more well-known *ondatra* or *ondathra*, found in Sagard's writings (see Steckley 2010, 85), which appears in no other source. It is used as the species name for muskrat.

11 If Kandiaronk was Wolf phratry, and Burnt Tongue was Deer phratry, this person would be representing the Turtle phratry.
12 The capitals are as in the original, which, it should be noted, was not written by someone with the Wendat language experience of Potier.
13 There is an earlier person by that name who died at an old age in 1694 (La Potherie 3:94–193, 222–3, 226; see Havard 2001, 203). The Baron that I am speaking of may well have been of his clan and his successor. Of course, he may have been named after some connection he had with Lahontan.
14 Jacob Te Hatontaratase was said by Potier to be that old in 1747 (Toupin 1996, 209).
15 In prayer, this term would appear as chie8endio st'a,ionnhe: "you are great in voice in our lives, our living." The term "Ha8endio," meaning "he is great in voice" was often used to refer to God.
16 This occurred with other labial (pronounced with the lips) sounds from non-Iroquoian languages. For example, an -m- was changed into a -w- in Jesuit Father Simon Le Moyne's last name: Wane (JR16:239). The same happened with the name Marie, which in 1636 was written (and presumably spoken) as "8arie" (JR10:72).
17 The -g- in both these names suggests that they were Iroquois. In Wendat there would be a -y- like sound there. In the second word the double -n- suggests an Iroquois language.
18 This last reference is to an aspect of their shared Iroquoian story of the origin of all things.
19 The first had been Father Paul Ragueneau, Superior of the Jesuits at Sainte-Marie Among the Hurons during the last years of the mission.
20 There was a Christian burial notice recorded in 1753 of "Marg: Saati (La la mothe) enceinte de 3 mois." It would seem that she had changed her Wyandot name, but not her French Christian name or the French surname that she was associated with.
21 This is an apparent reference to the long-term southern Ontario home of the Petun and the Huron.
22 Unfortunately, I can neither translate this name nor connect it with any name found in Potier's writings. I suspect it may have looked something like Chi hannon8tson.
23 Recollect Brother Gabriel Sagard wrote with reference to the verb root -*nnion,en*-, that it referred to the French as "iron people" (Sagard 1939, 79). However, it does not do so in the Wendat language as far as I can determine. Perhaps this term comes from the language of the St. Lawrence Iroquoians. A number of peoples' names in Sagard's dictionary came from that language (see Steckley 2012). In the Wendat dictionary that I composed, I referred to the verb root as meaning "to be French, pot, kettle" (Steckley 2007b, 195). It is not etymologically linked to any other Wendat term for "pot."
24 The causative suffix -t- is added to the verb root -*atati*- "to talk, speak" (Steckley 2007b, 40), giving it this meaning.

NOTES TO CHAPTER 4

1. The B followed by a number is the baptism number as recorded by Potier and/or Toupin.
2. In that year the Catawba were hit hard by smallpox. Perhaps this led them to seek alliances.
3. A census of "warriors" taken in 1736 (see NYCD9:1057–58) stated that the Wyandot of Detroit had two hundred warriors. The Ottawa were recorded as having two hundred in their Detroit village and another eighty in a village near the Saginaw River.
4. This word, meaning "it is very cold," is derived from the Wendat verb root -nd8st- "to be cold" (Steckley 2007b, 173–74), and refers to the cold water of a spring.
5. For another indication of Richardie's negative attitude towards Ang8irot, see Michigan 34:172.
6. Of the two words presented for "lion" in a French–Wendat dictionary, one is "Tiontara,onra," which can be translated as "where the lake is white" (FH1697:231).
7. It might be important to note here that the word Sandusky, where some of the Wyandot stayed, refers to a cold spring (see n4).
8. The Jesuits were not called Black Robes in the Wendat language. They were term "hatsihenstatsi," "they (m) are called charcoal," with the noun root -tsihenst- (Steckley 2007b, 262) and the verb root -as- "to name, be called" (Steckley 2007b, 69–70). This was their term for the colour black. As the Jesuits always wore black, this was an appropriate appellation.
9. For example, at a meeting of the Six Nations of the Iroquois and their allies with the governor of New York held at Albany in August and September of 1746, it was recorded that:

    > There is a Nation call'd the Messagues [Mississaugas], whose Delegates are here present: They consist of five Castles, containing eight hundred men, who are all determined, and do agree to join us, in this common Cause, against our Enemies the French, and their Indians. (Colden 1972, 177)

10. Some years later, Potier would use this method to prevent a large number of Wyandot from joining with the Ottawa resistance fighter, Pontiac. See chap. 5.
11. The first Huron name given to Chaumonot was the slightly different *Aronhiatiri* (JR33:169–71), which meant "he supports the sky" and comprises the noun root -ronhi- "sky" (Steckley 2007b, 236) and the verb root -atiri- "to support" (Steckley 2007b, 51). It does not appear again as a Jesuit name, but in 1769 ,aronhiatiri was the name of a baptized child's father (Toupin 1996, 893, B1213), and was a participant in an anniversary service (Toupin 1996, 945).
12. It is intriguing for me to speculate whether this implies that Hechon was a newly created Wolf clan name. The thinking here (which is not proof) is that if Chaumonot had been adopted by the Wolf clan, then any name he would come to bear would also be Wolf clan.

13 In all there were twenty-seven ages given, but three of them were repeated individuals.
14 In terms of the "sample bias," discussed in chapter 5, this moves them up five places in the ranking, which is significant.
15 Three of the names are repeated in two houses.
16 I have been unable to find a meaning for this word, other than to discover that it was a name of nobility in France—not, I think, what the Jesuits intended.
17 Of course, this clan's lack of participation in baptismal services might have made their adoption of Fox harder for researchers to detect.
18 The words "soeur ad," meaning "sister of," were written in the first census (Toupin 1996, 203), but did not say "sister of" whom.
19 The possibility exists that the name, which should have a final -t-, was used to designate rattlesnakes (see FH1697:210; Steckley 2007b, 248), meaning "one has rattles attached," with the noun root or stem -sta8ench- "turtle shell rattle" (Steckley 2007b, 248) with the verb root -ont- "to attach, be attached" (Steckley 2007b, 303).
20 A Pierre 8e8as was baptized as an adult in 1736 (B359). I suspect he was her brother, as he had a wife named Marie ,ahenhe, to whom he was married from the 1730s to 1759 (see B1024).
21 There was an Abenaki man named Taonda8is who was married in 1738 to a Wyandot woman named Nniendita (Toupin 1996, 845; B865). But she was listed as a widow in 1747 (see Appendix A).

NOTES TO CHAPTER 5

1 The actual term for baptism in the Wendat language employed the noun root -ndek8- "water" (Steckley 2007, 150–51) and the verb root -ae- "to hit, strike, run into" (Steckley 2007b, 15). Also added was the causative-instrumental root suffix -st-, giving the general meaning of "to cause to be struck with water" for baptism (see FH1697:22).
2 The word translated as "group" here, ,entiok8a, can also refer to matrilineal clan, as was discussed in chapter 2.
3 In this context it refers to godmother.
4 In this context it refers to godfather.
5 The age was presented when the person being baptized wasn't a newborn. Only rarely did the record spell out that the baptized was a newborn.
6 This refers to the fact that the baptizing priest did not know the name of the father. It does not necessarily mean that the mother did not. She might not want to have incriminated the father in the missionary's eyes.
7 In the system of kinship known to anthropologists as "Iroquoian," which is the system that Wendat kinship falls under, your mother's sisters' children and your father's brothers' children are considered your siblings.
8 It is possible that more than one person with this name was involved.
9 It is possible that more than one person with this name was involved.

10 As three of the times he was a godfather were after 1747 (1762, B1086; 1774, B1285; 1777, B1378; Toupin 1996, 884, 897, 903), it could be that he was on an elders' council after 1747.
11 This refers to being the first named of the female elders.
12 There might be two people who had this name.
13 She was eleven in 1747 (see PV10); she became a godmother long after 1747.
14 The form hon'da means "he is a spouse" and on'da means "she is a spouse." There was no separate verb or noun root for "husband" or "wife," "groom" or "bride." This reflects the Wendat language tendency to use verbs rather than nouns for identification, and that kinship terms are expressed in relationships between individuals.
15 The first part of the translation represents the Latin text; the second part represents the Wendat text.
16 This is one of a very small number of mentions of the Sturgeon clan.
17 The -tk- here, and in other examples in this chart, represents Potier's writing a superscript -k- to indicate what the Wyandot feature was. Wyandot had -ky- where the Wendake dialect of Wendat had -ty-.
18 The reference to the male gender was added in translation here because in the original French the two masculine nouns "le défunt" and "le nom" (JR60:34) are used, with the masculinity being just that of the noun, not the referents.
19 Raccoons were early referred to in seventeenth- and eighteenth-century French as "chat sauvage." Also see entiron, which means "raccoon" (FH1697:231; Toupin 1996, 914).
20 I translated it this way on the possibility that the word here is short for onnon'k8arota (Steckley 2007b, 204).
21 This makes reference to the one heading the council held in this ceremony, with the noun root -hach- , which typically refers to "flame" and "council," the latter especially when the verb root -en- "to put, lie" is used, as in this case (Steckley 2007b, 91, 83).
22 This makes reference to the one who sings or prays in sacred ceremony, with the noun root -rend-, "sacred ceremony, prayer, dance, song" (Steckley 2007b, 227) used with the verb root -en- "to put, lie" (Steckley 2007b, 83).
23 The verb root in the second word is -on'da- "to be a spouse" (Steckley 2007b, 295).
24 The verb root in the second word is -nd8en- "to be mother to" (Steckley 2007b, 172–73).
25 This is translated this way on the possibility that the word is ,ari8'ta "stone" (Steckley 2007, 234).
26 That is if the word is ,atsena. It could also be ,aten8aka "shirt" (Steckley 2007b, 255–56).
27 It is listed as being what in French is called a "tavelle" (Toupin 1996, 918), which I cannot find a translation for. Unfortunately, there is no apparent Wendat translation either.
28 It appears to be constructed from -8,ats- "flesh, meat" (Steckley 2007b, 215), and the verb root -,ete- "to carry" (Steckley 2007b, 121).

NOTES TO CHAPTER 6

1. In my work in this dictionary < > is used for translations from Wendat, while [ ] is used for translations from French.
2. In a catechism about Joseph written by an unknown Jesuit, his son, Jesus, was referred to as "Hoton8eientichichia,innen," meaning "he had achieved, completed the age of a young man" (Potier 1920, 567 line 22; my translation).
3. Unfortunately, this name does not appear elsewhere in Toupin's recording of Potier's records, so we cannot track this individual's life path prior to his death. There was an Armand Tseannon, who was a godfather in 1732 (Toupin 1996, 831, B197), but he was of the Porcupine clan.
4. This is the Detroit council concerning the Schieffelin Deed, 22 October 1783 (Curnoe 1996, 218).
5. Such was how Potier often recorded names. Jean Baptiste Te Horonhiateχa was known as "Piponette" and his mother was known as "la vielle pipon[ette]" (Toupin 1996, 216).
6. The "big" comes from this being a form of -,8annen- "to be large" (Steckley 2007b, 108).
7. The name 8ate,enronnon was used to refer to the Catawba in the eighteenth century (Toupin 1996, 231), but got switched to the Cherokee by the time Barbeau was collecting Wyandot stories. The name contains the noun root -,ate- "hole, cavern, cave" (Steckley 2007b, 113) and the locative "at," along with the populative -ronnon- "people of."
8. The noun root here is -nnenh- "corn" (Steckley 2007b, 183), which unsurprisingly was a common noun root employed in Wendat names, and the verb root is -a- "to be such a size, quantity" (Steckley 2007b, 13).
9. While technically the term *otrea* means "she has her as granddaughter," since all of these entries have *otrea*, none *hotrea*, which means "she has him as grandchild," I think that Potier only knew that it was a grandchild.
10. Here, as elsewhere, the -g- signals the Wyandot dialect form for which the Wendake dialect used -d-.
11. This makes reference to the name of a prominent French family in New France, not to being a small child.
12. This name does not appear elsewhere in the mourning rituals.
13. The "v" here is short for the Latin *vel* meaning "or."
14. The verb root involved here is -oren- "to split in two" (Steckley 2006b, 306).
15. The word *ha8endio* with the noun root -8end- "voice, word" (Steckley 2007b, 216) and the verb root -io- "to be great, large" (Steckley 2007b, 290) was usually used in the Jesuit literature to refer to the Christian God.
16. The noun root here is -tsinnontsir- "head" (Steckley 2007b, 208). The verb root is -ia,- "to break, cut" (Steckley 2007b, 127). In the second word, the noun root is -ond- "space (in time and place)" (Steckley 2007b, 295), but I am not sure what the verb root is. The meaning of the combination is "to have or be a space, place."

NOTES TO CHAPTER 6   283

17 The noun root here is *-ndi,onr-* "mind, thoughts" (Steckley 2007b, 163).
18 This noun root only appears with this verb, and its precise meaning is not known. I (2007b, 242) refer to it as simply meaning "war."
19 His name is recorded as "tia8endata defunto" (Toupin 1996, 863).
20 The noun stem is *-,entiok8-*, referring to a matrilineal clan or group (see chapter 2 for how it was used). The verb root is *-ndoron-* "to be valuable, difficult" (Steckley 2007b, 171–72). See Appendix D for another reference to him.
21 In the second census, Hondatorenha was mistakenly assigned to the hatindesonk or Hawk clan. He belonged to the Wolf clan. His name means "he finds villages," with the noun root *-ndat-* "village, community" (Steckley 2007b, 145), and the verb root *-oren-* "to find" (Steckley 2007b, 306).
22 The verb root here is *-ennon-* "to keep, protect, take care of" (Steckley 2007b, 275).
23 Note that this name is shared with a8innonke of the Large Turtle clan.
24 In Potier's dictionary, he goes through all the grammatically possible forms of this verb, including "atï,8annens" (Potier 1920, 254), but that is just a grammar exercise, not a clear reference to female elders.
25 The verb root here would appear to be *-tase-* "to turn, twist" (Steckley 2007b, 253). I have been unable to determine what the noun root is.
26 This is not a translation of his Wyandot name, which appears to be constructed with the noun root *-nnenh-* "corn." (Steckley 2007b, 183). I have not yet determined what the verb root could be.
27 The first word uses the verb root *-hetsaron-* "to encourage" (Steckley 2007b, 95–96). The second employs *-(r)io-* "to fight, kill" (Steckley 2007b, 234).
28 The verb root here is *-nnion,en-* "to be French" (Steckley 2007b, 195).
29 The verb root here is *-atati-* "to talk, speak" (Steckley 2007b, 40).
30 The -k- here was a superscript in the original, and exhibits a Wyandot dialect feature.
31 The noun root is *-rih8-* "affair, matter, issue, message, news" (Steckley 2007b, 233), and the verb root is *-8a,-* "to take, hold" (Steckley 2007b, 213).
32 The noun root is *-nnh8-* "door" (Steckley 2007b, 191–92) and the verb root is *-ra-* "to be on top" (Steckley 2007b, 221).
33 Another possible interpretation of this name is "He is a twisted double sky." Either way the noun root is *-ronhi-* "sky" (Steckley 2007b, 236), a common element in Iroquoian names (see n16), and the verb root is *-tase-* "to turn, twist" (Steckley 2007b, 253), which is also fairly common in Wyandot names.
34 This -te- could also be a dualic, rather than the negative, thereby taking away the negative meaning of the translation presented above.
35 The noun root is *-ronhi-* "sky" (Steckley 2007b, 236), and the verb root is *-ate,-* "to burn" (Steckley 2007b, 42).
36 This name is found with either a -t- or an -n- at the beginning.
37 The French word "tresor" is translated in Wendat with the verb *-nnondo-* as in the following: "Tresor, mine dor ou d'argent, ,annondo [Treasure, mine of gold or of silver]" (FH1697:214; Steckley 2007b, 199). There is a possibility that

this verb is composed of a noun root *-nnon-* (such as the one that means "deep water" or "chasm, precipice" (Steckley 2007b, 199) plus the verb root *-o-* "to be in water" (Steckley 2007b, 291–92).
38 This name comprises the noun root *-ontar-* "lake, large body of water" (Steckley 2007b, 304), as in "ontario," "it is a large lake," and the verb root *-tase-* "to twist, turn" (Steckley 2007b, 253). It can either mean "he is not a twisted lake" or "he is a lake twisted double."
39 The noun root has been previously mentioned (n13), and frequently found *-rih8-* "matter, affair," and the verb root is *-ndiont-* "to suspend, hang," (Steckley 2007b, 166). The name also appears as "harih8andinnontak," also written as "harih8andi,ontak" (Toupin 1996, 843, 851).
40 The verb root here is *-,annra-* "to look at" (Steckley 2007b, 107), with the imperative aspect.
41 I see two possibilities concerning the translation of this name. If the noun root is *-renh-* "treetops, branches" (Steckley 2007b, 228), with *-i8oin-*, which is probably *-,8annen-* "to be large" (Steckley 2006b, 108), then we have "large treetops, branches." However, if the noun root is *-ronhi-* "sky" (Steckley 2007b, 236), we have "large sky." Both of these noun roots appear in other names.

NOTES TO CHAPTER 7

1 The Narragansett, whose Algonquian language Williams was writing about, are associated with the Rhode Island area.
2 Potier in his dictionary lists all the plural forms: "a,8aï8annens [we (exclusive) are elders]…k8aï8annens [we (inclusive) are elders]…sk8aï8annens [you (pl) are elders]…hati,8annens [they (m) are elders]…ati,8annens [they (f) are elders]…eï8annens [they (indefinite) are elders] (Potier 1920, 254). It may be evidence that he heard the form, but it seems just as likely that he was showing all the grammatical possibilities, like any good language teacher would.
3 In the first word, the noun root here is *-at-* "body, something living" (Steckley 2007b, 70), and the verb root is *-ndoron-* "to be valuable, difficult" (Steckley 2007b, 171). In the second word, the verb root involved is *-nnhe'tien-* "to be a woman, female" (Steckley 2007b, 190). See its use in Appendix B2 and Appendix B4.
4 This is cognate with the word hati,8annens, mentioned earlier, but with a feminine pronominal prefix.
5 The word "gentile" (cognate with gene and genesis), used in early anthropological works, is derived from the Latin "gens" referring to clan or family. The term "Gentiles" referred in the Bible to peoples that were non-Israelites.
6 The word "sachem" is taken from an Algonquian word for "leader" or "head man." It is often used to refer to the fifty chiefs of the Iroquois Confederacy.
7 This was contested in 1957 for the early contact period by Cara Richards (in Spittal 1990, 149–51).
8 My reasons for suspecting this is that her son Pierre had the priest's name Sarenhes in 1747.

9 His wife was Ottawa, and her clan has not been identified. The Ottawa, like the Anishinabe, had clans.
10 She was a godmother between 1730 and 1740, but does not appear in the official record, or in the census, after that. Unfortunately, I have no clues as to her clan.
11 There might be two people who had this name.
12 She was eleven in 1747 (see PV10); she became a godmother long after 1747.
13 The noun root is -rend- "sacred ceremony, prayer, dance, song" (Steckley 2007b, 237) and the verb root -en- "to put, lie" (Steckley 2007b, 83).
14 This being twenty-one years after the 1747 elder list, other women noted here could have been elders at this time.
15 The noun root is -hach- "flame, council" (Steckley 2007b, 91); the verb root is -en- "to put, lie" (Steckley 2007b, 83).
16 The noun root is -ndient- "snow" (Steckley 2007b, 160), and the verb root is -as- "to name, be called" (Steckley 2007b, 69–70. This is the term for the colour white.
17 This word is translated as "she/he has him as child."
18 The noun stem comes from the verb root -8i- "to gird" (Steckley 2007b, 219).
19 See -,ennonhar- "cloth, fabric" (Steckley 2007b, 281).
20 A tobacco pouch (see -ng8ent- Steckley 2007b, 180) is a male-related article.
21 The verb root here is -arachi8- "to be a shoe" (Steckley 2007b, 26–27).
22 This word is translated as "she has her as maternal grandchild."
23 The term for "wampum bracelet" is -nnenstr- (Steckley 2007b, 186, some forms with -str- and one with -chtr-).
24 This word for cross literally means "one's arms are attached in two places," with the noun root -iachi- "arm, branch of a corn plant" (Steckley 2007b, 127), and the verb root -ont- "to attach, be attached" (Steckley 2007b, 303).
25 A woman named Tando,ares had her children baptized in 1761 (Toupin 1996, 882, B1050) and 1766 (Toupin 1996, 888, B1153); but they took place sufficiently after Tando,ares was an elder in 1747, so that it probably was not Hannenha's sister but someone who took up her name.
26 He repeats this reference to her being "La soeur du gros jacob [Hannenhasa]" in the census for PV18 (Toupin 1996, 215).
27 In the case of Atsironde and T'on8atsarandi, the son was listed as living in two different houses, one of those his mother's, not unusual in the census.
28 His name, written as "Ska~hou~mat," appears as one of the "Principal Chiefs of the Huron nation" at an important council of different nations that met at Detroit on 19 May 1790 (Curnoe 1996, 220).
29 In 1730 a female named "Susanna sendagnon" was baptized (Toupin 1996, 828, B132), with a Snake clan woman as her godmother, no parents being mentioned. The problem with this being Susanne Sendaniont is that there is no reference to this person being Fox (which usually occurred at this time), and she was stated as being two, too young for the person we are talking about here.
30 This appears to refer to an inedible tree root that was used for sewing up canoes (see Steckley 2007b, 256–57).

NOTES TO CHAPTER 8

1 He was also connected with the names d'ate,atak and taontierontie in the records of that time (Toupin 1996, 218).
2 It should be kept in mind here that Sendak8an and Nendeniont were in Sastaretsi's house, where he was the first listed, unusual among men, because he was the grand chief. Similarly, Sendak8an and Onnond8annon were listed as living in the house of Anastasie Ts8nde,en, the most influential of the Bear clan women.
3 It should be noted that she was the second wife of Ta,echiaten, the Wolf phratry leader listed first in her house.
4 It should be noted that she was the second wife of Ta,echiaten, the Wolf phratry leader listed first in her house.
5 Although her Large Turtle elder husband, Nicolas Taronhi8rens, has his name come first, there are more Porcupine clan members in the house.
6 She shared the honour with Bear clan leader A,a8as.

NOTES TO APPENDIX A

1 It is difficult to determine Catawba kinship patterns. Speck (1938) challenged the view that they were matrilineal.
2 She would appear to have been the wife of La 8aron, Wyandot for the Baron.
3 She is referred to as her "forte fille," which other than "strong daughter" has no meaning for me.
4 His third wife is mentioned on the list, but they had separated at that point.
5 Both he and Tia8endata are recorded as being his brother.
6 Their order is reversed in the second census.

NOTES TO APPENDIX B1

1 This word is used in reference to God.

NOTES TO APPENDIX B2

1 No one else seems to have had this name. It appears to have come from another Iroquoian language. Longueuil's name was also written as "ak8iechre" (Toupin 1996, 234, 261), the same name in another Iroquoian language.
2 The axe was a rich source of martial metaphors in the Wendat language (Steckley 2007a, 195; Toupin 1996, 284).
3 In the original it has the superscript -t- written over the two n's, a Wyandot dialect form.
4 The -,- does not seem to be appropriate there.

5 This is also the name of a Deer clan leader among the Wyandot (see chapter 7, n5).
6 This name began as an Iroquoian translation of the name of Governor Charles de Montmagny, governor of New France from 1636 to 1648. Later governors received the same name, as descendants of this governor.
7 There is a superscript -t- over the second -n- (Potier 1920, 69 "i8a,ennhe,e pendant l'ete").
8 FH1693:248; Potier 1920, 154.
9 It has -,- in the original.
10 On the night of 28–29 November 1745, five to six hundred French and Native allies attacked a small stockaded Dutch settlement called Saratoga, located within sight of Albany, New York. Some thirty inhabitants were reported to have been killed, with from sixty to one hundred taken prisoner. The figures given in this text seem to be somewhat inflated.
11 Kahnawake is a Mohawk community near Montreal. The word is cognate with the -,anda8a,e- part of the Wendat word.
12 The Wendat word -onnonta,e- is cognate with the word "Onondaga."
13 The -,- is added.
14 This is based on the verb root *-rhen-* "for day to come," referring to dawn (Steckley 2007b, 230–31). This in effect involves calling the English "people of the dawn, east."
15 It is possible that the verb root *-ri,-* "to join together, end to end" (Steckley 2007b, 234) is used here.
16 The verb root here may be *-ra,-* "to open up, pierce" (Steckley 2007b, 223, with "pierce" added). This might refer to the Straits of Mackinac, which narrowly join Lake Huron and Lake Michigan.
17 A superscript -t- is added over the -nn- in the original to reflect the Wyandot dialect. This is a metaphor that means "he invited us to council."
18 The Shawnee had just recently (1745) switched over from the English to the French sphere of influence.
19 The following is an entry in Potier (1920, 155) concerning the "Sonnioto" river: "s8gnioto v s8gnioocto *R. Vers la source d'otsand8ske [Sandusky] on fait portage pour y entrer." The Sonnioto was probably the present-day Scioto River.
20 This word appears to refer to a "lying tree or log," with *-ront-* "tree, log, pole" (Steckley 2007b, 236) and *-en-* "to put, lie" (Steckley 2007b, 83).
21 There is a Wyandot dialect superscript -t- between the two n's in the original. This is found in all uses in this text of the verb root -nnha- "to request, ask" (Steckley 2007b, 187).
22 In the original there is a superscript -g- over the -d-, reflecting the Wyandot dialect.
23 It would probably be better to have used *ennonchien* here.
24 This strikes me as being a made-up term by the writer. There are examples where he changes the form of this standard term.
25 I am as yet unable to determine what location this is.
26 This could also be "he."

NOTES TO APPENDIX B3

1 The noun stem here is the ‚entiok8a "clan, group" discussed in the second chapter.
2 Potier (1920, 102) "stan v stena." With tsinnonka it "means not anything."
3 The actual meaning of this word seems to be "where there is a lying log, tree." The noun root used is -ront- "tree, log, pole" (Steckley 2007b, 236), with the verb root -en- "to put, lie" (Steckley 2007b, 83).

NOTES TO APPENDIX B4

1 The -r- in this word marks it as being written in the Wyandot dialect of Wendat.
2 In the original there is a -g- over the two n's, as a sign of a Wyandot dialect feature.
3 This is another example of Richardie playing with the name Onnontio in a way that I believe the Wyandot would not.
4 On the night of 23–24 March 1746, Father de la Richardie suffered a paralytic stroke.
5 There appears to be a mistake here as the verb root -as- "to name, be called" (Steckley 2007b, 69–70) should be attached to the noun root -tsienst- "charcoal" (Steckley 2007b, 262), to refer to the black colour of their robes.
6 There is a -g- over the second -n-, a sign of a Wyandot dialect feature.
7 There is a superscript -g- over the -d- to show the presence of a Wyandot dialect feature.
8 There is a superscript -g- over the second -n-, showing the presence of a Wyandot dialect feature.
9 There is an extra -at- here that does not belong.
10 This is another word that Richardie seems to have made up using the name Onnontio.
11 The Wendat language distinguishes in some contexts between dual and plural.
12 In Cadwallader Colden's *The History of the Five Nations of Canada* (1747, xv-xvi), it was recorded that: "Corlaer, or Corlard...the Five Nations commonly call the Governor of New York by this Name, and often the People of Province of New York in general."
13 It seems to me that this imperative, and the one before it, should be plural and not singular, that a mistake has been made here.

NOTES TO APPENDIX B5

1 The word "mihi" is Latin, and is the dative case of the first person.
2 There is a -g- written as superscript over the -d-, indicating the Wyandot dialect form.

3 Father Pierre Daniel Richer was born in 1682, so would have been sixty-four in 1746.

NOTES TO APPENDIX C

1 This combination of the noun root *-rih8-* (Steckley2007b, 233) with the verb root *-ndera,-* "to be mistaken" (Steckley 2007b, 145) was from early days in the Jesuit mission used to express the idea of "sin."
2 It looks like there is a partially erased -h- at the beginning of this word, as seems true of the next use of this word.
3 An iota seems to come before the -8- here, as it does with ai8nnonratont.
4 In Potier (1920, 370n6) this is translated as "eau de vie."
5 The use of the masculine here looks to be a mistake.
6 There is a possibility that 2p (second-person plural) is involved here as with the verbs to follow.
7 Notice that the Jesuit writer here contrasts elders with women.
8 This appears to be the name of the Striped Turtle leader, otherwise known as Baby.
9 I think that there should be a dualic here, as that regularly occurs with this verb.
10 The -v- stands for the Latin word vel, meaning "or," referring in this case to another way of saying essentially the same thing.
11 This seems to be an invented word, as usually with this set of pronominal prefixes, with both a subject and an object, the causative-instrumental suffix is used.
12 This could be -io- with a mistake, or just mistaken added letters. There is a -g- placed over the -d- as a mark of a Wyandot dialect feature.

References

UNPUBLISHED

FHO. c. 1656. Dictionnaire Huron et hiroquois onontaheronon, MS. Archive Seminaire de Quebec.
FH67. n.d. French–Wendat dictionary, MS 67 (as cited in Hanzeli), Archive Seminaire de Quebec.
FH1693. c. 1693. French–Wendat dictionary, MS, Archive Seminaire de Quebec.
FH1697. c. 1697. French–Wendat dictionary, MS, John Carter Brown Library, Brown University, Providence, Rhode Island.
HF59. n.d. Wendat–French dictionary, MS 59 (as cited in Hanzeli), Archive Seminaire de Quebec.
HF62. n.d. Wendat–French section of MS 62 (as cited in Hanzeli), Archive Seminaire de Quebec.
HF65. n.d. Wendat–French dictionary, MS 65 (as cited in Hanzeli), Archive Seminaire de Quebec.
Steckley, John L. 2013. "Instructions to a Dying Infidel." Unpublished.
Sturtevant, Andrew K. 2011. "Jealous Neighbors: Rivalry and Alliance among the Native Communities of Detroit, 1701–1766." Doctoral diss., Dept. of History, College of William and Mary.
Warrick, Gary. 1990. "A Population History of the Huron–Petun, A.D. 900–1650." Doctoral diss., Dept. of Anthropology, McGill University, Montreal.

PUBLISHED

Anderson, Karen. 1991. *Chain Her by One Foot: The Subjugation of Women in Seventeenth-Century New France.* New York: Routledge.

Barbeau, C. Marius. 1915. *Huron and Wyandot Mythology*, Memoir 80. Ottawa: Dept. of Mines, Geological Survey.

———. 1917. "'Iroquoioan Clans and Phratries," *American Anthropologist*, vol. 19, no. 3, 392–402.

———. 1960. *Huron-Wyandot Traditional Narratives in Translation and Native Texts*. Bulletin 105. Ottawa: National Museum of Canada.

Brandão, José António. 2000. *Your Fyre Shall Burn No More: Iroquois Policy toward New France and Its Native Allies to 1701*. Lincoln: University of Nebraska Press.

Brockey, Liam Matthew. 2007. *Journey to the East: The Jesuit Mission to China, 1579–1724*. Cambridge, MA: Harvard University Press.

Callender, Charles. 1978. "Miami," in *Handbook of North American Indians*, vol. 15: *Northeast*. Washington, DC: Smithsonian Institution, 681–89.

Campbell, Chris Rabich. 1989. "A Study of Matrilineal Descent from the Perspective of the Tlingit NexA'di Eagles." *Arctic*, vol. 42, no. 2: 119–27.

Campeau, Lucien. 1987. *La Mission des Jesuites chez les Hurons, 1639–50*. Montreal: Editions Bellarmin.

Carr. In Spittal, 1990.

Chafe, Wallace. 1967. *Seneca Morphology and Dictionary*. Smithsonian Contributions to Anthropology, vol. 4. Washington, DC: Smithsonian Institute.

Champlain, Samuel de. 1632. *Voyages de la Nouvelle France*. Paris: Chez Claude Collet au Palais, en la Gallerie des Prisonniers, à l'Étoile d'Or.

———. 1929. *The Works of Samuel de Champlain*, vol. 3. ed. Henry Biggar. Toronto: Champlain Society.

Chapdelaine, Claude. 2004. "Review of the Latest Developments in St. Lawrence Iroquoian Archaeology." *A Passion for the Past: Papers in Honour of James F. Pendergast*, James Wright and Jean-Luc Pilon eds. Gatineau, QC: Canadian Museum of Civilization, 63–76.

Charlevoix, Pierre de. 1900. *History and General Description of New France*. Trans. and ed. by John Gilmary Shea, 6 vols. Chicago: Loyola University Press.

———. 1923 (orig. 1761). *Journal of a Voyage to North America*, 2 vols. Ed. Louise Phelps Kellogg. Chicago: Caxton Club.

Clarke, Peter Dooyentate. 1870. *Origin and Traditional History of the Wyandotts and Sketches of other Indian Tribes of North America, True Traditional Stories of Tecumseh and His League in the Years 1811 and 1812*. Toronto: Hunter, Rose and Company.

Clifton, James. 1983. "The Re-Emergent Wyandot: A Study in Ethnogenesis on the Detroit River Borderland," 1747, *The Western District: Papers from the Western District Conference*. Ed. K.G. Pryke and L.L. Kulisek. Essex County Historical Society and Western District Council, 7–8, 12–13.

Colden, Cadwallader. 1972 (orig. 1747). *The History of the Five Nations of Canada*. Toronto: Coles Publishing.

Colonial Records of Pennsylvania (CRP). 1851. *Minutes of the Provincial Council of Pennsylvania, from the Organization to the Termination of the Proprietary Government*, CRP vol. 5. Harrisburg: Theo Fenn and Company.

Connolly, William. 1900a. "The Wyandots." *Annual Archaeological Report, Appendix to the Report of the Minister of Education of Ontario*, 92–123.

———. 1900b. *Wyandot Folk-Lore*. Topeka: Crane and Company Publishers.

Curnoe, Greg. 1996. *Deeds/Nation*. London Chapter, Ontario Archaeological Society, Occasional Publications #4.

Farewell to a Beloved Land. 1843. Accessed 12 Dec. 2012. Retrieved from: http://www.wyandot.org/farewell.htm.

Fenton, William. 1998. *The Great Law and the Longhouse*. Norman: University of Oklahoma Press.

Firth, Raymond. 1957. *We, the Tikopia*, Sydney, Australia: Allen & Unwin.

Frishkopf, Michael. 2007. "Spiritual Kinship and Globalization." *Religious Studies and Theology*, vol. 22, no. 1: 1–25.

Garrad, Charles. 2011. *Petun to Wyandot: The Ontario Petun from ca. 1580*. Toronto: Petun Research Institute.

Hale, Horatio. 1883. *The Iroquois Book of Rites*. Brinton's Library of Aboriginal American Literature, no. 2. Philadelphia: D.G. Brinton.

———. 1894. "The Fall of Hochelaga: A Study of Popular Tradition." *Journal of American Folklore*, vol. 7, no. 124. Cambridge: American Folklore Society, 1–14.

Hanzeli, Victor. 1969. *Missionary Linguistics in New France: A Study of Seventeenth and Eighteenth Century Descriptions of American Indian Language*. The Hague: Mouton.

Havard, Gilles. 2001. *The Great Peace of Montreal of 1701: French–Native Diplomacy in the Seventeenth Century*. Montreal & Kingston: McGill–Queen's University Press.

Heidenreich, Conrad. 1971. *Huronia: A History and Geography of the Huron Indians 1600–1650*. Toronto: McClelland & Stewart.

Hunt, T. George. 1940. *Wars of the Iroquois: A Study in Intertribal Trade Relations*. Madison: University of Wisconsin Press.

Johnson, William. 1922. *The Papers of Sir William Johnson*, vol. 2. Ed. Alexander Flick. Albany: University of New York.

JR. *See* Thwaites.

Lafitau, Joseph-François. 1974. *Customs of the American Indians Compared with the Customs of Primitive Times*. E. Moore and W. Fenton eds. Toronto: Champlain Society.

Lahontan, Louis Armand de Lom d'Arce. 1970. *New Voyages to North America*, vol. 2. New York: B. Franklin.

Lajeunesse, Ernest J. (ed. and trans.). 1960. *The Windsor Border Region: Canada's Southernmost Frontier*. Champlain Society. Toronto: University of Toronto Press.

Lounsbury, Floyd. 1953. *Oneida Verb Morphology*. New Haven, CT: Yale University Press.

Margry, Pierre. "Decouvertes et l'etablissements des Francais dans l'ouest et dans le sud de l'amerique septentrionale 1614–1618, Paris 1888." Reprinted with AMS 1974, vol. 5. English translation of Margry, "Journal of Michipichy to the Miamis," originally 1702. http://gbl.indiana.edu/ethnohistory/archives/miamis4/M17-03_28a.htm.

Michelson, Gunther. 1973. *A Thousand Words of Mohawk*. Ottawa, National Museum of Man, Mercury Series, Ethnology Division, Paper No. 5.

Michigan. *See* Michigan Pioneer.

Michigan Pioneer and Historical Society. 1905. *Historical Collections*, vol. 34. http://archive.org/stream/michiganhistoric34/michuoft#page/n1/mode/2up.

Middleton, Richard. 2007. *Pontiac's War: Its Causes, Course and Consequences*. New York: Routledge.

Mooney, James. 1894. *The Siouan Tribes of the East*. Bureau of American Ethnology Bulletin, Washington.

———. 1900. *History, Myths, and Sacred Formulas of the Cherokee*. Washington, DC: Government Printing Office.

Morgan, Lewis H. 1877. *Ancient Society*, as reprinted in http://www.marxists.org/reference/archive/morgan-lewis/ancient-society/ch06.htm.

———. 1904. *League of the Ho-dé-no-sau-nee, Iroquois*. H.M. Lloyd, ed. New York: Dodd, Mead.

NYCD. *See* O'Callaghan.

O'Callaghan, Edmund B. ed. 1853–1861. *Documents Relative to the Colonial History of the State of New York*, vols. 5 (1855), 9 (1855), and 10 (1858). See also http://www.archive.org/details/documentsrelativ10brod. Albany, NY: Weed, Parsons and Company.

Ott, E.R. 1936. "Selections from the Diary and Gazette of Father Pierre Potier, S.J. (1708–1781). *Mid America* 18: 199–207, 260–65.

Parkman, Francis. 1894. *The Conspiracy of Pontiac and the Indian War after the Conquest of Canada*, vol. 1. Boston: Little, Brown and Company.

———. Reprint. 1966. New York: Collier.

Peckham, Howard H. 1947. *Pontiac and the Indian Uprising*. Princeton, NJ: Princeton University Press.

Pennsylvania. *See* Colonial Records of Pennsylvania.

Perrot, Nicolas. 1911. "Memoir on the Manners, Customs and Religion of the Savages of North America." In Emma Helen Blair, ed. *The Indian Tribes of the Upper Mississippi Valley and Region of the Great Lakes*, 3 vols. Cleveland: Arthur H. Clark.

Petersen, James B., et al. 2004. "St. Lawrence Iroquoians in Northern New England: Pendergast was 'Right' and More." *A Passion for the Past: Papers in Honour of James F. Pendergast*. James Wright and Pilon, Jean-Luc (ed.). Gatineau, QC: Canadian Museum of Civilization, 87–123.

Potier, Pierre. 1920. *Fifteenth Report of the Bureau of Archives for the Province of Ontario*. Toronto: C.W. James.

Powell, J.W. 1881. Wyandot Government, *Bureau of American Ethnology*, 1st Annual Report, 57–69. Washington, DC.

Quaife, Milo Milton, ed. 1958. *The Siege of Detroit in 1763: The Journal of Pontiac's Conspiracy and John Rutherfurd's Captivity*. Chicago: R.R. Donnelley.

Raudot, Antoine D., and Antoine Silvy. 1902. *Relation par lettres de l'Amérique*

Septentrionalle (années 1709 et 1710). Camille de Rochemoneix ed. Paris: Letouzey.

Richter, Daniel. 1992. *The Ordeal of the Longhouse: The Peoples of the Iroquois League in the Era of European Colonization*. Chapel Hill: University of North Carolina Press.

Robinson, Angela. 2005. *Ta'n Teli-ktlamsitasit (Ways of Believing): Mi'kmaw Religion in Eskasoni, Nova Scotia*. Toronto: Pearson Canada.

Sagard, Gabriel. 1632. *Dictionnaire de la langue huronne necessaire à ceux n'ont intelligence-d'icelle & ont a traiter avec les sauvages du pays*. Paris: Denys Moreau.

———. 1939. *The Long Journey to the Country of the Hurons*. Toronto: Champlain Society.

Seeman, Erik R. 2010. *Death in the New World: Cross-Cultural Encounters, 1492–1800*. Philadelphia: University of Pennsylvania Press.

———. 2011. *The Huron-Wendat Feast of the Dead: Indian-European Encounters in Early North America*. Baltimore: Johns Hopkins University Press.

Shiels, Eugene W. 1936. "The Jesuits in Ohio in the Eighteenth Century." *Mid-America*, Handbook of North American Indians 15, 404–5, 27–47.

Sioui, Georges E. 1992. *For an Amerindian Autohistory*. Montreal: McGill-Queen's University Press.

———. 1999. *Huron-Wendat: The Heritage of the Circle*. Vancouver: University of British Columbia Press.

Speck, Frank. 1938. "The Question of Matrilineal Descent in the Southeastern Siouan Area." *American Anthropologist*, New Series 40, no. 1: 1–12.

Spittal, W.G., ed. 1990. *Iroquois Women: An Anthology*. Ohsweken, ON: Irocrafts.

Steckley, John L. 1978. "Brebeuf's Presentation of Catholicism in the Huron Language." *University of Ottawa Quarterly* 48: 1–2, 93–115.

———. 1982. "Huron Clans and Phratries." *Ontario Archaeology*, 37: 29–34.

———. 1987. "An Ethnolinguistic Look at the Huron Longhouse." *Ontario Archaeology* 47: 19–32.

———. 1988. "How the Huron Became Wyandot." *Onomastica Canadiana* 70: 59–70.

———. 1990a. "Reciprocal Burial: The Aiheonde Relationship." *Arch Notes* 5: 9–14.

———. 1990b. "One Bear or Two?" *Arch Notes* 6: 29–33.

———. 1991a. "Rock and Southern Bear: Another Feature Shared." *Arch Notes* 4: 12–15.

———. 1991b. "Southern Bear's -chr-: How can a sound be like a bat's wing?" *Arch Notes* 6: 11–14.

———. 1992a. "The Warrior and the Lineage: Jesuit Use of Iroquoian Images to Communicate Christianity." *Ethnohistory* 39, no. 4: 478–509.

———. 1992b. "The Wendat: Were They Islanders?" *Arch Notes* 5: 23–26.

———. 1992c. "Tying the Cord with the Southern Bear." *Arch Notes* 2: 12–16.

———. 1992d. *Untold Tales: Four Seventeenth Century Huron*. Self-published.

———. 1993a. "Huron Kinship Terminology." *Ontario Archaeology* 55: 35–59.

———. 1993b. "Linguistically Linking the Petun with the Southern Bear." *Arch Notes* 2: 20–26.

———. 1997. "Wendat Dialects and the Development of the Huron Alliance." *Northeast Anthropology* 54: 23–36.

———. 2004. *De Religione: Seventeenth-Century Jesuits Telling Their Story in Huron to the Iroquois*. Tulsa, OK: University of Oklahoma Press.

———. 2007a. *Words of the Huron*. Waterloo, ON: Wilfrid Laurier University Press.

———. 2007b. *Huron Dictionary: Verb Roots and Noun Roots*. Lewiston, NY: Edwin Mellen Press.

———. 2008. *White Lies about the Inuit*. Peterborough, ON: Broadview Press.

———. 2010a. *Gabriel Sagard's Dictionary of Huron*. Evolution Publishing. ALR Supplement Series.

———. 2010b. *The First French–Huron Dictionary by Father Jean de Brébeuf and His Jesuit Brethren*. Lewiston, NY: Edwin Mellen Press.

———. 2012. "Trade Goods and Nations in Sagard's Dictionary: A St. Lawrence Iroquoian Perspective." *Ontario History*, vol. 104, no. 2: 139–54.

Steckley, John L., and Bryan Cummins. 2007. *Full Circle: Canada's First Nations*, 2nd ed. Toronto: Pearson Education Canada.

Steinbeck, John. 1989. *Steinbeck: A Life in Letters*. Elaine Steinbeck and Robert Wallsten, eds. Toronto: Penguin Books.

Thiong'o, wa Ngũgĩ. 2009. *Something Torn and New: An African Renaissance*. New York: Basic Books.

Thwaites, Reuben G. (JR). 1959. *The Jesuit Relations and Allied Documents*. New York: Pageant Book.

Tooker, Elisabeth. 1967. *An Ethnography of the Huron Indians, 1615–1649*. Midland, ON: Huronia Historical Development Council.

———. 1978. "Wyandot." In *Handbook of North American Indians*, vol. 15: *Northeast*. Washington, DC: Smithsonian Institute, 398–406.

Toupin, Robert, s.j. 1996. *Les Écrits de Pierre Potier*. Ottawa: Les Press de l'Université d'Ottawa.

The Treaty of Greenville. (1795). Prepared by Nancy Troutman. Retrieved from: http://www.wyandot.org/greenvil.htm.

Trigger, Bruce. 1969. *Huron: Farmers of the North*. New York: Holt, Rinehart and Winston.

———. 1976. *The Children of Aataentsic*, 2 vols. Montreal: McGill-Queen's University Press.

Vincent, Marguerite Tehariolina. 1984. *La Nation Huronne*. Quebec: Editions du Pélican.

Voltaire, François-Marie Arouet. 1767. *Ingénu*. Paris: Londres.

Warrick, Gary. 2003. "European infectious disease and depopulation of the Wendat–Tionontate (Huron–Petun)." *World Archaeology*, vol. 35 (2): 258–75.

White, Richard. 1991. *The Middle Ground: Indians, Empires and Republics in the Great Lakes Region, 1650–1815*. New York: Cambridge University Press, 1991.

Wilkie, Daniel, trans. 1831. "Grammar of the Huron Language, by a Missionary of the Village of Huron Indians at Lorette, near Quebec, found amongst the papers of the Mission, and Translated from the Latin." *Literary and Historical Society of Quebec, Transactions*, original series, vol. 2. See online at http://www.morrin.org/transactions/docsfromclient/books/77/77_f.html.

Wisconsin. *See* Wisconsin Historical Collections.

Wisconsin Historical Collections, vol. 16, 1902: http://content.wisconsinhistory.org/cdm/ref/collection/whc/id/13127.

———. vol. 17, 1906: httl://content.wisconsinhistory/org/cdm/compoundobject/collection/whc/id/1254/rec18.

Wyandot of Kansas website. http://www.wyandot.org.

Index

Abenaki, 88, 95, 103, 109, 115, 198, 221, 239–40, 245–46, 277, 286
adultery, 119–20, 160, 271
Aendi (f – Wolf), 115, 118, 130, 158, 181, 183–84, 199, 210, 213
A,a8as (m – Bear), 34–35, 73, 99, 154–56, 158, 161, 166, 168, 177–78, 186–87, 207–8, 212, 223, 286
(,)aennen(ch/s) (f – Striped Turtle), 100, 158, 179, 197–98, 209
(,)Ang8enta (f – Fox nation), 99–100, 285
(,)Ang8irot (m – Prairie Turtle), 81–84, 86, 92, 111, 134, 139, 142, 151, 156–57, 167–68, 185, 205–7, 212, 226, 279
Annend8ach (f – Bear), 122
Annien8indet, Barnabe (m – Snake), 35, 118, 158, 161, 177–78, 191, 207, 226
(a,)otiok8andoron (m – Striped Turtle), 15, 46, 86, 117, 147–48, 156–58, 168, 174, 183, 186, 195, 207–8, 212, 220, 223, 267–69, 283
(,)Arhonnens (f – Large Turtle), 108, 115, 118, 131, 139–40, 158, 163, 181–82, 186, 193, 196, 209, 213, 222, 228

(A,)Aronhiet (f – Porcupine), 158, 182, 196–97, 209
Aron-issa (m – Large Turtle), 155
Asenra,e-haon (f – Bear), 93, 158, 161, 184, 192–93, 209, 226
(,)Atera (f – Porcupine), 45, 130, 146, 153, 158, 182, 196, 209, 225
(H)Atironta (m – Deer), 10, 31–33, 41–42, 44, 113, 187, 189, 200, 232–33
Atsataion (ceremony), 24, 59–60
Atsironde (f – Porcupine), 77–78, 94, 99–101, 115, 118, 122, 130, 158, 164, 175, 177, 180–81, 183–87, 195–96, 209–10, 213, 219, 285
A8(oi/e)ndaara (f – Striped Turtle), 158, 198, 209, 231
A8endii (f – Snake), 118, 161, 177, 181, 201, 221
A8(oi/e)ndgiandii. *See* (Sa)8(oi/e)ndgiandii
A8innonke, Anne (f – Large Turtle), 35, 101, 103, 130, 158, 179, 194–95, 209, 220, 283
A8innonke (Christine; f – Bear), 35, 73, 120, 158, 179, 191–92, 195, 209, 229, 231, 283
A8innon-8oin (f – Snake), 122

baptism, 13, 33, 35–36, 40–41, 47, 78, 81–83, 89, 91, 93, 97, 99, 101, 103, 105, 107–17, 119–21, 127, 129, 133–34, 142, 144, 148–49, 152, 154, 156, 160–61, 163–67, 180, 187, 189, 192, 194–96, 198–201, 203, 276, 279–80
Barbeau, Marius, 17–19, 42–45, 82, 141, 282, 292
Bark-Carrier (m – Roundhead), 14–15, 146
Baron (8aron; m – Prairie Turtle), 61–63, 74, 80, 205, 278, 286
Bear clan, 5–6, 27, 34–35, 40–41, 44, 47–49, 56, 60, 63, 69, 72–74, 90, 92–94, 97, 99–102, 104–5, 110–18, 120–23, 130–34, 164–66, 158, 160–66, 168, 176–78, 181–86, 188, 191–94, 197–99, 204, 207–13, 219–20, 223–27, 229, 231–34, 286
Bear nation, 19, 23–25, 37–38, 41–42, 44, 163, 254, 273, 275, 295–96
Beaver clan, 40, 48, 139
Brandão, José Antonio, 21, 275, 292
Brébeuf, Father Jean de, vii–iii, 8–9, 17, 23, 29–31, 34, 47, 90, 123–24, 173, 261, 275, 295–96

Cadillac, Antoine Laumet de la Mothe, Sieur de, 12, 50, 61–62, 69–72, 94
Catawba, 2, 5, 79, 83, 95–98, 102, 104–5, 115, 118, 141, 160, 177–78, 181, 222, 224–25, 227, 231, 233, 243, 246, 279, 282, 286
Cayuga, 19, 21, 24, 27, 40, 58, 65, 239, 245
Champlain, Samuel de, 8–9, 18, 22, 31, 43, 274, 292
Charlevoix, Father Pierre François de, 62, 67, 75–76, 136–37, 151, 173–74, 179–80, 195, 292
Chaumonot, Father Pierre, 17, 30, 34, 39, 90, 193, 205, 261, 279
Cherokee, 15, 25, 96, 141, 150, 282, 294

Chickasaw, 95–96, 102–3, 115, 154, 176, 188, 220, 224
Chihoatenhwa, Joseph, 10, 275
Choctaw, 96
Clifton, James, 53, 292
Cord nation, 23–25, 37, 275

Deer clan and phratry, 5–6, 16, 31, 33, 35, 38, 40–44, 46–49, 52, 56–57, 63, 72–74, 77–78, 81, 89, 92–95, 98–100, 103–5, 110–18, 121–22, 127, 130–34, 137–39, 142, 145, 149, 152–54, 156–57, 159, 162, 164, 167–68, 175–78, 180–83, 186–90, 197, 200–1, 204–7, 209–13, 221, 223–25, 223–33, 278, 287
Deer nation, 23, 25, 38, 46
Denonville, Governor Jacques-René de Brisay de, 57–60
divorce, 119–20, 271–72

Eñie8indet, Etienne (m – Deer), 35, 118, 157, 159, 186, 188, 191, 207, 224, 228
En(n)ons (m – Bear), 34, 101, 118, 154–56, 158, 168, 176, 199, 207, 226
Entaron8oin (m – Large Turtle), 97, 123, 177, 194, 222
exogamy, 3, 36, 40–41, 50, 57, 63, 166, 206

Fox clan, 39–40, 48, 276
Fox nation, 12, 15, 76, 78, 95, 97–102, 105, 115, 160–61, 165, 175–76, 190–91, 195, 219–26, 229–31, 233, 276, 280, 285
Frontenac, Louis de Buade, Conte de, 53–55, 64, 66

Garrad, Charles, 17, 22, 274, 293
godfathers, 35–36, 63, 83, 91, 93, 99, 110–13, 116–17, 139, 142, 144, 148–49, 152–54, 160–65, 167, 181, 189, 193, 197, 280–82

godmothers, 97–103, 110–12, 116, 118–19, 153, 167, 181, 187–94, 197–200, 280–81, 285
Gonnor, Father Nicholas de, 89, 94, 176

Hannenhasa (m – Prairie Turtle), 46, 152–55, 158, 166, 185–86, 199, 208, 221, 227, 285
Hannenratendi (m), 97, 157, 160, 195, 207, 222, 224
Harih8andiniontak (m – Striped Turtle), 158, 165–66, 192, 208, 284
Harih8a8a,i (m – Bear), 93, 163
Ha8endaraties (m – Bear), 34, 108
Hawk clan, 24, 36, 39–40, 46–48, 112, 204, 283
Hechon (m), viii, 17, 30, 90, 261–63, 279
Heidenreich, Conrad, 10, 22, 43, 275
(H)ochienda,ete (m – Bear), 158, 162, 186, 191, 207, 231
Honarak (m – Bear), 72, 158, 163, 191, 197, 207. *See also* Onh8arak
Hondatorenha (m – Wolf), 113, 117, 149, 156–58, 168, 200, 207–8, 212, 223, 230, 283
Hondechiaren8(oi/a)n (m – Large Turtle), 158, 164, 194, 207
Horonhia,ete (m – Wolf), 90–91, 167
-h8atsira-, noun root 'matrilineal lineage,' 107–8, 273
Hubert, Father Jean-François, 93–94, 163

Illinois, 24, 59–60
incest, 36, 166

Jaunay, Father Pierre de, 85

Kahnawake (Mohawk community), 79, 84–85, 87–88, 173, 239–40, 245–46, 287

Kandiaronk (a.k.a. Rat, m – Wolf [?]), viii, 12, 28–29, 49, 51–53, 55–59, 61–68, 74, 151, 164, 205, 278
Kaoindi (f – Striped Turtle), 158, 209

Lafitau, Father Joseph, François, 173–75, 293
Lahontan, Louis Armand, Baron de, 28–29, 52, 57–59, 278, 293
Lake of Two Mountains (Kahnesatake), 70, 79, 84–85, 88
Large Turtle clan, 5, 35, 38, 45–48, 63, 90, 92–93, 97–99, 101–5, 110–15, 117–18, 120–23, 128–34, 139–42, 145–47, 153, 155–56, 158, 160, 163–64, 167–68, 177–78, 181–82, 184, 186–87, 193–94, 196, 198, 204, 206–9, 211–13, 220–25, 227–31, 234, 283–84, 286
Laval, Bishop Francis-Xavier (François) de Montmorency, 93–94, 163
Longueuil, Charles le Moyne, Baron de, 55
Longueuil, Paul-Joseph, le Moyne, Chevalier de, 61, 87, 97, 143, 237, 245–46, 286
Loon (part of Sturgeon clan), 40, 47–48

marriage, 13, 29, 36, 40–41, 50, 89, 91, 97, 108, 119–23, 126, 134, 138, 142, 145, 162, 173, 180, 185, 187, 190, 194–96, 203, 206, 217, 221, 223, 225–26, 228, 230–31, 271–72
Miami, 24, 53–54, 61–62, 64, 68–69, 72, 87–88, 95, 103, 142, 163, 228, 238, 245, 277, 292, 294
Michilimackinac, 12, 18, 24, 49, 53, 55, 57–61, 64, 69–70, 85, 102, 107, 240–41, 246
Michipichy, Mishibichy, 63–64, 70, 294
Mohawk, 9, 18–19, 21, 24, 26–27, 41, 43, 47, 58–59, 70, 79, 85, 87–88, 154, 173, 256, 259, 277, 287, 294

-ndask8-, noun root 'prisoner, domesticated animal,' 64, 67, 239, 262
Ndikaratase (m – Snake), 158, 161, 186, 190–91, 207, 221
Nendaentons (f – Deer), 78, 100, 113, 153, 157, 164, 175–76, 186–89, 200, 209–10, 213, 221, 227, 229, 232–33
Nendeñiont (f – Deer), 103–4, 145, 157, 176, 186, 188, 209, 224, 286
Nenditaχon (f – Wolf), 158, 200, 210, 230, 233
Nenniense (f – Fox nation), 99, 101
Nentechien (f – Porcupine), 122
Neutral, 8, 22–26, 37–39, 50, 90, 105, 203, 205, 274
Niendaharonk (f – Bear), 118, 130, 158, 181–84, 188, 191–92, 209, 231
Nondeaon (f – Wolf), 178, 200, 210, 230
Northern Bear, 19, 23, 163

Ochron,oti (m – Large Turtle), 121–23
(H)ondachiate,en (m – Snake), 43, 117, 134, 153–54, 156, 167–68, 177, 187, 207–8, 212, 221
Onda8annhont (m – Deer), 95, 139, 152–53, 167, 193, 207
Ondechientonk (f – Deer), 95, 178, 223, 229
Ondechi8ri (f – Prairie Turtle), 91, 127
Oneida, 19, 21, 24, 27, 39, 41, 47, 58, 274, 276–77, 293
Onh8arak (m – Bear), 231. *See also* Honarak
Onnond8 (f – Bear), 101, 118, 130, 158, 181–85, 192, 209, 226, 232
Onnond8annon (f – Deer), 118, 130, 157, 181–83, 188, 190–92, 209, 286
Onnonrachien (f – Porcupine), 34
Onondaga, 11, 19, 21, 24, 27, 40–41, 58–59, 239, 244–45, 297
On(n)ontio (Great Mountain, name for French Governor of New France), 44, 54–55, 57, 64–65, 68–70, 72, 80, 138, 143, 238, 240–41, 244, 251–53, 255–58, 262, 288
Orontondi (m – Porcupine), 12, 15, 18, 60–61, 80, 83–89, 97, 105, 117, 122, 133, 143, 152–53, 155–56, 158, 167–68, 197, 205–7, 212, 217, 220, 232
(O)sk8arak, Angelique (f – Large Turtle), 102, 158, 194–95, 209, 220, 223
Ota8ata (f – Large Turtle). *See* 8ata8ata
Otiok8andoron. *See* A,otiok8andoron
Otren-i8oin (m – Prairie Turtle), 143, 158, 167, 208
Otre8ati (m – Snake), 93, 118, 122
Ottawa, 13, 24, 26, 55, 61–64, 69–72, 79, 85, 88, 95, 97, 102–3, 140, 146–48, 155, 185, 220, 222, 225, 243–44, 246, 279, 285

Petun, 8, 10, 12, 17, 22–26, 38, 50, 52–53, 63, 72–73, 102, 159, 162–63, 203, 273–74, 277–81, 291, 293, 296–97
Pierson, Father Philippe, 13, 49, 107–8
Pontiac, 12–13, 18, 92, 140–42, 145–48, 167, 185, 279, 294–95
Porcupine clan, 5–6, 12, 14, 34, 45, 48–49, 56, 59–60, 63, 74, 77–78, 80, 83, 89, 92–94, 97, 99–102, 104–5, 110–18, 120, 122–23, 127, 130–34, 149, 152–53, 155–56, 158, 164, 168, 175–78, 180–82, 184–86, 193, 195–96, 198, 204–13, 219–20, 224–26, 229–30, 232, 234, 282, 286
Potawatomi, 24, 53, 62, 66, 72, 79, 87–88, 95, 103, 115, 146–47, 192, 231
Potier, Father Pierre, 1–2, 11, 13, 18, 36, 39, 47, 77, 80–81, 86, 88, 90–92, 94, 96–97, 105, 107, 109, 113, 115–16, 119, 121, 126–28, 134, 141, 143, 145–46, 148–49, 152, 167, 171–72, 175, 177, 179, 182–83, 185, 195,

203, 205, 208, 217–19, 235, 237, 247, 261, 265, 267, 271, 277, 279, 281–83, 294

Prairie Turtle clan, 5–6, 34, 46, 48, 61, 63–64, 74, 80–82, 91–95, 97, 99, 103–5, 110–15, 117–18, 121, 127, 132–34, 139, 141–47, 149, 155–58, 166–68, 178, 182, 185–87, 192, 198–99, 202–4, 208, 210–13, 221–24, 226–30

Quarante Sols (m – Bear), 49, 56, 60–61, 63–64, 68–74, 161–62, 164, 204

Richardie, Father Armand de, 18, 69, 76–81, 83–91, 94, 97, 105, 108–9, 111–13, 115–16, 119, 126, 134, 142, 165, 175, 180, 187, 190, 195, 205, 208, 210, 235, 237, 249, 251, 258, 261, 265, 279, 288

Richer, Father Pierre-Daniel, 17, 30, 34, 89–90, 261–63, 289

Rock nation, 23, 25, 31–32, 41–45, 196, 275

Sa,ents8a't (m – Large Turtle), 86, 139–41, 155, 158, 163, 167, 186, 206–8

Sagard, Brother Gabriel, viii, 9–10, 18, 22, 32, 274, 277–78, 295–96

Sainte-Marie Among the Hurons, viii, 8–9, 18, 126, 278

Salleneuve, Father Jean-Baptiste de, 93–94

Sastaretsi (m – Deer), 16, 28–29, 41, 50, 52–57, 63, 69–71, 73–74, 78, 86, 89, 103–4, 113, 117, 121, 127, 137–40, 149, 151, 153–54, 156–57, 159–60, 167–68, 177–78, 180, 183, 186–91, 201, 204, 206–7, 212, 224, 233, 255, 259, 275, 277, 286

Sauk, 15, 24, 62

Sa8end8at (m – Striped Turtle), 46, 100, 158, 165, 208, 223

(Sa)8(oi/e)ndgiandii (f – Large Turtle), 158, 178, 186, 194, 209, 228, 234

Seeman, Erik, 7, 123–25, 172, 295

Sendak8an (f – Deer), 157, 209, 286

Sendañion(t) (f – Fox nation, Snake), 93, 99–100, 149, 157, 190, 197, 209, 213, 221, 285

Seneca, 16, 21, 24, 37–38, 40, 53, 55, 57–59, 62, 65–66, 68, 71–72, 82, 95, 101–2, 109, 115, 140–41, 144, 166, 229, 233, 242, 244, 246, 292

Shawnee, 14, 87, 241–44, 246, 287

Sk8atandi (f – Striped Turtle), 63, 100, 123, 176–77, 179, 198, 201, 209, 222–23

Sk8ate(,)enre (f – Deer), 100, 104, 108, 118–19, 181, 188–89, 201, 209, 224

Sk8(8)tache (m), 51, 59–61, 73–74, 164, 177, 195, 205, 220

Sk8enderonk (f – Prairie Turtle), 149

Sk8ndak8a (m – Sturgeon), 47, 152–53, 156, 168, 178, 207, 232

Snake clan, 5–6, 35, 42–44, 48, 63, 92–95, 97, 99–100, 102, 104–5, 110–18, 120–22, 132–34, 149, 153–54, 156–57, 159–61, 166–68, 177–78, 181–82, 186–87, 189–91, 195, 197, 201, 204, 206–9, 211–13, 219–24, 226, 230–33, 280, 285

Sohondinnon (m – Bear), 72–73, 99, 158, 161–63, 168, 186, 188, 191, 207–8, 224, 231. *See also* Quarante Sols

Southern Bear, 23, 193, 273

Striped Turtle clan, 5–6, 34–36, 45–46, 48, 60, 63, 86, 89–90, 92–97, 99–100, 104–5, 110–15, 117–18, 121–23, 128, 130–34, 145–47, 149, 156–58, 160–61, 165–68, 176–79, 181–86, 190, 192–93, 195, 197–99, 201, 204, 207–13, 219–23, 225, 228–29, 231, 269, 289

Sturgeon clan, 40, 47–48, 112, 121, 123, 152–53, 156–57, 168, 204, 207, 211, 232, 281
Sturtevant, Andrew, 63, 72, 75, 109, 127, 291

Taι(e/a)nnrak (m – Prairie Turtle), 145, 158, 166–67, 186, 199, 208, 284
Ta,echiaten (m – Wolf), 83, 89, 113, 117, 139, 149, 151, 156–57, 167–68, 177, 190, 197, 200, 206–8, 212, 221, 225, 286
Tahatie (m – Prairie Turtle), 92, 117, 141–45, 147–49, 158, 167, 185, 208, 226
Tandere-i8oin (m – Wolf), 158, 167, 208
Tando,ares (f – Prairie Turtle), 158, 185–86, 199, 210, 227, 285
Taniendonien (m – Prairie Turtle), 34, 143, 167, 227–28. *See also* Otre-ni8oin
Tannenhochre (m – Snake), 43, 158, 161, 207, 233
Taretande (m – Bear), 117, 158, 162–63, 186, 191, 198, 207, 231
Tarhe (m), 14–15, 146
Taronhi8rens (m – Large Turtle), 117, 152–53, 158, 168, 177–78, 196, 207, 225, 286
Te aïas (f – Bear), 158, 192, 226
Te,atak (m – Large Turtle), 117, 122, 141–42, 147–48, 198, 225, 228, 286
Te horonhiate (m – Striped Turtle), 122
Te horonhi8teχa (m – Large Turtle), 117, 158, 164, 186–87, 207, 227
Tendiho (f – Prairie Turtle), 223
Te ondise8a and Tiaondese8a (f – Snake and Striped Turtle), 35, 120, 157, 161, 166, 186, 190–91, 198, 209, 231
Te 8arachiarande (f – Striped Turtle), 178–79, 197, 209, 225

Ti(a)o(n)8endata (m – Porcupine), 60, 78, 94, 118, 153, 155–56, 167–68, 176, 206–8, 220, 283, 286
Tonti, 75, 95, 151–52
T'on8atsarandi (m – Porcupine), 49, 56, 155, 158, 164–65, 186, 196, 207–8, 219, 226, 285
Tooker, Elisabeth, 4, 10, 296
Toratati (m – Wolf), 91, 121–22, 150–51, 228
Totarach. *See* Aron-issa (m – Large Turtle)
Toupin, Father Robert, 13, 36
Trigger, Bruce, 10, 22, 119, 275, 296
(T)sa8ointondi (f – Prairie Turtle), 115, 155–56, 158, 166, 185–86, 198–99, 210, 213, 223
Tso,a8enda (m – Striped Turtle), 36, 158, 155, 208
Tsa8(oi/e)ndask8a (f – Bear), 69, 101, 158, 164, 178, 192, 209, 225, 234
Ts8chiaen (f – Porcupine), 60
Ts8ndehe (f – Striped Turtle), 60, 115, 149, 158, 179, 183–84, 186, 190, 197–98, 209, 213, 221, 225, 229
Ts8ndendora (f – Snake), 118, 122, 178, 181, 191, 209, 230, 234
Ts8nde,en (f – Bear), 72, 102, 115, 118, 130, 162–63, 178, 181–87, 209–10, 213, 231, 286
Ts8teses (f – Bear), 160
Turtle (clan), 27, 37–38, 40
Turtle (phratry), 6, 38, 40, 44–45, 47–49, 56, 81, 83–84, 86, 90, 95, 112, 134, 141–42, 145, 147, 149, 153–54, 158, 164, 167–68, 204–6, 211, 228, 278

Warrick, Gary, 22, 291
8asañion (m – Snake), 117, 154, 157, 160–61, 207–8, 222
8ata8ata (f – Large Turtle), 130, 153, 158, 164, 178, 184–87, 194, 209, 222, 227

Wendake (Lorette), 2, 7–8, 12, 17–18,
  24, 31, 33, 68, 73, 76, 107, 162, 193,
  251, 254, 259, 261, 276, 281–82
Wenro, 26–27, 37–38, 139, 274
8entïhaon (f – Prairie Turtle), 143,
  167, 178, 226
8en8(oi/e)n (m – Large Turtle), 103,
  118, 122, 132, 158, 163–64, 186,
  193, 207, 228
8ndaenton (f – Deer), 178, 188, 190,
  209–10, 229

Wolf (clan and phratry), 5–6, 23–24,
  36, 38–40, 46–49, 56–57, 63, 74, 83,
  89–95, 99, 104–5, 110–15, 117–18,
  121–23, 127, 130–34, 139–40,
  149–51, 153–54, 156–58, 164,
  167–68, 175, 177–78, 181–84, 190,
  197, 199–200, 204–8, 210–13, 219,
  221, 223–25, 228, 230–33, 278–79,
  283, 286
8tsia (f – Deer), 100, 104, 176, 187,
  189, 209, 221

**Books in the Aboriginal Studies Series
Published by Wilfrid Laurier University Press**

Blockades and Resistance: Studies in Actions of Peace and the Temagami Blockades of 1988–89 / Bruce W. Hodgins, Ute Lischke, and David T. McNab, editors / 2003 / xi + 276 pp. / map, illustrations / ISBN 0-88920-381-4

Indian Country: Essays on Contemporary Native Culture / Gail Guthrie Valaskakis / 2005 / x + 293 pp. / photos / ISBN 0-88920-479-9

Walking a Tightrope: Aboriginal People and Their Representations / Ute Lischke and David T. McNab, editors / 2005 / xix + 377 pp. / photos / ISBN 978-0-88920-484-3

The Long Journey of a Forgotten People: Métis Identities and Family Histories / Ute Lischke and David T. McNab, editors / 2007 / viii + 386 pp. / maps, photos / ISBN 978-0-88920-523-9

Words of the Huron / John L. Steckley / 2007 / xvii + 259 pp. / ISBN 978-0-88920-516-1

Essential Song: Three Decades of Northern Cree Music / Lynn Whidden / 2007 / xvi + 176 pp. / photos, musical examples, audio CD / ISBN 978-0-88920-459-1

From the Iron House: Imprisonment in First Nations Writing / Deena Rymhs / 2008 / ix + 147 pp. / ISBN 978-1-55458-021-7

Lines Drawn upon the Water: First Nations and the Great Lakes Borders and Borderlands / Karl S. Hele, editor / 2008 / xxiii + 351 pp. / illustrations, maps / ISBN 978-1-55458-004-0

Troubling Tricksters: Revisioning Critical Conversations / Linda M. Morra and Deanna Reder, editors / 2009 / xii+ 336 pp. / illustrations / ISBN 978-1-55458-181-8

Aboriginal Peoples in Canadian Cities: Transformations and Continuities / Heather A. Howard and Craig Proulx, editors / 2011 / viii + 256 pp. / colour and b&w photos / ISBN 978-1-055458-260-0

Bridging Two Peoples: Chief Peter E. Jones, 1843–1909 / Allan Sherwin / 2012 / xxiv + 246 pp. / 15 b&w photos / ISBN 978-1-55458-633-2

The Nature of Empires and the Empires of Nature: Indigenous Peoples and the Great Lakes Environment / Karl S. Hele, editor / 2013 / xxi + 350 pp. / 3 b&w photos / ISBN 978-1-55458-328-7

The Eighteenth-Century Wyandot: A Clan-Based Study / John L. Steckley / 2014 / x + 306 pp. / ISBN 978-1-55458-956-2